Unemployment Insurance

THE AMERICAN EXPERIENCE, 1915–1935

Unemployment Insurance

THE
AMERICAN
EXPERIENCE
1915–1935

Daniel Nelson

THE UNIVERSITY OF WISCONSIN PRESS
MADISON, MILWAUKEE, AND LONDON

1969

Published by the
University of Wisconsin Press
Box 1379, Madison, Wisconsin 53701
The University of Wisconsin Press, Ltd.
27–29 Whitfield Street, London, W. 1

Printed in the United States of America by
George Banta Company, Inc.
Menasha, Wisconsin

Standard Book Number 299–05200–1
Library of Congress Catalog Card Number 69–16114

TO
Lorraine

PREFACE

AMERICANS, LIKE citizens of other economically advanced nations, long ago recognized the need to provide temporary relief to men who were thrown out of their jobs during depressions. But unlike citizens of the major European nations, most Americans had considerable difficulty understanding the need for a long-term program, created with the same objective but in anticipation of, rather than in response to, unemployment. The purpose of this book is not to probe the reasons for this reluctance to embrace unemployment insurance; if this were its objective, it would duplicate the work of many other historians. Rather, its purpose is to show how and by whom this reluctance was overcome and how the results, the unemployment insurance legislation of the mid-1930's, reflected the interests and ideas of the people who played major roles in bringing about the change.

Perhaps unlike other social welfare programs of that time or this, unemployment insurance appealed primarily to specialists. It was designed largely for industrial workers and the employers of industrial workers and they, quite logically, took the greatest interest in it. Economists, labor legislation experts, and proponents of social insurance legislation were also involved in its development; but since unemployment insurance was considered separately from relief and since "good" and "evil" were seldom apparent in the discussion of the issues, there was at first relatively little popular interest in the subject. The Depression of the 1930's changed this situation and shifted the focus of the debate from what type of unemployment insurance was desirable to what type of legislation was desirable. After 1930 this debate became part of the larger discussion of government action to meet the economic and social crisis produced by the Depression. Appropriately, the federal-state system of unemployment insurance legislation created in 1935 was part of the most important social welfare program in American history.

To simplify the complex issues and interests that were involved in the development of unemployment insurance before 1935 I have distinguished between a "European" approach, or those programs, first initiated in Europe, which emphasized the worker and his economic needs, and an "American" approach, or those programs which looked to the employer, often encouraging him to "prevent" unemployment. It is true that all unemployment insurance plans provided for some form of monetary benefit and that most of the European-style legislation of the 1930's included some form of incentive to permit employers to reduce their payments to the state fund. Yet I believe it is important to recognize that virtually all the private unemployment insurance plans adopted before 1930 were designed, in theory, to help the employer perform more efficiently. And this theme, of helping the employer help himself, had a strong and in some cases decisive influence on the legislation enacted in the 1930's. If a single generalization were required to summarize the development of unemployment insurance in the United States, it might be that unemployment insurance was, and to some extent is today, intended to do much more than provide benefits to workers who lose their jobs.

Because of the importance of the American approach and the European precedents, I have devoted relatively little attention to grass-roots origins of the demands for a social insurance program in the 1930's. The social workers, union leaders, and reformers who urged such legislation seldom—with important exceptions—displayed much interest in the specific issues of unemployment insurance legislation, except to express support for a program providing benefits adequate to keep the able-bodied off the relief rolls. Unlike the businessmen, whose lack of unity was largely due to their obsession with details, these reformers generally had a simple view of unemployment insurance, a result of their exposure to the unprecedented distress of the unemployed in the 1930's. And because they drew their ideas from the British and German experiences and contributed little to the theory of unemployment insurance (as distinct from the mechanics of various administrative plans), I have done little more than enumerate the various groups that advocated unemployment measures as part of a social insurance program in the 1930's.

I have used the term "unemployment insurance" to cover a wide variety of programs, many of which were not based on insurance principles. This usage presents certain problems when the true insurance bills of the 1930's are considered, but nearly any other phrase would encounter similar difficulties at one point or another. My operational definition depends, then, not on whether actual insurance was involved, but rather on whether a specific plan was put into effect to pay benefits to jobless workers for either the workers' or the employers' ultimate gain. Undoubtedly a few employers or unions established programs that were in some respects similar to those I have considered but which have been forgotten. It hardly seems unfair to conclude, however, that knowledge of these experiments—even if it could be obtained—would not alter the trends that have been described.

For their kindness in allowing me to use and quote from manuscript collections I would like to express my appreciation to John Osgood Andrews (Andrews Papers), The State Historical Society of Wisconsin (Leiserson, Commons, Witte, Blaine, Huber, Clausen, American Federation of Labor, Wisconsin State Federation of Labor, D. C. Everest, and Federated Trades Council of Milwaukee Papers), Raymond S. Rubinow (Rubinow Papers), Mrs. Abraham Epstein (Epstein Papers), the Franklin D. Roosevelt Library (Roosevelt Papers), Georgetown University, Washington (Wagner Papers), Bergengren Memorial Museum Library of CUNA International, Inc. at the Filene House, Madison (Edward A. Filene Papers), the AFL-CIO (William Green Papers), Frank E. Mason (Herbert Hoover Papers), and the Amalgamated Clothing Workers of America (ACWA Papers).

I am also indebted to many individuals who have helped at various stages in the preparation of the manuscript. In particular I wish to thank Professor E. David Cronon of the University of Wisconsin for his generous advice and encouragement; Elizabeth Brandeis, Paul A. Raushenbush, Harold Groves, and J. F. Friedrick, who discussed their experiences with me; and most of all my wife Lorraine, whose editorial skills and typing prowess have been repeatedly overworked. I am, of course, solely responsible for the content.

CONTENTS

ILLUSTRATIONS

Unemployment Insurance

THE AMERICAN EXPERIENCE, 1915–1935

1 | ORIGINS OF AN AMERICAN APPROACH

"IT HAS taken the community a long time," observed the editor of the *Independent* in 1908, "to grasp the truth that under modern industrial conditions great numbers of working men out of work are not personally blameworthy for their misfortunes." For two centuries Americans had lived near the land. The outgrowth of this experience had been "a colonial or frontier philosophy" that emphasized the ability of every man to acquire property and manage his own affairs. Any man who was not lazy or improvident could provide for himself and his family in good times and bad. "But the day of such conditions is gone by. . . ." The growth of cities, factories, and a market economy had changed everything. "Industrial progress has put hundreds of thousands of wage-earners at the mercy of other men, who in turn are at the mercy of the great rhythmus of business prosperity and adversity."[1] Yet the editor underestimated the strength of the old beliefs. More than twenty years passed before substantial numbers of Americans were entirely convinced that this change had indeed taken place and that unemployed workers should be treated as victims of circumstances beyond their control.

The "colonial or frontier philosophy" did not, however, prevent the development of increasingly sophisticated relief programs in the nineteenth century. Haphazard public and private efforts gradually gave way, under pressure from the unemployed and the growing body of professional social workers, to a more systematic approach. The first signs of this appeared in the 1870's; by the 1890's most communities had made considerable advances, manifested in better organization of relief, often through city-wide coordinating committees, and a shift from public to private leadership. At the same time there was in-

3

creased emphasis on work relief and less on soup kitchens, which it was felt often led to the degradation of the unemployed. Yet despite the establishment of permanent charitable agencies, the hiring of professional full-time workers, and the acceptance of more systematic relief methods, the late-nineteenth- and early-twentieth-century efforts to meet the threat of unemployment were generally inadequate. Relief payments were often incredibly low; relatively little was done to establish effective employment agencies; work relief was costly and inefficient; and relief remained purely a community function.[2] There persisted, moreover, the conception of the unemployed worker as a victim of his own vices. As Thomas Nixon Carver, the economist, wrote, "Nothing could more effectively demoralize the laborer than the idea that he need not 'hustle' for himself."[3]

Even though the organization of community relief improved significantly toward the end of the nineteenth century, there was little agreement on measures to cope with unemployment on a long-term basis. In the 1870's, for example, Greenback leaders had proposed free transportation to carry unemployed workmen to the West.[4] Conservative unionists, on the other hand, favored public works, immigration restriction, and other measures to increase the amount of work or decrease the number of laborers. Socialists eschewed such remedies for a more fundamental restructuring of society. The depression of the 1890's produced many other proposals for remedies. Some observers called for state-sponsored savings plans to aid displaced wage earners, and a short-lived unemployment insurance company was even established in Chicago.[5] John R. Commons, a staff member of the Industrial Commission appointed by Congress in 1898, believed that unemployment was the "most serious of all our industrial problems. . . . the one," he emphasized, "which goes to the root of all other social problems."[6] Like other reformers of the 1890's, he called for currency and tariff reform. Unlike most of his colleagues, however, he defended the socialists' concept of the "right to work," albeit through moderate measures. "In lieu of economic reform giving stability to industry," he wrote, "the right to work during depressions is more or less protected by employment bureaus, labor colonies and public emergency works."[7] A Massachusetts investigating commission suggested an extensive, if modest, program that included returning workers to farms, a shorter work day, restricted immigration, extended industrial education, and improved state employment offices.[8] The sociologist Edward A. Ross admitted candidly, in reply to a request for an analysis of the problems facing labor, that he had no cure for unemployment. "I confess frankly," he added, "I am a good deal in the dark on that question."[9]

Insofar as they were able to agree on a long-term program, most reformers favored public works. This was in part a response to the popularity of public construction projects as a means of relief for the unemployed during the 1890's. But it was also a reflection of the attitude, held by a growing number of progressive thinkers, that government must ultimately assume responsibility for the welfare of the jobless. The economist Herbert Joseph Davenport foreshadowed the new concern in his well-known *The Outlines of Economic Theory* (1886), when he called for the postponement of public works until times of "labor stagnation." To finance construction during slack times, he proposed that government borrow during depressions and pay off its debts when prosperity returns.[10] Reform leaders such as Washington Gladden, Samuel M. "Golden Rule" Jones, Richard T. Ely, and B. O. Flowers, editor of the *Arena,* generally agreed with this idea. "It is much better," Ely explained, "that subsistence should be furnished in return for work rather than without work."[11]

But that few Americans—even few experts—had thought very far beyond relief was evident from a discussion that took place at the convention of the American Economic Association in 1901. Charles A. Tuttle, a professor at Wabash College, proposed a plan of indemnification for workers displaced by new machinery, a system similar to what would later be known as unemployment insurance. Tuttle argued that workers bear the full cost of technological change; therefore they should be compensated through a tax on the employer and the public —the primary recipients of the benefits of such change. Tuttle's colleagues, nevertheless, were unconvinced. One commentator remarked that such payments might "deaden individual enterprise" and that Tuttle's tax plan "would be difficult, if not impossible, to put into effect." Samuel MacCune Lindsay, an economist sympathetic to labor reform, struck a responsive chord when he suggested that state interference might check the efforts of private employers to keep their men regularly employed. Other critics of the paper predicted a variety of ills from such a system, but the most frequent themes were that it would promote idleness and that it was impractical. Only Commons, in fact, endorsed Tuttle's idea. He argued that Tuttle had a good point but that other ideas should also be considered: ". . . we can find lessons from other countries and different states, and draw upon our economic foundation for plans which would be practical and which would combine theory and practice."[12]

The European Experience

FORTUNATELY, THE few Americans who were ready to consider a long-term program had ample opportunities to "find lessons from other countries." In Europe there developed widespread interest in social insurance and unemployment measures in the late nineteenth and early twentieth centuries. Most European governments had a fair indication of the extent of the unemployment problem, either through trade union or government statistics, and had taken steps to provide compensatory benefits to the victims. A wide range of government relief programs of varying magnitude and effectiveness were in operation. Many labor unions also provided out-of-work benefits for their members. But government relief was often considered undesirable because of its costly administrative procedures and duplication of the union efforts, and the union funds were inadequate. The logical step seemed to be a combination of the two, a public contribution to the union funds. The beginning of this practice marked a new role for government in combating unemployment, and the first example of the European approach to unemployment insurance.

In the 1890's a number of Swiss and Belgian towns had started to assist their unions in paying out-of-work benefits. The first important scheme of this kind, instituted in St. Gall, Switzerland, in the late 1890's, was a compulsory, comprehensive benefit system that soon failed. Thereafter most municipal governments, following the example of Ghent, Belgium, merely subsidized union benefit funds to avoid the administrative problems of a government program. Though limited both in coverage and theory, since only a minority of wage earners in any country were union members and the employer did not participate in such a system, the Ghent plan was widely acknowledged as a success. In little more than a decade it had spread throughout Belgium, the Netherlands, Germany, Italy, and Switzerland. There were, in all, seventy such plans in existence in western Europe, though the heaviest concentration remained in Belgium and the Netherlands.[13]

Municipally subsidized trade-union benefit plans, once they had proved their merit, were adopted at the provincial and national level in many European countries during the first decade of the twentieth century. France began financing union unemployment-benefit funds and other similar programs in 1905. Norway followed in 1906, and Belgium and Denmark adopted the Ghent plan on a national scale in 1907. The Netherlands, Spain, Czechoslovakia, Finland, and Yugoslavia joined the list in the succeeding quarter century. Only Great Britain and Germany, among the important industrial nations of Europe, hesitated to adopt some form of the plan.

In Britain it had many partisans, but there was also a substantial group of labor leaders and intellectuals who wanted a more ambitious program. Their position was ably summarized by William Beveridge in his *Unemployment, A Problem of Industry*. Beveridge pointed out that subsidies to union funds would never be sufficient, because they did not attack the causes of unemployment. It was necessary, he maintained, to recognize that unemployment resulted from a "maladjustment between the supply and the demand for labour" and that the solution lay in "meeting without distress the changes and fluctuations without which industry is not and probably would not be carried on."[14] This could best be accomplished, Beveridge believed, through the establishment of a nationwide network of employment exchanges which would identify specific problems and bring together employers seeking men and men seeking employment.

Beveridge's analysis came at an auspicious time. The manifest inadequacies of the Poor Law relief system were well known and widely discussed. A Royal commission, appointed in 1905 as a result of persistent criticism, was conducting a study of ways to improve the operation of the system. Soon Beveridge was able to build a large following among those who believed that something more than the existing union exchanges was needed, and among his recruits were the influential Fabian socialists Sidney and Beatrice Webb.[15] Together they worked for the creation of an employment office system that would provide something more than mere relief payments for the worker.

Employment offices, however, provided no answer to the larger problem of what to do about workers who still were unable to obtain work. And on this point Beveridge and some of his followers were sharply divided. He recognized that the exchanges, by organizing the labor market, might substantially reduce needless unemployment. But he believed that industrial fluctuations would create a certain residual amount of unemployment no matter what the state of the economy. Unemployment was, in his opinion, "in some degree inevitable." The job of government was to find a means of coping with what remained. Thus by a series of economic reforms the state might further eliminate unnecessary joblessness and take important steps toward guaranteeing a minimum standard of living. "To a very large extent . . . it must suffice to aim at preventing not unemployment itself," he wrote, "but the distress which it now involves." He proposed a flexible system of wages and hours to keep pace with economic circumstance, the systematic planning of public works to counteract the business cycle, and unemployment insurance to compensate workers between jobs.[16]

The Webbs, on the other hand, agreed with Beveridge's analysis of the problem but saw in the establishment of employment offices the first step toward what Beatrice Webb termed "the more revolutionary scheme of dealing with unemployment." Unlike more radical and dogmatic socialists, they believed in gradualism; yet their ultimate aim was a fundamental change in the life of the working class.[17] To achieve this goal the Webbs proposed nothing less than "the prevention of destitution," a basic requirement of which was the elimination of joblessness. The problem was not so much the loss of income resulting from unemployment, but the fact that the unemployed wage earner "is suffering degeneration in skill, in health and in character, and that he is running grave risk of demoralization."[18] By providing economic security for the worker, they later wrote, "we should prevent at least nine-tenths of the destitution."[19] Prevention entailed a number of specific measures to reduce the incidence and extent of unemployment. To check the fluctuation of the business cycle, Sidney Webb proposed a program of compensatory spending, "the regularisation of the national aggregate demand." For noncyclical unemployment he proposed the dovetailing of seasonal work and the formation of a central pool of casual labor. By this means industry would continue to operate in its normal fashion but the worker would be assured a regular wage. The number of surplus workers eliminated from the labor market by these changes would be reduced by shorter working hours, the end of child labor, and a retraining program for the unfit or inefficient. An explicit feature of this approach was the regimentation of the labor force. "For every class of society," Webb wrote, "the deliberate organisation of leisure is as necessary as the organisation of work."[20]

Thus there were significant differences between the plans of Beveridge and the Webbs. Beveridge proposed to counteract an undesirable economic situation with a minimum of interference in the worker's daily life; the Webbs hoped to reform the individual laborer as they reformed society.

By 1908 the winds of reform in Britain were blowing strong. Agitation among workingmen and growing popular interest in foreign legislation led to new demands for action. The failure of the Poor Laws to prevent the pauperization of the jobless resulted in the formulation of several unemployment measures. A revamped Liberal ministry, which took office in 1908, soon devised the most ambitious social insurance program of any European country—one that included old age pensions, health insurance, a national system of labor exchanges, and a program of unemployment insurance more advanced than any yet adopted anywhere. One of the younger members of the new cabinet—Winston Churchill, the president of the Board of Trade—had a strong personal interest in unemployment, and responsibility for the drafting of legislation. His policies marked an important extension of the Ghent plan and a reaffirmation of the European approach to unemployment insurance.[21]

For a few months after he took over the Board of Trade, Churchill worked closely with both groups of reformers. Beatrice Webb rejoiced that he seemed to be "casting his lot" for "constructive state action" and was "most anxious to be friendly."[22] But it soon became apparent that Churchill had decided on a practical program that would avoid the most extreme elements of the Webbs' plans. In late 1908 he asked Beveridge, who had joined him at the Board of Trade, to draw up a workable unemployment insurance plan to accompany an employment exchanges bill. From this time Churchill moved rapidly away from the Webbs; repelled by the paternalism implicit in their plans, he embraced the more moderate social insurance program sponsored by Beveridge. And his choice proved to be decisive. Compensation, with no strings attached, was to be the hallmark of the British system. The reports of the Poor Law Commission, published in early 1909, emphasized the difference between the two approaches. The majority report advocated employment exchanges and unemployment insurance, but the dissenting minority report, written by the Webbs, proposed their prevention plan and the Ghent system. Beveridge suspected that the latter provision was tacked on as a "last-minute concession to the inevitable," since the Webbs knew of Churchill's intention to introduce an insurance measure.[23]

Although much less ambitious than the Webb's approach, Churchill's policy was, as Beveridge observed, "a risky adventure into the unknown."[24] No other nation in the world had contemplated compulsory unemployment insurance. Many contemporary students of unemployment reform agreed with Cyril Jackson that the only types of plans "which can claim any measure of real success are those based upon the trade unions themselves."[25] Parliament nevertheless passed the labor exchanges bill in 1909 and in 1911 pushed through the unemployment insurance plan that the Board of Trade reformers had drawn up two years before as Part II of the National Insurance Act. (Part I created a system of national health insurance.) The 1911 act established a compulsory system for workers in certain industries with high unemployment records; the total covered numbered about 2,250,000. Contributions were required from employers and employees, and a state subsidy amounting to one-third of the sum paid by the two groups increased the total available for benefits. This tripartite system of contributions became the distinguishing characteristic of the British plan. Although the emphasis of the act was on compensating the jobless, relatively strict limitations prevented unnecessary benefit payments, and modest incentive provisions allowed workers and employers with good employment records to claim refunds (a provision that was dropped in 1920). In deference to the Webbs, subsidies were offered to trade unions. While it rejected prevention, the 1911 act was sound financially, limited, moderate, and based, insofar as possible, on insurance methods.[26] It was, moreover, consistent with the principle of the Ghent plan in providing benefits while minimizing the regimentation of the labor force.

The impact of the events of 1909–11 was profound. Ten other countries, including Germany, adopted compulsory unemployment insurance during 1919–30. American reformers enthusiastically debated the Ghent plan and the ideas developed by Beveridge and the Webbs, and began working for a system of public labor exchanges, planned public works, and unemployment insurance. Few people seriously considered the Webbs' scheme for the United States, but a program similar to the British act was at least within the realm of possibility. "Little origination is now to be expected in the analysis of the problem," wrote William M. Leiserson, an early American student of unemployment. "In the United States everything remains to be done in working out practical laws and administrative machinery to put the theoretically sound remedies into practice."[27] But Leiserson exaggerated if he meant by "theoretically sound remedies" any more than the principle of compulsory unemployment insurance. For the emphasis on workers' benefits, the basis of both the Ghent and the British plans and hence of the European approach, was sure to clash with the "colonial or frontier philosophy." A conflict between prevention and automatic and adequate benefits was destined to play an important role in the American attack on unemployment, although in radically different form.

American Involvement

IF LEISERSON misjudged the theoretical importance of the British act, his statement was nevertheless an indication of its immense psychological impact. Events in Britain acted as a catalyst on American reformers. Suddenly the precedent for a workable long-term program existed. In the following years there appeared in the United States numerous reports on unemployment and equally numerous assessments of the relative merits of the Ghent and the British plans. Relatively few Americans, perhaps, changed their ideas about unemployment, but among the small groups of scholars and writers who were interested in unemployment, the British act had a remarkable influence.

From the beginning, however, it was evident that Americans would not merely copy the European approach to unemployment insurance. In a country where even the experts had been unable to devise a satisfactory program, it was presumptuous to expect the public to endorse a sophisticated unemployment insurance program in a single step. But unemployment insurance might be palatable if it were adapted to the prevailing values of American society. Thus having accepted Beveridge's argument that unemployment was a problem of industry, American reformers made the logical deduction that they should look to industry for a helping hand in solving the problem. This emphasis on the employer's ability to affect unemployment was apparent from the beginning of the American interest in unemployment remedies. But until the period of World War I it was merely a complement to the conventional European social insurance approach. After all, the 1911 British act offered financial rewards to employers who improved their employment records. The literalness with which Americans took the word "industry" in Beveridge's famous phrase became apparent only after the war, when, for reasons that will be explored later, many of the prewar reformers became ardent champions of unemployment prevention.

The writings of American economic and labor legislation experts on unemployment insurance between 1910–15 indicate the degree to which they had absorbed the ideas of the European reformers and adapted them to American conditions. On the eve of the passage of the British act, Henry R. Seager, a Columbia University economist, published the first important work on unemployment to appear in the United States. Like Beveridge, he recognized the importance of the "maladjustments" which accounted for "the growing seriousness of the problem of unemployment," yet he was critical of the Ghent system. American unions were so small and powerless that such a program would have a negligible effect. On the other hand, the absence of unemployment statistics would hamper the effectiveness of any government-sponsored program in the United States. Instead, Seager argued, American reformers should emphasize the ability of employers to stabi-

lize production and sales.[28] Louis D. Brandeis, long a critic of inefficient business management, also recognized the relative weakness of
American unions and the power of the American businessmen. He
argued that the employer rather than the union leader held the key to
the solution of the unemployment problem. "Society and industry," he
maintained, "need only the necessary incentive to secure a great reduction in irregularity of employment. In the scientifically managed business, irregularity tends to disappear."[29] Judge Elbert H. Gary, head of
the New York City Mayor's Commission on Unemployment, sounded
the same note several years later when he explained that "the problem
of unemployment is essentially one of business and of business management, and must be met by business statesmanship."[30]

It was Leiserson, however, who made the most thorough attempt to
apply the foreign experience to American conditions. As a special investigator for the Wainwright Commission of the New York legislature, he traveled to Europe in 1910 and presented a paper to the First
International Conference on Unemployment describing the benefit
plans of American unions and the operation of public employment
offices.[31] He also had the opportunity to hear the leading European experts debate the virtues of trade-union unemployment insurance versus
the anticipated merits of compulsory schemes like that being considered in Great Britain.[32] His report, published the following year, reflected his experiences. "Unemployment is," he concluded, "a permanent feature of industrial life everywhere." He urged the creation of
an effective public employment office system, planned public works, the
restriction of immigration, and unemployment insurance. However, he
did not believe that state-sponsored unemployment insurance was feasible "until we establish an exchange for labor and compile careful statistics of the supply and demand."[33]

Similar suggestions appeared in Isaac M. Rubinow's comprehensive
Social Insurance, published in 1913. Rubinow described the foreign
methods of coping with unemployment and the prerequisites for an
American program; he pointed out the absence of adequate unemployment statistics in the United States and the need for more information
before any plan could succeed. But he left no doubt about the importance of such an effort. Unemployment insurance would constitute the
"pivotal point" of a comprehensive social insurance system. And he
recognized the dilemma that would face all advocates of unemployment insurance in the next two decades: insufficient statistics made the
establishment of a genuine insurance system difficult at best, but without an unemployment insurance program "it is almost impossible to
trace all existing unemployment." Rubinow's answer—a compulsory,

subsidized unemployment-insurance system—won far less acclaim and attention than his analysis of the problem.[34]

The many American writings on unemployment that appeared after 1910 were only one indication of the stimulus that the British experience had provided. Equally important—and in the long run perhaps more so—was the increased attention that the American Association for Labor Legislation paid to the problem of unemployment. The AALL, founded in 1906, was a symbol of the growing American interest in labor legislation in general and social insurance in particular. It was modeled after similar organizations in Europe and included among its membership many progressive intellectuals, social workers, and professional reformers. It was originally formed for the immediate purpose of agitating for workmen's compensation legislation, but under the direction of its secretary, John B. Andrews, it soon became active in promoting a wide variety of labor reforms. In the period between 1910 and the First World War, it became the chief agent in directing the new interest in unemployment into support for a number of specific measures, including unemployment insurance legislation.

Although virtually everyone who wrote about or was in any way connected with unemployment measures was an AALL member, three men were primarily responsible for shaping the unemployment policies of the association. Andrews was, of course, the central figure. As secretary he not only managed the day-to-day activities of the AALL but was responsible for many policy decisions. In this activity he closely followed foreign developments, but he also relied on the advice of John R. Commons, the second major figure in the association's work. In 1904 Commons had joined the faculty of the University of Wisconsin, and in the following years had trained a number of outstanding graduate students, including Andrews. In 1911 he began a two-year term as an administrator of the Wisconsin workmen's compensation act. During this period he concluded that employers under the pressure of the compensation law had managed to reduce substantially their accident rates.[35] From this observation he generalized that the proper financial incentive would induce employers to prevent other social ills. Commons' doctrine of prevention differed in several respects from the Webbs' plan: it was based on a minimum of state interference and focused on the activities of the employer rather than those of the government or the trade union. Andrews wrote in 1915 that "Professor Commons and I . . . have thought first of prevention and second of relief in dealing with each form of social insurance in this country."[36]

The third man who played a decisive role in the prewar unemployment work of the AALL was Charles R. Henderson, professor of sociology at the University of Chicago. Like Commons, Henderson had long recognized the importance of unemployment and had closely followed European developments. As early as 1898 he had noted the ill effects of industrialism and improved technology on the workers' security; employers, he contended, could partially alleviate these threats "by making their plans to keep their work going more steadily and avoid the rush of specially active seasons."[37] But he also called for a public policy to offset the "defects" of industry which "result in widespread misery and ruin."[38] His chief contribution to the advancement of unemployment insurance was, however, his organizing ability. In 1912 he headed a Chicago city committee to study the unemployment problem in that area. This committee recommended only improvements in the employment-exchange system, but its successor, the Chicago Industrial Commission, likewise a product of Henderson's influence, called for unemployment insurance "by state or nation"—significant first steps toward a legislative program.[39]

These men first raised the issue of AALL involvement in unemployment work at the December 1911 annual convention. Andrews scheduled William Hard, a reformer-journalist, to speak on "Unemployment as a Coming Issue" and Henderson to review recent events in Europe. After the speeches Henderson introduced a resolution calling for the establishment of an American section of the newly created International Association on Unemployment. He was then selected to head a committee to contact the International Association and make the official arrangements.[40] Henderson, Andrews, and Lee K. Frankel, an insurance company executive, attended a conference of the International Association in Zurich in September 1912, where the American section was officially chartered.[41] Andrews later explained Henderson's strategic role in the creation of this body: ". . . Professor Henderson's desire [was] to extend to the United States, a movement that is rapidly gaining ground in Europe, for the purpose of avoiding unnecessary duplication of effort among organizations like our own."[42] The American section as such was seldom heard from afterward, but this activity did serve to commit the AALL to an active role in the struggle for unemployment legislation.

It was also indicative of a growing belief, expressed by Andrews, that unemployment "is not only the most difficult but the most important problem with which we will have to deal in the coming years."[43] This belief led the AALL leaders to organize or at least introduce the unemployment issue in a series of conferences in 1913–14. The first of these was the First American Conference on Social Insurance, held in 1913 in Chicago. Andrews, Henderson, Rubinow, Seager, and others had founded a social insurance committee of the AALL the previous year to organize the conference. They had used this pretext to study social insurance "in preparation for legislation next year," but there is no evidence that they contemplated the immediate introduction of unemployment insurance bills.[44] At the conference itself Henderson discussed unemployment insurance. He emphasized the need to "prevent or indemnify unemployment" and endorsed the British system. Yet he and the other conference delegates concluded, as Rubinow later reported, that "little thought has been given in this country to the insurance method of meeting this problem."[45] To stimulate additional thought the association sponsored an unemployment conference in early 1914 to examine the entire problem and decide on ways of proceeding in the future.

The First National Conference on Unemployment, which met in New York in February, was devoted to a general discussion of the unemployment problem. More than three hundred delegates, including officials from twenty-five states and fifty-nine cities, considered various aspects of the unemployment problem. They reported on the extent of unemployment in their areas and then discussed long-term remedies. At the opening session Henderson called on the delegates to ponder new ideas, including unemployment insurance legislation. Seager then summarized the British system, which he believed to be on the verge of solving the problem of unemployment in Great Britain.[46] The delegates passed resolutions emphasizing the need for improved statistics, a national system of employment exchanges, improved industrial education, the "regularization" of business, and compulsory unemployment insurance. One observer noted "a prevailing sentiment in favor of the ultimate adoption in America of some form of unemployment insurance for working men supported jointly by the Government, employers, and employees."[47]

The February conference, coupled with a fortuitous (at least from the reformers' point of view) downturn in the business cycle occasioned by the outbreak of the European war, created the momentum to sustain the AALL's unemployment work in the following months. As a result of the conference Andrews raised "quite a substantial fund to continue the work started under such favorable circumstances."[48] Taking advantage of the increased public interest in unemployment, he initiated a series of studies to discover what changes American conditions would require in the European programs. These included a study of seasonal employment conditions in Boston directed by Juliet S. Poyntz, a student of the Webbs, a survey of unemployment in Oregon, reports on public employment bureaus, public works, and women's wages, and a detailed examination of the British unemployment insurance system.[49]

The continuing unemployment problem and the reports that Andrews received from his field workers were the subjects of the AALL's Second National Conference on Unemployment, held in Philadelphia in December 1914. The meeting itself attracted less attention than the First National Conference because of the many emergency committees and conferences that competed for attention during the recession period and because it was devoted to the consideration of reform measures rather than to an immediate relief program. Nevertheless, a number of papers were presented to the conference by academic experts and public officials, suggesting the scope of the problem and offering many ideas. But more important was the formal presentation of a document which was to serve as a blueprint for much of the unemployment agitation in the United States during the following twenty years, *A Practical Program for the Prevention of Unemployment.*[50]

The *Practical Program* was a synthesis of Commons' ideas and the findings of the recent AALL studies that Andrews drew up for the delegates. It called for the creation of efficient employment offices, advanced planning of public works to counteract cyclical fluctuations, unemployment insurance, and the regularization of employment by individual employers. The first three of these proposals, which had earlier appeared in the Poor Law Commission reports and the Webbs' proposals, reflected the strong foreign influence on American thinking. But the last proposal, and to some extent the section on unemployment insurance, revealed the influence of Commons' prevention theory. While the American reformers envisioned a less radical transformation of society than the Webbs, they were no less ambitious; by adjusting the employer's unemployment insurance contributions to his employment record, they sought to persuade employers to do what their English counterparts sought to achieve through the reeducation of the labor force—prevent the recurrence of joblessness. Though Andrews incorporated certain features of the British act, notably the provision for contributions from employers, employees, and the state, his attitude differed markedly from that of Beveridge or Churchill on the purpose of unemployment insurance. "Of crowning importance in the movement toward regularization of industry," he wrote, "is the careful development of this form of insurance with its continuous pressure toward the prevention of unemployment."[51] Within a few months the AALL distributed 22,000 copies of the *Practical Program* and began a twenty-year campaign for what increasingly became an American approach to unemployment insurance.[52]

Legislative Efforts

DURING THE brief period between the program's publication and the entry of the United States into World War I, compulsory unemployment insurance became an objective of progressive reformers, much as other advanced measures were belatedly incorporated in the platforms of national and state progressive groups. As such, the demand for unemployment insurance was part of the larger drive for social insurance legislation which gathered momentum during the same period. While it was probably the least popular and least understood of the various insurance proposals, it had the backing of a variety of reformers. At this early time the problems that would plague the movement in later years were not yet apparent. For this reason the AALL-backed plan received a relatively enthusiastic reception where it was proposed; in time, it appeared, the United States might join Great Britain in implementing a compulsory plan of unemployment insurance.

The most important attempt to secure unemployment insurance legislation before World War I occurred in Massachusetts, where the AALL study developed into a full-scale assault on unemployment. An anonymous observer wrote that Miss Poyntz returned to Boston in December 1914 and "made arrangements with Mr. Robert Valentine by which he was to form a Massachusetts Committee on Unemployment as a branch of the American Association on Unemployment [sic]."[53] Organized in early 1915, Valentine's committee included subcommittees on relief, rural resources, labor exchanges, industrial education, public works, and unemployment insurance, the last of which included Olga Halsey, Felix Frankfurter, and Ordway Tead, a prominent management engineer, among its members.[54] After several meetings this group decided to introduce a bill in the 1916 Massachusetts state legislature "following the general principles of the English Unemployment Insurance Act."[55] With the assistance of the social insurance committee of the AALL and an AALL representative named Joseph Cohen, Frankfurter and Arthur D. Hill, a Boston attorney, then proceeded to draft a bill similar to the British law but "adapted to American conditions"—meaning the inclusion of definite prevention provisions.[56]

In its final form this bill covered workers in various specific industries who made less than $25 a week, who had been employed for a designated period before their layoff, and who were capable but unable to find work. The employer and the employee would each contribute one-fourth of the total, and the state would add the remaining one-half. Benefits would vary from $3.50 to $7.00 per week depending on the worker's average wage and would last no more than ten weeks in a given year. At the end of the year the administrators of the fund would refund one-half of the employers' and wage earners' remaining contributions in the hope of encouraging employers to keep their men on the job. As a result of a "vigorous campaign to induce the legislature next year to pass such a measure," the bill received the endorsements of the Massachusetts Republican Party, the Massachusetts State Federation of Labor, the New England Typographical Union, and several progressive employers.[57] On January 4, 1916, the Valentine Committee sponsored the introduction of the first unemployment insurance bill in American history.

It is doubtful that Valentine or his colleagues were optimistic over the prospects of their bill, at least in 1916, for they proposed a resolution calling for a commission to study social insurance at the same time. Cohen, in fact, wanted two distinct commissions in order to keep the question of health insurance separate from unemployment.[58] Their position was well taken because the original bill aroused sufficient opposition among employers to convince the Joint Rules Committee not to return a favorable report. The committee report did, however, urge the passage of the social-insurance commission resolution, and the legislature complied by a wide margin.[59] The report of this commission, submitted in February 1917, also seemed to confirm the wisdom of the reformers' strategy. The legislators professed to be "in general accord with the ideas of Mr. John B. Andrews" and did not deny the desirability of unemployment insurance. In fact they called on businessmen to set up their own plans of unemployment reserves in order "to prevent unemployment and not to relieve it."[60] Yet they refused to endorse compulsory action, and in the end this refusal was decisive. With the return of prosperity public interest in unemployment flagged and Valentine's committee gradually disbanded, leaving the field to the progressive employers of Massachusetts who, like the legislative committee members, were "in accord with" Andrews' ideas but who also emphasized the importance of education and self-interest rather than government compulsion in achieving their goals.

If the immediate consequences of the reformers' activities in Massachusetts were disappointing, in Illinois they were even less satisfactory and left no legacy to build on in the future. Henderson's long efforts to educate the people reached their zenith early in 1915 when he reported to Andrews that the "public mind is ripening for unemployment insurance."[61] As head of the Chicago Industrial Commission he had found that local businessmen were reluctant to cooperate in the creation of a relief fund because it included no provision for unemployment prevention. Henderson hoped that this deficiency would arouse "the business world to a serious effort to grapple with the evil in some thorough and earnest fashion."[62] With this end in mind he therefore began to work with Andrews and other AALL officials in an unemployment insurance bill for the Illinois legislature. Such a measure probably would have resembled the Massachusetts bill if it had ever been introduced.[63] But in mid-March Henderson became ill from overwork and unexpectedly died several weeks later. Henderson's death effectively ended whatever possibility there had been for a sustained drive to enact unemployment insurance legislation in Illinois.

The leadership of AALL representatives in Massachusetts and Illinois should not, however, obscure the fact that in this period many other groups became involved in the promotion, or at least the discussion, of unemployment insurance legislation. There were a few legislative proposals, none of which received serious consideration, and a wide variety of public and private studies. Numerous state legislative committees and one congressional group, the United States Commission on Industrial Relations, gave some attention to unemployment insurance. The reactions of the former were frequently negative or inconclusive, but the latter, aided by Commons and several of his students, took a more benevolent view. Early in the commission's investigation Leiserson, who was the staff specialist on unemployment, asked the commissioners to consider unemployment insurance and advised a thorough examination of employment office practices as a practical first step toward this end.[64] The majority report of the commission reflected this approach: it noted the desirability of unemployment insurance but emphasized the immediate need for better employment offices.[65] The minority report, on the other hand, did not go so far. Although Commons, who wrote this statement, considered unemployment the greatest evil facing American workmen, he noted that "such measures as . . . unemployment insurance evidently require a large amount of investigation before they can be recommended. Their principal object should be the cooperation of employers and employees in the prevention of . . . unemployment."[66]

The appropriateness of Commons' warning became apparent in 1916 when a congressional committee considered a proposal by the Socialist representative Meyer London for a social insurance commission, raising for the first time the question of unemployment insurance before Congress. A number of reformers, in most instances members of the AALL, testified in favor of compulsory unemployment insurance.[67] Rubinow summarized European developments in general and Miss Poyntz explained the British system.[68] But their efforts made little headway after Samuel Gompers, president of the American Federation of Labor, occupied more than half the committee's time with a virulent attack on compulsory social insurance and socialism, which he seemed to equate. Gompers also offered a counterresolution calling for a study of voluntary social insurance.[69] His opposition was more than sufficient to end any serious consideration of London's bill.

The social insurance campaigns of 1918–19, a postscript to these efforts, were essentially a continuation and in some cases an extension of the earlier actions. Buoyed by the idealism of the war period and foreign radicalism, many progressives sought to continue the prewar campaign for social insurance legislation. In most cases their efforts were aimed at health insurance or old age pensions, but unemployment insurance was also frequently mentioned. A few union leaders broke with Gompers and endorsed the enactment of compulsory unemployment insurance. Religious groups such as the American Catholic Bishops and the Federal Council of Churches urged similar action in their postwar reconstruction programs.[70] Other organizations, both public and private, added their approval, although there were occasional reservations about the practical problems of devising an unemployment insurance program. Governor Alfred E. Smith's Commission on a Permanent Unemployment Program, for example, forecast difficulties for unemployment insurance unless an improved employment office system and a vigorous stabilization effort preceded it.[71]

These events indicated both the promise and the inherent problems in any effort to create a system of compulsory unemployment insurance in the United States. Many economists and reformers—notably those who were active in advancing other forms of social insurance—welcomed the idea but agreed that the time was not ripe for legislation. Noting the British experience, they pointed to the absence of adequate public employment facilities and the slight prospect of obtaining them. At the same time, public interest in the plight of the unemployed was uncertain with the return of peace, and the opposition of employers, commercial insurance companies, and political conservatives was growing. By 1919 the movement for unemployment and other forms of social insurance legislation had reached a turning point; the events of the following years would determine the future course of such legislation and, indeed, the status of unemployment insurance in the United States.

Prospects for Legislation, 1919–

BEFORE 1920 the campaign for unemployment insurance was almost wholly a political movement, derived from European precedents and nurtured on growing public support for social insurance legislation. Whether it would continue as a political movement in an increasingly hostile atmosphere depended on a number of considerations that were only indirectly related to the activities of the men who had initiated the struggle in the prewar years. The policies of organized labor, which are treated at greater length in later chapters, the ability of reformers to implement the other provisions of the *Practical Program,* the performance of the European plans, and the extent of unemployment, so important in the successful British campaign and the American efforts of 1914–16—all profoundly affected the prospects for compulsory unemployment insurance in the following years.

No development better revealed the problems ahead for unemployment insurance legislation than the failure of the other legislative provisions of the *Practical Program,* particularly employment exchanges. In part this failure resulted from the rapid growth and frequent mismanagement of employment offices before and during the First World War. In 1917, after ten years of agitation, there were over ninety public employment bureaus in the United States.[72] Yet the administration of these offices was invariably inefficient and occasionally scandalous; moreover, the bureaus offered little effective competition to the often corrupt private fee-charging agencies. Even during the war, when the nation, as never before in its history, faced the task of rapidly organizing and allocating its human resources in a systematic manner, the establishment of a national employment service was essentially a "war afterthought."[73] Although the federal government began the preliminary steps in mid-1917, the United States Employment Service was not officially created until early 1918. Then it faced a virtually impossible task with little time to organize and insufficient funds. By October 1918 there were, however, 832 offices throughout the nation attempting with mixed success to handle the vast manpower problems of the nation.[74] The decline of this jerry-built system occurred even more rapidly than its rise. Complaints of employers, union officials, and cost-conscious politicians doomed the organization; retrenchment began soon after the armistice, and after March 1919 the USES's financial resources practically vanished. By the end of the year nearly all the offices had been closed or turned over to the states, and the USES, despite a few feeble efforts at rejuvenation, began a decade and a half of virtual inactivity.[75]

A second provision of the *Practical Program*, planned public works, encountered similar difficulties during the 1920's. The first serious efforts to organize public works with the goal of counteracting the business cycle took place during World War I. Otto T. Mallery, a vigorous exponent of such planning, developed a program to schedule public works to coincide with the downswing of the business cycle.[76] But the end of the war also marked the end of popular interest in economic planning of the type Mallery favored. Nevertheless, planned public spending remained a topic of discussion, though not action, in the following decade. Herbert Hoover endorsed the idea and Wadill Catchings and William Trufant Foster popularized it in their writings. Many other political leaders were free with their praise if not their votes. The agitation for public works planning culminated with the Jones "prosperity reserve" bill of 1928 and a congressional campaign under the sponsorship of Senator Robert Wagner of New York that dragged on, with little success, until 1931.

Though these developments augured ill for compulsory unemployment insurance, the operation of the unemployment insurance systems in Europe, particularly Great Britain and Germany, had an even more direct effect on the receptiveness of the American public to such legislation. In Britain the war and the postwar depression placed increasing pressure on the unemployment insurance system. Before 1918 most British observers anticipated increased unemployment in the reconstruction period and sought to plan for it.[77] These preparations, however, proved to be inadequate; many industries, particularly those that had been the basis of the nation's economy before the war, suffered a continuous decline. Unemployment reached 2,500,000 in 1921 and was never below 1,000,000 in the following decade.[78]

Unfortunately for the unemployment insurance program in Britain, the magnitude of the postwar slump was much worse than even the most pessimistic economists had forecast. Meanwhile the system, which included munitions workers after 1916, was again expanded in 1920 to cover nearly all laborers under the same contributory provisions. Before sufficient funds accumulated to pay tremendously increased benefits, the economic downturn rapidly increased the ranks of the unemployed. Beginning in 1921 the government extended the benefit periods to help workers who had exhausted their eligibility and had no other recourse but charity. Thus began the period of the "dole," as

American opponents of unemployment insurance legislation termed it. Between 1921 and 1930 Parliament constantly revised the basic legislation to meet the demands of the depression. By 1927 benefit periods were almost indefinite and payments bore no relation to contributions.[79] Undoubtedly there were many errors in the planning and administration of the system; yet as one expert noted, "The patchwork system was characteristic of British methods and escaped serious criticism mainly because no responsible persons had anything better to propose."[80]

The British unemployment insurance program, despite constant reorganization, performed well under incredibly adverse circumstances. Indeed, it is hard to imagine an alternative under similar conditions. The people, as Harold J. Laski reported, were "insistent that the government produce a thorough-going plan for coping with the evil."[81] While the addition of relief provisions to the insurance scheme angered purists, it was still far superior to the traditional relief programs and prevented the jobless from starving. The British employer B. Seebohm Rowntree contended that "our system of insurance, inadequate as it is, has, in my opinion, saved us from something like revolution."[82] But it also provided a wealth of ammunition to business groups and insurance companies in the United States, who invariably pointed to the British plan as an example of how political interests would soon change an actuarially sound program into a mere handout.

If the British experience with compulsory unemployment insurance left any doubts in the minds of Americans, the German experience seemed to confirm their belief that such a system would inevitably degenerate into a dole. Though the Weimar government had adopted a systematic relief policy in 1919 which carried through the immediate reconstruction period, the recurring economic crises of the 1920's forced the adoption of a variety of expedients, including public works, subsidies to private firms, and finally unemployment insurance.[83] Under the act of 1927 the employers and employees were to pay equal contributions, and any deficit was to be made up from a national reserve fund. No provision for regularization by employers appeared in the act because German experience with unemployment relief indicated that individual employers could do little.[84] But like Great Britain, Germany suffered a sharp economic depression and widespread unemployment almost at the time the act went into effect. Thereafter the ranks of the jobless constantly swelled, until more than 6,000,000 were out of work by 1932.[85] Consequently the fund, which the government designed to cope with a much smaller volume of unemployment, had to be supplemented from the public treasury. After 1928 the deficits grew large; soon the German situation closely resembled the British. The economic debacle made the German efforts to operate on strict insurance principles hopeless. A contemporary student of the German system wrote that the depression "has necessitated the development of a thorough-going system of unemployment insurance at the same time that it has created conditions with which no unemployment insurance system alone can cope."[86] While most Germans considered unemployment insurance preferable to what they had had before, this was little consolation to American reformers.

Unlike Europe, there was in postwar America no large and politically vocal group of jobless wage earners. The exceptional years of 1920–22, when the collapse of the postwar boom threw millions out of work, produced the usual demands for reform as well as relief. But the rapid recovery of 1922 and the relatively full employment during the rest of the decade helped cut short this agitation. Despite the fact that the great majority of states made little effort to collect unemployment statistics, the estimates of joblessness for the period from 1917 to the Great Depression are sufficiently accurate to question the implication of Professor Irving Bernstein that high unemployment was a distinctive social problem of the 1920's.[87]

In spite of the paucity of statistics, students of unemployment have reached surprisingly similar conclusions on the extent of joblessness in the United States before the Depression. As early as 1918 Hornell Hart, an economist and social worker, estimated that total unemployment for the period 1902–17 averaged 9.9 percent annually.[88] Though Hart's methodology was frequently criticized, other studies seemed to confirm his conclusion. In 1929 Leo Wolman and Meredith Givens reported that unemployment had averaged 7.8 percent between 1920 and 1927. The authors admitted that this figure probably underestimated the actual total and provided no indication of seasonal fluctuations in employment.[89] Shortly thereafter Paul H. Douglas published his pioneering study, *Real Wages in the United States,* which included an estimate of unemployment based on the work of Hart and Wolman and Givens. For manufacturing and transportation Douglas concluded that average unemployment between 1889–1926 was 7.5 percent. When he combined this with the figures for construction and mining, he reached an overall average of 10.2 percent for 1897–1926.[90] Using a somewhat different technique David Weintraub later calculated that more than 10 percent of available manpower had been unemployed in the 1920's.[91]

A more recent investigator, Stanley Lebergott, has seemingly questioned the implication of these studies. "High-level employment," he has maintained, "characterized the performance of the American economy in the past half century."[92] Yet upon closer observation it becomes apparent that the difference between Lebergott and his predecessors is not as great as one might first suspect. In fact, they differ only in evaluating the importance of the extent of unemployment. They agree that average unemployment in prosperous years remained about the same and that there was no trend toward greater unemployment after the turn of the century. Lebergott, moreover, qualifies his judgment by acknowledging that 10 to 15 percent of urban wage earners were able to find only part-time work even before the 1930's.[93] Though there seems little doubt that unemployment was remarkably high during this period, it was apparently no more serious after 1910 than in the previous years when it received relatively little attention from economists, public officials, or reformers.

Yet it is also true that joblessness, even if merely an irritant to the economy as a whole, was a major problem in the few key industries in which it was concentrated after 1917. The "sick" industries, such as coal and railroads, obviously made substantial contributions to the totals of Douglas, Wolman and Givens, and Lebergott. Perhaps more important, because they were subject to "maladjustments" rather than to mass unemployment, were the manufacturing industries. As early as 1911, a congressional committee had found that only 63 percent of the nation's steelworkers were employed an average of forty-four hours per week whatever the state of the economy. "This striking situation" was attributed to the "business policies followed in the industry."[94] The same policies resulted in considerable hardship for wage earners in other industries. Robert S. and Helen Lynd found in the 1920's that Middletown workers were so concerned about losing their jobs that they preferred steady employment to high wages or the opportunity for advancement.[95] But irregular or casual work was only one aspect of the problem; more than 1,000,000 wage earners were seasonally employed and thousands of others lost their jobs as a result of technological improvements. Weintraub estimated that an average of 250,000 men per year were displaced during the 1920's by technological changes and that the average worker was jobless for nearly nine months before finding other work. After 1926 "the absorptive capacity of the manufacturing industries had already begun to lag behind the displacement effects of improved productive technology."[96]

Unstable employment was magnified by the rapid growth of American manufacturing in the early decades of the century. The production increases dating from the recovery of the late 1890's were unusually high and were accompanied by an equally significant rise in the number of factory workers. The number of wage earners engaged in manufacturing increased from 4,500,000 in 1899 to a peak of nearly 8,500,000 in 1919.[97] Lebergott's figures show that the number of persons added in all manufacturing occupations was double the total increase in any other nonfarm sector of the economy between 1900 and 1909, and quadruple the number added in the next decade.[98] Increased output was in large part a result of the continuous influx of new workers over this twenty-year period.[99]

In the postwar era manufacturing output continued to rise at its previous rate, but, contrary to the earlier tendency, the number of employees engaged in these industries remained virtually stationary. Substantial productivity increases rather than new workers accounted for the growth of the 1920's. In part, managers may have shifted to labor-saving machinery as a result of the rise in real wages that accompanied the wartime labor shortage and persisted through the 1920's. But doubtless of equal significance was their tendency to devote more attention to the organization and administration of their factories. Frederick C. Mills, writing in 1932, was among the first economists to note this development. He observed that "integration and concentration of production in establishments turning out constantly larger quantities of goods, have proceeded more rapidly during the last decade than in any similar period."[100]

This interest in improved managerial technique, and the high rate of unemployment—particularly of the casual, seasonal, and technological variety—in manufacturing, had an important effect on the campaign for unemployment insurance in the 1920's. The decline of political progressivism, reflected in the reformers' failure to enact the Practical Program, helped focus the attention of many of the same men on the activities of businessmen. At the same time the European depression discredited, at least for American conservatives, the European approach to unemployment insurance, and enhanced the ideas developed by Commons and men like Brandeis. Thus the unemployment prevention campaign of the 1920's and the Depression years was the successor to the early activities of the AALL and the social insurance movement. Beveridge, Churchill, and the Webbs had performed a distinct service in emphasizing unemployment as a problem of industry. It remained, however, for American reformers, many of whom disavowed the source of their ideas, to carry this theme to its logical conclusion.

Looking back ten years after the *Practical Program,* the pioneering Massachusetts campaign, and other developments in the broader field of social insurance of the prewar era, Isaac M. Rubinow assessed the results of the decade's work. "In the United States there is at this moment," he reluctantly acknowledged in 1926, "no very active movement for social insurance." Unlike Europe, where the war's destruction of life and property had generated a new demand for social welfare programs, notably compulsory unemployment insurance, the United States experienced prosperity and a political reaction following the war that halted virtually all progress in the direction of an adequate social insurance system. The reaction, he recalled, had come suddenly and "lasted longer than most of us had reason to expect." There were, nevertheless, "a few symptoms of the beginning of a recovery." Improvements in workmen's compensation legislation and mothers' assistance laws had proceeded in spite of the adverse political climate. He could also have cited the few old-age pension and assistance laws that passed state legislatures and the even fewer unemployment insurance bills (twenty in number) that reformers—generally socialists interested in extended relief programs—had introduced in the 1920's without success. These efforts, modest though they were, indicated that many Americans still realized that "the problems themselves will not be solved by mere disregard of conditions." And of even greater importance, he added perceptively, were "the groping efforts of American employers and employees to meet these problems, sometimes together, sometimes separately."[101]

2 | BUSINESS AND THE "NEW EMPHASIS"

IF THE era of normalcy signified the decline of political progressivism, it also witnessed a new awakening to the problems—and potentialities—of business management. American businessmen resolved, as Henry S. Dennison, a Framingham, Massachusetts, tag and paper manufacturer wrote, to "deal in a businesslike way with business problems."[1] They devised new processes, new techniques, new strategies of organization. A few experimented with innovations in top-level administration—the creation of multidivision firms with central planning departments—but many more developed an increased awareness of the importance of efficient plant operation.[2]

As Howard Coonley, a Boston businessman argued, a "revolution" seemed to have occurred. The "weapons" of the revolution were "marketing analysis, thorough budgeting, sound scheduling, and broadminded personnel cooperation."[3] This preoccupation with higher production and lower costs also led to a wider realization of the losses resulting from unemployment, for, as Herman Feldman, a business-school professor, noted, there was "a greater chaos of inefficient management of sales, finance, production and personnel" behind the "confusion of fluctuating labor requirements."[4] To deal with the problem realistically it would be necessary to forget the remedies of the political reformers and to adopt a new approach, indeed, a "New Emphasis," to prevent unemployment where it occurred—in the factory. Many American businessmen agreed to the occasional use of Coonley's weapons to prevent joblessness; a few realized that the only lasting solution, the only way to insure their continuous attention, was to stake their profits on the New Emphasis through a program of unemployment insurance.

The employers of the 1920's were not entirely original in emphasiz-

28

ing voluntary prevention. Louis D. Brandeis, the lawyer and jurist, had developed what was essentially the New Emphasis approach at the turn of the century when he and William H. McElwain, owner of a Boston shoe company, had worked out a plan for year-round production to maintain continuous employment.[5] He had come back to the idea in 1910, when he created the Protocol, a plan to stabilize production and reduce seasonal layoffs, for the New York garment industry. By 1911 he had formulated a plan for dealing with irregular employment, the basis of which, he wrote, was the premise that "irregularity can be overcome in large measure." To achieve this ambitious goal he sought to provide businessmen with an incentive to systematize their operations by establishing a fund which "would therefore have not only the advantage of providing an incentive to make the employment regular, but it would also provide something like a benefit or insurance fund for current payments during the idle period."[6] Before 1916, when he was appointed to the Supreme Court, Brandeis elaborated on his ideas to a wide variety of correspondents and associates.[7] He told the United States Commission on Industrial Relations that "industry has been allowed to develop chaotically, mainly because we have accepted irregularity of employment as if it was something inevitable. . . . a business can not be run profitably unless you keep it running, because if you have to pay [wages or benefits] whether your men are working or not, your men will work."[8] While company unemployment funds were too radical for most businessmen, Brandeis' approach, if not his specific suggestions, offered many promising avenues for action.

Although Brandeis outlined the New Emphasis in the prewar era, businessmen and their spokesmen were primarily responsible for popularizing it in the 1920's. Feldman wrote, in one of the most important discussions of the new approach, that the "Indifference of Management" was the "one common cause of unemployment." And while he rejected the British approach to unemployment insurance, he suggested that the creation of a company fund to cover operating expenses in slack periods or provide unemployment benefits might be feasible.[9] A group of businessmen and economists concluded in *Can Business Prevent Unemployment?* that compulsory unemployment insurance was impractical for the United States but that managers could do a great deal to improve efficiency and reduce joblessness.[10] Edwin S. Smith, Massachusetts Commissioner of Labor, warned businessmen "not to gamble against a heavy loss" by unnecessary expansion and contraction in his *Reducing Seasonal Unemployment*.[11] *Waste in Industry* (1920), sponsored by the American Engineering Council, concluded that poor management was responsible for tremendous wastes in nearly every area of business activity. Wesley C. Mitchell, summarizing the economic changes of the postwar period, found that "the old process of putting science into industry has been followed more intensively than before."[12]

Of the themes that appeared consistently in the New Emphasis literature, the least logical but perhaps most instructive was the outright rejection of the European experience. Andrews once complained that the British employer B. Seebohm Rowntree, an early advocate of unemployment benefits, was receiving inordinate attention from his American audiences, but he need not have worried.[13] Nearly all American businessmen peremptorily rejected the British experiment. To a degree this reflected the widespread belief that the British emphasis on compensation had opened the door to a dole, but the fact that the British system did not emphasize the businessman's role in combating unemployment was more important. Feldman was perhaps most vociferous in attacking the "backwardness" of British writers and their inability to understand "the possibilities of industrial administration."[14] As the British depression made heavier demands on the unemployment insurance system, the absence of prevention incentives appeared, to an increasing number of American employers, the fatal defect. The National Industrial Conference Board made an important contribution to this contention with its "scientific" studies of the English system and unemployment insurance in general. By the early 1930's even the outright supporters of compulsory unemployment insurance were almost unanimous in their condemnation of the British "dole"—and in their demands that any American system emphasize the possibilities that lay in management initiative.

As they dismissed European methods, the New Emphasis businessmen had no trouble identifying what were the right men and means for a proper attack on the problem of unemployment. The practical scientist, the engineer, was their champion; they rejected the rule-of-thumb methods of the past for the "engineer mind" and the "engineering approach."[15] If Hoover was the popular symbol of the engineer's ascendancy, the Taylor Society and other organizations which stressed the applicability of broad engineering principles to the problems of management also received their share of acclaim.

Nor, as one might expect, did these business spokesmen and their intellectual allies envision a conflict between regular employment and the profit motive. Fundamental to their attitude was the notion, expressed in a United States Chamber of Commerce publication, that the primary purpose of employment stabilization was "to bring about more efficient and more profitable operation of business." The rejection of paternalism was as much a part of the New Emphasis as the role of the engineer-manager.[16] A. Lincoln Filene emphasized this when he wrote that "betterment cannot be lasting, unless it is made to pay for itself, unless it is pursued for business reasons, and in a business manner."[17] His brother Edward was even more specific. "My big hope out of state [unemployment] insurance," he wrote, "lies in the fact that my own experience . . . shows that it is possible to get added business profit by keeping people steadily employed. Toward this end, such insurance would force better business methods, and a steady and more successful fight on waste."[18] Time and again when business propagandists recited the virtues of unemployment prevention, they explained that their efforts, with or without the incentive provided by an unemployment insurance fund, would result in greater, not reduced, profits. The value of the additional incentive was that the actual use of this fund, as a Massachusetts employer wrote, "should be looked on as a penalty on management for overestimating its labor needs, or failing to adequately stabilize its labor demands."[19] While the penalty feature elicited greater enthusiasm from academicians than employers, its appeal should not be underestimated.[20] As late as 1935 a few businessmen continued to insist that management bear the entire financial burden of unemployment insurance.

The employers' approach to the unemployment problem, despite its emphasis on scientific analysis, raised almost as many questions as it proposed to answer. No one, for example, was exactly sure what type of unemployment it aimed to prevent. Proponents usually talked in terms of reducing seasonal and irregular or casual joblessness, but they were ambiguous when it came to cyclical fluctuations. Nor did they consider the possibility that part-time employees might be permanently discharged under stabilization programs or that workers unemployed as a consequence of technological changes would be unaffected. Officials of the NICB were unusually candid when they reported that layoffs would be reduced except "in the event of a major business depression. [Then] . . . the problem of lay-off assumes a far more serious character and management is . . . confronted with a necessity rather than a choice, in reducing its work force."[21]

Problems no less perplexing arose when business leaders tried to explain what the New Emphasis encompassed. To some, stabilization or regularization referred only to the adoption of a general program of economic planning. The Walworth Company of Boston, for example, devised new methods of production and inventory control which "enabled us to eliminate some of the chance and guesswork. . . . We feel we have been able to steer our course more intelligently and have gained some of the benefits of stabilization."[22] To others much more specific and detailed methods were involved. Dennison found that unemployment had been prevented through the "standardization of products, better planning, scheduling production, inducing customers to buy more regularly, additional or specialized warehousing facilities, training employees to be versatile, manufacturing for stock, working repairs in with production, and adding complementary lines of goods."[23] Other lists included virtually every aspect of production and personnel management. But whatever their methods, most businessmen agreed that a smooth-running, stable economic order would result if they were given sufficient time. The trouble was that by 1929 stability, as the authors of a personnel management manual noted, remained "the exception rather than the normal state of employment."[24]

Business Involvement

UNEMPLOYMENT PREVENTION and the development of improved managerial methods were two sides of the same coin, as far as the progressive businessmen of the first third of the twentieth century were concerned. The expansion of manufacturing that had subjected workmen to unstable employment also led employers to consider the potential benefits of more efficient production. Their interest, quite logically, focused on the operation of the individual shop or plant, where irregular work, whether due to poor planning, indiscriminate layoffs, high labor turnover, or improper use of the available manpower, was obviously a problem. Thus it was no coincidence that the management reformers of the early twentieth century took a deep interest in the alleviation of unemployment, or that the members of the Taylor Society, the interpreters of "scientific management," and the personnel reform groups formed the vanguard of the movement to prevent it.

From the beginning, the members of the Taylor Society, the small band of Frederick W. Taylor's disciples that organized in 1910, adopted a broader outlook than their teacher. The Cleveland clothing manufacturer Richard A. Feiss was probably the first to note the applicability of scientific management to the reduction of layoffs; yet his ideas were closer to the older paternalistic approach than to the "engineering" methods that his colleagues adopted in the 1920's. "Steadiness of employment," he contended in 1915, "must be considered not only from the point of view that is desirable for reasons of profit."[25] More representative were Morris L. Cooke, the engineer-reformer who attacked unemployment as "something that must be reduced to a minimum—yes, removed from our industrial system," and Harlow S. Person, president of the society and a leader of the group that sought to explore the social implications of Taylor's teachings.[26] Together these men paved the way for other members who in the postwar period embraced employment regularization as part of a plan of wholesale industrial reform. Their influence and the progressive atmosphere of the scientific management movement were most apparent in the fact that virtually all the business leaders who led the campaigns for unemployment insurance were society members.

The same industrial conditions that attracted attention to Taylor's original studies also generated interest in improved personnel relations, which unlike scientific management were the concern of every employer threatened with diminished profits due to labor turnover, labor unrest, and haphazard hiring and firing. Modern personnel management grew out of the personnel practices of employers like Feiss, and the more widespread "welfare work" (company libraries, recreational facilities, medical care, and home-purchase plans) that was popular at the turn of the century.[27] Despite this relatively late beginning, interest in employment practices grew rapidly; by 1911 a sufficient number of specialists operated in the Boston area to form an Employment Managers Association under the leadership of Meyer Bloomfield, a friend of Brandeis, who maintained close contact with the International Association on Unemployment and presumably with its American section.[28]

This interest received its greatest impetus, however, from the publication of a number of reports during the depression of 1914–15 on the extent and cost of labor turnover resulting from irregular personnel practices. The best known of these was a study written by Magnus Alexander, an executive of the General Electric Company and later the head of the NICB. Alexander contended that turnover averaged nearly 100 percent per year in many firms and resulted in a loss of $50 to $200 per employee in wasted training costs.[29] Other reports produced equally startling estimates. The reformers maintained that the real significance of this waste, as Sumner Slichter observed, was not "as a cost in itself, but as a symptom of conditions which are sources of loss to the employer."[30] When employers recognized the relationship between efficient management and a stable labor force, they took a major step toward accepting the idea of unemployment prevention, or so the leaders of the employment managers' associations believed.

While the reformers made substantial progress before 1917, the World War, by magnifying all the existing problems and creating others, greatly accelerated the process of educating the business community. The apparent need for rapid production, the rise in labor turnover, and the shortages of materials and transportation made managers aware of the possibilities for improvement. Increased labor turnover in particular prompted the creation of employment relations or personnel departments in as many as two hundred companies, though most of them concentrated exclusively on hiring and firing. Often the creation of a personnel department signified the beginning of a virtual revolution in labor relations encompassing a multitude of welfare and representation plans.[31] Equally important was the training of a large number of employment managers who retained a vested interest in good personnel relations.[32] But the establishment of personnel departments was not the only wartime development that contributed to the postwar interest in eliminating unemployment. Labor radicalism led many employers to adopt "industrial democracy" plans which, among other things, forced them to take a greater interest in personnel work, if only to undermine labor unions. In a few cases "industrial democracy" even led to the creation of unemployment insurance funds.

Other activities more directly related to the war had a similar effect. Many business leaders served on the War Industries Board, the Commercial Economy Board of the Council of National Defense, and its successor the Conservation Division of the WIB, all of which stressed the elimination of waste, the simplification of styles, and the standardization of parts.[33] Other businessmen assisted in the mobilization of the nation's resources, an effort that grew out of a conference sponsored by the United States Chamber of Commerce in September 1917. The chamber's leaders considered ways of alleviating unemployment in future depressions, while emphasizing the need for eliminating waste at all times.[34] To further these objectives they established nearly four hundred war service committees with the intention of bringing every businessman under their jurisdiction. The chamber's president, Harry A. Wheeler, described these groups as the machinery by which the government "has put into operation measures of conserving raw materials and of saving labor and transportation to the end of waging war more efficiently. . . . If out of the emergency conditions of war," he added, "American industry finds a way of eliminating waste, of simplifying processes of manufacturing, of introducing greater economy in the use of basic materials, of providing uniform systems of cost accounting and of introducing a more sympathetic and cooperative system of dealing with the factor of labor, the war will have given us by-product advantages which never could have been acquired under the highly competitive conditions of peace."[35] As a consequence of the war service committees' activities nearly every important executive of the 1920's had had some exposure to the New Emphasis, and as late as 1931 the possibility of an unemployment insurance program based on unemployment prevention attracted considerable support within the chamber itself, the largest of the businessmen's organizations.

Building on the legacy of the wartime experience, the scientific and personnel management movements attracted even greater attention in postwar America. Many observers felt the war had marked a turning point for the Taylor Society; henceforth it would completely abandon Taylor's narrow outlook and enter, in the words of Person, the "period of the larger conception of scientific management."[36] This was also the view of Cooke and others who had always chafed at Taylor's preoccupation with the factory work process. In the introduction to a book which attempted to document this trend Edward Eyre Hunt, a close associate of Hoover, maintained that "in a few years since the war, the function of the management engineer has amazingly broadened. Not mechanical but human problems are in the foreground."[37] If scientific management did not hold the key for all of society's ills, at least it promoted a broadened conception of efficiency and good management practice.

For many businessmen the new concern also meant a concerted attack on unemployment, especially that associated with seasonal or irregular work resulting directly from management policy. The Taylor Society established a research committee to study underemployment in 1919, and individual members frequently described their work in reducing labor turnover.[38] Feiss and Stanley King, vice-president of the McElwain Shoe Company, were active in this endeavor, and Dennison, by this time an outspoken advocate of unemployment insurance, contributed regularly to the organization's meetings.[39] Person summarized their achievements when he wrote that "the advocate of unemployment insurance is consciously or unconsciously an advocate of scientific management."[40] The leaders of the American Management Association, successor to the prewar personnel reform movement, also took an interest in these efforts to guarantee employment and establish unemployment insurance programs.[41] Yet because of the diverse membership of the AMA and anti-union tone of much of its work, the theme was not as pronounced as it was in the activities of the Taylor Society. An economist who attended an AMA convention found that the speakers' views on stabilization were "muddled," although such a situation was not unusual when businessmen discussed their long-term goals.[42] The fact remains that the formation of the AMA, like the creation of the Taylor Society, represented the broadening of the effort to promote managerial reform, which in both cases led to the consideration of un-employment and ultimately to the acceptance of prevention as a legitimate goal for alert businessmen.[43]

Normalcy and the "New Emphasis"

WHILE THE New Emphasis was a product of private enterprise, the businessmen of the 1920's were fortunate enough to have the backing of government leaders who were sympathetic to their problems and to at least some of their proposed remedies. This assistance was not at first the product of a deliberate policy, although Herbert Hoover, the Secretary of Commerce, seemed to share the views of the business community's most progressive spokesmen in this matter. Rather it was an accidental commitment arising from the necessity of combating the severe postwar recession of 1920–22, the worst economic downturn since the turn of the century, which left from three to five million jobless (according to contemporary estimates) and businessmen complaining of high debts and unsalable inventories. In early 1921 Hoover worked out a program that established several precedents for federal activity in later years. The solution to the unemployment problem as he saw it involved two activities: an immediate "reconnaissance" to help local agencies coordinate temporary relief measures and a more thorough study of the steps necessary to prevent similar crises in the future. The Administration's unemployment conference of September–October 1921 was designed to advance both the short- and long-term phases of this plan. When his aide, Edward Eyre Hunt, suggested that the major problem of the conference was to devise new ways of handling relief, Hoover replied that "what we are really going to do is to tackle the fundamentals of unemployment."[44]

Hoover's preconference preparations—whether he desired it or not—insured that the fundamentals of unemployment would receive more than cursory consideration. Though the immediate purpose of the conference was to decide on ways of coordinating state and local relief programs, Hoover so limited the prerogatives of the delegates—he merely wanted to bring together men "who can influence the action of employing forces and who can influence public opinion"—that they could do little more than ratify the Administration's plans.[45] At the same time he was determined to prevent the arguments between employer and labor representatives over the open shop which had been the major stumbling block of previous postwar industrial conferences and had distracted public attention from the real problems at hand. His careful planning insured a significant role for the New Emphasis employers, one they might not have enjoyed had a drastic new relief program been contemplated or had the unionists and conservative businessmen been allowed to continue their running debate over collective bargaining.[46]

While the coordination of relief activities necessarily had to await the convening of the conference, the work of defining the Administration's long-range unemployment policy started in early September. According to Hoover's plan a group of experts, called the Economic Advisory Council, met quietly before the conference to prepare a report on the causes of and possible solutions for the depression. The EAC consisted of nearly everyone who had taken part in the AALL's unemployment work of the previous six years, including Andrews, Dennison, Sam A. Lewisohn, Henry Seager, Otto Mallery, and Leo Wolman.[47] Andrews, acting chairman of the subcommittee on unemployment prevention, set the tone for much of the work of the council when he wrote to Hunt in early September, that "it is particularly important that there be strong representation of the industries of the country and that employers known to be sincerely and constructively interested in meeting the problem of irregular employment be given opportunity early to present their views. . . . The responsibility and opportunity of industrial managers should, I think, be strongly stressed."[48] At the same time he sent Hoover a summary of the new unemployment insurance plan of the Cleveland garment industry, a description of the plans of private employers, and a résumé of the AALL's legislative efforts.[49]

The EAC held three meetings during September to discuss unemployment statistics, temporary measures, and permanent measures that might be considered. While the committee on permanent measures was made up of Seager, Edwin F. Gay, a Harvard economist, Samuel McCune Lindsay, an officer of the AALL, and Andrews, much of the work was done by other EAC members or outsiders, who presented summaries of their findings. Thus Seager reported on the gathering of unemployment information, Dennison on "depression insurance," and Lewisohn on company unemployment-insurance plans in the United States.[50] The consequence of this activity was an unequivocal endorsement of unemployment prevention. In their confidential report to Hoover the EAC members concluded that "most promising of all is the opportunity now offered to bring home to the public mind the significance of the business cycle and enlist the individual enterprise of business managers . . . in this work of regularizing employment within their own establishments."[51] Their final report to the conference also listed specific measures that employers might undertake to stabilize employment conditions, and described existing union out-of-work funds and company insurance systems. In summary they suggested that "any forms of unemployment insurance which would create an economic motive to regularize employment is [sic] worthy of the most careful consideration."[52]

Thanks to Hoover's skillful planning, the unemployment conference, which proceeded, as the *New York Times* reported, "with the smoothness of well-oiled machinery," had ample opportunity to consider long-range policies.[53] To simplify the problems of the conferees in drafting a relief program, the President declared at the first session that he would accept no solution "which seeks either palliation or tonic from the public treasury."[54] While this left little room for meaningful action, it facilitated the task of drafting the recommendations on unemployment relief during the first week of deliberations. As Hoover had anticipated, the President's message and his "guidance" minimized dissension. The delegates duly ratified his proposals for coordinated activities by mayors' committees and adjourned for a week to consider the EAC report and the role of government in future crises.[55] When the conference reconvened in the second week of October the delegates' recommendations indicated the importance of the preliminary work of the EAC. Their final report called for the elimination of waste, the regularization of employment, the strengthening of the USES, and the planning of public works.[56] The conference also decided that a permanent organization, in the form of a standing committee, should explore the causes of unemployment and the business cycle. Andrews was elated at this virtual endorsement of the *Practical Program*. Hoover deserved, he felt, "a great deal of credit for the way in which he handled the conference."[57]

But the delegates' failure to consider unemployment insurance legislation also disappointed many people. The *Survey's* reporter, William L. Chenery, attacked the conference as a "business affair" and chided the delegates for their timidity.[58] Andrews similarly recognized this weakness and requested that Hoover include the study of compulsory jobless benefits in the agenda of the standing committee.[59] But Otto T. Mallery, the public works expert, took a different approach. Though he admitted that "a number of members of the Conference" favored such legislation, a proposal of this sort, he argued, would have been impractical. It would only have led to "distraction from and public hostility to, the recommendations that it did make and is now energetically urging . . . ." Furthermore, he asked: "What instances can be cited where the federal government has pioneered in such a far-reaching field . . . before any state had tried it out?"[60] Probably a majority of the delegates favorable to unemployment insurance legislation agreed with Mallery's view.

Despite this neglect of insurance legislation, the Washington conference was an unprecedented event and Hoover's greatest achievement in the field of unemployment policy. For the first time the outstanding American students of unemployment had been brought together under official auspices. Since Gompers and the AFL leadership, as well as most businessmen, opposed legislative programs to alleviate or prevent unemployment, there was no real possibility for a more advanced program. But the decision to establish a committee to study business fluctuations and unemployment problems indicated official interest in combating unemployment on a long-term basis. The work of this group in the following years revealed the extent to which the conference had served to coordinate the policies of Hoover and the Administration with those of the reformers.

Like most organizations dominated by businessmen in the 1920's, the standing committee, organized a month after the conclusion of the conference, displayed a zealous interest in the study of unemployment but an even stronger reluctance to explore the possibilities of unemployment insurance, at least when achieved through legislation. Hoover and his advisors recruited Wesley Mitchell to report on business cycles, and sponsored studies of the construction and bituminous coal industries; yet they peremptorily rejected compulsory jobless benefits because, as Andrews, a member, reported, they were "already of [the] opinion that the European plans are not well adapted to American needs."[61] If there was any doubt about the validity of such a position, Hoover must have exerted a strong influence in its favor. He wrote that "one of the great objects" of their investigations was "to eliminate from the American mind, if possible, a number of hallucinations transported from Europe as to the adaptability of their various relief plans, and to develop by consideration, some of the sound business and financial plans gradually emerging from American industry and the handling of public works."[62] Yet at least in the preparation of Mitchell's study it was impossible to dismiss the consideration of unemployment insurance so easily. At a meeting in October 1922 the issue was openly debated, with Matthew Woll, a representative of organized labor, and Joseph DeFrees, a representative of organized management, opposing compulsory benefits and Mitchell and Mary Van Kleeck, a prominent social worker, taking the other side.[63] Significantly Mitchell's tentative report, completed several months later, proposed a program of jobless insurance, although it did not recommend a specific plan. A group of economists who examined the document were similarly divided; the minority, led by John R. Commons, was unable to obtain more than a general endorsement of unemployment prevention.[64]

In spite of these disagreements, the report on business cycles and unemployment, the major product of post-conference investigations, did endorse the other provisions of Andrews' *Practical Program*. It called for the systematic collection of unemployment statistics, for planned public works, the regularization of employment by individual employers, and voluntary unemployment insurance funds, without actually dismissing the possibility of a compulsory system.[65] The economist Leo Wolman explained in a supplementary statement that the problem was not one of opposition to jobless insurance in principle but of wide disagreement over the specific features of a satisfactory plan. He viewed this situation with optimism, since it was impossible to know in 1923 that such differences of opinion would be the major stumbling blocks to unemployment insurance legislation in the future.[66] While the report on business cycles was only the first of a number of documents that grew out of the unemployment conference, the later studies steered clear of this sensitive area. Considering the composition of the conference, its standing committees, and the state of public opinion, the failure of these efforts to result in an endorsement of unemployment insurance legislation was less important than the fact that Hoover and his aides had given the businessmen's approach to unemployment an important boost.

The "New Emphasis" and Unemployment Insurance

WHATEVER THE position of the federal government, the acceptance of unemployment prevention without the acceptance of some form of unemployment insurance made little sense to men like Commons, Andrews, or Brandeis, who realized that a commitment to pay benefits was essential if the stabilization methods were to be taken seriously. The number of businessmen who reached a similar conclusion in the 1920's, though significant, was surprisingly small in view of the enthusiasm for the New Emphasis, and undoubtedly reflected the limited commitment of the average employer to prevention. Yet whether they established jobless insurance plans in their own plants or merely urged others to do so, this group achieved a remarkable visibility before the Depression. Through their speeches and writings they were responsible for much of the contemporary discussion of unemployment remedies. But they were important not only for their writings, but also for their activities in the 1930's, when their knowledge and experience in the field exercised an important influence on legislation that was being framed.

For more than twenty years Henry S. Dennison, "one of the keenest-minded, clearest-thinking practical employers . . . in this country," was the unofficial leader of this group.[67] As factory manager and later president of the Dennison Manufacturing Company, he took a special interest in shop conditions and the employees' welfare, complaining that he did not understand "how we can get very far ahead . . . if the last word lies with a group of men who have never visited the factory."[68] But like other employers who rejected absentee control, Dennison also condemned trade unions that sought to align labor against management. Rather, he believed, the individual firm was a microcosm of all society and should be treated as an integrated unit. "Your problem," he told a meeting of employment managers, "is simply one part of the whole problem of social structure. Your problem is simply part of and parallels the general political problem."[69] To guide his actions, Dennison argued, the manager must realize that if there is "any such applied science as social engineering, its ultimate objective cannot differ much from the demand of the Christian ethic."[70] His broad view of the employers' role led him to introduce a number of innovations at his own plant, including a profit sharing program, an employment department, and the first employer-financed unemployment insurance plan in the United States. He also supported the AALL Massachusetts legislative campaign of 1915–16, but he was more concerned, as he wrote to Andrews, that "employers should be urged to work hard at the problem before it becomes an active legislative question."[71]

Like other New Emphasis employers, Dennison was fond of citing the benefits of the new approach. He boasted in 1922 that it was "not difficult to keep in the course if one studies the present as growing out of the past."[72] On another occasion he attributed most of the nation's economic ills "to the fact that the majority of business managers have no definite plan for normal growth and are heedless of fundamental economic conditions."[73] But he also maintained that unemployment insurance was an integral part of an overall program of stabilization, since it "should exert a balance of influence toward regularizing unemployment."[74] This approach caused some confusion when, for example, he appeared before the Wisconsin legislature to speak for an unemployment insurance bill and spent most of his time discussing his company's efforts to prevent layoffs through production and sales planning.[75] It also led him—and other businessmen who shared his viewpoint—to see in their efforts a virtual panacea for the nation's economic problems. Dennison insisted, and pointed to his company's record as verification, that cyclical unemployment could be prevented or at least greatly reduced. As early as 1916 he predicted that "when a majority of businessmen are wise enough to foresee the occurrence of a depression, say 18 months hence, and begin to counteract it, business depressions will be less acute."[76] Understandably, he was perplexed at the seeming irrelevance of his theories to the Depression of the 1930's.

Dennison's wide interests and inexhaustible energy insured that his views would receive maximum exposure. As an AALL member and president of the Taylor Society (1919–21), he explained his ideas and policies in innumerable speeches and articles. In the late 1920's he helped sponsor Edwin Smith's *Reducing Seasonal Unemployment* and wrote the chapter on management for the authoritative *Recent Economic Changes*. He backed Roosevelt in 1932 and wrote several years later that he was "fanatically for the NRA and almost every angle of the New Deal."[77] During the Depression Dennison served on the Commerce Department's Business Advisory and Planning Council, the Industrial Advisory Board of the NRA, the National Labor Board, and the National Resources Planning Board.

While Dennison was an important figure in his own right, his influence was considerably greater because many employers who thought like him were located in the Boston metropolitan area, Yankee heirs to a long reform tradition.[78] Their collective leadership was most clearly evident in the activities of the Boston Chamber of Commerce, which in the years before World War I assumed to a high degree the policies of its most farsighted members. The largest organization of its kind in the United States, the Boston chamber soon developed a reputation for fostering improved labor relations and employee welfare plans.[79] But its most important achievement before the war was to provide the impetus for the formation of the United States Chamber of Commerce, an organization that retained much of its Boston influence until the mid-1930's.[80]

Of Dennison's Boston associates Brandeis, of course, remained a staunch supporter of unemployment insurance long after he went to the Supreme Court. Henry Kendall, who served as president of the Taylor Society in the late 1920's, introduced scientific management at the Plimpton Press and later at Kendall Mills, a textile firm.[81] Like Dennison he recognized unemployment as a matter of the "utmost importance."[82] Though he did not immediately share Dennison's enthusiasm for unemployment insurance, he served on the Massachusetts Special Commission on the Stabilization of Employment, a body, appointed by the legislature in 1931, which endorsed unemployment reserves legislation. Thereafter he became a member and later chairman of the Business Advisory and Planning Council and an advisor to the Department of Labor. Edward A. Filene, another member of this group, also believed that employers should be encouraged to establish their own jobless benefit plans.[83] If done properly, he felt, "employers will adopt their own private insurance and will be able more and more to avoid discharging their employees, because under the pressure of the need of eliminating the preventable expenses of unemployment, they will succeed in eliminating the extraordinary wastes that still exist in production and distribution."[84] His younger brother A. Lincoln Filene served as Massachusetts representative to the Interstate Committee on unemployment in 1930–31 and wrote the committee's final report, which called for unemployment reserves legislation. Later he added that "there is no force today which makes the businessman pay any particular attention to seasonal unemployment. Unemployment reserve legislation is such a force."[85]

Others, such as Howard Coonley, president of the Walworth Company, Henry I. Harriman, a textiles and utilities executive, and Stanley King of the McElwain Shoe Company also recognized the value of insurance funds.[86] Harriman, whose special interest was economic planning, promised, as president of the Boston Chamber in 1917, that he and his colleagues would give "careful and sympathetic attention" to proposals for a system of social insurance; and, as president of the United States Chamber of Commerce in the early 1930's, he was in a position to redeem that pledge.[87]

Outside the Bay State Ernest G. Draper, a New York business executive, was probably the most articulate supporter of unemployment insurance in the 1920's. As treasurer of the Hills Brothers Company, a food products firm that specialized in the importation and marketing of dates, he initiated a program of employment stabilization in 1920 that insured year-around production and ended seasonal layoffs, as a first step toward an insurance plan. Thereafter he traveled extensively, telling of his own experiences and explaining the possibilities of unemployment prevention. As a long-time member and officer of the AALL he maintained close ties with the supporters of compulsory as well as voluntary unemployment insurance.

Draper, like Dennison, stressed the importance of the businessman and of his voluntary effort. Unemployment insurance was "particularly an obligation of the employer," he wrote in 1921, "because, after all, he is not only interested, for material reason . . . but no real advance, short of compulsory legislation or ultimate revolution by the workers can be made without his cooperation."[88] Characteristically he argued that "diminished unemployment would mean stabilized industry, even more production and thus freer opportunities to increase business profits.''[89] He also stressed the analogy between workmen's compensation legislation and unemployment insurance, but unlike Dennison clearly distinguished between employment regularization and insurance.[90] He praised the New Emphasis employers who planned their production and sales; yet until stability had been achieved, he feared the cost of unemployment insurance: ". . . it seems to me that it is more or less academic until we make production in our plants more regular. It is perfectly ridiculous to talk about giving insurance to individual employees—unemployment insurance—until you regularize your employment, because if you do it without making your employment regular you are liable to . . . break the company."[91] Most of all, Draper opposed the creation of a national unemployment insurance system that did not provide incentives for employers to regularize employment. "What gives one pause," he warned in 1928, "is the inflexibility of such an organization built, as it would be, upon such a gigantic scale."[92] During the Depression he became a strong backer of the legislative campaigns for unemployment reserves, a Roosevelt partisan, a member of the Business Advisory Council, the National Labor Board, and in 1935, Assistant Secretary of Commerce.[93]

Equally close to Dennison in his approach was Morris E. Leeds, the "Quaker employer" of Philadelphia and a pioneer in the introduction of scientific management and company welfare programs. Like Dennison he was suspect of absentee ownership and devised a stock-dividend plan with control vested in the company's executives.[94] He, too, considered trade unions outmoded, and headed the Metal Manufacturers Association of Philadelphia, an open shop organization, from 1924 to 1930.[95] While Leeds seldom went so far as to suggest that unemployment insurance should be legislated, he was devoted to the theory of unemployment prevention and actively supported practical experiments in reducing joblessness. Of his own company's plan, which he introduced in 1923, he reported: "It has created in our management a state of mind that, having accumulated that fund, we do not intend to spend it if we can possibly help it. We intend to do the other thing and keep them regularly employed."[96] In 1930 he led a study group under the auspices of the Philadelphia Chamber of Commerce that devised a program to stabilize employment. The committee's report stated that "it is [our] hope that . . . [the] good judgment of American businessmen will lead them to different industrially-controlled measures which will put the major emphasis on providing employment."[97] Leeds also supported the work of the AALL in combating unemployment and helped subsidize the 1931 Swarthmore unemployment project. During the 1930's he served on the Industrial Advisory Board of the NRA and the Business Advisory and Planning Council of the Department of Commerce.

Sam A. Lewisohn, president of the AMA from 1923 to 1928, was more a student of business than an active employer, but he shared his friends' concern for improved factory operating methods—an interest that also led him to endorse the naive appeals of the business apologists of the 1920's.[98] He urged voluntary reform to avoid government coercion and felt that "trade unionism [is] a most valuable institution but I cannot see how it can hope to compete in leadership with the employers' personnel people."[99] Consequently he felt the key to better industrial conditions was the "scientific study of the art of management, particularly labor relations."[100] The businessman's duty was "not only to carefully prepare for matters by guarding against too much expansion . . . but also by statistical research to attempt to forecast approximately when the slump is likely to come in the particular business."[101] In 1928 Lewisohn proposed the establishment of unemployment insurance plans through private insurance companies, since legislation would be enacted "many many years from now."[102] By 1933, however, he was a strong supporter of compulsory unemployment reserves controlled by business and combined with a program of employment stabilization. In the following years he insisted that "unemployment insurance . . . is no longer to be classed as a social humanitarian problem. . . . It is a problem not solely for the social workers but for the financial and business economist."[103]

Of the many other businessmen who played some part in the promotion of unemployment insurance, Gerard Swope, president of the General Electric Company, and Marion B. Folsom, treasurer of the Eastman Kodak Company, were perhaps the most outstanding. Of the two, Swope received the greater publicity. Backed by his colleague, Board Chairman Owen D. Young, who considered unemployment the "greatest blot on our capitalist system," Swope personified the popular image of the engineer-reformer.[104] He considered the failure of employers to provide steady work "one of the severest indictments of our modern civilization" and believed that only the employer had the resources to solve this most serious of all industrial problems.[105] Folsom, if less well known, was equally vigorous in pursuing the same objectives. As early as 1922 he had attempted to inaugurate a company-financed unemployment insurance system at Kodak. He strongly opposed a compulsory system, however, until businessmen had had an opportunity to experiment with their own plans.[106] "My contention," he stated, "is that it would be almost impossible to prevent government from making those changes [that is, to the "dole"] once a plan is in operation."[107] Still, Folsom's primary argument was that unemployment insurance under employer control would provide an incentive to employers for reducing joblessness: "Economies in production costs, brought about by reduced fluctuations in employment, lower turnover, and better morale of the force, would go a long way to offset the employer's appropriations to the fund."[108]

These men and a few others bore a major share of the responsibility for promoting the distinctive American approach to unemployment insurance first developed by Commons and Brandeis. If their statements often lacked consistency and focus, it was because they were practical men of differing backgrounds whose common characteristic was a conviction that unemployment prevention required more than the occasional use of up-to-date managerial techniques. The importance, indeed the vital role, of their approach in determining the nature of the unemployment insurance system ultimately established in the United States is considered in a later chapter. Their opinions, insofar as they were the result of the experience and observation of company-initiated plans, were a distinctive development of the period. For the New Emphasis businessmen of the time the performance of these efforts seemed to warrant the promise of their optimistic pronouncements; for later observers the evidence is less clear.

3 | COMPANY PLANS: PURPOSE AND PERFORMANCE

THE EVIDENT lack of enthusiasm for voluntary unemployment insurance among businessmen was not a result of their dislike for it in theory; indeed they welcomed the plans that a few employers began, as sure signs that unemployment would be "prevented." The real problem was their underlying skepticism toward the New Emphasis, a genuine though seldom articulated distrust that made them reluctant to stake money on their ability to provide steady work. The absence of widespread, or at least of increasing, unemployment before 1930 also made a wait-and-see policy possible and even expedient. And if full employment was not enough to sidetrack any consideration of unemployment insurance, the purported outcome of the British and German experiences made caution the better part of valor. The result was less the repudiation of unemployment insurance than the indefinite postponement of any action. Perhaps the extraordinary thing was not that so few firms actually adopted some form of unemployment insurance but that any did at all.

At least twenty-three company unemployment-insurance funds, covering approximately 60,000 workers, were in operation at one time or another between 1916 and 1934. There were never more than sixteen plans in effect at one time, and this peak was reached only in 1931. The Bureau of Labor Statistics estimated that in that year approximately 50,000 workers, most of whom had hard-to-replace skills or high seniority, were eligible to receive out-of-work benefits.[1] This select group represented slightly less than one-third of the total number of workers covered by unemployment insurance under company, union, or joint union-company plans.[2] Since the largest employers, the General Electric Company and the Eastman Kodak Company, began their

47

funds after the stock market crash, the statistics for 1930–31 show sizable increases in the number of employees qualified for compensation. After 1931, however, the number of plans remained almost constant, but the number of workers affected declined drastically. One observer estimated that the company systems covered no more than 32,000 workers in July 1933, and it is unlikely that this figure increased before the beginning of compulsory unemployment insurance under state and federal laws.[3]

It is relatively easy to understand why most American businessmen preferred to confine their activities to less radical aspects of the New Emphasis in the 1920's, but it is more difficult to explain why there were a few who did adopt unemployment insurance. Undoubtedly New Emphasis psychology was an important, though often intangible, factor in their decisions. The widespread interest in efficiency, productivity, and "industrial democracy" of the war and postwar periods was another influence that, while impossible to measure, was obviously present. But there apparently were more concrete factors, at least in the early years, that simplified the commitment. Before the Depression all of the companies that became involved were small or medium-sized, with payrolls that ranged from barely one hundred to several thousand. The limited scope of the typical plan meant that administrative problems were minimal. Most, but not all, of these companies also manufactured traditional consumers goods such as foods, paper products, and soap; neither the sick industries nor the new industries of the postwar era were involved before 1930. Because they produced goods for which there was a fairly constant demand year after year, the companies that adopted unemployment insurance were largely immune from disastrous economic fluctuations and thus able to concentrate on solving such basic problems as unemployment.

It would nevertheless be a mistake to overemphasize such characteristics, since Eastman Kodak and General Electric and to a lesser degree the Procter & Gamble Company, the most important firms to adopt company plans, were neither small nor engaged in the manufacture of traditional consumers goods. If there was a decisive factor that can be pinpointed, it was not the size, function, or profitability of the company but its leadership. The employers who adopted unemployment insurance were, with few exceptions, deeply committed to the New Emphasis. They pioneered in the introduction of management of reforms, both to streamline the administration of their factories and to provide their employees with an environment conducive to increased productivity. Dennison, Leeds, and others who took an active role in promoting the New Emphasis had been among the first to accept scientific management and the most up-to-date personnel reforms. In most cases they implemented Taylor's ideas, and established personnel departments, profit-sharing plans, company unions, employee insurance funds, and related services before they established unemployment insurance systems. Either these programs had proven so successful that they were able to convince their less daring colleagues of the potential of unemployment insurance, or they had sufficient power (either through family ownership or innate ability) to disregard their associates' objections. In either case, their experiences during World War I and the postwar period formed the catalyst for their subsequent actions. Their often arbitrary rule did not mean, however, that they were less interested than conventional executives in the traditional objectives of a business enterprise. Like other New Emphasis spokesmen, they believed that unemployment insurance would force them to recognize ways of operating more efficiently, and hence more profitably.

The employers who developed unemployment insurance plans were also sensitive to the apparently increasing gap between society's haves and have-nots—in particular, the growing impersonalization of employer-employee relations. They sought, in addition to steady production, increased earnings, a stable labor force, and the open shop, to create a renewed sense of community, they said, in order to counteract the process of social fragmentation that seemed to accompany the rise of big business. This explains in part their opposition to financiers, bankers, and absentee executives who, they believed, had been responsible for the separation of ownership from management and of management from production. It also accounts for their emphasis on stock distribution to their employees, profit sharing, and other measures to give management and employees a continuing interest in the operation of the firm. And though they seldom attempted to devise a program of social change, or even carefully spelled out their thoughts on unemployment, their vision of a stable industrial society appeared piecemeal in their statements of the 1920's, and later in the early Depression years formed the basis for a more ambitious program with the same ultimate purpose—a productive, smoothly operating economy.[4]

The statistics of the company plans do not suggest the extent of the problems encountered during the Depression by the firms which had adopted them. An authoritative survey of 1932 reported that "even in cases where comparatively restricted benefits are paid . . . the depression has put such a strain on the funds that in most instances they have been maintained only with the greatest difficulty."[5] While it is impossible to judge the degree to which the apparent success of the company plans in the 1920's reinforced the popular commitment to the New Emphasis, it is evident that their frequent failure in the 1930's contributed to the reassessment of the premises of unemployment prevention and to the growing disillusionment with unemployment insurance as a broad reform measure. But these perils were unforeseen in the formative period of unemployment insurance, when optimism was possible and when a small group of executives were able to arouse considerable interest in voluntary unemployment insurance, the last step in the businessmen's campaign against unemployment.

Employer-Financed Reserves Plans

STUDENTS OF unemployment insurance have often distinguished between the company plans that actually provided reserves for the payment of unemployment benefits and the plans that merely guaranteed employment for a designated number of weeks or days per year. Since the firms that set up reserve funds usually limited their liability to the extent of the fund and made all the contributions, there was little difference in practice between the two approaches before 1930. Indeed, the events leading to the adoption of unemployment insurance, the motivation of the executives involved, and the accompanying policy changes, that is, the commitment to a program of prevention, were so similar in most cases that the validity of such a distinction is questionable. Yet in one respect the separation of reserves and guarantee plans appears meaningful, for it emphasizes the fact that employers who favored company reserves had clearly distinguished between stabilization and unemployment insurance and were often ready, by the early Depression years, to advance some form of legislative action.

The Dennison Manufacturing Company originated and maintained for nearly two decades the best known of the reserves plans. The narrow range of the company's products—jewelers' boxes, shipping tags, crepe paper, and a few specialized holiday items—and the limited, relatively stable demand for them made this policy possible, but the influence and imagination of Henry S. Dennison made it a success. Beginning in 1906 Dennison initiated a series of factory reforms, including "the beginning of functionalization, divisional control, emphasis on accounting methods, the establishment of a research department, a methods department, and the nucleus of a planning department," that served as the background for his later experiments with unemployment.[6] An employment department, organized in 1913 to handle the growing burden of personnel work, also provided a useful administrative organization, and Dennison's profit-sharing program established a precedent for direct payments to the workers.[7] But it was only the depression of 1914–15 which revealed the inadequacy of these policies and ultimately led to the creation of the unemployment insurance fund.

The prewar economic downturn caught Dennison unprepared and unprotected; his sales dropped sharply and layoffs were necessary. When good times returned he resolved to prevent the recurrence of such hardship, both for the firm and the employees, in the same manner that he had attacked other personnel problems in earlier years. The direction of his thinking became evident in February 1915, when he asked Andrews if other employers had experimented with jobless benefits. Andrews replied that they had not, but hoped "that the Dennison Manufacturing Company would . . . [create] an establishment fund for the purpose of paying out-of-work benefits." Dennison noted that his employment manager was compiling the necessary data, though "we are not even far enough along to predict whether we shall want to install unemployment insurance or not."[8] Progress was evidently rapid, however, for in the next year, 1916, he initiated the first company-financed unemployment insurance program in American history.[9]

The Dennison company contributed nearly $150,000 in the next three years for unemployment benefits, and Dennison, in cooperation with representatives of the company union, formulated the benefit provisions. He agreed that employees with more than six months' service should receive at least half of their average weekly wage when laid off and that other workers who might be transferred to different jobs at lower rates should receive partial compensation. He also insisted that benefits might be terminated after a week if the employee had failed to look for other employment.[10]

On the other hand, the primary purpose of the plan, if not altogether clear in 1916, was soon defined as unemployment prevention. The company rules described it as "not charity; it has a business basis and must rest upon considerations of mutual advantage."[11] In subsequent years Dennison and his subordinates often repeated their contention that unemployment insurance was designed to prevent rather than compensate unemployment. H. N. Dowse, a company representative who assisted in administering the fund, told a conference of employment managers that "the Dennison Manufacturing Company has not done a tremendously big thing along the insurance lines but we have done a beautiful job in the way of prevention." When other employers argued that the Dennison experience would not apply to their establishments, Dowse scoffed at them. "Fundamentally," he asserted, "all business is about the same."[12]

The stresses of the war period resulted in an intensified effort to maintain continuous employment by stabilizing production. Despite rising profits, war mobilization meant increased production schedules, new problems in obtaining raw materials and transportation, and a higher labor turnover, a situation that made Dennison wary of the future; he had not forgotten his experiences of 1914–15. Consequently he prepared for a postwar depression, ordering cuts in advertising expenditures, the spreading of salesmen's orders, the end of short-term hiring, and the retraining of permanent employees so they could shift to other jobs in the event of a depression. The rules of the company union were also liberalized, and the profit-sharing plan extended to include factory workers.[13] By 1920, when payments from the unemployment insurance fund began, Dennison and his colleagues had worked out a comprehensive stabilization program based on the company's past experiences and anticipated future needs that paid important dividends in the following years. Dennison cut wages by 10 percent during the postwar depression, but the workers suffered few other ill effects. Those who were unfortunate enough to be laid off or transferred received unemployment benefits or supplemental wages, but the company's total outlays for unemployment compensation from 1920–22 amounted to only $23,000, a figure that indicated the success of the stabilization plan.[14]

Unfortunately for the later history of Dennison's experiment, the lessons of 1920–22 were as deceptive as they were beneficial. Because the postwar depression was the worst since the 1890's, Dennison, like other businessmen, generally agreed that measures adequate to meet the demands of 1920–22 would be sufficient for any future crisis. Using this experience as a guide, he limited the reserve fund to the amount necessary to cover short, relatively sharp cyclical fluctuations and concentrated on eliminating seasonal unemployment. A Dennison official wrote in 1923: "As we have placed our greatest emphasis and our hardest work upon prevention of unemployment rather than the relief of it, and as we have been relatively successful . . . it hardly seems necessary just now to consider the desirability of increasing the fund."[15] There were in fact so few layoffs after 1921 that the company fund disbursed only $57,000 in the next seven years, most of which went to pay supplemental wages to men transferred to other jobs.[16] Dennison testified that "we work so hard to keep our people on the pay roll that our scheme is in effect a guarantee of employment."[17]

The beginning of the Depression in 1930, however, almost immedi-

ately revealed the program's vulnerability to periods of sustained unemployment. The steady drain on the reserve during that year led the
company to scale down the benefit provisions, but this change had little effect. By March 1931 only $35,000 remained; by December only
$28,500. Another $14,000 was paid to unemployed workers before the
fund was suspended in June 1932.[18] Not only did the unemployment
insurance reserve leave the employees unprotected early in the Depression, but the Dennison labor force, which had numbered between
2,000 and 3,000 in the 1920's, was reduced to approximately 1500 in
1930–31, and another 300 employees were dismissed before the end of
unemployment payments a year later.[19] Most of these people were permanently discharged and were therefore ineligible for unemployment
benefits. Apparently the employment guarantee that Dennison boasted
of in 1928 applied, in effect, to less than one-half of his workers.

Next to the Framingham paper firm, the Leeds and Northrup Company of Philadelphia developed the best known and most widely discussed unemployment-reserves plan of the postwar years. Like Dennison, Morris E. Leeds was independent, strong-willed, and committed to
increased productivity and the identification of his employees' interests
with his own.[20] To retain control of the firm "in the hands of those
who are experienced, competent, and in full sympathy with the company's policies," he began a stock distribution plan in 1915.[21] Although
he considered this the keystone of his management system, his reputation as a progressive employer stemmed from his Cooperative Association, a special type of company union whose formation was due less to
Leeds' benevolence than to the exigencies of the war period. The rapid
growth of the company in 1917–18 created friction between management and labor and finally prompted Leeds to send a delegation of
workers to Boston to study the employee representation plans of the
Filenes and Dennison. On receiving their report Leeds and a number
of other Quaker employers engaged Robert Bruere, a management engineer, to draw up a plan of "industrial democracy" out of which grew
the association, composed of all employees, that was the first step toward the introduction of a program of unemployment insurance.[22]

The formation of the association marked a turning point in Leeds'
relationship with his employees. Together with the employees' representatives he worked out his most pressing postwar personnel problems. The apparent willingness of the association leaders to place the
interests of the company above their own welfare so impressed Leeds
that he was not unfavorable to an extension of his personnel
program.[23] The New Emphasis then became the deciding factor. Working with the association leaders and his Quaker associates, he began a
study of unemployment insurance to ascertain the practicability of a

plan for Leeds and Northrup. After examining various proposals, he concluded that individual employers could reasonably assume a limited liability for out-of-work benefits, and initiated an unemployment insurance plan in February 1923 that closely resembled the Dennison system.[24] The company contributed a total of $55,000, a sum that seemed adequate to cover any situation. "We worked," wrote the factory manager, "on the assumption that the 1920 experience is the most violent depression in a lifetime, and its force measures the maximum depression which we are likely to encounter."[25] Eligibility for benefits varied with the individual worker's seniority: an experienced employee could receive up to twenty-six weekly payments in a year, but no one who had less than three months' experience or made more than $2600 per year was eligible for benefits. The administration of the fund was the responsibility of a joint committee of executives and representatives from the Cooperative Association.[26]

The virtual exclusion of the workers most likely to be laid off, the prosperity of the period, and the company's stabilization policy kept the fund intact through the 1920's. Leeds indicated that the threat of having to pay benefits had been a major factor in the inauguration of a coordinated program of work sharing, manufacturing for stock, and special sales campaigns.[27] He testified in 1929 that these activities had resulted in insignificant demands on the fund; only five eligible workers had been laid off, and they had collected a mere $500. "We have to go through a bump of unemployment," he added, "before it will become significant."[28] But Leeds' fund was somewhat less valuable in the hard times of the 1930's than it had been in the good times of the previous decade. The $68,000 that the company had set aside by 1930 was exhausted in less than two years. At the same time, permanent discharges reduced the number of eligible employees from 900 in 1930 to less than 500 in 1932, when the company suspended benefit payments.[29] Leeds and his associates nevertheless favored the resumption of contributions as soon as economic conditions permitted, and in 1939, after the beginning of federal-state unemployment insurance, initiated a supplementary benefit plan.[30]

A third well-known unemployment reserves plan of the early 1920's, that of the S. C. Johnson Company of Racine, Wisconsin, differed only in detail—and in its ultimate results—from the two already described. In 1917–18 Herbert F. Johnson, president of the family firm, began a program of employment stabilization that included most of the conventional methods. He hired full-time salesmen, expanded his advertising budget, and trained workers to handle more than one job.[31] But Johnson, like Dennison and Leeds, was not content with these halfway measures. "We . . . feel that there should be something more permanent and more definite for the average working man."[32] The postwar recession and the New Emphasis provided the answer—unemployment insurance. Johnson's plan, started in 1922, resembled the others except for a provision requiring employee contributions. And it seemed to contribute to the overall objective of reducing joblessness, since yearly benefit payments averaged only about $800 between 1923 and 1934, when they increased slightly.[33] Two other factors—the company's remarkable success, and the practice of discharging new workers before they became eligible for benefit payments—probably had a favorable influence on this record. Johnson's fund contained approximately $22,000 when the Wisconsin unemployment reserves act went into effect, a record that was the basis for his claim that he had licked the Depression through unemployment prevention.[34]

Three other reserves plans of the 1920's, while less well-publicized, were clearly products of the New Emphasis approach. The funds of the Dutchess Bleachery of Wappingers Falls, New York, and the John A. Manning Company of Troy, New York, were both parts of broader reform plans initiated after the First World War. The Manning plan, begun in 1919, included provisions for health, life, and accident insurance and an employment guarantee that was changed to a reserves system three years later. The company created no special fund to compensate its workers, but it did agree to pay $9 a week for a maximum of eight weeks a year.[35] The Bleachery scheme grew out of a postwar "industrial democracy" arrangement based on a Partnership Plan.[36] "Employee representation" was an important part of all such efforts, but at Dutchess Bleachery the company union existed alongside a trade union. The Partnership Plan also included profit sharing, provisions for stock purchases by the workers, an employee savings program, life and health insurance, and two unique sinking funds.[37] One fund was established to insure the payment of a 6 percent annual common stock dividend, but the other, the "employees'" fund, was established to pay half wages to all unemployed workers. Between 1918 and 1922 over $80,000 was paid into the unemployment insurance fund. In 1920 the Bleachery management established a similar plan at its Garnerville plant, the Rockland Finishing Company, by contributing $100,000 to a fund for the Rockland print-and-dye workers.[38]

The success or failure of these plans apparently depended on factors beyond the control of Management. The instability of the textile industry in the 1920's was a disadvantage that no amount of managerial competence could overcome, and the Bleachery funds were consequently being drained at the very time that the firm had no money with which to replenish them. The Garnerville company paid out $80,000 in benefits during 1920 alone.[39] By mid-1923 the original appropriation was exhausted and the plan was suspended. Some years later an executive of the firm recalled that the fund had helped reduce labor turnover while it was in operation.[40] The Bleachery itself spent large sums on unemployment relief during the 1920's. This drain, amounting to at least $70,000 between 1920 and 1929, destroyed the original rationale for the fund; yet it helped create an interest in efficiency among the workmen: "The Partnership Plan has revolutionized the attitude of the operatives toward production. All the foremen have perceived a new alertness . . . among the men."[41] Though the company reported it made no contributions to the fund after 1922, a sufficient amount remained to pay benefits during the early 1930's. This sum totaled more than $3,100 in 1932. Apparently the Bleachery workers, long accustomed to insecure employment, acclimated themselves to the Depression with relative ease. The Manning Company, on the other hand, had no such problems. It paid less than $500 in benefits between 1919 and 1927.[42] One manager commented that such payments had rarely been necessary and were only a "final safeguard."[43] Manning executives were fairly successful in maintaining this policy during the Depression. Layoffs remained relatively low, at least until 1933, indicating the company's ability to devise other expedients to maintain steady work.[44]

Of the other firms that established unemployment reserves funds in the 1920's, none were as publicized or as important as the six that have been reviewed. For the most part their plans covered only small numbers of workers, were highly experimental in nature, and lasted only for short periods. The American Cast Iron Pipe Company of Birmingham, Alabama, and the United Diamond Works of Newark, New Jersey, exhausted their funds before the advent of the Depression. The Delaware and Hudson Railroad began paying "dismissal" wages in 1922, and the Consolidated Water, Power, and Paper Company of Wisconsin Rapids, Wisconsin, paid unemployment benefits for a brief period in 1929. The Brown and Baily Company of Philadelphia was the only one of the group to set up a conventional reserves plan, and it suspended payments in 1932 after two years of operation.[45]

Guaranteed Employment

OF THE firms in the 1920's that guaranteed employment only two established plans of any consequence, and of these the plan of the Procter & Gamble Company of Cincinnati, Ohio, by far overshadowed the other in almost every respect. Without the activities of William C. Procter, the company president and principal owner, guaranteed employment would hardly have warranted special attention. And yet Procter's background, his ideas, and his methods of attacking unemployment were anything but unique.

Since the 1890's Procter had taken an interest in the firm's personnel relations; his creation of a profit-sharing plan before the turn of the century was only the first of many innovations designed to improve industrial life and management. In 1919 he wrote that "the chief problem of 'big business' today is to shape its policies so that each worker . . . will feel he is part of the company, with a personal responsibility for its success. . . . To bring this about, an employer must take the men into his confidence."[46] In addition to profit sharing Procter had begun a plan of sickness, disability, and life insurance, old age pensions, a company union, the eight-hour day, and employee representation on the board of directors.[47] Gradually, however, he realized that this was not enough; stock ownership, insurance, and other welfare programs were meaningless to workers without steady employment. He had long believed that "too much stress cannot be placed upon the advantage of being able to retain the same employees year after year," and in the period following World War I he initiated a full-scale campaign against irregular employment.[48]

The unemployment problem at P & G was a result of the company's dependence on wholesale jobbers who purchased soap for resale to retailers. Customer demand actually varied little from season to season, but the jobbers, intent on making a quick profit, only ordered from P & G when low raw material prices reduced the wholesale price, making production dependent on their speculative activities. To combat this practice Procter proposed a drastic change in policy: he decided to circumvent the middlemen and sell directly to the retailers. Such a plan involved tremendous difficulties; traditional lines of authority would have to be redrawn and a large sales force recruited. But in spite of the objections of many subordinates, Procter began marketing directly to his retailers in July 1920.[49]

Under this plan P & G stabilized employment in its soapmaking plants within eighteen months. The newly expanded sales department divided the country into sections and assigned sales quotas to its field representatives. When the quotas had been set the salesmen were committed to filling them. The company, moreover, refused to make large or irregular deliveries; orders had to be filled from the scheduled production, a job that was accomplished with the aid of strategically located warehouses and a fleet of trucks. To complement these changes a number of factory reforms were undertaken. The superintendents postponed repairs during good times, created a single utility department to do odd jobs, transferred men between jobs to keep them continuously employed, and adjusted their machinery to assure steady production.[50] By 1923 Procter was ready for a second step. In what the *New York Times* called "the boldest attack on uncertain tenure of jobs—and the industrial and social ills entailed thereby—that has been made in this country," he guaranteed the jobs of more than five thousand workers for forty-eight weeks a year.[51]

This guarantee was not only a sensational move but a highly successful one. All employees with at least six months' seniority who made less than $2000 per year and who participated in the profit-sharing plan were eligible, with the notable exception of the workers at several southern cottonseed oil plants, where irregular work was "too hard for the company to solve."[52] Not a single worker covered by the guarantee was laid off between 1923 and 1933. Procter reported in 1931 that labor turnover was drastically reduced and the company had lowered production costs by as much as 5 percent. "The close scrutiny of all details of the business," he wrote, "would, of course, increase the efficiency of the organization and profits of the business, and it has at least demonstrated that Guaranteed Employment is practical."[53] Herbert Feis, who made a detailed study of P & G labor policies in the late twenties, found that regularized production based on the employment guarantee had resulted in substantial savings to the company.[54] A P & G employee attributed the firm's success to the acceptance of the "spirit and methods of scientific management," and Beulah Amidon, a journalist, concluded that "regularization of production and of employment was faced and solved by Procter and Gamble as a management problem."[55]

The Columbia Conserve Company of Indianapolis, Indiana, initiated an equally daring experiment in 1917, when its president, William P. Hapgood, brother of the social critics Norman and Hutchins Hapgood, began what Paul H. Douglas described as a "unique experiment in industrial democracy."[56] Hapgood's objectives were the substitution of salaries for wages—making, as he said, "the first principle of our business the abolition of irregular employment"—and the gradual transfer of ownership to the employees.[57] Any worker approved by his fellow employees was guaranteed year-round employment and made a member of the works council, which was involved in the formation of all company policy after 1921. This arrangement worked well, and the company prospered in the 1920's. "The workers have proved themselves increasingly capable of wise and efficient government and of whole-souled co-operation in working for the best interests of the concern. In practically every case when an issue has arisen between their immediate self interest and the welfare of the company, they had adopted the altruistic course with little hesitation."[58]

But it was the employment guarantee which had the greatest impact on Columbia Conserve employees. After the beginning of the plan, all but the workers who were temporarily hired during the peak fall season came under the guarantee. Because of this constant overhead cost, the company had to find ways to utilize its labor force. After the 1920–22 recession Columbia Conserve began a policy of developing versatility in its workers, getting early orders, and adding new lines of goods to manufacture in the off-season. Hapgood reported in 1928 that 97 percent of the employees were covered by the guarantee.[59] The unemployment policy of Columbia Conserve reflected his view that "society ought to undertake to employ every man who is out of employment. A man that has no voice in the management of the business is not responsible for his unemployment."[60]

Despite the many advantages of Columbia Conserve's industrial democracy plan, the Depression created enormous hardships for the workers. In June 1930 the works council formally assumed control of the business, but this merely added to the difficulties of maintaining shop discipline. As profits declined the workers' representatives were forced to cut their salaries until by the summer of 1932 the average employee's income was little more than half that of 1931. Dissension grew and reached a peak in 1933, when Hapgood insisted upon the dismissal of several workers whom he considered insubordinate. A committee of four, including Douglas, mediated the dispute and found that Hapgood had acted in an autocratic manner toward the workers who were apparently trying to organize a labor union. Industrial democracy, the investigators concluded, had disappeared.[61] For some time these problems and the company's financial difficulties seemed to forecast the end of Columbia Conserve. But with the economic upturn of the early New Deal period the company made a remarkable recovery; by 1935 salaries were nearly back to their 1930 level.[62]

There were other efforts to guarantee employment that were neither as successful as the Procter & Gamble plan nor as far-reaching in their implications as the plan of Columbia Conserve. The Crocker-McElwain and the Chemical Paper Manufacturing Company of Holyoke, Massachusetts, guaranteed employment in 1921 but limited their plans to those workers with five or more years' company service who promised not to join a labor union.[63] This rather unique approach was, nevertheless, combined with a stabilization program that significantly reduced labor turnover in the following years. The guarantee was revised in 1931–32, but it continued to include most of the firms' employees.[64] The Samarkand Company, a small San Francisco food concern, adopted a guarantee plan in 1929 and subsequently reported that its rate of labor turnover had declined and that its employees' morale had improved. Poor business conditions forced it to suspend the guarantee in 1932.[65] Such efforts were, by the third year of the Depression, risky experiments that only well-established and prosperous enterprises dared embark on.

Employer Plans of the 1930's

WHILE THE Depression of the 1930's left most companies unable to experiment with any type of employment reform, it also convinced many businessmen of the need for unemployment insurance. The group that did manage to implement some form of reserves or guarantee plan had the advantage of following the precedents of the 1920's, and these men learned their lessons well. Most of the new experimenters had long been devoted to the New Emphasis and had the same ostensible objectives as the employers who adopted unemployment insurance a decade before. Their programs consequently included, with the exception of employee contributions—which became popular only after 1929—few ideas that had not appeared in the earlier plans. Yet 1931 was not 1921 and the severity of the Depression forced many changes, including the abandonment of much of the New Emphasis in practice, if not in theory, in favor of unemployment relief.

The experiences of the General Electric Company illustrate the factors of continuity and change in the plans inaugurated after 1929. GE had nearly 100,000 employees in 1929, many times the number who worked at Procter and Gamble, the largest firm to adopt unemployment insurance in the 1920's. It had also prospered by manufacturing many of the products of the postwar era that had radically changed living and working conditions in the United States. And, in the 1930's, size and earning power were important prerequisites for a company unemployment-insurance system. Even Gerard Swope, president of GE and architect of its unemployment scheme, later admitted that under the circumstances of the early 1930's such a plan was "too ambitious . . . for any one company to undertake."[66] Offsetting these differences was the presence of Swope and Young, who had initiated or updated a number of benefit programs since 1922.[67] In 1924–25 they drew up an unemployment insurance program based on joint contributions from the company and workers, but the employees rejected it. Five years later Swope revived the plan and the workers accepted it without hesitation.

The GE unemployment insurance system went into effect in 1930 under Swope's personal supervision. To protect the most vulnerable workers he limited eligibility to workers in the producers' goods departments. He also demanded a small contribution from the employees so the program would involve a cooperative approach to solving the problem of unemployment. He told a congressional committee that "the cardinal principle of our plan is that unemployment benefits should be accumulated from employees and from the company. Personally, I feel quite strongly on the subject and believe it is the only constructive way to do it."[68] In late 1930, as sales dropped, the company substituted an emergency program for the original plan. The new scheme required contributions from all employees not covered under the scheme except those in the incandescent lamp department. Between 1931 and 1934 the insurance fund received approximately $5,000,000 and paid out more than $3,600,000 in benefits. During the first year and a half of the plan's operation, 23,000 workers received unemployment benefits. Yet these statistics, while impressive, did not tell the whole story. In 1934 Swope admitted that the company had on its payroll 30,000 to 40,000 fewer workers than in 1929 and that the benefits had gone "to people whom we expect to call back into the industry as soon as we can find work for them."[69]

Despite the problems that he encountered with the insurance fund, Swope offered the employees in the lamp works an employment guarantee in 1931. While this step was possible because the demand for incandescent bulbs varied only slightly with economic conditions, the guarantee, which originally covered 50 weeks per year, was later reduced to 1500 and then 1250 hours; the workers, moreover, had to contribute 1 percent of their wages.[70] Swope's experiences, perhaps more than those of any other employer, revealed the inability of private businessmen, even those with abundant resources at their command, to cope with the unemployment problem of the 1930's.

Second only to the GE experiment in its scope was the 1931 Rochester plan, essentially the creation of the Eastman Kodak Company and its treasurer, Marion B. Folsom. Kodak executives had already undertaken an extensive employment stabilization program; planned production, purchasing, and sales had enabled them to end virtually all seasonal layoffs.[71] "Not only from the point of view of stabilizing employment," wrote Folsom, "but also from the standpoint of investment in plant equipment, we have found it more practical to produce at a constant rate throughout the year."[72] And this was a major consideration in his and his colleagues' decision to promote a city-wide program of unemployment insurance, but it was apparently not the only one. A pamphlet published by the Rochester Industrial Management Council explained: "The companies are opposed to compulsory unemployment insurance. They are opposed to legislation that would establish either state or national unemployment insurance. They believe that plans similar to theirs . . . is [sic] the best way, the American way, of dealing with the problem involved."[73]

The plan that emerged under the auspices of the Rochester Chamber of Commerce and the Civic Committee on Unemployment provided for a multicompany attack on joblessness. Fourteen (later nineteen) local firms agreed to set up separate but identical unemployment insurance programs. Each agreed to contribute 2 percent of its payroll and to begin benefit payments in 1933. All the workers covered were to be compensated according to a single, uniform scale: 60 per cent of their average weekly wage or at least $22.50 for six to thirteen weeks per year, depending on the length of each employee's service to his company. No provision was included for compulsory employee contributions. The impression of a joint community effort that these employers sought to convey was nevertheless misleading. Of the 26,000 workers originally covered under the agreements, more than half were Kodak employees, and Kodak executives, notably Folsom, assumed the primary responsibility for directing the program. Of the eighteen other companies that pledged to create unemployment insurance funds, many ran into trouble almost immediately; only seven actually established funds and of these all but one laid off many workers before benefit payments started in 1933. By 1934 the seven participating firms, including Kodak, employed only 12,000 workers. The benefit provisions were also revised in 1932 to reduce payments to 50 percent of the average wage or a maximum of $18.75 per week.[74] Paradoxically, these problems led several employers who had sought to forestall government action to advocate compulsory unemployment insurance.[75]

Of the four other company plans of the early 1930's, only one, the Mauthe Fond du Lac scheme, achieved any degree of success. Between 1930 and 1934 William Mauthe of Fond du Lac, Wisconsin, established unemployment insurance funds at four separate plants that covered a relatively small number of employees but were quite successful at three of the factories. Eligible employees could receive benefits for a maximum of 100 days per year.[76] The Fond du Lac voluntary plan ended in 1934 when the Wisconsin unemployment reserves act went into effect—a law Mauthe had helped enact. Another Wisconsin firm, the J. I. Case Company of Racine, began an unemployment insurance program in November 1931, probably in an attempt to undermine the 1931–32 Wisconsin legislative campaign for unemployment insurance. The Case employees, moreover, had to contribute 50 percent of the fund and received only meager benefits. Even with these limitations the Case plan was no more successful as a relief program than it was as a political tool; poor business conditions prevented an adequate trial, and Case officials reluctantly accepted compulsory unemployment insurance in 1934.[77] The voluntary programs of the Minnesota Mining and Manufacturing Company and the William Wrigley Company of Chicago, begun in 1932 and 1934 respectively, were similarly disappointing in their results.

Thus a small group of employers, usually with inadequate preparation and often slight success, demonstrated their faith in the businessman's approach to unemployment insurance. That they failed was due not to their lack of imagination but to the impact of the Depression, which revealed how limited their control actually was. Before that time, however, they had shown that management reform and reduced unemployment were indeed related, and had provided experience to support the assertion that America was unique and need not adopt the bankrupt remedies of Europe—an idea that drew strength from more than the practices of this small group of employers. It was accepted, too, by labor leaders of widely divergent political complexions, in some cases after considering more conventional approaches to unemployment insurance, and incorporated into their policies for varying periods. Because of the activities of both groups, unemployment prevention remained a major approach to be considered when popular attention shifted from voluntary to compulsory unemployment insurance in the 1930's.

4 | ORGANIZED LABOR:
THE AFL

For the American labor movement, unemployment was always a problem of real or potential significance. During depressions union members suffered many of the hardships of unorganized workers; in prosperous times they were subject to seasonal layoffs and technological changes. For some unions unemployment was relatively infrequent or was anticipated and adequately provided for by higher wages.[1] But for other unions it was a constant menace that required much more elaborate countermeasures. The policies of individual labor organizations therefore varied widely, depending on the composition, leadership, and objectives of the union. On one matter, however, there was near unanimity. Unemployment insurance, whether compulsory or voluntary, was rejected as dangerous or impractical by the majority of the unions of the AFL.

For nearly four decades Samuel Gompers served as president of the AFL and spokesman for the executive council. At first a confirmed socialist, he quickly became immersed in the day-to-day details of organizing and bargaining and wrote, as early as 1887, that "no successful attempt can be made to reach those ends [of socialism] without first improving present conditions."[2] While he soon disavowed any interest in radicalism, his early flirtation with socialism left him with a strong sense of class consciousness that left a deep imprint on the AFL and was a major factor in the development of its policies toward unemployment insurance. Gompers insisted that the unions rely on their own resources for social change. All they required, he argued, was the right to organize and bargain collectively, just as other groups, notably employers, had the right to organize and protect their interests.[3] His approach was reflected in the federation's narrow concentration on immediate goals, on "organization, jurisdiction, eight hours, assessments, and strike policies," that were the essence of "pure and simple" unionism.[4] It was also evident in the federation's policies toward specific hazards such as unemployment, and remained a major stumbling block to the acceptance of unemployment insurance legislation long after Gompers had passed from the scene.

Gompers' insistence that the workers solve their own problems was not, at least in the case of unemployment, an excuse for inaction. Indeed, he was among the most vociferous critics of an industrial system that permitted joblessness.[5] "Next to the intensity of my desire to protect child life," he wrote, "was my resentment of unemployment."[6] The solution to the unemployment problem—and he assured his colleagues it could be solved—was the responsibility of the unions.[7] To achieve this end, as well as to help their jobless members, Gompers and the AFL unions developed a series of policies that fall under three general headings: the call for the shorter workday, historically the most important of the union demands; the rejection of the idea that production levels, and wages and employment, should be related, an important consideration in the unionists' relations with the New Emphasis employers; and the relief of the jobless, significant in this regard only insofar as it reflected the federation leaders' attitude toward government interference and voluntary unemployment insurance.[8]

The traditional unemployment policy of American unionists was a demand for shorter hours. Since the 1860's both conservative and radical unionists had emphasized the eight-hour day as the solution to a variety of evils, including unemployment.[9] The rationale behind this demand was simple enough: if workers were given more leisure, say an eight- rather than a ten-hour day, they would—all other things being equal—produce less. Thus the shorter workday would create a demand for more labor and automatically spread employment. Since the workers would need more money to finance their new leisure, shorter hours would also—or so the federation's theory ran—lead to a demand for higher pay.[10] This method of raising wages and reducing unemployment, which radical unionists soon subordinated to other demands, remained a basic tenet of AFL policy for many years.

The same somewhat narrow outlook was apparent in the federation's disregard for productivity, which had a direct bearing on its unemployment insurance policy. Gompers' jealousy of labor's prerogatives was the basis of the unions' approach to production. Since workers could never be certain of receiving wages based on the value of their contribution—and for that matter could never rely on outsiders to provide accurate advice—they must disregard the claims of economists and others that productivity should determine wages, and instead, demand more regardless of output. This approach dictated policies designed to help individual union members, both by restricting the supply of labor and by prolonging the available work. High membership fees, long apprenticeships, the restriction of output, agitation for curbs on immigration, regulation of overtime, work sharing, and opposition to incentive schemes of the sort that Taylor's followers proposed were methods used by individual unions and the AFL to combat unemployment, much to the distress of the "outsiders" who took a larger view of the problem. The unions' insistence on impeding production to reduce unemployment inevitably precipitated a long and acrimonious debate with the engineers.[11] At a time when reformers were taking a more sophisticated view of unemployment and its remedies the spokesmen for the labor movement clung to their self-centered approach, a disparity that accounted in large measure for the fact that most New Emphasis employers ran open shops.[12]

Since even Gompers acknowledged that the unions would solve the unemployment problem only in the long run, the federation's relief policies were also of considerable importance. During depressions the AFL supported the use of public works to employ the unemployed, a tradition Gompers began in the 1890's when he endorsed "General" Coxey's march on Washington. At the same time he vigorously opposed government appropriations for outright relief, since industrious workingmen wanted productive labor, not charity.[13] Some unions, particularly the American affiliates of British labor organizations, also established out-of-work benefit funds. Gompers, in fact, actively supported the creation of unemployment funds during his career as an officer of the Cigar Makers' Union. He introduced an unemployment benefit system in his New York local in the early 1870's and proposed a union-wide fund at the 1876 Cigar Makers' convention. In 1889 the union finally established a jobless benefit plan, which it maintained as part of its welfare program until 1920.[14] Although nine other national unions, notably the International Typographical Union, made halfhearted attempts to develop a system of worker-financed unemployment insurance before 1919, the burden of caring for the unemployed was usually left to the local union.[15] The efforts that resulted were largely makeshift, though most locals managed to make some provision for their members. David P. Smelser, who studied these activities in 1919, found two reasons for the "slight development" of the trade union plans: ". . . first, the unwillingness of the average union member to acquiesce in the necessary increase of dues; and second, the apparent inadequacy of the administrative agencies of the union to secure a just distribution of the benefits."[16]

Despite the wide range of union unemployment policies, the measures that Gompers and his colleagues rejected were ultimately as important as those that they accepted. For apart from their demand for public works during depressions, they denied the need for government assistance either to help them solve the problem or to aid the jobless directly. Their reliance on voluntary action, or "voluntarism," was part and parcel of their doctrine of self-help. Gompers, the best-known exponent of this theory, believed voluntarism to be the "cornerstone" of the house of labor. "I want to urge devotion to the fundamental of human liberty," he told the AFL convention a few days before his death. ". . . no lasting gain has ever come from compulsion. If we seek to force, we but tear apart that which united is invincible."[17]

But there were other more concrete reasons for his and his successors' rigid adherence to voluntarism. It had, after all, been an effective strategy. Labor unions were seldom able to rely on government, and the courts remained generally antagonistic to their purposes and methods. Unlike the radicals, the AFL leaders accepted this situation as a fact of life and concentrated on collective bargaining, strikes, boycotts, and the union label to advance their cause. They thus became conditioned to acting alone and, more important, had developed a vested interest in independent action. A sudden emphasis on legislation or the formation of a labor party would mean not only an assumption that government had somehow become more accessible to organized labor, but a decisive defeat for the old guard leadership of the federation.[18] This did not mean, of course, that the leaders of the AFL opposed all government activity. They supported legislation in matters such as women's suffrage, business regulation, child labor, accident compensation, and factory inspection, that were either outside the immediate realm of labor-management relations or had no equivalent enforceable by the unions.[19] But there were definite limits to their acquiescence in legislative action, and these stopped well short of social insurance. For the AFL in the era of Gompers, state-sponsored old age pensions, health, or unemployment insurance were taboo.[20]

Opposition to unemployment insurance legislation developed as part of the federation's general anti-State policy. Gompers characterized it as a "utopian dream" and called upon the workers to maintain their pay scales and, if necessary, spread work in hard times.[21] He attacked not only the proposal but the reformers, labeling them "professional representatives of social welfare" whose objectives were to do "things for the workers . . . that will prevent their doing things for themselves."[22] But since there was relatively little sentiment among American unionists for compulsory social insurance before World War I, Gompers' views probably had a greater impact on the legislatures than on the unions. In April 1916, for example, he testified before the congressional committee which was considering Meyer London's social insurance commission bill. He denounced all compulsory insurance for making the worker surrender his freedom; he was, as he stated, "more concerned . . . with the fundamental principles of human liberty and refusal to surrender rights to government agencies, than I am with social insurance."[23] His practice of rejecting social insurance in general and unemployment insurance legislation in particular remained a traditional practice of AFL leaders until the Depression of the 1930's forced a reassessment of voluntarism.

After 1917 the federation's unemployment policies underwent a significant, though largely unplanned, even unconscious, transformation. The AFL gradually repudiated its former attitude toward production and its rationale for shorter hours. It reemphasized its old demand for increased public works during depressions and adopted several of the reformers' proposals. Slowly it seemed the federation might accept unemployment insurance as an instrument of industrial stability.

Policy Changes and Challenges

THE YEARS of World War I and the immediate postwar period inaugurated an era of union resurgence and militancy seldom equalled in American labor history. Organizing proceeded at an unprecedented pace: the membership of the AFL unions rose from 2,500,000 in 1915 to nearly 4,000,000 in 1921, and the aggressiveness of the members increased as their numbers grew. At the same time "industrial democracy"—an amalgam of wartime idealism, the new interest in labor productivity, and a fear of trade unions—became popular with many businessmen. Welfare programs, "works councils" or "employee representation" plans, and generous wage increases seemed to signal a new and more cooperative era in labor relations. The depression of 1920–22 terminated both of these developments but it did not halt the efforts to evolve a fresh approach to business and business problems.

An immediate effect of the war was to force Gompers to reconsider his attitude toward government and business. Before 1917 he had established good relations with the Wilson Administration, largely because of his moderate position and conciliatory approach.[24] But mobilization introduced a new phase in this relationship, as Gompers became a star performer in the preparedness effort. As a member of the Advisory Commission of the Council of National Defense, an Administration advisor on labor policy, and a staunch opponent of socialism and pacifism, he proved to be a valuable asset to the government. The honors and the influence that accompanied these roles, as well as the opportunity to view labor-management relations from a different perspective, were reflected in Gompers' statements. In contrast to his former position he stressed the need for "continuity" in production, and the fact that "we established a going machine upon a basis of business efficiency."[25] His antipathy toward the engineers also cooled, thanks largely to the efforts of Morris L. Cooke, and Gompers endorsed various efforts to promote mutual understanding—the first, hesitant steps by the AFL toward the New Emphasis.[26]

Federation policies in the immediate postwar era similarly indicated that old ideas had given way to new. The socialist editor of *Justice,* the journal of the International Ladies' Garment Workers' Union, proclaimed in 1919 that "the AFL is a great force, a growing force . . . ."[27] The involvement of the AFL in the steel strike and its endorsement of the Plumb Plan for the nationalization of the railroads seemed to substantiate this conclusion. The 1919 AFL convention adopted a reconstruction program that proposed the establishment of shop committees to cooperate with management in solving production problems. But on other postwar issues, particularly social insurance and unemployment measures, the evidence of change was less clear. The reconstruction platform called for higher wages to allow the workers to save for periods of layoff and, in Gompers' words, for "government—national, state, and local—to adopt every measure necessary to prevent unemployment," which meant, however, the restriction of immigration and the use of public works during depressions.[28]

While the new approach to production embodied in the reconstruction platform was an important factor in federation policy-making in the 1920's, it was overshadowed in the immediate postwar years by other, and from the point of view of many union members more appealing, programs. Increasingly, radical union leaders abandoned the federation's methods and goals for more ambitious ones, specifically the creation of an independent labor party, modeled after the British Labour Party, and a wide-ranging legislative program. They were inspired by the success of the British party and by its postwar reconstruction platform, an avowedly socialist document written by Sidney Webb that pledged the party to seek "the universal enforcement of a national minimum."[29] Webb argued that the national minimum demanded the use of public works, employment exchanges, vocational training, unemployment insurance, and the subsidization of trade union out-of-work benefit funds to prevent unemployment.[30] He thus coupled his proposals of 1907–10 with compulsory unemployment insurance, which even the indomitable Fabians now recognized as a *fait accompli,* if not an altogether desirable policy. The American unionists, in turn, drew from the British platform in what became their first somewhat haphazard attempt to promote unemployment insurance legislation.

Agitation for independent political action based on the British program occurred in many parts of the country, but it was strongest in Illinois, where the Illinois State Federation of Labor and the powerful Chicago Federation of Labor, under the progressive leadership of John Fitzpatrick, organizer of the steel strike, formed the nucleus for a local, state, and national movement. In November 1918 the Illinois leaders enthusiastically endorsed a reform manifesto called "Labor's Fourteen Points" to serve as their statement of aims. This document, which had been drafted by Frank P. Walsh and Basil Manly, formerly officials of the United States Commission on Industrial Relations, drew on traditional socialist demands, the social insurance programs of the prewar progressives, and the British reconstruction platform; it called for the nationalization of transportation and communication facilities, "democratic control of industry," the eight-hour day, social insurance, and minimum wages. It demanded the "abolition of unemployment by the creation of opportunity for steady work . . . through the stabilization of industry" as well as by public works during depression periods.[31] In the spring of 1919 the Chicago leaders ran state and local tickets on the Fourteen Points; they demanded, in particular, full pay for the unemployed and a comprehensive social insurance program.[32] Radical union groups in New York adopted a similar platform in December 1918.[33] In the spring of 1919 important independent labor parties developed in Pennsylvania, Ohio, Indiana, Washington, Minnesota, North Dakota, and Kansas.[34] In November 1919 the radicals held their first national convention and advanced a platform calling for financial aid for the unemployed, stabilization of industry, and support for socialist and farmers' organizations.[35]

The growth of the labor party movement, with its promise of radical political action, caused Gompers and his close associates considerable anguish, if few long-run problems. John P. Frey, a leader among the old guard, warned the federation's president of a "new set of dreamers" who were a "menace" to the labor movement.[36] Gompers himself was sorely perplexed at these developments, fearing that by independent political action "we shall be either submerged" or driven "into ultra-radicalism and impotent, furious Bolshevism."[37] They were nevertheless successful in maintaining their ascendancy over American labor—a tribute to their consummate political skills and an indication of the limited appeal of their opponents, whose attempts to rally various dissatisfied groups under a single banner only created dissension. The farmers had little interest in such purely labor issues as unemployment insurance, and succeeded in subordinating many of the labor demands to agrarian measures without contributing much popular support. In 1920 a coalition of labor, farmer, and progressive elements formed the Farmer-Labor Party, unsuccessfully attempted to draft Senator Robert M. La Follette as their presidential candidate, and lost much of their support to the Socialists.[38] The Illinois labor party, which was the strongest of the state groups, suffered a series of election disasters that reduced it to impotence. In 1923 William Z. Foster's Communists administered the *coup de grâce* to the labor party movement by capturing control of the Farmer-Labor Party. The legacy of postwar labor radicalism, the 1924 Progressive campaign, lacked nearly all of its forerunner's characteristics, including the demand for unemployment legislation. Only in the 1930's, when widespread joblessness turned many union members to radicalism, were there new demands for political agitation and compulsory unemployment insurance based on the British precedent.

Yet the labor party movement was not the only, or even the most serious, threat to the old guard and voluntarism in the postwar period. The depression produced new demands for unemployment insurance legislation, although the focus shifted from the radicals' quasi-British approach to the more conservative program of the AALL. Most of the union leaders who promoted unemployment insurance legislation, either in union meetings or in the state campaigns, had played some part in the AALL legislative drives for social insurance legislation in the postwar years. Despite the opposition of the federation, they had sponsored the introduction of health insurance bills and had nearly secured the passage of one such measure in New York.[39] Among the larger unions, the United Mine Workers took a strong position in favor of social insurance measures. The chief sponsor of this legislation among the miners was William Green, who called upon the AFL at its 1921 convention to begin "defining for the workers of America a complete, definite, simple social justice program." Green refused to consider unemployment insurance at the miners' convention of the same year only because it "would divert from the concentration upon the other two social justice purposes [old age pensions and health insurance] and thus weaken our chances and lessen our influence."[40]

Other unionists were less reluctant to advance specific unemployment proposals. While the legislative campaigns for unemployment insurance backed by the AALL never approached in number the earlier efforts for health and old age benefits, they did signify widespread interest in the possibility of combating unemployment through political action. By far the most important of these efforts developed in Wisconsin, where the state labor federation and a group of university professors nearly convinced the legislature to enact an unemployment insurance law.[41] A similar but less auspicious movement developed in Pennsylvania under the sponsorship of the Pennsylvania State Federation of Labor and the Women's Trade Union League of Philadelphia. James Maurer and Frieda S. Miller, the respective heads of these organizations, asked Andrews to draft a bill for the Pennsylvania legislature. Miss Miller explained that "We have no chance to enact the bill into law at this session. On the other hand, large groups of organized workers, e.g. textile workers, miners, railroad workers . . . are now much occupied with the question and will give serious consideration to any proposal to remedy it. . . . Two years hence, or as soon as we do get a more favorable legislature, we will have this sentiment to build on."[42] But unfortunately for the Pennsylvania labor leaders, Andrews' bill, which was modeled after the Wisconsin measure, did not have the desired effect of awakening the interest of the "sick"-industry workers.[43]

These efforts, indicative of the growing unrest within the unions, nevertheless had little direct effect on AFL policy. In response to queries about compulsory unemployment insurance, Gompers emphasized the importance of voluntarism, the evils of government interference, and the experimental nature of such legislation.[44] He maintained that state employment offices, through which unemployment insurance would be administered, would provide a means of spying on the workers, and that union members might have to accept drastic wage reductions to qualify for benefits. All such programs, he concluded, would make joblessness a "permanent evil." "Anyone who advocates compulsory unemployment insurance simply aggravates the evil of unemployment and harms instead of helps those it is . . . desired to aid."[45] When the machinists' delegation introduced a resolution at the 1921 convention calling for employer-financed jobless benefits, he emphasized the reluctance of the workers to "place themselves under the guardianship of the government of the country" and the fact that in Europe jobless insurance "has not reduced unemployment one iota."[46] The machinists' spokesman, perplexed at this misunderstanding of the recent AALL bills, replied that a charge on industry would induce employers to keep their men on the job, but the convention would hear no more.[47]

Although they refused to recognize Andrews' rationale for unemployment insurance legislation, Gompers and the old guard leaders had, by 1921, accepted virtually every other feature of the *Practical Program*. The federation had, of course, long supported increased public construction to absorb the jobless during depressions, and this became its chief demand for government action in 1921. Gompers insisted that public improvements would eliminate unemployment; he lashed the Harding Unemployment Conference for attempting to "pass the buck" to the states when Congress should supply the necessary appropriations.[48] With somewhat less consistency he also demanded the strengthening of the United States Employment Service. But the best indication of the changes wrought by the previous four years' activities was his attack on business for causing the depression. "Bad management," he argued, "means waste—unnecessary high costs of production. This waste is cumulative and finally becomes too heavy for the productive process to carry."[49] Moreover, he added, in a statement on unemployment: "It is within the power of management to discourage this evil to a marked extent."[50]

This rather anomalous position was characteristic of the AFL in the 1920's. The demands of the war period had made certain policy changes necessary or at least expedient. The role of Gompers and the federation leaders in war mobilization and the cries of the dissidents had led to important shifts in AFL unemployment policy. Yet Gompers and his associates never altered their basic ideas, a fact that became clear whenever the issue of unemployment insurance was raised. Despite the acceptance of much of the businessmen's rhetoric and of many of the programs that Andrews and other reformers proposed, unemployment insurance remained, they thought, a demand of the radicals, who favored the European approach. This attitude continued to prevail in the following years, and the disparity between the statements of the federation policy-makers and their actions became ever wider.

AFL Policy: the 1920's

GOMPERS AND his colleagues had often chosen to sacrifice consistency and ideological commitment for short-term gains before the war; in the 1920's they had little choice but to continue this practice, with even less expectation of success. Welfare capitalism, the "American plan," and the decline of important unionized industries ate away at the ranks of organized labor. Adverse public opinion and the courts further restricted union activities. In an attempt to preserve what strength they had, the AFL leaders continued to reject unemployment insurance legislation while they became increasingly receptive to the New Emphasis, a policy that was most accurately reflected in the strengthening of business unionism. This approach involved a host of conservative measures, but it amounted to an attempt to work out better relations with employers. Unlike the early years when Gompers and other leaders succeeded by stressing their unconcern for the employers' problems, the policy-makers of the 1920's took a different view of the situation. To justify their existence under unfavorable circumstances, they attempted to show that organized workers could contribute more to the employers' success than the growing army of the unorganized. Increasingly they sought to convince the employers rather than the workers of their relevance to the "new era."

While many of the measures embraced by federation leaders in the 1920's are beyond the scope of this study, one is particularly relevant, the improvement in their relations with the engineers—perhaps the best indication of the new direction in AFL policy. The unions' acceptance of scientific management had, of course, begun during the war, but it was only afterward that the reconciliation really took effect. Signs of it were abundant in *Waste In Industry*, the engineers' chronicle of management malpractice, and in Gompers' call during the unemployment conference of 1921 for the adoption of lower production costs as an official goal.[51] Numerous articles and conciliatory statements followed. The engineers also changed their tactics to meet the unions' objections. They professed to consider the individual worker in their calculations and, contrary to Taylor's teachings, permitted union representatives to take part in determining production standards.[52] But this conciliatory atmosphere was best reflected in the federation's "new wage policy" that grew out of the labor-management cooperation programs of the decade. The plans themselves were uniformly unsuccessful and scarcely warranted the attention they received. In truth, cooperation was a defensive technique, tried only in declining industries after more conventional methods of increasing productivity and profits had failed. Yet under these plans the unions permitted the introduction of production standards, accepting what they had formerly rejected—the relation of wages to productivity. The new wage theory seemed to mark a sharp theoretical break with the past, but it was in fact merely another step in the drift toward the employers' approach to labor problems.

The policy changes apparent in the new relationship with the engineers and the new wage policy were also evident in the federation's approach to unemployment. Gompers' espousal of New Emphasis became more pronounced in 1921–22; he headed a group studying unemployment whose conclusions indicated the extent to which the AFL had officially accepted the employers' arguments. Stabilization and regularization, their report maintained, were necessary to prevent unemployment: "We believe that the economic problem of stabilizing employment must be worked out in the various industries by the groups associated together in production. . . . Stabilization of employment will be in part the outgrowth of efforts to improve the methods and policies of production and development of a spirit of cooperation."[53] While this report reflected the rising sentiment in favor of union-management cooperation, it also stressed the responsibility of management for joblessness. The committee went so far as to declare that "each industry must care for its own workers including the reserve force it requires."[54] It was, however, unwilling to extend this demand beyond calling for labor-management conferences to consider appropriate action for the future.

As the labor movement became more sympathetic to the engineers' ideas, the New Emphasis rhetoric also became more pronounced in AFL policy statements. Matthew Woll, a labor representative on the Committee on Business Cycles and Unemployment, reported that the burden of preventing unemployment rested on management. He even endorsed the experience of Dennison and other employers: "That the losses and suffering of periods of depression may be mitigated or even eliminated is evident from the achievements of the best informed and efficient managements."[55] On other occasions the AFL leaders lauded the efforts of business and government to eliminate waste, and they were as effusive in their praise of Secretary Hoover as the progressive businessmen. By 1925 the federation had completely rejected the discredited idea of restricting production to reduce unemployment, and seldom mentioned the arbitrary shortening of the work day. Typically, when President Green appeared before the Taylor Society, he emphasized the connection between management theory and unemployment prevention.[56]

The AFL leaders' new appreciation of the relation between inefficiency and unemployment resulted in two important conferences during 1927. Under the auspices of the Philadelphia Central Labor Union and the Philadelphia Labor College, a Conference on the Elimination of Industrial Waste was held in April. Representatives from the unions and the Taylor Society vied with each other in expressing their devotion to the techniques of scientific management. They agreed, moreover, that unemployment was the most prevalent form of waste.[57] Several months later the Philadelphia Labor College sponsored another conference, devoted entirely to the problem of unemployment, which resulted in few original suggestions but many more assertions of the role of economic planning and labor-management cooperation in preventing joblessness. A representative of the International Ladies' Garment Workers' Union explained his union's unemployment insurance program, but no substantive action was taken on the question of out-of-work benefits. The most significant result of the conference, the decision by AFL leaders to begin collecting statistics on unemployment from their member unions, indicated no change in fundamental policy.[58]

Ironically, the acceptance of the New Emphasis was not accompanied by a commensurate willingness to reconsider the relationship between unemployment insurance and the elimination of unemployment. Green, who never had an independent power base within the federation, made no effort to alter its official position on unemployment insurance legislation. After 1923, when the AFL convention again endorsed old age pension legislation, opposition to compulsory jobless benefits became a test of voluntarism. In 1924 and 1925 pressure from the AFL hierarchy helped defeat unemployment insurance bills in New York and Illinois.[59] Because unemployment was not a serious menace to the craft unions until 1928–29, this opposition consisted largely of symbolic proclamations, reminders in periods of decline and compromise that the AFL held fast to its traditional values. Unemployment insurance legislation, the bête noire of the Gompers era, thus continued to be equated with socialism, subsidized indolence, and all the things that employers like Dennison and Leeds and intellectuals like Commons and Andrews insisted it was not.

This lack of direction was also evident in the relation of union out-of-work benefit funds, the equivalents of the company plans, to that policy. Though the leaders of the labor movement agreed with many of the New Emphasis employers that compulsory unemployment insurance was undesirable, they made little effort, unlike the businessmen, to develop an alternative approach. Union out-of-work benefit plans seldom bore any relation to efficiency or increased production techniques and remained, as they had always been, relief funds to assist jobless workers. This was due in part to the defensive nature of the federation's policy, which lacked the commitment to rationality and economic order inherent in the employers' methods. Other factors, such as the autonomy of the constituent union organizations which reduced the AFL to a coordinating body, inhibited any positive move by the executive council.[60] Yet neither Gompers, who had devised the Cigar Makers' plan of the 1880's, nor Green, who had spearheaded the UMW's social insurance campaign after World War I, made any effort to use his influence to this end. Nor did the latter, for example, attempt to make unemployment insurance a feature of union-management cooperation. Since they were unwilling to endorse government subsidies as the British trade unions had done, the AFL leaders had little chance of winning rank and file backing for increased assessments to support plans that were often considered prohibitively expensive.

The unions' lack of interest in voluntary unemployment insurance is obvious when the list of union-financed plans is examined. No important labor organization, after the decline of the Cigar Makers, initiated such a program. The Diamond Workers, Deutsch-Amerikanische Typographia, Siderographers, Pocket Book Makers, and Print Cutters' section of the United Wall Paper Crafts—insignificant organizations with no more than a few hundred members—were consequently the only national unions paying out-of-work benefits in the 1920's, and their plans were national only because their members were concentrated in a few locals. There were, in addition, forty-five locals with approximately 50,000 members that provided regular out-of-work benefits at the end of the decade.[61] Of these, twenty-two were locals of the Typographical Workers, Photo-Engravers, Lithographers, Stereotypers and Electrotypers, and Printing Pressmen, whose members enjoyed relatively stable employment.[62] Nearly all of their plans were initiated in the 1920's, when the printers shared in the nation's prosperity but were threatened with technological unemployment. There is no evidence that any of the printing crafts designed their funds for anything but relief.

The remainder of the locals with out-of-work benefits were distinguished only by their insignificance. Many were obscure groups whose plans had no influence outside a small circle of eligible members. A few systems, like that of Buffalo Local No. 16 of the Bakery and Confectionery Workers, dated back many years, but most were developed after the First World War. These plans, like other union benefit funds, had one redeeming feature: they survived the early Depression years. As long as the unions were able to maintain their existence, they usually managed to adjust their plans to economic conditions. Hence, of the forty-eight local-union benefit funds of 1931, only ten failed, and three were added in the next three years. Though their benefits were usually inadequate, most members were thankful for the small amounts they received.[63]

Far more important were the joint agreements, financed or managed by the employers and workers, that became popular in the 1920's. Often these plans were the result of aggressive leadership by men who had little sympathy for the federation's approach and who hoped for the eventual enactment of unemployment insurance legislation. Because they often involved larger unions, required complex administrative procedures, and frequently were instituted in declining industries, they were also less likely to succeed. Of twenty-six agreements, only five managed to survive until 1934.[64] The plans of the Wall Paper Craftsmen, Lace Operatives, United Hatters, Cleaners and Dyers, and Hosiery Workers were relatively short-lived and inconsequential. On the other hand, the joint agreements of the industrial unions of the needle trades covered many more workers than all the union-financed plans and were based on a different rationale. In addition to compensating irregularly employed workers, they were designed to remedy the serious economic problems of the needle trades. In short, they embodied the systematic approach that was notably absent in AFL policies.

5 | THE NEEDLE TRADES: REFORM AND RELIEF

BETWEEN 1919 and 1928 the Amalgamated Clothing Workers of America, the International Ladies' Garment Workers' Union, the International Fur Workers, and the United Cloth Hat and Cap Makers (after 1924 the Cloth Hat, Cap, and Millinery Workers), nominally socialist or "radical" unions, adopted the most far-reaching unemployment insurance plans of the postwar decade. This was not an entirely unnatural development; the radicals often embraced programs that the conservative Gompers and his allies had shown little interest in. But this case was different, for the needle trades officers combined the objectives of the New Emphasis employers with the aims of the conventional union benefit plans in formulating their "joint agreements." The explanation for this seeming anomaly lies in the economic situation that faced the needle trades union leaders after World War I and in the abilities of the leaders themselves.

Two aspects of the economic situation deserve special attention in an analysis of the needle-trades unemployment insurance plans. First, the fact that the bulk of the workers were new immigrants—East European Jews and Italians—differentiated them from other union members. As socialists (in the main) they were contemptuous of "pure and simple" unionism, but as ambitious newcomers they were eager for opportunities to better their lot in life. This combination meant that the needle trades workers were often willing to adopt a more flexible position on a given issue than the more dogmatic and conservative AFL members.

Second, it is important to note that the outstanding problem of the needle trades unions after the war was unemployment. This was not a new problem; irregular employment had long plagued the clothing,

79

cap, and fur workers. Nor was it the same type of unemployment problem that the New Emphasis employers or the other AFL officials faced. It included long-term joblessness resulting from the postwar decline of the garment industries, as well as seasonal and technological unemployment. Studies of the garment industries during this period document with considerable detail the severity of the problem. Interestingly, the causes seemed readily apparent to contemporary observers. The increasingly fickle buying public encouraged frequent style changes and a minimum of long-range planning. The result was highly seasonal production and employment. Easy entry into the business (enough cash to rent a room, purchase a few sewing machines, and pay wages) reinforced the trend toward sporadic production and employment. Layoffs due to declining demand in the large shops and the low capital requirements for production led to a multiplication of small shops, each one attempting to draw business from the others by reducing overhead cost and engaging new workers in insecure jobs. The vicious circle of declining demand, layoffs, increased competition, and further layoffs continued through the 1920's. A simple rule-of-thumb served as a guide to employment opportunities in a particular city or "market": the more firms, the greater the competition and the greater the unemployment.

The structure of the industry also increased the difficulty of introducing reforms, for it required the unions to deal simultaneously with a variety of manufacturers and shops. The "inside" factories, the large organizations that performed the manufacturing process within a single establishment, were the most stable and, from the point of view of the unions, the easiest to deal with. Union leaders found that their success in promoting improvements varied in direct proportion to the size of the shop and the power of the employers with whom they were bargaining. But the inside shops often farmed out some of their work to "contract" shops, which were makeshift in organization and impermanent in character. The contractor theoretically was an independent producer; yet he usually worked for one or more inside manufacturers on a seasonal basis. The contractor's employees did most of the work, but the inside manufacturer retained control over the financing, the cutting (the first step in the manufacturing process), and the subsequent sale of the garment to the wholesaler or retailer. In the postwar period the jobber and submanufacturer often replaced the inside manufacturer and contractor in the ladies' cloak, dress, and suit industry. The submanufacturer would purchase his materials on consignment from the jobber, a wholesale merchant, who had nothing to do with the production of the garment. The financing and marketing of the final

product were the responsibilities of the jobbers, while the submanufacturers were accountable for the employees who performed the actual
work.[1]

The high incidence of unemployment and the chaotic organization
of the industries posed two basic questions for the needle-trades union
leaders. On one hand, what were they to do about the instability of the
industries, the apparent trend toward increased competition, more and
more small impermanent shops, and cost reductions at the expense of
the employees? The answer here was not difficult: any program that
made the employer financially responsible for his workmen would halt
the deterioration of employment conditions. At least such a program
would increase the cost of "irresponsibility" and promote steadier employment. But, as everyone realized, this approach might work only in
the long run or perhaps not at all. On the other hand the second question, what to do about the workers who suffered from lengthening
periods of layoff, provided immediate headaches for the union leaders.
From the point of view of the rank and file this was, of course, a problem of paramount importance. The need for temporary relief had been
a recurring difficulty for many years, but the post-1919 situation made
more apparent the necessity for prompt and thorough action.

In the prewar years the needle trades leaders had been aware of the
unemployment problem and had developed a number of policies to
deal with it. These did not differ greatly from conventional union policies: they advocated shorter hours, restricted production (although
they could not, as predominantly immigrant unions, advocate limitations on immigration or easily restrict entrance to the trade), and government relief. Several local unions experimented with worker-financed unemployment benefit funds. As befitted their emphasis on
labor solidarity, the needle trades unions also placed strong emphasis
on the equal division of work in slack periods. But only after the war
did they begin to become aware of the long- and short-term aspects of
the problem and consider a systematic approach. The man who first
realized the apparent applicability of unemployment insurance to this
situation—the possibility of preventing unemployment and compensating the workers at the same time—was Sidney Hillman, the youthful
president of the Amalgamated Clothing Workers.

The Chicago Plan

AN INTENSE, enigmatic man, Hillman had shown, by the
time of the war, that he was a stripe above the ordinary union leader.

In a few short years he had guided the Amalgamated from the position of a breakaway, "dual" union to that of a major power in the men's clothing industry.[2] As Hillman's genius for planning and organizing became apparent, it was equally obvious that he would not allow ideology to stand in the way of building an even more powerful union. While ostensibly a socialist, he had little interest in abstract theory; he was, a later observer noted with only slight exaggeration, "a pragmatist to the core."[3] Thus he recognized at an early date that, despite his colleagues' talk of revolution or nationalization, they would remain powerless to effect any change in employment conditions throughout the industry until they controlled the labor force. Thereafter he set his sights on achieving this control and using the power that would grow out of it to implement his own type of practical revolution.[4]

The wartime demand for clothing, the reduction in the civilian labor force, and the temporarily benevolent attitude of the government permitted him to take the first steps toward realizing his goal. In 1916 the ACWA had a membership of 50,000; by 1920 this number had more than tripled and the union controlled 85 percent of the industry's labor force.[5] Only the large New York market, where the prevalence of small shops made organizing difficult, remained uncertain. The power that this new control represented was precisely what Hillman had worked for; from this point, as Joseph Schlossberg, the union's secretary general wrote, the Amalgamated would "lead the working class in this country in the realization of the new consciousness."[6] To take advantage of his position Hillman rapidly developed an ambitious program of personnel reforms and member benefits. In 1920, when he presented his blueprint for labor-management cooperation, worker cooperatives, and unemployment insurance to the annual convention, the *Advance,* the organ of the ACWA, accurately termed it a plan to bring about a "reorganization of the market."[7]

While his organizing campaign was in progress, Hillman gave his first serious thoughts to an unemployment insurance program. He had long been aware of the threat of unemployment and the need for some form of relief. He recalled his own early career and how "uppermost in all our minds was 'Who will be thrown out next.' "[8] Yet at the time he began to consider unemployment insurance, employment remained steady and there was little distress—unlike the situation that was to exist after 1919. Hillman was also familiar with the work of the New Emphasis employers, although this influence too was not at first clearly apparent in his activities. Most likely, therefore, his immediate consideration was the agitation of British labor groups during the war. The Amalgamated leaders, like those of other radical unions, had paid considerable attention to the wartime activities of the British labor leaders. Hillman in particular followed their successful campaign to extend the coverage of the 1911 unemployment insurance act. He hoped American unionists would demand the adoption of a similar program, but he admitted that to expect this would be overly sanguine. He and his colleagues nevertheless found a parallel between their ideas and the work of the British Building Trades Parliament, which was engaged in a nationwide bargaining campaign to win recognition of unemployment benefits as a direct cost of production. Jacob S. Potofsky, a rising young leader of the ACWA and Hillman's eventual successor, wrote that "we are highly interested in the unemployment feature of the Building Trades Parliament, as it has a direct bearing on a similar proposal in our industry here."[9]

Hillman first notified the manufacturers of his interest in unemployment insurance in January 1919, when he told the National Association of Retail Clothiers that the industry was responsible for continuous employment "not six or nine months a year, but twelve months a year." If this was impossible, "funds for unemployment should be provided so the workers will not be uneasy concerning what may happen to them."[10] The following summer he called for a 10 percent tax on payrolls to finance out-of-work benefits. "This move will lend a powerful stimulus to production. Some workmen feel now that by increasing their output they are 'working against themselves' by hastening the approach of the slack season. This fear will be removed by unemployment insurance."[11] He adopted the same approach at the famous 1920 convention, urging unemployment insurance "by which the terrible evil of unemployment will be once and for all abolished."[12]

But it was one thing to explain the workers' needs and another to convince the employers to finance an unemployment insurance program, as Hillman soon discovered. In 1919 the ACWA demanded the establishment of unemployment insurance funds in New York, Rochester, and Baltimore, and in Chicago, the most stable of the markets.[13] Under Hillman's direction the Chicago workers asked the employers to contribute 5 percent of their payrolls into a fund to pay jobless benefits.[14] The Chicago manufacturers as well as those of the other markets rejected the union's demands in 1919. But Hillman, undaunted, introduced the same proposal the following year, with the threat that he might demand further wage increases so the employees could establish their own fund if the manufacturers balked.[15] The influence of Leo Wolman, an economist who had been added to the Amalgamated's staff in 1919, also became apparent at this point. He provided Hillman and the negotiators with a long brief explaining, in much the same terms that the New Emphasis employers were using, how unemployment insurance would reduce joblessness. The *Advance* reported that the union believed "the experience of the workmen's compensation laws had shown that specific allocation of responsibility for accidents upon employers had already done much to stimulate the movement for prevention of accidents in industry. The union held that an unemployment fund scheme would provide a similar financial incentive to the employer to reduce unemployment."[16] Yet the results of this effort were again disappointing. The arbitrators rejected the union's demands and an investigatory committee, consisting of Wolman, a representative of the manufacturers, and Leiserson, the impartial arbitrator of the Rochester market, was unable to work out a satisfactory plan.[17]

Despite this failure the Amalgamated officers, with Wolman's help, began to develop a clear theoretical position on unemployment insurance, something few other labor leaders accomplished before the 1930's. Hillman had been aware of the argument that there was a relation between jobless benefits and efficient management. But there had been at first no clear-cut commitment to unemployment prevention from the union. Between 1919 and 1922, under Wolman's direction, the Amalgamated gradually accepted this rationale. While never neglecting the importance of compensation for the workers, Hillman increasingly emphasized that "unemployment is nothing more than a bad habit of industry" and that inefficient employers should be required to pay for their reserve labor supply.[18] The best statement of the Amalgamated's position, however, came from Wolman. He criticized union-financed out-of-work benefits since they made "no provision for the examination and removal of those factors that themselves produce unemployment. . . . [their] effect, therefore, is to mitigate the influence of an evil but not to remove the evil."[19] He concluded that unemployment "is not only not inevitable but it is reducible in extent if steps to reduce it are taken. Where that is the case, the more progressive employers will turn their attention to the problems of industrial organization."[20] For many years this approach remained a basic aspect of the union's policy. Hillman maintained in 1927 that "unemployment insurance . . . will establish that balance between the consuming and producing powers of the country without which sound functioning of industry is not possible."[21]

By 1922 the economic conditions of the industry had improved sufficiently for Hillman to resume his campaign for an unemployment fund. This time he concentrated on Chicago, where the union was already experimenting with a variety of expedients to reduce layoffs.[22]

Though the employers remained obdurate about the benefit plan, they did permit Hillman to establish a single employment office for the Chicago market and to resubmit the question of unemployment insurance in 1923. When the employment office was functioning smoothly, Hillman and Wolman, with the aid of Earl Dean Howard, the labor manager of Hart Schaffner & Marx, worked out the particulars of an unemployment plan. In return for Howard's cooperation the union leaders agreed in December 1922 to drop their demand that the employers make the entire contribution, thus establishing a precedent for the later joint agreements.[23] Even with this understanding the employers at first refused to grant wage increases or the unemployment fund, and the Chicago chairman appointed an arbitration team that included Leiserson and John R. Commons to settle the dispute. Their proceedings began in April. "The one thing which stood out particularly," reported the *Advance,* "was the definiteness with which all present urged that every effort should be made to establish an unemployment fund."[24] After several weeks of discussion, the arbitrators granted a 10 percent wage increase which included the employers' contributions to an insurance fund for 20,000 Chicago workers.[25] "Conceivably, when the industrial history of 1923—or even the decade is written," speculated the editors of the *Survey* in a November editorial, "the unemployment fund set up in the Chicago garment trades will stand out as the most prescient development of the time."[26]

Contributions under this agreement began in June, but it was many months before the details were worked out. The plan called for the employers to pay 1.5 percent of their payrolls and the workers to pay an equal percentage of their wages. Each firm was to maintain a separate fund, at least in theory, so that a two-year limitation on the accumulation of contributions would constitute a financial incentive for employers to provide continuous work. Employees would receive no more than five weekly payments per year, and all benefits would be calculated at 40 percent of the average wage up to a maximum of $20 a week. To insure the funds' solvency, no benefits were to be paid until the spring of 1924. Bryce Stewart, director of the employment office, and Howard were to work out office procedures for administering the agreement, and Professor Commons was designated to head the board of trustees, the administrative body that was to handle the contributions and oversee the payment of benefits.[27]

To facilitate the administration of the plan, the employers and Amalgamated officers devised several procedural short cuts. So the clothing workers would be certain of receiving their benefits, they pooled the contributions of two hundred and fifty small contracting houses in one fund and those of fifty medium-sized firms in another. This left only eighty large establishments with individual house reserves. Similar action was taken with regard to the administrative boards that were to govern the use of the funds. Because they were dealing with a single union, the employers agreed to have one board for all the contracting houses, another for the pooled-fund establishments, a third for other large firms, and one board each for Hart Schaffner & Marx and for B. Kuppenheimer and Company, the largest manufacturers. The five groups agreed to meet on the same day, thereby easing the work of the trustees.[28] Commons spent the following January in Chicago where, with the assistance of Stewart's staff, he organized the necessary procedures for putting the plan into operation. For eighteen months he presided over the increasingly routine meetings of the administrative boards.[29]

Even with an efficient administrative organization there remained the problem of making ends meet—a crucial but undramatic assignment for the trustees and the union officials. The continued recession in the clothing industry made the collection of contributions difficult and led the trustees to delay the start of payments until the last moment. Each employee finally received about $35 in the spring and fall of 1924, considerably less than the amount originally stipulated.[30] In all, Stewart's office distributed approximately 70,000 checks at a cost which the union estimated at 6 percent of the total fund—a remarkable record for an insurance enterprise. In the first year of its operation the unemployment fund paid more than $1,000,000 in benefits.[31]

Realizing the workers' need for increased compensation, the union leaders made repeated efforts to strengthen the Chicago system in the next five years. When the trustees reduced the benefit schedule in 1925 because of a lack of funds, the Amalgamated officers began a new campaign to require the employers to increase their payments. In 1928 they persuaded the employers to raise their contributions to 3 percent. At the same time they cooperated with the trustees in a unique experiment. Drawing one-third of the total from the unemployed fund, the trustees paid $500 apiece to 150 cutters in the form of a dismissal wage on the condition that they leave the industry.[32] Nor did the union leaders forget their broader objectives. In 1926, for example, they opposed a rank and file demand for a more extensive pooling arrangement because "it might remove from certain manufacturers the incentive to regularize their business or give greater employment."[33]

The decline of the Chicago market in the late 1920's and the Depression of the early 1930's made the continuation of the unemployment insurance program difficult, but the local leaders managed to pay reduced benefits through the mid-1930's. The Chicago tailors received an unprecedented $5,000,000 in unemployment benefits between 1924 and 1929 and an additional $2,000,000 between 1930 and 1932.[34] It was Commons' belief that the unemployment insurance program also reduced unemployment and promoted increased production.[35] If indeed the Chicago experiment encouraged unemployment prevention, the effect was negligible, at least as far as the overall standing of the market was concerned. It seems more likely that the long-range value of the Chicago plan was in delaying or retarding the effects of the industry-wide dislocations of the 1920's, hardly an encouraging result when it is remembered that the Chicago firms were the strongest of all the needle trades establishments. On the other hand the Chicago operation provided the inspiration, the impetus, and the experience necessary for efforts in other more difficult markets—intangible effects that outweighed any immediate consequences.

ACWA Plans: New York and Rochester

FROM THE time of their initial success, Hillman and his aides had looked upon the Chicago system as a foundation upon which to build until every worker in every market was similarly protected. Believing that unemployment insurance would alleviate the threat as well as the distress of unemployment, they remained optimistic despite the decline of the industry in the early 1920's. At their December 1923 General Executive Board meeting they voted to extend the system as soon as possible, a decision which the rank and file leaders ratified at the 1924 convention the following summer.[36] With this backing Hillman concentrated on New York City and Rochester, the second and third largest men's clothing centers, in the following years.

It would be hard to imagine two more dissimilar labor markets than the New York centers. New York City was the most important single market of the needle trades industries; its men's clothing manufacturers specialized in inexpensive clothing and employed large numbers of contractors. The small shops, undisciplined workers, and willingness on the part of the manufacturers to move to other cities rather than submit to the union's demands had long made it a union organizer's nightmare. The ACWA locals that did survive were jealous of their rights and often uncooperative. Rochester, on the other hand, presented a completely different situation. Dominated by a few large inside shops, the Rochester industry seemed to offer a much more favorable atmosphere for the introduction of unemployment insurance. Yet in both cases political rather than economic considerations determined the timing and the success of the Amalgamated's unemployment insurance programs.

Hillman's plan for New York City, introduced in 1924, was designed to cope with the distinctive economic problems he encountered there. As part of a general reform effort that included the introduction of minimum wages and the restoration of the arbitration machinery which the employers had destroyed in 1921, he demanded unemployment insurance to provide, as the *Advance* reported, "some system of relief for our members during periods of unemployment."[37] The purpose of such a plan, at least as defined by the union during the negotiations, was thus to furnish the New York tailors with a much-needed steady income. Prevention was seldom discussed, and then only in general terms.[38] The contract, concluded with relatively little difficulty, reflected this shift in emphasis. The workers and employers would each contribute 1.5 percent of the workers' average wages. But unlike the Chicago arrangement, these funds would go into a single market fund. This was necessary to protect the workers in the contract shops, which often closed after a season or two, but it also eliminated the incentive feature that had won wide praise from Commons and others associated with the Chicago experiment. Jacob Billikopf, the impartial arbitrator, conducted a series of meetings between Wolman and the manufacturers' representatives during the summer and fall to iron out the final details. By mid-November they had completed preparations for the beginning of contributions, leaving only a few minor questions unresolved.

But Hillman, Billikopf, and the ACWA leaders failed to take into account the political conflict that was dividing the needle trades unions in the New York market into right and left factions. Beginning in 1922 the Trade Union Educational League, the labor-organizing arm of the Communist Party, had made substantial progress in recruiting members within the needle trades unions. Exploiting the discontent arising from the depression and the widespread radicalism of the period, the TUEL established powerful groups in many locals, including some of the Amalgamated. Despite growing conflict in the ILGWU and Fur Workers' union, the ACWA was at first immune from outright dissension. The Communists' cooperative attitude was apparently a response to Hillman's tacit support for the TUEL in the early 1920's and his acquiescence in the Communist influence in New York Coat Operators Local 5.[39] On the eve of the negotiations of 1924 Earl R. Browder, writing in the *Labor Herald,* the League's official journal, observed that the Amalgamated "brings a refreshing breeze of proletarian spirit" to the American labor movement.[40] The Communists also welcomed Hillman's new agreement, singling out the unemployment fund as one of its important achievements.[41] By the summer of 1924, however, they had decided on a direct attempt to gain control of the needle trades unions. They now included the Amalgamated in their plans, since Hillman had refused to intercede on behalf of the Communist delegates who were excluded from the July convention of the Conference on Progressive Political Action. Suddenly the unemployment insurance program became "altogether inadequate" and dissension increased in the New York locals.[42]

The ACWA officers, eager to remain aloof from the conflict, at first tried to work with the Communists. The *Advance* argued that "the A.C.W. of A. is not a political or philosophical sect, but an economic mass organization."[43] But when pressure from the "lefts" increased during the autumn and the fate of the union in New York City seemed endangered, Hillman decided on a change of policy. To the General Executive Board, meeting in St. Paul in November, "he characterized as 'hypocrisy' the contentions of one group that the terms of the unemployment insurance agreement in New York are not sufficiently favorable to the members." It was impossible, he maintained, to continue the "constructive work" of the union until all factionalism had ceased.[44]

Hillman's speech brought the dispute into the open and precipitated a violent conflict between the union and the Local 5 leaders in late 1924 and early 1925. The ACWA suspended the local officers and assigned a loyal man to take control of the renegade group. The Communists retaliated by attacking the Amalgamated members and condemning Hillman's policies. Thus the unemployment insurance program was an example of "class collaboration," since the employers did not pay the entire cost.[45] These actions never threatened Hillman's power in New York City, but the conflict insured that the unemployment insurance plan operated—if at all—only under severe disadvantages. With the union unable to control the shops, many manufacturers "forgot" to make their required contributions, and the contractors, the hardest group to discipline, flatly refused to pay. Hillman soon realized the impossibility of operating under these circumstances and reluctantly agreed to suspend the entire program until conditions had returned to normal.[46]

For the next three years Hillman and the Amalgamated officers busied themselves with the task of repairing the damage caused by the Communists. During this period of recuperation they continued to raise the issue of an unemployment insurance program each year, but the manufacturers replied that the creation of such a fund would be "premature."[47] Not until 1928 did Hillman again feel that the union was strong enough to make unemployment insurance the most important of its demands. At the bargaining sessions of that year, "the Union's insistence on establishing an Unemployment Insurance Fund without further delay was constantly in the foreground."[48] After a month of negotiation, the manufacturers conceded defeat and signed an agreement creating an unemployment benefit plan which would cover all 30,000 New York workers, whether they worked in inside or contract shops. The employers agreed to pay 1.5 percent of their payrolls if the workers would contribute an equivalent amount. All contributions, scheduled to begin in September, would be deposited in a single unsegregated fund for the entire market.[49]

Interestingly, there was disagreement over the purpose of the plan. Once the manufacturers had accepted it, they insisted that unemployment insurance was good business and not merely a system of charitable payments to unfortunate workmen. C. D. Jaffe, a prominent employer, reflected this sentiment when he maintained that "unemployment insurance will strengthen the impartial machinery established four years ago and will help stabilize the industry."[50] But the continued instability of the New York market and the discouragingly slow progress in Chicago had a marked effect on the attitudes of the union officers. By 1928 Hillman and his associates were increasingly emphasizing the immediate goal of relief. In Wolman's words, unemployment insurance "is no longer considered in the terms of 1920 and described vaguely as a charge on the industry and as a solution of the problem of unemployment. . . . it will take some time before insurance has completely solved the problem of unemployment for the members of the organization."[51]

The operation of the New York City insurance fund between 1928 and the mid-1930's tended to confirm Wolman's view. Adverse business conditions and rising unemployment made the job of collecting contributions difficult. The poorly paid workers often failed to cooperate with the union in forcing their employers to comply with the rules. By 1928–29 the economic situation in New York City had become so bad that the Amalgamated had to resort to strikes to enforce the agreement. Billikopf also had to use part of the fund to relieve the plight of the needy, regardless of the amount of their contributions. The trustees consequently distributed nearly $150,000 in 1929, over $200,000 in 1930, and similar amounts in later years. No actual reserve was ever accumulated and benefits went to the unemployed on the basis of need. As late as 1936 the workers voted to continue the New York plan in order to supplement the state system, but the impact of the Depression had made the limitations of the Amalgamated program abundantly clear.[52]

In Rochester, despite the prevalence of inside shops, a combination of employer resistance and left-wing factionalism prevented the introduction of unemployment insurance in 1924 and encouraged the manufacturers to resist the union. The manufacturers argued that "unemployment is a problem pertaining to the state or community as a whole, rather than to any particular industry or factory."[53] In the meantime the ACWA leaders began to prepare for the time when these problems would be less acute. To hold the leftists in line, the local officials, with Hillman's backing, threatened punitive action against any member guilty of making "irresponsible remarks on a matter so vital to the union." And Hillman made a special appearance at a local meeting to answer the objections of the opposition.[54] Finally in the 1928 negotiations the union representatives agreed to drop their demands for the forty hour week in return for the establishment of an unemployment fund covering 10,000 Rochester clothing workers.[55] This plan required the employers to contribute 1.5 percent of their payrolls immediately and the workers to contribute a like amount beginning in 1929. No benefits were to be paid until a large fund had accumulated, and though emergency relief payments were drawn from the fund as early as June 1929, no actual compensation was paid until May 1930. At that time the union set the maximum benefit period at two and one-half weeks per season and limited payments to $31 per worker. Even with these restrictions the Rochester clothing workers received a total of $500,000 between 1930 and 1936.[56] For them, as for many other clothing workers throughout the country, unemployment benefits, drawn from the insurance funds, were the only defense against destitution in the early Depression years.

While the Amalgamated's New York City and Rochester programs were introduced too late in the decade to have much effect on the industry as a whole, most union members, from Hillman to the lowliest tailor, would have agreed that they had succeeded. The benefits, if inadequate, helped mitigate the hardships that accompanied seasonal layoffs, particularly during the Depression, and represented at least a modest step toward stabilizing the workers' incomes. Hillman, moreover, refused to concede that stable employment was impossible in the men's clothing industry. He speculated in 1930 that if other groups had followed the clothing workers' example "we would then have been spared the terrible catastrophe which is confronting so many people. We, in our industry, have demonstrated that the problem of unemployment can be remedied, that it is not a fatal catastrophe about which we can do nothing but sit by and helplessly look on."[57] In fact, other unions had followed the Amalgamated and forced their employers to assume responsibility for continuous employment, although, for a variety of reasons, their efforts failed to achieve the same degree of success.

Other Needles Trades Plans

THE OTHER needle trades leaders either rejected or disregarded unemployment insurance in the early 1920's, only to reverse themselves in later years. This shift was due in part to the decline of the industries and the existence of a serious—and seemingly permanent—unemployment problem. But the economic crisis was not the only factor in their decisions: for the ILGWU and the Fur Workers' leadership the Communist pressure was equally important. As the left-wing insurgency spread in 1924–25, it produced a willingness to experiment that had often been lacking in more normal times. In short, the prospect of continued high unemployment, increasing dissatisfaction on the part of the rank and file, and loss of power to the Communists resulted in a reconsideration of unemployment insurance and the ultimate acceptance of Hillman's approach.

Though the ILGWU leaders had long exhibited a deep interest in industrial reform, they showed little interest in the union plans common before World War I.[58] Since the turn of the century they had emphasized the need for work-sharing during hard times and the responsibilities of the manufacturers for their employees.[59] They had also endorsed the efforts of the New York Protocol organization to standardize labor costs and eliminate unfair competition between 1910 and 1916, but had made no attempt to devise a more comprehensive policy. Indeed, many ILGWU leaders protested when the New York manufacturers' association proposed a benefit fund for seasonal employees financed by contributions from the employers and the regularly employed workers.[60] Gradually, however, they became more interested in controlling the labor supply and providing each worker with a regular wage. During World War I they demanded the replacement of piecework with "week work." Many top ILGWU officials, including Morris Sigman and David Dubinsky of the New York Joint Board, saw the weekly wage as the solution to many of the workers' problems despite the fact that the union bureaucracy, whose jobs involved the setting of piece rates, and the employers, who were afraid of losing control of their employees, vigorously opposed it. The insurgents were persistent, nevertheless, and at the GEB meeting of August 1917 were victorious.

As part of a "programme of reform" designed to "lengthen the working season," the officers endorsed week work as well as the forty-eight hour week and minimum wages.[61]

Ironically, this decision, instead of marking a step toward the ultimate adoption of unemployment insurance as it might have with the Amalgamated, had exactly the opposite effect. This was due to the unfortunate association of unemployment insurance with scientific management in the Cleveland market of the ladies' garment industry. Before the war the Cleveland manufacturers, whose inside shops were unique to the trade, had used welfare capitalism and scientific management to thwart Meyer Perlstein, the ILGWU organizer. But the threat of crippling strikes during the war and widespread sentiment for "industrial democracy" led them to reconsider their position. In 1919 Morris A. Black, the head of the employers' association, agreed to recognize the union in return for Perlstein's pledge to drop his demand for week work and accept a wage plan based on production standards.[62] In December 1919 Black and Perlstein signed a revolutionary new contract that called for labor-management cooperation and the introduction of production standards in all the shops. The Cleveland plan became one of the most important postwar experiments in "industrial democracy" and the first step toward the introduction of unemployment insurance in the ladies' garment industry.

The introduction of production standards did not have the beneficial effects both sides had anticipated. In 1929 the new system was introduced, but with little success. During the three years that the Cleveland market operated on production standards, there were interminable disputes over the details of the plan.[63] Morris L. Cooke, who became chairman of the referees in 1923, wrote that "the accuracy of these standards varies quite a good deal from shop to shop and probably from season to season. The basic work . . . hasn't been followed up as assiduously as it should have been."[64] More serious, however, was the effect of this agreement on relations between Perlstein and the ILGWU leadership. Benjamin Schlesinger and Morris Sigman, respectively president and vice-president of the union, were appalled when they learned that Perlstein had forsaken week work. They attacked his policies as "detrimental to the best interests of the union." The editors of *Justice,* the ILGWU newspaper, summarized their sentiments when they wrote: "Not the slightest compromise on the question of week work can or will be made by our organization."[65]

Perlstein, however, disregarded his superiors' criticisms and made the best of his situation. In early 1920 he discussed with Fred C. But-

ler, the employers' representative, a plan to guarantee employment for
forty-one weeks per year. Butler agreed that such a program would encourage the manufacturers to stabilize production and they submitted
the plan to mediation.[66] In April 1921 the referees announced that the
manufacturers would have to promise forty weeks' employment per
year for approximately three thousand workers and insure this guarantee with a deposit of 7.5 percent of their payrolls. If a worker was laid
off for more than twelve weeks a year he would receive a portion of his
average wage, drawn from his employer's fund. The referees also encouraged stabilization by specifying that manufacturers who satisfied
the terms of the agreement by providing the required weeks of employment might reclaim their contributions at the end of the year.[67] The
program they established seemed to mark a significant step toward
"making the industry partly responsible for the enforced idleness of
the workers and of supplying an incentive to the employers to reduce
seasonality of employment."[68]

While generally well administered and a temporary aid to many
workers in the 1920's, the unemployment insurance program of the
Cleveland garment workers was hardly more successful than the attempt to introduce production standards. When the industry began to
revive in 1922 the referees modified the system to allow employers who
increased their reserves to make a corresponding reduction in their employees' wages, but they received little response.[69] The referees then reduced the benefits from two-thirds to one-half of the worker's average
wage in 1924 and took up the question of an additional out-of-work
fund for the slack season, a proposal which the union constantly demanded and finally won in 1927.[70] Even with these changes the plan
failed to increase the profits of the firms that were involved, and the
Cleveland shops lost ground along with the rest of the industry. Many
companies failed in the late 1920's, adding to the overall burden of unemployment, and the whole system was abandoned in 1931.

Judged by the degree to which it aided the Cleveland garment workers and garment firms, Perlstein's guarantee plan was a distinct failure.
But like so many similar programs of the period it had a psychological
impact that far outweighed its economic importance. The New Emphasis employers and their intellectual allies, in particular, viewed the
Cleveland experiment with enthusiasm. Herman Feldman saw in the
employers' right to claim the unused fund a definite advantage over
the Amalgamated's Chicago plan.[71] John B. Andrews published several
accounts of the prevention features of the Cleveland system. Butler,
the employers' agent, wrote: "The primary purpose of the Cleveland
plan is the elimination of seasonal unemployment through the device

of offering an incentive to the only one who has it in his power to attempt it—the employer."[72] Even the National Industrial Conference Board, no friend of unemployment insurance or radical labor unions, reported that the agreement had effectively reduced unemployment in the Cleveland market.[73]

But the ILGWU leaders took a different view. Since Perlstein had accepted production standards, they had taken a dim view of anything connected with the Cleveland plan. In their most generous statement the GEB members acknowledged that guaranteed employment should be "regarded as an experiment and this experiment . . . might be tried out under certain circumstances and might even turn out to be a success."[74] Yet coupled with their antagonism toward Perlstein was a more fundamental objection to unemployment insurance. Led by Schlesinger—"the socialist trade unionist par excellence" in the words of Benjamin Stolberg—the leaders of the ILGWU were committed to advancing the workers' interests through class solidarity, not labor-management cooperation, and rejected in principle any plan that took power from the wage earner and gave it to the employer.[75] While the brilliant but erratic Schlesinger remained as president, the union's position on unemployment reflected his insistence on worker control of any plan. Though he agreed that the members needed protection, he wrote that "this insurance must be made by and through the union, for it is the duty of the union to insure the workers' livelihood not only when there is work to do . . . but always and at all times."[76] In his 1922 report to the union convention he strongly reiterated his belief that any program involving joint administration was unacceptable. Such a system, he contended, "would hamper the [workers'] freedom of action" and place them in "greater dependence" on the employers. He succeeded in getting all consideration of unemployment insurance referred to the GEB for "study," stating "that the way the matter appeared . . . it would not be adopted even in principle."[77]

By 1923, however, Schlesinger's ideological approach to union policy was rapidly losing its appeal. The failure of the industry to revive after the 1920–21 recession, most evident in the disastrous decline of the cloak and suit trade, the basis of the New York market, and the continued growth of submanufacturing, exposed the union's weaknesses. As jobs became scarcer and the workers' demands louder, the locals were often slow to react. Revelations of corruption in several local organizations also embarrassed the Schlesinger administration. But the most obvious manifestation of rank and file unrest, the rapid growth of Communist influence, was the decisive factor in prompting a change in leadership and a change in policy toward unemployment insurance.

Left-wing dissatisfaction with Schlesinger and his colleagues had been evident since 1917, and the newly formed Communist Party, acting directly or through the TUEL, found it relatively easy to gain a following among the garment workers.[78] Aware of the growing threat to themselves and the union, the GEB members finally resolved to dump Schlesinger. When he threatened to resign rather than submit to criticism at the board meeting in March 1923, they quickly accepted his offer and replaced him with Sigman, who had a record of both solid achievement and anti-Communism as head of the New York Joint Board.

Sigman immediately initiated an ambitious campaign to purge the leftists and at the same time began a program of economic reform that would strike at the roots of rank and file dissatisfaction. Acting through the GEB he outlawed Communist groups within the New York locals, brought prominent "lefts" to trial in various cities, and attempted a thorough house cleaning. But his arbitrary actions also transformed the conflict into a near civil war, with the Communists and the International officers often trading blows as well as invective.[79] Fortunately for the union Sigman's economic reform program got off to a more promising start. At the same GEB meeting which replaced Schlesinger with Sigman, the officers began working on industrial reform measures, and at the October meeting Sigman unveiled a comprehensive plan calling for the forty-hour week, an employment guarantee similar to the Cleveland agreement, and an unemployment insurance fund financed by the employers and the workers—an indication of the remarkable change of attitude that had taken place. The heart of Sigman's program, like Hillman's, was the regulation of the manufacturer. The unemployment measures were designed to make the "jobber-manufacturer responsible in an industrial sense and will prevent his engaging more contractors than he actually needs for his work, thus checking unnecessary competition in the trade."[80] The GEB adopted these proposals as the union's 1924 contract demands and began a belated effort to reform production methods in the New York ladies' garment industry.

While guaranteed employment and the joint agreement were unthinkable under Schlesinger's administration, their inclusion in the reform program could hardly be said to represent a revolutionary change in 1923. Sigman and the ILGWU leaders were undoubtedly aware of Hillman's work in the early 1920's.[81] The new president also led a special committee that studied the Cleveland plan in the summer of 1923 —an indication, at least, that they felt no implacable hostility toward

Perlstein's work.[82] There is also evidence of local union support for un-employment insurance, especially in New York, where the Cloak Makers Joint Board had considered the adoption of a fund for its members in March 1923 and where Local 35 leaders had discussed unemployment benefits only to find the "general stand of the members is against [them]."[83] The ease with which Sigman shifted his thinking is apparent from his statements about the new policy. "Unemployment in the cloak trade," he told a meeting of workers, ". . . does not always go hand in hand with a long work week. There are other influences that contribute toward it and that is why the insurance fund for unemployment is an industrial measure in which all the employing interests in the trade must concur."[84]

If the leaders of the Fur Workers' Union were somewhat less resistant to new ideas, it was only because they had faced a strong threat from the Communist-backed left wing at an earlier date. In fact the furriers' president, Meyer Kaufman, exhibited little interest in reforms of any type until he barely managed to survive a struggle for leadership with the radicals under Ben Gold, in 1920–22. Faced with this ever-present threat in the following years, the "right" leaders suddenly became more aggressive in their efforts to strengthen the organization and consolidate their power. They managed to increase the membership of the New York locals but were still confronted with serious economic problems. The small shops were unable to stabilize their production and often resisted the introduction of reforms that might have increased their profits in the long run. In their search for a solution, the union leaders began to consider unemployment insurance at their February 1923 GEB meeting. After animated discussion the officers established a committee to study the question and urged rank and file interest. Kaufman wrote that it was their wish "that this question be made one of the most paramount questions of today and should receive the necessary attention and consideration of all the members who feel like we do, that the Union cannot afford to put it off any longer."[85] The newly created ACWA plan was apparently an important factor in this decision; one Fur Workers' official reported that until the Chicago experiment, unemployment insurance "looked like a dream." Hillman's success, however, gave them "sufficient reason to believe that we are coming nearer to the time when the idea of establishing such a fund will become popular with the great mass of our people and the employers."[86]

In their 1923 contract negotiations with the fur manufacturers, the Furriers' officials submitted a series of demands that included the establishment of an unemployment fund based on a 4 percent contribution divided evenly between the employers and the employees.[87] They contended that "an insurance fund would tend to stabilize conditions" and "remove causes of friction and dangerous situations in the industry."[88] Their January 1924 contract provided for the creation of an unemployment insurance fund within a year, as well as a limitation on the use of apprentices and restrictions on the small contracting and submanufacturing shops. While this contract applied only to the New York market, the Fur Workers' officers made it clear that they intended to extend jobless benefits throughout the industry.[89] As an indication of their seriousness they employed Benjamin Squires, Commons' successor in the Chicago men's clothing industry, to assist in the preparation of a specific plan. Squires conducted meetings between the union and employers in July and again in October, and concluded that the existing Chicago plan was unsatisfactory for New York. He advised instead a single market-wide pooled fund, joint contributions, and the beginning of benefit payments in 1926.[90] His suggestions formed the basis of the plan that was finally agreed upon.

Faced with widespread unemployment among their membership, the leaders of the United Cloth Hat and Cap Makers' Union approached unemployment insurance from a somewhat different direction. As early as 1915 the union considered a relief fund, and by 1918 at least three Cap Makers' locals had set up formal out-of-work payments based on accumulated contributions. But the attitude underlying these efforts was that "while unemployment is a phase of our social and economic system which we cannot eliminate, we can . . . to some extent relieve the suffering among the unemployed."[91] Not until 1921, when their convention called for "fundamental reform in the present arrangements of industrial life," did the Cap Makers begin to think in terms of Hillman's approach, and two more years passed before the union convention authorized the officers to devise a workable plan.[92] Subsequent events were to show that the old conception of an unemployment insurance fund did not die easily.

The events of 1923–24 thus marked a turning point in the policies of the needle trades unions. The depression, the left-wing insurgency, and Hillman's work had had a tremendous impact. By 1924 whatever opposition there had been to unemployment insurance had been swept away. But there remained two important problems for the unions to solve: the hostility of the manufacturers to any plan that would increase costs in a period of declining profits and the willingness of the Communists to sabotage any program that might give an advantage to their opponents. The leaders of the Garment Workers, Furriers, and

Cap Makers attacked these problems in 1924–26 with at least initial success; but the situation had deteriorated to such a point that their initial victories did not insure continued success.

The major effort of 1924–26 took place in the ladies' garment industry. At the 1924 convention Sigman and his advisors announced that they would implement their plans for reform. Perlstein, no longer in official disfavor, presented a report on unemployment insurance.[93] The delegates ratified Sigman's program at the same time that they refused to permit the Communist representatives to take their seats—an action indicating their cooperation with Sigman's two-pronged attack.[94] The purge of the Communists did not, however, pave the way for acceptance of unemployment insurance. When the reform program was introduced to the manufacturers in 1925 they resisted so strongly that the governor of New York, Alfred E. Smith, appointed a five-man commission to avert a crippling strike. The commissioners studied Sigman's reform proposals and agreed that an unemployment benefit fund (but not guaranteed employment) was necessary for the New York market. They proposed joint contributions, with the manufacturers paying 2 percent of their payrolls and the workers 1 percent of their wages. The ILGWU leaders, the submanufacturers, and the inside-shop operators agreed to a contract based on these recommendations, and the jobbers, who had the most to lose from such a plan, joined them after a short strike. Sixty thousand New York workers were eventually covered under these agreements.[95] For the first time a governmental body had successfully sponsored a program of unemployment insurance in the United States.

But the problem of actually putting the contract provision into effect still remained. Under the direction of Arthur D. Wolf, one of the governor's commissioners, representatives of the union and the manufacturers worked out an administrative plan based on the 1924 New York ACWA proposals. The wisdom of not following the original Chicago agreement, with its system of funds tailored to the manufacturers' needs, became evident in August and September when contributions from the 850 shops—650 of them small submanufacturing establishments—began.[96] They also decided that the workers should only be paid after nine weeks' unemployment per season and be eligible for only twelve weeks' compensation per year. At $10 per week no worker covered by this plan could receive more than $120 per year.[97] Yet even with these precautions the chaotic state of the New York market and the absence of an effective employment office system seriously compromised their efforts.[98] Although more than $1,000,000 was paid to the workers during the first season, the trustees reported that a $300,000 deficit had been incurred and that $150,000 had been paid to workers who had not qualified for benefits.[99] The union officials and the governor's commissioners devoted considerable time and effort to improving the administration of the program and held the payments to $200,000 in the 1925–26 season.[100]

Ultimately, however, the continued deterioration of the industry and the increasing Communist agitation posed insurmountable problems for the union. The Communists won control of the New York locals in 1925 and nearly removed Sigman from office. They then rejected a compromise contract offered by the governor's commission and accepted by Sigman and the inside manufacturers, and struck in July 1926.[101] During the six-month strike that followed, the local ILGWU leaders worked closely with Charles Ruthenberg and Benjamin Gitlow, the Communist leaders in New York, to advance their own political aims. They siphoned off much of the strike benefit fund and authorized extravagant expenditures before the strike was lost and the right-wing leaders returned to office. The trustees did pay an additional $700,000 in unemployment benefits, but with the union divided and bankrupt the future of the fund was not long in doubt.[102] The right-wing leaders who returned to power simply were unable to enforce the payment of contributions. By February 1927 the employers were more than $250,000 delinquent in their payments, and in March the ILGWU officers suspended the operation of the fund until 1929.[103]

The Furriers, fewer in number and without benefit of the governor's assistance, encountered even more formidable problems. The fur manufacturers, having accepted unemployment insurance, did their best to delay the beginning of contributions. Since similar plans were scheduled to go into effect in Boston, Chicago, and Philadelphia after the beginning of the New York fund, the union leaders resolved "to bend every effort in the direction of starting the promised fund as speedily as possible."[104] After extended negotiations, they forced the employers to agree to begin contributions in May 1925.[105]

In the intervening period a "progressive" group of "neutrals" joined Gold and his followers in an attempt to oust the "rights" in the New York locals. They succeeded in calling a special election one week before the starting date for contributions and won control of the Joint Board.[106] In the accompanying confusion the unemployment fund was all but forgotten. The "rights" charged that the Communists "killed the unemployment insurance fund and thereby saved the manufacturers tens of thousands of dollars," but to no avail.[107] The Communists quietly suspended the existing plan and demanded an unemployment insurance fund financed entirely by the manufacturers in January

1926. When the employers rejected this and other union proposals, the leftists began a market-wide walkout.[108] The seventeen-week furriers' strike of 1926 was marred by violence and corruption and greatly weakened the union.[109] The contract that was finally agreed upon scarcely benefited the workers, and in a unique provision prohibited the consideration of unemployment insurance before 1929.[110]

The fate of the Furriers' and Garment Workers' plans in the following years provided little more than a footnote to the events of 1926. Sigman continued to preach the industry's obligation to the workers until he was replaced by Schlesinger in 1928. The latter, in turn, proposed unemployment insurance as part of a plan to rebuild the union and convinced the employers to accept—in principle—his proposals in 1929, 1930, and 1931, although nothing actually came of their concessions.[111] A similar plan which paid approximately $22,000 to unemployed ILGWU members in the Chicago market in 1926 was discontinued after a short period of Communist leadership.[112] The Fur Workers, on the other hand, not only lost their chance to establish an unemployment insurance program but were unable to rid their membership of Communist influence. The Kaufman administration and the leaders of the Communist dual union that came into existence after the "rights" returned to power both proposed unemployment insurance funds in the 1930's, but were prevented by economic conditions from realizing their objectives.[113]

The Cap Makers' leaders, starting at the same time, encountered quite different problems in devising and implementing an unemployment insurance program. At the end of the 1923 convention the Cap Makers' GEB had assigned a committee to draw up a plan for submission to the rank and file. For more than four months this group labored over its task, and presented its conclusions to the next meeting of the union's hierarchy in late September. The committee's report contained two alternatives: a union out-of-work benefit system or a joint agreement with the employers. After much discussion the officers rejected, in a reversal of their earlier position, the former suggestion in favor of an employee-manufacturer-financed scheme. The final plan, which resembled those of other needle trades unions, provided for 1.5 percent contributions from the workers and their employers and six weeks of benefits per worker per year.[114] In mid-November the GEB submitted this proposal to the locals for ratification. The result, however, was an unexpected defeat; in the eighteen locals that responded, the vote against the proposal was nearly six to one. Perplexed at this response after the previous enthusiasm for unemployment insurance, the GEB analyzed the reasons for the rejection. The officers found that the workers disliked the idea of contributing to the fund. Some locals, moreover, "took the attitude that they would rather have the manufacturers pay their 1.5 per cent directly to the workers as an increase of wages."[115] As a consequence the question of unemployment benefits was left, much to the officers' chagrin, to the individual locals and joint councils of each market.

That the rank and file was opposed to employee contributions, and not to unemployment insurance, was apparent in the following years. Plans financed entirely by the employers were negotiated in eight cities. The first of these was initiated in St. Paul, where, in November 1923, the union negotiated an agreement providing for an employment guarantee of forty-eight weeks a year, with benefits for workers who missed more than four weeks of work.[116] In March 1924 the Chicago local demanded a similar guarantee and after extensive negotiations won a single employer-financed fund. The Philadelphia, Boston, Baltimore, Milwaukee, and Scranton locals had similar provisions written into their contracts in 1925.[117] None of these agreements, however, matched in importance the plan of the Cap Makers Joint Council of New York, which the local officials first demanded in May 1924 when they called for a program to "bring about greater stabilization" in the industry while protecting the workers against the "worst effects of unemployment."[118] They explicitly recognized the relationship between employer-financed benefits and industrial stability: ". . . only by guaranteeing the worker more or less regular employment . . . with the further provision that the employer failing to provide such employment increases his labor cost of production will there be sufficient inducement to both the manufacturers and the bigger buyer to take effective measures to lengthen the busy seasons and shorten the periods of unemployment."[119] The New York contract of July 1924 subsequently established a 3 percent employer-financed fund under union control.

Although by 1925 the Cap Makers' leaders had achieved their original goal and begun to look forward to the time when the various local plans would be brought in line with the New York provisions, the economic problems that originally led them to consider out-of-work benefits also prevented any further advance. During the first twenty months the funds paid a total of $175,000 to 3,900 jobless workers and encountered few unusual problems.[120] In New York the system worked so well that union leaders decided to increase the benefit payments. But it soon became apparent that this was a mistake. The industry slumped badly after 1926 and the funds were quickly depleted. As conditions became worse the national officers unsuccessfully proposed a uniform, national plan to help stabilize the industry and spread the cost of compensation, but they were too late. Six local funds were declared insolvent and discontinued between 1927 and 1930. The New York system, which was the strongest, ceased payments in 1931.[121]

The performance of the Cap Makers' unemployment insurance plans, like those of the Ladies' Garment Workers and Furriers, strikingly revealed the limitations of voluntary efforts in the face of adverse economic conditions, a fact that the leading New Emphasis employers did not fully comprehend until the Depression years. In the men's clothing industry Hillman's remarkable leadership and the power of the ACWA permitted the union to provide modest benefits for its jobless members, although not without a protracted initial struggle and continuous supervision. But the experiences of the other unions reduced the significance of even this achievement. Faced with a long-term decline in the demand for labor, and beset by weak leadership and Communist agitation, they were uniformly unsuccessful in reforming their industries and compensating their members. Progressive employers in particular might have given heed to the experience of the needle trades unionists, for economic conditions in the depressed clothing, fur, and hat industries suggested, long before the stock market crash, the necessity for political action if unemployment was to be adequately prevented or compensated.

6 | WISCONSIN AND THE COMMONS SCHOOL

THE PREVAILING conception of the purposes of unemployment insurance did not entirely foreclose the possibility of legislation in the 1920's. To be sure, bills modeled after the European laws and introduced by socialists and other radicals received scant consideration. But proposals that followed the precedent of the 1916 Massachusetts bill, that sought to use, in Andrews' words, "that powerful element of social compulsion" to achieve prevention, were quite another matter.[1] They were introduced in several states in the early 1920's, usually under AALL auspices, only to die from lack of support and the stubborn opposition of legislators and employers who rejected legislation with the same zeal they embraced the "engineering mind," the open shop, and frequently the New Emphasis. Only in Wisconsin, a state with relatively little industry but a long tradition of progressive government, did unemployment insurance legislation come close to passage. This was due in part to the unique political situation that existed in Wisconsin and in part to the presence of an extraordinary individual, the ubiquitous John R. Commons, who, as Joseph Dorfman has written, "more than any other economist was responsible for the conversion into public policy of reform proposals designed to alleviate the defects of the industrial system."[2]

When Commons came to the University of Wisconsin in 1904, he brought to the state a keen mind, indefatigable energy, and an understanding of the problem of unemployment that had few parallels. As early as 1893 he argued that all wage earners should be guaranteed against arbitrary discharge, since the "only way in which these people can get access to . . . production is through recognition of the right of employment."[3] Six years later he called for the establishment of employment bureaus, labor colonies, and public works projects during depressions to insure the "right to work."[4] He told the United States Industrial Commission in 1900 that unemployment was the "most serious of all our social problems,"[5] and that no permanent solution was possible until the economy was stabilized.[6] But his first important practical contribution came in 1910, when the Milwaukee city council asked him to help reorganize the mismanaged municipal employment office. With his help William M. Leiserson, fresh from the New York Wainwright Committee study, completely revamped the operation of the employment office and made it a model of efficient service. Commons was impressed with Leiserson's work and "comprehensive program" of reform, which included the creation of a sinking fund to compensate the jobless, but he saw the greatest immediate value in the reform of the employment service.[7] He wrote that "the reason why it [unemployment insurance legislation] is not taken up in this country is because our administration of labor exchanges has been so very ineffective."[8]

More important in shaping Commons' approach to unemployment was his early experience with workmen's compensation legislation. Employer-financed accident benefits, like other forms of industrial insurance, originated in Europe; there was little agitation for workmen's compensation in the United States until the passage of the British act in 1897. In 1909 the Wisconsin legislature appointed an interim committee to study the possibility of legislation, and in the 1911 session passed a law that removed the old defenses against the claims of injured workmen and encouraged employers to insure against accidents and attempt to lower their premium rates by accident prevention. An important purpose of the law was to bring "pressure upon the employer both to safeguard his place of employment and instruct and discipline his employees."[9] The lawmakers also established the Industrial Commission, an impartial body of experts to administer the law with the help of advisory committees of employers' and workers' representatives. As a member of the Industrial Commission from 1911 to 1913, Commons was in a strategic position to assess the results of the act.

From this experience he developed his theory of "prevention." Almost immediately he was impressed by how "accidents could be prevented by safety experts if employers could be furnished an inducement to hire them for the purpose."[10] It was clear, he came to believe, that the state, by threatening businessmen with additional taxation, could persuade them to reduce the original need for compensation. "Insurance and compensation are secondary," he wrote. Workmen's compensation "is much better described as a kind of social pressure brought to bear upon all employers in order to make them devote as much attention to the prevention of accidents . . . as they do to the manufacture and sale of their products."[11] This was possible, Commons argued, because businessmen were the dynamic factor in the economy. "They are ingenious, alert, they take chances. . . . They are also quite superior to our politicians and other government officials."[12] The reformer's duty was to make them act in a constructive way by providing the only incentives (that is, those reflected in the profit margin) that they understood.[13] This was a limited but all-important function. It permitted the expert, under the aegis of the state, to force employers to be better businessmen. Accordingly, Commons believed that legislation could achieve through coercion and education what the Taylorites achieved through education alone. Efficiency, stability, and increased profits thus were the potential by-products of properly designed accident, health, or unemployment legislation.

Preoccupied with other activities between 1914 and 1920, Commons deferred to Andrews in the application of his theory to unemployment.[14] But he kept in close touch with the AALL and endorsed the work of the unemployment conferences. "I am particularly anxious," Andrews wrote when sending a copy of the *Practical Program*, "to have you see the treatment of unemployment insurance with the emphasis on prevention of unemployment."[15] But the best indication of their relationship was the arrangement they made for the preparation of their book, *Principles of Labor Legislation*, published in 1916. Under an agreement reached two years before, Commons recognized his student's expertise in the field of unemployment: "Mr. Andrews," the document stated, "will take care of Unemployment Insurance."[16] Andrews subsequently wrote the section on insurance legislation, maintaining that it would eliminate unemployment and that the provisions of the 1916 Massachusetts bill might serve as suitable guidelines for any contemplated future legislation.[17]

But as the British reformers discovered to their immediate benefit between 1903 and 1911 and Andrews learned to his distress in 1915–16, unemployment insurance legislation was politically feasible only in periods of mass unemployment. The upswing of the business cycle in 1916, accompanied by substantially increased employment, quieted the public clamor over the plight of the jobless.[18] Commons remained absorbed in other interests; he paid relatively little attention to unemployment, except to note the importance of the employer in regularizing work and to call vaguely for a tax on layoffs to force employers to reduce them.[19] This was partly because in Wisconsin, as in most states, unemployment insurance legislation took a back seat to other forms of social insurance legislation. A legislative committee appointed in 1917 to study the subject decided to devote full time to the question of health benefits. Unemployment insurance was not considered, the committee report stated, because "the problem of unemployment . . . would not require legislative action until the economic conditions of the country experienced a radical change."[20]

The 1921 Campaign

WHILE THE legislature and Commons were devoting their attention to other activities, the wartime growth of labor militancy was providing the impetus for unemployment insurance legislation in Wisconsin, much as it provided the background for a host of labor-backed political demands. Militant politicking was not, however, a new role for the Socialist-led Wisconsin labor movement, which had backed Victor Berger's powerful Milwaukee Socialist organization since the 1890's.[21] Nor for that matter was the union leaders' interest in state-sanctioned unemployment benefits. As early as 1910 the general organizer of the State Federation of Labor, Frank Weber, had demanded pensions for the jobless and two years later proposed that receipts from the inheritance tax be deposited in a fund to aid the unemployed. In 1914 he argued that "the time is close at hand when municipal and state governments will be bound to take up the matter of introducing insurance which must protect the workers against the untold sufferings and misery of unemployment."[22] Yet it was the new energy of the postwar era, coupled with the fear of increased unemployment during demobilization, that gave direction to these sentiments. At their July 1918 state convention, Wisconsin union leaders introduced a tentative plan of postwar reconstruction which included a long section on the prevention of unemployment. They called for unemployment insurance, dismissal pay, the stabilization of seasonal industries, retraining of workers, advance planning of public works, and the opening of new land for settlement. The state executive council requested that a committee study these proposals and draw up a systematic statement of postwar aims. There was, however, no attempt to evade the issues; Henry Ohl, general organizer of the state federation, advised that "social insurance should be made a subject of closer attention."[23]

The reconstruction platform of the Wisconsin unionists, entitled "The Next Steps for Wisconsin," appeared in 1919 and resembled many similar statements of the period. It combined familiar socialist objectives with less radical reform demands. Hence it called for public ownership of basic industry, more democratic government, cooperatives, and various programs to benefit the workers. Under "social insurance" it demanded old age, health, and unemployment benefits. Perhaps reflecting the union leaders' experience with reformers like Commons and Leiserson, the platform stressed the need for better employment statistics before an insurance program went into effect. Until that time it demanded a dismissal wage: "Because we have neglected to make provisions . . . for the prevention of unemployment, we believe it is incumbent on the state to pay an out-of-work allowance to those who are unable to find employment. This should be a temporary measure to be superseded by a permanent system of unemployment insurance."[24] Yet for more than a year Wisconsin union leaders made little effort to advance this demand. In fact it was not until their 1920 convention, held in La Crosse in late July—and which Commons was invited to address—that they once again raised the issue of unemployment insurance.

Outwardly little occurred at the La Crosse convention that a close observer of the Wisconsin labor movement might not have anticipated. The delegates endorsed the labor party movement and industrial unionism and condemned Gompers' rule as "autocracy."[25] They had, however, voiced these sentiments before and their 1920 resolutions constituted more of a rhetorical exercise than a call for action. Commons' speech of July 21 also contained little that differed from his past statements. He discussed the charges of employers that unions restricted production, called for a study of production techniques to determine whether organized labor or management was primarily responsible for the inefficient operation of industry. But he devoted the body of his address to the question of social insurance legislation. In accordance with AALL policy and his own efforts of the past year, Commons urged special attention for health insurance. He justified this measure in terms of improved efficiency. Citing the Wisconsin experience with workmen's compensation, he contended that employers could reduce costs by preventing disease just as they had saved money by preventing accidents. He added, as a corollary, "that unemployment insurance would decrease unemployment, stabilize industry and speed up production."[26]

The potential significance of his final statement can only be appreciated when it is remembered that the postwar boom of 1919–20 had begun to collapse. Factory employment in Wisconsin started to decline in February; by the time of the convention the decline had become "abrupt." By October factory employment was nearly 11 percent below February's and 9 percent below July's.[27] The Industrial Commission reported that "Wisconsin has not been hit anywhere near as hard as the eastern states by the present depression," but there can be little doubt that unemployment increased substantially after July in all fields.[28] By the following July factory employment was 37 percent less than the same month the year before and nearly 10 percent below the figure for the first quarter of 1915, the trough of the prewar recession.[29] This situation, more than the programs of the AALL or the state federation's reconstruction platform, attracted the union leaders to Commons' final reference. After informal discussions at La Crosse they created a committee consisting of J. J. Handley, secretary of the state federation, Ohl, and a relative newcomer, Jacob F. Friedrick, to meet with Commons and his students to draft an unemployment insurance bill for the next legislature.[30] The committee began its work soon after the convention—work that marked the beginning of the decade-long campaign for unemployment insurance legislation in Wisconsin.

The principal problem that the committee members had to face was the question of which precedent to follow, the British plan, as refined in the 1916 Massachusetts bill, or the Wisconsin workmen's compensation act. Commons, who had received numerous copies of the Massachusetts bill from Andrews, proposed that they include employee contributions and base the effort to prevent unemployment on the adjustment of the employers' payments. The union leaders objected, not to the prevention feature but to employee contributions, and demanded a bill more closely approximating the workmen's compensation act.[31] In September Handley wrote that "it should be worked out along the same line as that of the workmen's compensation act. I am satisfied the results will be the same . . . ."[32] Their reasons were twofold: they knew that the rank and file might reject any measure that forced them to contribute and, as Handley told the Wisconsin Conference of Social Work, "If the burden of this fund rests upon industry it will be more apt to cause the employers to take an active part in working out rules and orders that will eliminate and eventually prevent unemployment rather than the payment of a small pittance of unemployment insurance."[33] This argument proved so convincing that Commons became a convert; thereafter the proposal for employee contributions, a legacy of the foreign experience with unemployment insurance and of the 1916 Massachusetts bill, was dropped from the Wisconsin measures.

The bill they presented to Senator Henry Huber for introduction followed in principle the workmen's compensation act. The employers' contributions (there were of course no employee or state contributions) were to provide thirteen weeks of annual benefits per worker at $1.50 a day. To help businessmen reduce unemployment—and thus their taxes

—the employers were to establish mutual insurance companies that would classify industries and adjust rates to reward firms with records of steady employment. This arrangement, which was modified in May to provide for a single mutual insurance company, resembled many of the pooled plans with merit rating that reformers proposed in the 1930's.[34] Huber introduced the bill in the state senate on February 4, 1921.

Meanwhile Commons, his students, and the union leaders had begun an intensive campaign to sell the bill to the legislature. Friedrick advised Milwaukee labor leaders in December to be prepared for "a bill providing for unemployment insurance, which will have the effect of penalizing industry in case of unemployment."[35] Commons made numerous public appearances in response to his students' complaints that "our resources are rather scant in the way of worked arguments and facts."[36] He told the Madison Rotary Club, for example, that joblessness was the cause of labor unrest and the restriction of production; unemployment insurance, by relieving the employee's fear of layoff, would reward the employer.[37] Organized labor made its contribution in mid-February when the state federation's annual legislative conference coincided with the first hearing on the Huber bill. More than 250 labor leaders "unanimously endorsed" unemployment insurance after Allen B. Forsberg, one of Commons' students, had described the bill to them. They then adjourned to attend the hearing at which Commons was scheduled to speak, appeared at the Capitol in a body and, at the completion of the session, called on their individual representatives to urge passage of the bill.[38]

Despite the nature of his support, Commons directed his speech to the businessmen rather than the workers. He maintained that the Huber bill was a replica of the compensation act; that businessmen like Dennison had solved the problem of business instability through similar means; that the Huber bill had no relation to "relief" legislation in Great Britain; and that unemployment prevention was the key to ending "socialistic agitation" in the United States. The employer, he claimed, was the only one who had the power to alleviate instability and should therefore make the entire contribution. "It might seem that if the thing was unpreventable then it would be proper for the workingman to contribute. . . . The workingman cannot prevent it." Only the "employer or business man and the banking system . . . can prevent unemployment."[39] Commons' reference to the banking system was a reflection of his broad view of unemployment insurance and its relevance to national stability. Individual businessmen would reduce seasonal employment fluctuations to avoid paying benefits; the bankers, on the other hand, would exercise more caution in granting loans during periods of economic expansion if they knew that employees could not be laid off without financial loss.[40]

In the relatively short period between February and May, when the state senate would finally consider the Huber bill, Forsberg made in Commons' words "a remarkable campaign through this state for the enactment of the law."[41] To attract the farmers he argued that depressions reduced the demand for farm products; by preventing overexpansion the Huber bill would give the farmers and workers a degree of control over production.[42] As for the unionists, Commons reported that Forsberg, himself a carpenter, "is canvassing the state, in each case inducing the local labor people to go after the retail merchants who are responding quite favorably by writing letters to members of the legislature."[43] As a result the lawmakers received nearly one hundred petitions, only one of which was unfavorable to the Huber bill.

When the conservative senators refused to act in spite of the pressure, Commons and Huber prepared a substitute measure. The new bill modified the original proposal by reducing the workers' compensation to $1.00 per day, providing that benefits could be further lowered in hard times, and creating a single employers' mutual fund.[44] After another hearing, at which Commons repeated his earlier statements, the judiciary committee favorably reported the bill. When the measure reached the senate floor, however, Frederick H. Clausen, spokesman for the manufacturers, and A. L. Osborn, representative of the lumber interests, led a group of businessmen in arguing that the bill would adversely affect the state's seasonal industries. Commons, Handley, and leaders of several religious and civic groups contradicted them, but the senate, sympathetic to the employers, voted sixteen to thirteen, on strict conservative-progressive lines, for indefinite postponement.[45] After a conference with Commons, Forsberg, and several moderate opponents, Huber moved to reconsider the bill with an amendment exempting seasonal industries. Commons and most observers thought this concession would reverse the negative vote.[46] The passage of the reconsideration motion by a narrow margin raised new hope in the progressives and greater determination on the part of the conservatives to block passage of the bill. The final debate was a "field day of accusations and challenges," but Huber was unable to prevent the conservatives from amending his bill to extend its coverage to farm as well as industrial labor. Because of the strong farm representation in the upper house, this was tantamount to killing it, and Huber himself moved for indefinite postponement.[47] The 1921 campaign nevertheless demonstrated what could be accomplished by carefully organizing the interests with a stake in unemployment insurance—a lesson that Commons and his students did not forget.

The Campaign Renewed: 1923

"THE UNEMPLOYMENT insurance bill will have to be passed at the next session of the legislature," wrote Edwin E. Witte, head of the Wisconsin Legislative Reference Library, "if this form of social insurance is to get any foothold in this country in the next decade."[48] Many observers shared Witte's concern and would have agreed with his analysis. The 1921 campaign had attracted relatively little attention from the employers until near the end of the session. Their continued opposition would make the passage of any bill more difficult while another defeat, coupled with the return of prosperity, might demoralize the reformers and their supporters. The stakes were high as both groups prepared for the 1923 session, the last time, as Witte predicted, that unemployment insurance legislation was seriously considered before the Great Depression.

Having won a narrow victory in 1921, Wisconsin businessmen, nearly all of whom opposed the Huber bill as "socialistic" and costly, determined to prevent the recurrence of the near-disaster. Under the leadership of the Wisconsin Manufacturers Association they conducted an extensive campaign against unemployment insurance legislation.[49] Yet the men who led the opposition were not unmindful of the workers' problems. Generally the WMA adopted a more conciliatory approach to labor legislation than, for example, the Milwaukee Employers Council, which led the open-shop campaign.[50] Clausen, president of the manufacturers' association and the most prominent of the opponents, argued that few employers enjoyed the advantages of Procter or Dennison; since they could not control their sales or production, they should not be penalized for failing to stabilize their operations. Still he admitted, not unlike the New Emphasis businessmen, that the "problem of employment more than any other is disturbing the minds of economists and factory managers . . . [who] have long since learned that continuous operation means efficiency as compared with intermittent shut downs. My purpose in directing your attention to the importance of steady employment is to emphasize the obligation of management so that our industry will do everything possible to keep its house in order."[51]

As if to answer Clausen and the employers, Commons wrote what may have been the definitive statements of the prevention theory. In two articles prepared for the *Survey* and Andrews' *American Labor Legislation Review* he contrasted his views with those of his opponents. Instead of the "paternalistic and philanthropic" or "socialistic" British plan, he and his followers espoused the "business-like way," which "induces the business man to make a profit or avoid a loss by efficient labor management." This was because "the business man is the dynamic factor . . . . He is the Captain of Industry." Consequently the Huber bill "abandons the idea that the state can operate the system successfully or that the trade unions can operate it." Rather "if there is enough money in it . . . [business] can accomplish more than any other agency." Such an achievement was possible because the manager, through the personnel department and industrial engineer, could reduce turnover, dovetail jobs, train workers for several positions, transfer employees, and in other ways stabilize employment. Furthermore the banks would counteract cyclical fluctuations just as individual managers would prevent seasonal and irregular unemployment. "Any improvement that looks to the prevention of unemployment must go back to the period of inflation and prevent the overexpansion that caused the unemployment." This was feasible when the workers were guaranteed out-of-work benefits, because "the banks would prevent [businessmen] from overexpanding."[52]

From this theoretical position Commons, his students, and the unionists prepared for their second campaign. After the 1921 session, Forsberg and Olga Halsey, another graduate student, continued to organize public support for the Huber bill. Their tireless devotion to the cause was a key factor in whatever success it achieved. Realizing that the backing of organized labor was insufficient, they attempted to attract other allies in 1922. Forsberg obtained funds to reprint Commons' articles and distributed them throughout the state. A primary objective of his work was to win the support of the farmers, whose representatives controlled the senate and had opposed the Huber bill in 1921. "Our problem," he wrote in the spring of 1922, "is to sell the idea to the farmers. . . . We are now preparing articles for farm papers, and speaking at farm meetings, presenting the problem as a marketing problem . . . with fair success."[53]

While Forsberg attempted to stir up public interest, Miss Halsey devoted her time to research and propaganda. She prepared much of the campaign literature and became an unofficial advisor to Senator Huber, who, as leader of the senate progressives, agreed to reintroduce his bill in 1923. She was also a persistent fund raiser who continually badgered Andrews for donations. After a long series of exchanges, during which the AALL head, none too certain about his own financial future, argued that out-of-state financing would be detrimental to the campaign if the conservatives found out about it, she was partially successful. Andrews helped her secure a $500 personal grant from Sam A. Lewisohn, "on account of her research on unemployment insurance that he desires to have investigated."[54]

These contacts with the AALL were another example of the widening of the Wisconsin legislative campaign. During 1922–23 the association became deeply involved in the drive for passage of the Huber bill. In addition to providing nominal monetary assistance, Andrews helped promote the Wisconsin effort and even persuaded Henry Shattuck, a Massachusetts legislator, to introduce a similar bill in his state. Late in January 1922 the association sponsored a conference on unemployment insurance legislation which Commons, Leo Wolman of the ACWA, and Ernest Draper attended. They favored the single statewide mutual provision of the Huber bill over a clause in the Shattuck bill which permitted a number of insurance organizations.[55] The conference and Andrews' work in 1921–22 helped convince businessmen like Dennison, Draper, and Lewisohn that legislative proposals such as the Huber bill were identical in principle to their voluntary insurance plans and offered, under the proper circumstances, an appropriate method of implementing their ideas.

Commons' participation in the AALL conference was also an indication of the Wisconsin reformers' strategy for 1923. Forsberg had no trouble in winning the endorsement of organized labor for the new legislative campaign, but the opposition of Wisconsin businessmen was a serious threat to its success.[56] On one occasion Forsberg was hooted down by an employers' convention.[57] To solve this problem the reformers pursued two courses. They modified the Huber bill to permit the Industrial Commission to limit benefit payments to the busy seasons in seasonal industries.[58] And they recruited several New Emphasis employers to offset the impression that all businessmen opposed unemployment legislation. Commons persuaded Henry Dennison to appear in behalf of the bill when the judiciary committee conducted public hearings in February. The Framingham tag maker responded with a strong endorsement of the Huber bill. He explained his efforts to prevent unemployment and told the committee that he was "definitely convinced that a bill of this sort will act as a constant spur upon management to make steady progress in correcting the conditions of irregular employment."[59] Clausen and Osborn replied that unemployment insurance would merely represent an "added burden" for the majority of businessmen who were unable to prevent joblessness. Roger Sherman Hoar, a Milwaukee lawyer and reputed expert on insurance law, backed their contentions with a violent attack on the British program and, by insinuation, the Huber bill.[60]

But the reformers had other tricks in their bag. In mid-May they recruited Herbert Johnson, the wax manufacturer, to help them publicize the Huber bill. With Forsberg's help Johnson explained his methods and his ideas for combating unemployment. The Huber bill, he explained, would encourage industry "to cooperate on a gigantic scale to tackle this very problem of business irregularity which brings on unemployment. . . . It assists industry in correcting a most damaging condition to business."[61]

With the business opposition at least partially neutralized, Commons and his students turned their attention to the farmers. In numerous articles written for the agricultural journals, they argued that unemployment insurance would keep farm youths from migrating to the city in good times, only to fall victim to vice and degradation when the inevitable layoffs came. When the judiciary committee favorably reported the Huber bill on April 5, they publicized a statement by one of the farm representatives that unemployment insurance would mean increased purchasing power for city workers in hard times, which would stabilize the demand for agricultural goods.[62] It is unlikely, however, that their work made much of an impact: most Wisconsin farmers were more concerned about the immediate prospect of losing their labor supply if idle men received out-of-work benefits than the evils of city life or the stabilization of long-term demand for their products.

When the senate considered the Huber bill in early June the farmers' suspicions as well as the continued opposition of the employers were apparent. Commons, Osborn, Clausen, and Hoar appeared before the lawmakers to make their final statements. There was some support in the upper house, but Commons soon realized that many of the legislators were unconvinced. Since this left the reformers a few votes short of victory, he and Forsberg decided to lower their sights and try to salvage at least a moral victory. They accepted "an offer made orally by the Manufacturers' Association to drop the bill and have a thorough investigation by an interim committee."[63] Senator William Titus of Fond du Lac then introduced a substitute bill calling for a legislative interim committee to study unemployment insurance legislation and report in 1925. Apparently the Governor, John J. Blaine, favored this measure; like many others he considered it certain of passage.[64]

Two weeks later, when the Titus bill came before the senate for consideration, most observers still believed it would pass. According to rumor Huber would head the interim study group and friends of the bill would fill at least two more of the projected five places. In the meantime, however, other controversial measures had created splits in the ranks of the senate progressives. As adjournment drew near and tempers grew short, bills that had passed the overwhelmingly progressive state assembly were defeated in the senate. The Titus proposal, not considered until the last days of the session, was caught in the last-minute rush. On June 27, after a short debate, the Titus bill was killed by a vote of seventeen to sixteen. Witte believed that it would have passed despite these problems except that the "Manufacturers' Association tricked the friends of the bill." They called for an investigation, he asserted, "solely to sidetrack the original bill and then turned around and also killed the investigation."[65] Whatever the cause, the result was disaster for unemployment insurance legislation in Wisconsin during the 1920's.

Division and Defeat

IF THE opposition of the manufacturers and the apprehensions of the farmers undermined the reformers' campaign of 1922–23, there was little reason to expect a different outcome in the following years. Economic conditions in Wisconsin, reflecting national trends, provided little basis for continued public enthusiasm for unemployment insurance legislation. Businessmen prospered and the farmers were generally more successful than their counterparts in other states. Factory productivity rose substantially, and manufacturing employment dropped at approximately the same rate as elsewhere. These changes apparently intensified the problem of technological unemployment, but since they coincided with the decline of organized labor, the workers were relatively powerless to alter their situation.[66] High business profits, the temporarily secure state of agriculture, and a decline in union membership militated against legislative reform experiments —including unemployment insurance.

Wisconsin businessmen, especially the manufacturers, also contributed to the general indifference to unemployment legislation by undermining the farmer-labor coalition that Commons and his followers had worked to create in 1921–23. They appealed to the farmers to recognize their common interests as property owners and entrepreneurs. The Milwaukee Association of Commerce specified: "It is our duty to dignify and stimulate the business of farming by placing at the disposal of the farmer the advantages of adequate financing, scientific production and efficient distribution."[67] They also stressed the interdependence of agriculture, industry, and commerce. Businessmen provided markets for farm products, they argued; industrial development, by accelerating this trend, was as much the farmers' interest as the factory managers'. Although this appeal was primarily nonpolitical, it also emphasized that increased taxation of any type was a deterrent to continued growth.[68] The results of this effort were mixed; the farmers seldom agreed among themselves, much less with the manufacturers, but it helped plant additional seeds of discord that bore fruit in the form of legislative inaction.

A second and equally effective device used by the manufacturers was welfare capitalism. Often this was not their ostensible motive, but the effect was the same; group life-insurance, pension plans, sick benefits, and stock-purchase plans, as well as increased wages, quieted the noisy radicalism of the postwar era.[69] With several notable exceptions, Wisconsin manufacturers did not adopt unemployment insurance plans, but many of them gave lip service and, in some cases, sincere consideration to ways of regularizing their labor requirements. Clausen boasted that his colleagues understood the causes of unemployment, which was why they took "great care . . . in obtaining accurate information on the demands of each territory, so laying out schedules that these demands will be met in season without excess inventories which in themselves defeat regular employment."[70] In the same terms manufacturers justified the productivity increases of the late 1920's which displaced many factory workers. "Industrial plants must produce efficiently at a high rate of speed," observed one writer. "Obviously the use of machinery has not caused factory unemployment in Wisconsin but has resulted in an improved industrial and social condition."[71]

Commons also recognized the growing indifference to unemployment insurance legislation. Increasingly he considered Hillman's Chicago plan as the best hope for the future, especially since it was "a system of unemployment insurance practically identical with . . . the Huber . . . bill."[72] As a result, he modified his original views in one important respect. In 1920–21 he agreed with Andrews that the manner of segregating contributions had little effect on the possibilities of unemployment prevention. By 1923 he began to reconsider his position and examine the idea of allowing large firms to maintain their own plans instead of paying their contributions into mutual insurance funds. Noting his experience with the Chicago clothing market he wrote, "Only from the large establishments, and not from the smaller establishments, nor from the employees, nor from the state, can any material progress be made towards prevention of unemployment."[73]

Meanwhile the Wisconsin reformers, disappointed but not discouraged, planned another effort for the 1925 session of the legislature. Commons and Forsberg once again did most of the work. In public appearances Commons restated most of his previous arguments, emphasizing that the Heck bill (named after Huber's successor, Senator Max Heck of Racine) would not increase taxes and would actually lower the employers' costs. Using the Chicago plan as an illustration, he contended that unemployment insurance reduced labor unrest and promoted cooperation. Ernest Draper, whom he persuaded to appear before a senate committee, endorsed the Heck bill because "it emphasized the American idea of prevention as opposed to the European idea of relief." Representatives of the Catholic Benefit Societies and the State Federation of Labor also appeared on behalf of the bill, and delegations from the Milwaukee Employers Council and WMA opposed it.[74] At the same time Forsberg headed an Unemployment Insurance Association which coordinated the reformers' propaganda activities. He distributed Commons' articles, many of which compared the Heck bill with the Chicago plan and attempted to interest farm groups in unemployment insurance.[75] But the results of these efforts were again disappointing. Although the senate committee on labor and industries favorably reported the Heck bill, the committee on finance, to which the bill was then referred, recommended indefinite postponement. On June 3 the senate voted twenty to twelve to concur with the recommendation.[76]

Two final efforts of the decade, in 1927 and 1929, proved no more successful. Indeed, they indicated the continued decline of whatever interest Commons and his graduate students had created in 1921–23. The 1927 bill, introduced by Assemblyman William Coleman, a Milwaukee socialist and labor leader, suffered a quiet but overwhelming defeat. Andrews reported that "the local labor people reintroduced the bill, but made no very strong fight for it."[77] The unions nevertheless persuaded Assemblyman Robert Nixon to introduce another bill in 1929. While it generated greater public interest than the Coleman bill, neither Commons, who was absorbed in other matters, nor his former assistants appeared to defend it against a formidable group of employers. As a result, the lawmakers indefinitely postponed the Nixon bill on June 6 by a vote of fifty-six to thirty-three.[78] Commons, distracted perhaps but not discouraged, optimistically assured Andrews that "the bill is not dead."[79]

Depression and Triumph

THE ADVENT of the Depression in 1930 reawakened the nation to the social and economic costs of joblessness. Within a few months, employment in Wisconsin had fallen 25 percent from the

1925–27 level, and unemployment had become a major problem. The new urgency did not mean, however, the automatic acceptance of unemployment insurance. Various proposals were made and many plans tried. The new governor, Walter Kohler, like most state executives of the period, formed a citizens' committee to direct and coordinate the anti-Depression work of the state and of private employers.[80] Kohler's committee performed valuable services, particularly in organizing local relief and public works, but it soon proved inadequate for the immense job that it faced. A cry arose for more drastic measures, not only to supplement the activities of the citizens' committee, but also to protect against future hardship. And as a result of the activity of the 1920's, Wisconsin became the scene of the strongest movement for unemployment insurance legislation to develop in any state.

Wisconsin businessmen were among the first groups to recognize that, at least in their state, a more fundamental solution to the problem of unemployment than community relief, work sharing, or shorter hours was needed, or in any case would be demanded.[81] W. F. Ashe, a paper company executive, conjectured that the "Commons bills of a few years ago will be resurrected, possibly re-written and passed." He called on representatives from the paper industry to study the subject, with the objective of modifying any bill that would be introduced because, he emphasized, "the last bill placed the entire burden on the employer."[82] Many other employers shared this sentiment, not the least of whom was Governor Kohler, himself a manufacturer. Although he opposed the unemployment insurance bills of the 1920's, he gave qualified support to a plan that included employee contributions. In doing so he again revealed the gulf that existed between employers who talked about preventing joblessness and those who were willing to stake money on the idea; nevertheless, as the *Wisconsin State Journal* reported, "the attitude of Governor Kohler in support of unemployment insurance has greatly aided the standing of that question as a legislative issue."[83]

Rather than the businessmen, however, it was the university reformers and the labor leaders who exploited the renewed interest in unemployment. Under Commons' tutelage a new generation of economists had inherited the mantles of Forsberg, Halsey, and others. This group included Witte and Arthur J. Altmeyer, senior members who were primarily administrators rather than agitators; Paul Raushenbush and his wife Elizabeth Brandeis, daughter of the Supreme Court Justice, who were the intellectual leaders of the Wisconsin movement and, significantly, were influenced as much by the elder Brandeis as by Commons; Harold Groves, a taxation expert and close acquaintance of Philip La Follette, Kohler's successor at the statehouse; and Merrill Murray, who specialized in labor-law administration. Beginning in 1930, they devised a new legislative approach to unemployment insurance that incorporated the theory and experience of Commons, Brandeis, and the progressive employers and satisfied many of the objections of Wisconsin businessmen.

During the summer of 1930 the Raushenbushes and Groves met with La Follette, then a gubernatorial candidate, and subsequently worked out the major provisions of what was later called the Groves bill. Early in June Miss Brandeis noted that "a number of us here have been discussing the subject of unemployment insurance. . . . We are considering a number of changes in the Huber bill which might allay the opposition."[84] Their major innovation, which Groves first suggested and Raushenbush developed, was a new method of collecting the employers' contributions. Instead of the mutual insurance companies which had been provided for under the Huber bills and which generally followed the pattern of the workmen's compensation act and the 1916 AALL bill, they proposed a system of individual accounts for each employer. This idea of unemployment reserves rather than insurance was based on the experience of the progressive employers, notably Swope at General Electric, whose activities Groves had studied, and the work of Commons with the Chicago clothing workers. It was not per se an insurance plan; each employer's fund would be separate and his liability limited to that amount. Specifically, each employer would contribute a fixed percentage of his payroll until his fund reached a certain level. After that point he would cease further contributions as long as he prevented unemployment and did not have to pay benefits. The workers, on the other hand, could rely only on their employer's fund for benefit payments. The reserves idea marked a further refinement of the prevention theory and an important deviation from the workmen's compensation precedent.

Indicative of this change was the fact that Commons did not play a leading or even an active role in formulating this plan. Having passed his sixty-fifth birthday and beset with personal problems, he became less involved in legislative affairs; nevertheless he endorsed his students' efforts and gradually became more enthusiastic about the Groves plan, since it expanded upon his contention that self-insurers, particularly the large firms, were best able to prevent unemployment.[85]

While the Groves plan was calculated to win the approval of the progressive employers, it had precisely the opposite effect on many former supporters of the Wisconsin movement. Andrews, who was engaged in drawing up a model bill for introduction in the legislatures of many states, was particularly disturbed. He had twice visited Commons in Madison and thought he had the support of the Wisconsin reformers for a new version of the Huber bills. He was therefore "astounded" when he found that he could no longer count on his Wisconsin friends. He wrote Commons of reported rumors that the Raushenbushes "are advising some of their friends not to give financial or other support to the Association's proposal."[86] Raushenbush's comments about the "glaring defects" in the AALL plan did little to alleviate his fears.[87] When Commons came out in support of the reserves plan, Andrews realized that his case was hopeless and subsequently made his peace with the new generation of Wisconsin reformers. This proved to be only the first of a long series of disputes among the friends of unemployment insurance that often resulted in their fighting one another as vigorously as they fought conservative employers and politicians who opposed all legislation.

Of more immediate danger to the Wisconsin reformers was the antagonism of organized labor to the Groves plan. The state federation had not only rejected the employer's suggestion of employee contributions but now questioned the idea of individual plant reserves. With their members becoming increasingly interested in adequate compensation, Handley and Ohl had the 1929 Nixon bill reintroduced with slight modifications. The major change they made also dealt with the handling of the employers' contributions. Instead of the mutual insurance company previously proposed, the unionists supported a single fund under state control. From their point of view the reserves plan provided too little for the workers and too many concessions to the employers. Though they promised to give careful consideration to the Groves bill, there was friction between the state federation and the university people.[88] Witte reported in late 1930 that the situation was still "up in the air."[89]

Meanwhile Groves and several graduate students worked out the details of the reserves bill in January 1931. By the middle of the month Commons reported that they were "just winding up the final draft."[90] It followed, with the exceptions of the reserves feature and provisions which permitted the benefit funds to be used in financing public works or vocational education under certain circumstances, the earlier Wisconsin measures. The modest contribution rates, benefit schedule, and length of benefit payments reflected the continued emphasis on the employer rather than the worker. The reserves approach also introduced the possibility that individual funds might be exhausted very quickly in a long depression. Groves, who had been elected to the assembly in 1930, introduced his bill on February 6, 1931.

The immediate opponents of the Groves bill, not to mention the

Nixon measure, were the spokesmen of the WMA and other organized business groups. Well aware of the certain popularity of any measure that promised to alleviate unemployment, Clausen, Osborn, George Kull, executive secretary of the WMA, and H. W. Story, an Allis Chalmers executive, attacked both bills as visionary and impractical. They maintained that an additional financial burden would retard recovery and drive business out of the state. They also offered a number of alternate plans, probably with the intention of delaying consideration of any measure. Osborn, for example, pleaded the virtues of voluntary insurance, and the Milwaukee Association of Commerce argued that "the voluntary plan has the distinct advantage of lessening the curse of industry . . . labor turnover."[91] Clausen suggested a more sophisticated proposal, reminiscent of Governor Kohler's earlier plan; he called for joint contributions which would only begin after the unemployment crisis had ended. Ultimately, however, the employers counseled delay; they wanted an interim commission to study unemployment insurance and report to the next session of the legislature.[92]

Although the businessmen's arguments made the reformers' job more difficult, it was dissension within their own ranks that did the greatest damage. Despite numerous efforts to compromise, the supporters of the Groves and Nixon bills were unable to decide on a common position. As early as February 28 Witte wrote: "Chances for the passage of unemployment insurance seem to me to have decreased. The labor people do not like the Groves bill. . . . and in consequence prospects for unemployment insurance looks [sic] less hopeful than some time ago."[93] Commons, though embarrassed at being caught in the feud between his friends, performed yeoman service in publicizing unemployment prevention before the legislature and the public. He favored conciliation and supported efforts to bring the two sides together. Two formal conferences were held in March and April, but they produced no agreement. During those months Groves and Raushenbush, with the help of several others, worked out a substitute amendment for the original bill. This measure retained the reserves idea but restricted overtime work and clarified the administrative procedures. By the time Groves introduced it, however, the legislators had decided that further study was necessary.[94] Governor La Follette endorsed their call for a legislative commission to study unemployment legislation and report to a special session in November 1931. The legislature then created an interim committee consisting of Groves, Nixon, three other legislators, and Clausen and Handley, who would serve as representatives of the employers and workers.

During the summer of 1931 the reformers, with Andrews' aid, began

a new campaign emphasizing the principle of unemployment prevention rather than any specific bill. Returning from conferences on unemployment insurance in several midwestern states, Andrews stopped
in Madison for a few days. "I conferred with several of my old
friends," he recalled, "and started the organization of the state committee to organize the various industrial centers in advance of the public
hearings . . . . We shall therefore concentrate most attention upon Wisconsin during the next few weeks."[95] The reformers consequently organized a Wisconsin Committee for Unemployment Reserves Legislation
under Murray and Harry Weiss, another graduate student. Commons
suggested that his students "stir up as much discussion throughout the
state in the newspapers as possible and see to it that the interim committee is kept on its toes . . . ."[96] Much more difficult, however, was the
matter of raising the $1500 they estimated would be required for an
effective campaign. During July Andrews solicited many of the AALL's
most prominent supporters, but the only encouragement he received
was from Morris E. Leeds, who agreed to make a modest donation if
the Wisconsin forces settled their differences and agreed on a single
bill.[97] Just as the situation appeared desperate, Raushenbush stepped
in. He asked Andrews if the state federation would require the proposed organization to favor the Nixon bill. To the latter's reply that
the unionists would not dictate policy and that Murray and Weiss
would work for unemployment insurance legislation and not a specific
bill, he replied that prompt action was necessary. "Elizabeth and I are
able, and eager, to contribute substantially to the cause." Rather than
finance a campaign solely for the Groves bill, they agreed to cooperate
with the association. He enclosed a check for $500 and the assurance
that "we should . . . be able to keep the work going adequately, once it
gets started."[98]

The prospect of another defeat with victory in sight also put the
labor leaders in a more conciliatory mood. Handley tentatively agreed
to the substitute bill, and the state federation convention of July
strongly endorsed unemployment insurance legislation. While they did
not openly endorse the reserves plan, the union officials did agree that
a unified effort was necessary if any bill was to pass.[99] This concession
to expediency, coupled with the Raushenbushes' financial aid, considerably brightened the outlook for unemployment insurance in Wisconsin. By the time the interim committee began public hearings in late
August, the reformers were adequately financed, moving toward a unified position, and more optimistic than they had ever before dared to
be.

Although the interim committee considered a variety of unemployment measures, including public works and poor relief, unemployment insurance attracted the greatest public interest and received the most thorough treatment. The committee hearings also indicated the divergence between the business community and other groups on this issue. Of the sixty-seven people who testified on unemployment insurance before the committee, thirty-two—twenty-eight of whom were employers —opposed any legislation. Conversely only four employers favored an unemployment insurance law. While many of the opponents supported some alternative action, most of the alternatives suggested were voluntary plans.[100] This sharp division between the employers and nonemployers was characteristic of the social and political conflicts of the early Depression years and suggested the limited appeal of unemployment prevention to businessmen when translated into compulsory— even though moderate—measures.

The committee conducted hearings throughout the state, but the most significant and disputed sessions occurred at Madison, September 15–16, and at Milwaukee, September 28–29. At the former Commons and his students appeared; Ohl testified for the state federation, and Leiserson and Andrews represented expert out-of-state opinion. Osborn, Story, and Noel Sargent, labor legislation consultant of the National Association of Manufacturers, opposed unemployment insurance legislation. Don D. Lescohier, a university economics professor, caused a mild sensation when he seemed to question the idea of preventing unemployment through the use of reserves. Leiserson made the longest and one of the most convincing addresses; he excoriated the employers for irresponsibility and pleaded for an insurance plan. His accusations commanded greater respect when Osborn admitted that the employers "see no way out of the woods." Sargent was as inept as Leiserson was effective. He read a long statement and made a poor impression, and Andrews, who attended this session, cynically advised a California colleague: "If your commission is to have some representative of the N.A.M. from New York, I suggest you get Sargent!"[101] Later, at Milwaukee, Friedrick and former Governor Francis McGovern appeared in support of unemployment insurance. The businessmen, led by Hoar, were again unimpressive.[102]

In the meantime the work of mobilizing public opinion was proceeding at a rapid pace. Commons headed a formidable list of supporters who served on the Wisconsin committee. They included former governor McGovern; William Mauthe of Fond du Lac plan fame; John A. Lapp of Marquette University; Ohl; Barney J. Gehrman, state president of the American Society of Equity; Max Leopold, a Farm Bureau official; and Madison's mayor, A. G. Schmedeman, the state's Demo-

cratic leader. Under the terms of the arrangement between Raushenbush and Andrews, all the funds for this work officially came from the
AALL. This rather circuitous method was chosen because Raushenbush preferred not to be linked with the financing of the Wisconsin
committee. As the system operated, he or his wife would send money or
instructions to Andrews who would in turn forward the designated
funds to Murray. Additional monies from the labor movement or private contributors such as Leeds were also channeled into the Wisconsin
committee by this route. Despite these elaborate efforts Murray was
often short of financial resources, particularly after Andrews failed to
obtain the assistance of Edward A. Filene and Dennison, who were
"deeply interested" but financially hard pressed.[103]

What they lacked in tangible resources the reformers compensated
for in enthusiasm, especially after the poor showing of the employers
in Madison and Milwaukee. By early October Elizabeth Brandeis reported that the manufacturers were "talking very mildly" in compari-
son with Murray and Weiss, who were performing well.[104] Treading
the paths of Forsberg and other earlier Commons students, Murray
crossed the state, arranging for supporters to speak at the hearings and
drumming up public interest. After a trip through northwest Wisconsin he recalled: "The report of the hearing at La Crosse yesterday was
very favorable. I had lined up the mayor, the secretary of the Eagles . . .
and a good labor representation. Only one employer appeared against
unemployment compensation. Eau Claire was a tough nut to crack . . .
but [I] think there will be a good hearing at Superior."[105]

While they sought the support of all groups, the Wisconsin committee members knew that, for the practical purpose of passing a bill,
farm backing was essential. For this reason Weiss spent much of his
time explaining the relationship between unemployment and agricultural prosperity. He produced figures showing the dependence of farm
prices on urban purchasing power; he also argued that farmers paid
for unemployment relief through their property taxes.[106] This work
and the steadfast support of Gehrman and Leopold produced the most
valuable dividends of the entire campaign. At the October meeting of
farm organizations, the "Farmers Get Together" at Shawano, Gehrman
and Leopold, aided by William Kirsch of the Department of Cooperative Marketing, and a resolution drafted by Raushenbush, persuaded
the delegates to endorse unemployment insurance legislation.[107] Less
than a week later the Pure Milk Products Cooperative, representing
five thousand dairy farmers, resolved to support unemployment insurance. Finally Gehrman's militant Equity added its backing to the resolutions of the other farm organizations. After a decade of indecision or

opposition, the state's farmers had fallen in line within a week; in the words of Elizabeth Brandeis, this was "probably the turning point in the campaign."[108]

On November 16, a few days after the farmers' meetings, the interim committee released its report. The committee endorsed the provisions of the substitute Groves bill and called for unemployment reserves as a more "orderly" method of relief and an incentive to stabilize employment. Concluding that the "idea of individual plant reserves appeals strongly to employers," it considered the Groves plan the most practical from a political standpoint and the one that would achieve the purposes of unemployment insurance. But, as a concession to the employers, the committee suggested that contributions be postponed at least until July 1, 1933. In a bitter dissenting statement Clausen and Ira Burtis, a conservative assemblyman, attacked all compulsory schemes and proposed as alternatives state assistance to business, and voluntary efforts to promote "thrift" among employees.[109]

The WMA, probably anticipating the committee report, made a last ditch effort to thwart a new legislative campaign at its November convention. Two themes ran through the proceedings, which were largely devoted to unemployment insurance. On one hand the employers freely admitted the necessity of some type of provision to protect their workers. Hoar, Clausen, Story, and G. H. Whyte, president of the organization, stressed this point, but they were not alone: "The members of the association from all parts of the state seemed more impressed with the necessity of 'getting some form of unemployment insurance' than they were in 1930. . . . [observers] admitted that there had been a decided change in the attitude of the old 'hard shelled' manufacturers . . . ."[110] On the other hand there was no commensurate change in the employers' attitude toward compulsory insurance. Attacking legislation as the first step toward the dole, an assault on prosperity, or more realistically as a transfer of their power to the state or the labor unions, the delegates unequivocally rejected the Groves bill. As a countermove they invited Bryce Stewart, who had left the ACWA to join the Industrial Relations Counselors, a Rockefeller-sponsored research group, to speak to the convention on voluntary methods and then voted to employ him to devise a voluntary program.[111] In a move that may have been related to the WMA strategy, Leon R. Clausen, president of the J. I. Case Company and brother of Frederick Clausen, announced that his company had established a voluntary reserves plan.

These events provided the background for the dramatic special session of the legislature which met in late November. As one of a number of crucial anti-Depression measures, the Groves–interim committee bill attracted widespread discussion. This was particularly true when La Follette, in a move to weaken the opposition, called for an amendment providing that the act would not go into effect if Wisconsin employers established voluntary plans covering at least 200,000 workers by June 1, 1933. After this move the approval of the assembly, which was dominated by progressives, was a foregone conclusion. When the bill was presented on December 21, the lower house voted sixty-nine to fifteen in favor, almost without debate. But the reformers knew that the decisive battle lay ahead, since the upper house was evenly divided between conservatives and progressives. There were, in fact, fifteen senators who opposed the Groves bill, fourteen who supported it, and three who were undecided but potential supporters.[112] The backing of the latter became less certain when the representatives of the Milwaukee Association of Commerce succeeded in having the senate vote postponed until early January.

During the ten-day interim period the reformers focused their attention on the three crucial senators. Philip E. Nelson of Douglas County had pledged to support unemployment insurance legislation in his election campaign and was thus seemingly committed; yet Witte felt he would approve any amendments the Milwaukee businessmen offered.[113] Walter Polakowski, a Milwaukee socialist, also presented a problem. He had formerly introduced his own measure and had expressed deep dissatisfaction over the Groves bill, although it was unlikely that he would vote with the employers. The final and least certain of the three was Bernhard Gettleman, representative of a Milwaukee constituency, who had supported the bill in committee but who often deferred to the policies of the Association of Commerce. Gettleman, however, was known to be something of a maverick and had acted independently of Republican regulars in and out of the legislature before; Murray hoped that appeals from constituents, from labor and women's organizations, and from Father Oberle, a strong supporter of the bill, would strike a responsive chord. They did, and Gettleman voted for the bill.[114]

With the reformers, the governor, the farmers, and organized labor calling for passage of the Groves bill, the conservatives had little success in emasculating it when it came before the senate in early January. They did win senate approval of amendments to exempt workers in interstate commerce, and to reduce the number of employees required to be covered under voluntary plans (from 200,000 to 175,000) before employers could be exempted from the compulsory. The senate then voted nineteen to thirteen for passage. Murray exulted: "We are almost certain of victory."[115] The senate and assembly ironed out the differences between their respective bills and La Follette signed the final act on January 28, 1932. The first unemployment insurance act in American history required each employer of ten or more workers to contribute 2 percent of his payroll (beginning in 1933) to a state-controlled individual fund until he had accumulated $55 per employee, then 1 percent until he had $75 per employee. After the fund reached this point no further contributions were required as long as no benefits were paid and the accumulated contributions remained at $75 per worker. The wage earners, on the other hand, would receive a maximum of ten weeks of benefits per year, at a rate of 50 percent of their average weekly wage, not to exceed $10 in any week. Advisory committees of workers and employers were to help the Industrial Commission administer the act.

After the passage of the Groves bill Wisconsin employers began to look at unemployment insurance in a different light. Since no one wanted to take the first step, they made only feeble efforts to enact voluntary plans. Instead, they soon became enthusiastic backers of the Groves law. As neighboring states seriously considered more costly plans, Wisconsin employers rejoiced that they had gotten off so easily. Clausen and Kull, who served on the employers' advisory board, and Story became active propagandists for unemployment reserves. As a result of their new policy, they succeeded in getting the beginning date set back to 1934 rather than 1933. The first consideration of the employers was the lower cost of the Groves bill, but there was more to their friendlier outlook, once the pressures of the legislative campaign had passed, than the lower tax rate. They had always taken a nominal interest in the idea of business reform through unemployment prevention; in 1931–32 these concepts became familiar to every businessman in Wisconsin and throughout the nation.

7 | 1928-1932
TRANSITION YEARS

IN 1928, despite evidence of increasing unemployment among seasonal workers and certain skilled groups, the typical workman in the United States was steadily employed and relatively prosperous. In 1932, as the nation approached the trough of the worst depression in its history, the same workman was likely to be unemployed or working part time and worried about the next month's rent or mortgage payment. Approximately 4,000,000 wage earners had lost their jobs by early 1930, another 9,500,000 by late 1932. The advent of the Depression obviously had a profound effect on public attitudes toward unemployment insurance. While this effect is often difficult to document with any degree of precision one fact is clear: as more and more people came face to face with unemployment they became increasingly preoccupied with the need for an income dependent on their willingness to work, not on the success or failure of the economy to provide steady employment. This concern marked the early Depression years as a decisive stage in the development of unemployment insurance in the United States that had important political implications for the New Deal period.

No groups or institutions better revealed the friction between the traditions of the past and the pressures of the present than the executive and legislative branches of the federal government, where the influences of Herbert Hoover and Republican conservatism were paramount. Under Hoover's guidance, the government had accepted the rhetoric of progressive management; the 1921 unemployment conference, the work of the committee on seasonal construction work and business cycles, the campaign against waste, the simplification movement, the collection of business statistics, and the promotion of trade associations all bore the indelible mark of the drive for more efficient business techniques. There was somewhat less concern over efficiency and industrial order in Congress, where public works planning and proposals for an effective national employment-office system received relatively little attention. But with the deepening of the Depression and the rise of popular interest in labor legislation, the balance shifted. Congress became more receptive to reform proposals while the new President, the architect of the government's alliance with the businessmen of the 1920's, clung steadfastly to the lessons of the past.

At the time of his inauguration Hoover's record on unemployment gave every indication of a progressive outlook. He had, at one time or another, endorsed the four major points of the *Practical Program*. In 1928 he had even asked William Trufant Foster, of the team of Foster and Catchings, to explain to the Governors' Conference public works planning as a method of eliminating unemployment.[1] He had also proclaimed the advantages of regularized employment and unemployment insurance, though on the latter he showed far less understanding than Dennison, Leeds, or Commons would have hoped. He paid little attention to private, employer-financed plans and the apparent influence they had on industrial stability. At most he stressed the maintenance of purchasing power and the reduction of labor turnover during periods of cyclical unemployment. Without unemployment insurance, he stated on one occasion in 1923, "there is lost time and added expense in gathering new workers and fitting them into their jobs."[2] Instead he thought of jobless insurance as a means of self-help by which the employee, perhaps with the aid of the employer, provided himself with a subsistence wage.[3] Such an approach attracted little attention from either the workers, who traditionally opposed deductions from their wages, or employers, who saw no relation between this scheme and industrial stability. On this issue the oracle of business in the 1920's was strangely out of tune with the times.

In this matter Hoover differed not only from the management experts and union leaders but also from the more progressive Republican congressional leaders, of whom James Couzens, a Michigan businessman and former associate of Henry Ford, was a leading spokesman. In response to evidence of rising unemployment—which led the Socialist representative Victor Berger of Wisconsin to introduce the first unemployment insurance bill in the House, only to have it die in committee —the Senate authorized an investigation of unemployment in 1928 by Couzens' Committee on Education and Labor. From the beginning the Senator rejected any consideration of European compulsory schemes as a "waste of time" and suggested that progressive industrialists were

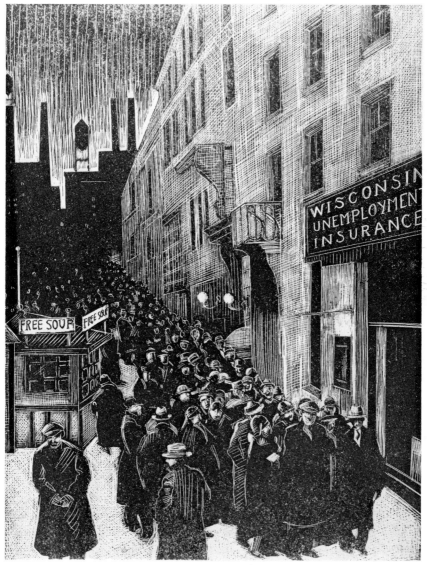

"Wisconsin Turns its Back on the Soup Kitchen." Frontispiece drawing by Charles Silver for the February 15, 1932, issue of *The Survey*. Wisconsin's Unemployment Compensation Act had been signed eighteen days earlier.

Wide World Photos

SIDNEY   HILLMAN

State Historical Society of Wisconsin

JOHN R. COMMONS

Dennison Manufacturing Co.

HENRY S. DENNISON

Brown Brothers Photo

JOHN B. ANDREWS

State Historical Society of Wisconsin

WILLIAM M. LEISERSON

Courtesy Mrs. Abraham Epstein

ABRAHAM EPSTEIN

State Historical Society of Wisconsin

EDWIN E. WITTE

Wisconsin Department of Industry, Labor, and Human Relations

Governor Philip La Follette signing Wisconsin's pioneering Unemployment Compensation Act, January 28, 1932. Left to right: Henry Ohl, Jr., Elizabeth Brandeis, Paul A. Raushenbush, John R. Commons, La Follette, Henry A. Huber, Harold M. Groves, and Robert A. Nixon.

Wide World Photos

The signing of the Federal Social Security Act of 1935. Grouped around President Franklin D. Roosevelt, from left to right, are Representative Robert L. Doughton, Senator Robert F. Wagner, Secretary of Labor Frances Perkins, Senator Pat Harrison, and Representative David J. Lewis.

"gaining much ground." With the assistance of Isador Lubin of the Brookings Institution, Couzens and his staff concentrated on the idea that "the problem of unemployment was largely one which would have to be solved by industry itself." They sought to "impress the employers with the thought that this [unemployment insurance] is a good business proposition."[4] As a result the Couzens hearings, held in late 1928 and early 1929, were largely devoted to consideration of the theory and practice of unemployment prevention.

The Couzens Committee investigation revealed both the seriousness of unemployment in the late 1920's and the relative success of many businessmen in dealing with it during periods of general prosperity. Lubin's staff reports indicated a high degree of joblessness among elderly and seasonal wage-earners and the difficulties these workers had in finding new positions.[5] On the other hand the employers who testified, including nearly all those who experimented with company plans, proclaimed the efficacy of voluntary plans in reducing unemployment. Probably the most influential statement, however, came from Commons, who cited the Huber bill and his work with the Chicago clothing workers as proof of the vital role management must play in stabilizing employment. The committee's final report emphasized the professor's findings and the experiences of progressive employers. It suggested the creation of individual reserve funds but rejected European-style unemployment insurance or a program initiated by the federal government. It repeated the managers' argument that "the employer who does not stabilize his employment . . . is the employer who is going to fail" and found "there is general accord on the proposition that [unemployment insurance] . . . is 'good business,' that it has increased profits."[6] Couzens concluded that unemployment prevention together with better employment exchanges and planned public works "require the serious consideration of those who are concerned with the establishment of stable industrial conditions."[7]

While Couzens and the employers considered some of the avenues open for action, Hoover made little effort to keep pace until the stock market collapse provided abundant warning that time was growing short. As late as July 1929 Robert P. Lamont, his Secretary of the Treasury, had excused his refusal to take part in an unemployment conference sponsored by the American Management Association with the explanation that "he has the notion that the matter is not sufficiently urgent at this time."[8] Only after the crash did he move: recalling the precedents of 1921 he scheduled conferences with industrialists and bankers to promote wage stability, confidence in the economy and —belatedly—the type of management reforms that had been discussed at the Taylor Society and the AMA for more than a decade. Hoover's policy, as it developed from these activities, aimed at both relief and recovery, the former through the mobilization of local resources and the latter through the work of such organizations as the National Business Survey Conference which he sponsored in December 1929. Designed to promote private construction and coordinate federal public works projects, the Survey Conference was also intended to insure employment stability. In his December 5 speech announcing the formation of the NBSC Hoover stated that "all these efforts have one end—to assure employment and remove the fear of unemployment."[9] Convinced that events in 1930 would parallel those of 1921, Hoover invoked the New Emphasis with increasing frequency as the months passed. Speaking to the AFL convention, for example, he praised the federation's new wage policy and experiments in labor-management cooperation, asserting that these ideas, applied to the nation as a whole, would constitute a "practical system of unemployment insurance."[10] Such a development, he added, would be far more advantageous than the practice of European countries where they "patch up the old system with doles of various kinds which limit the independence of man." The task facing the United States, then, was to reform the practice of business: ". . . most of these problems are problems of stability. With the job secure, other questions can be solved with much more assurance. . . . To establish a system that assures this security is the supreme challenge.[11]

Yet Hoover and his supporters were not the only ones who urged a more definite commitment to the New Emphasis in 1930, and this fact had an important effect on the President's policy. Senator Robert F. Wagner of New York, since 1927 the most effective critic of Republican unemployment policies, had introduced much of the old AALL program—bills for an effective employment office system, public works planning, and adequate unemployment statistics—in 1928, and begun a long controversy with the Coolidge and Hoover Administrations.[12] He reintroduced these bills in January 1930, as the first steps in a larger prevention program. He made this clear when he explained that they aimed at "the future control of the unemployment problem."[13] Andrews, who threw his organization into the fight for the Wagner bills, also gauged the importance of employment bureaus, planned public works, and accurate employment statistics: "For many years this Association has studied the problem of unemployment *prevention*," he wrote, "and we are convinced that these bills are not only important but are necessary steps in any permanent constructive program."[14] Other employers and management experts of a similar mind, like William T. Foster, Dennison, Coonley, Edwin S. Smith, Edward A. Filene, and a group of economists from the President's relief agency, the Emergency Committee for Employment, also took an active role in the fight for the Wagner bills. More significant, however, was the support of a large number of liberal economists, clergymen, and social workers. Lillian Wald, Francis J. McConnell, Stephen Wise, Paul Douglas, and Frances Perkins enthusiastically and publicly endorsed Wagner's provisions against unemployment—introducing another element into what ultimately became a campaign for unemployment insurance.

Despite its wide support Wagner's program encountered considerable opposition from Congress and the White House. Although employers' organizations, such as the National Association of Manufacturers, and conservative politicians voiced their anxiety over the Wagner bills, it was Hoover who was most responsible for the trouble. He signed the statistics bill into law in July 1930 but made no serious effort to comply with its provisions. Obviously piqued that Wagner had succeeded in having an estimate of unemployment included in the 1930 census, his performance was nevertheless inconsistent with his past interest in business and labor statistics. The public works planning bill also encountered difficulties; the President managed to prevent its passage, although planned construction was his favorite anti-depression measure of the 1920's, until February 1931. Then he curtailed the activities of the Federal Employment Stabilization Board, set up to administer the act, and thus insured the failure of advance works-planning in the 1930's. When Congress passed the most important of the Wagner proposals, the employment office bill, Hoover overruled his subordinates, including the Secretary of Labor, and returned it with a stinging veto message.[15]

Thus in early 1931 Hoover seemed to repudiate the New Emphasis in a series of steps that disillusioned many of his erstwhile followers and contradicted his oft-expressed support for unemployment prevention. Two reasons apparently account for this seemingly inexplicable action: the President's aversion to increased federal obligations that would further unbalance the budget, and his disdain for Wagner and his Democratic allies. Irving Bernstein, who has made the most thorough study of the Wagner bills, credits the first as the decisive reason. But Hoover stressed, both in his veto message and his *Memoirs,* the intent of his political opponents. In the latter he argued, incorrectly, that the employment office bill "would have put workers' jobs in control of political machines, such as Tammany in New York, or the Hague gang in Jersey City," while the Democrats had "ditched" his own program.[16] Whatever his reason for sabotaging Wagner's 1930 program, Hoover's distrust of the Senator accounted for his attack on the unemployment insurance bills of 1931–32.

While the battle over public works planning and employment offices was in progress, Andrews prepared for the next step in the unemployment prevention campaign—the introduction of federal unemployment insurance legislation. In March 1930 he sent Senator Couzens a model bill designed to allow the states considerable flexibility in enacting their own programs; the federal government would merely subsidize the cost of the state systems. But Couzens was hesitant to become involved until the Wagner bills had been disposed of.[17] Andrews then sent the same bill to Wagner and asked if he would be willing to introduce it, only to discover that he too was reluctant to advance another measure before Congress acted on his 1930 bills. Complaining that his opponents were using the "opening wedge" argument against his current proposals, Wagner advised that "it is still important that we pass these bills . . . and it is perhaps inadvisable to frighten away possible support by introducing other legislation which they are not yet ready to follow."[18]

Despite his tactical objections to an unemployment insurance bill in 1930, Wagner made preparations, alone and in conjunction with the AALL, to introduce such a measure at the following session. In addition to Andrews' model bill, which he considered overly ambitious in view of the conservatives' strength, he studied a more modest proposal to provide tax exemptions to employers who established voluntary reserves plans. He made several inquiries in regard to the latter, including a request that Swope send him a copy of the General Electric plan.[19] By the beginning of the December session Wagner had decided to introduce a series of bills as "part of my general program for the prevention of unemployment"; he submitted the Andrews plan and the tax exemption measure in late 1930 and early 1931.[20] But he counted most on another measure that called for an investigation of various insurance schemes, explaining that the senators needed time to compare existing alternatives and that unemployment insurance should not be considered as emergency legislation.[21]

Though the Senate refused to debate Wagner's tax exemption and federal subsidy bills, it passed his resolution for a study committee in late February—a move that produced another clash with the President. According to Senate custom, Wagner was entitled to the chairmanship of this committee. Assuming this practice would be followed, he proceeded to organize the investigation, despite the reluctance of Republicans Felix Hebert of Rhode Island and Otis Glenn of Illinois to schedule an early meeting. When the committee did meet, the two Republican senators overruled Wagner and named Hebert to the chairman's post. It was widely believed that the President dictated this breach of senatorial tradition. Since Hebert and Glenn acted soon after Hoover vetoed the employment offices bill, it is likely that the Chief Executive considered the investigation another effort to embarrass his Administration.[22]

Hoover's apparent opposition to the investigation was another indication that by 1931 he was prepared to reject anything that Wagner proposed. But it was also an outgrowth of the President's dedication to what a recent student has called his "second program."[23] Fearful of more radical proposals, Hoover abandoned the field in which he had won a reputation for special competence and focused his attention exclusively on restoring the nation's financial institutions. He subsequently urged congressional action on a number of measures relating to these problems and in 1931–32 successfully backed the Reconstruction Finance Corporation, the war-debt moratorium, Federal Land Bank appropriations, the Home Loan Bank act, and the Glass-Steagall Credit act. At the same time he ceased his appeals to businessmen to maintain wages and stabilize employment, judging from experience if not from conviction that the New Emphasis was a dead issue. Instead, the President's unemployment policy became one of urging voluntary community relief efforts through such organizations as the Gifford Committee and the Teagle "Share the Work" movement. The failure of these modest efforts further undermined Hoover's popularity and threw the unemployment insurance issue into anti-Administration hands.

Having turned from his former business allies and their emphasis on voluntary unemployment prevention, Hoover became increasingly hostile to unemployment insurance legislation. As his distrust of Wagner grew, he worked more closely with Glenn and Hebert to insure that the committee's report did not advocate federal action. On several occasions the President made clear his opposition to any legislation the committee might propose, noting to an Indianapolis audience, for example, that "we have had one proposal after another which amounts to a dole from the Federal Treasury. The largest is that of unemployment insurance." Recalling that he had supported private plans, he argued that "the moment the Government enters into this field it invariably degenerates into the dole."[24] His opposition became more obvious in August when Hebert returned from "studying" unemployment insurance in Europe and spent a weekend at the President's summer retreat. The *New York Times* reported that Hoover had reached a turning point; if he decided to oppose federal action, "it would be necessary to lay plans for combatting efforts to have it passed at the next session."[25] Hebert emerged to attack unemployment insurance: "I am firmly convinced . . . that the institution of such a system in the United States would be the first step toward a national dole." Shortly thereafter Senator Simeon Fess, the conservative head of the Republican national committee, told reporters, after conferring with Hoover, that "every possible effort will be made to avert such an expedient."[26]

Apparently determined to oppose any federal action on unemployment insurance, the President devoted considerable energy to justifying his position. He studied the General Electric plan and Bulletin 544 of the Bureau of Labor Statistics, which described voluntary plans in the United States.[27] He sent Hebert a memorandum of criticism on Swope's proposal "and intimated that it might be necessary for him to talk to the Senator over the phone about it, since he understands it is to be launched under important Democratic auspices during the next week." And he met with the Rhode Island senator several times in September to discuss ways of opposing Wagner's maneuvers.[28] Hoover also asked his attorney general for an opinion on the constitutionality of unemployment insurance, to which his legal advisor obligingly replied that federal action was unconstitutional except in the case of interstate industries.[29]

While the President made no public statement, the work of the Hebert committee accurately registered what had happened behind the scenes. Hebert managed to delay any action until the autumn by an agreement with Glenn that no meetings would be held until two of the three senators were so disposed.[30] Much to his chagrin, the worsening economic situation only increased public interest in unemployment legislation during the summer of 1931. When the hearings began, virtually everyone who appeared, including businessmen like Swope, Folsom, and E. A. Filene, urged some form of federal activity. Under Wagner's adept if informal leadership, the hearings offered overwhelming evidence of the need for positive action. The chairman, out of desperation, finally ended the sessions before many witnesses had had a chance to appear. Yet even Hebert and Glenn were not entirely immune from what had happened. In their report of June 30, 1932, they condemned overt federal sponsorship of unemployment insurance but upheld Wagner's earlier bill to grant tax exemptions to employers who established their own plans. The senators also favored private employer plans while admitting that the states would almost certainly act.[31] Wagner, who had been urged by his supporters for many months to file a dissenting statement, disregarded his colleagues' objections to compulsory systems and urged legislation by the states.[32]

Perhaps the most important consequence of the Hebert committee hearings was the further enhancement of Wagner's reputation as the champion of labor reform legislation. Certainly this was more significant for the future of unemployment insurance than the actual revelations of the committee, for it marked a shift from the traditional approach represented by men like Couzens. The New Yorker had few ties, by politics or inclination, with the business community, and while he willingly espoused the doctrines of the AALL he was never wholly committed to the prevention theory. In late 1930, when he introduced Andrews' model bill, he had in fact described unemployment insurance as a benefit program for the unemployed, a systematic alternative to charity or state poor relief.[33] Usually, however, he was more ambiguous. To a constituent he wrote: "All my efforts in the field of unemployment have been predicated upon the theory that mass unemployment is preventable. I expect unemployment insurance, however, to take care of that residual amount of unemployment which will inevitably occur. . . . It will, in addition, tend to stimulate regularization of employment. . . ."[34] On another occasion in early 1931 he described unemployment insurance as part of the "war on want" that had to be waged until stable employment was achieved.[35]

While Wagner enhanced his reputation, Hoover had in 1931 abnegated his role as the sponsor of the New Emphasis approach to unemployment reform. Determined to avoid increased expenditures wherever possible and irked by Wagner's aggressive and, in his opinion, partisan tactics, the President had sacrificed his reputation among labor economists, progressive employers, and management experts by unwisely undermining the Wagner-Hebert investigation. He succeeded in sidetracking federal unemployment insurance, just as he was able to sidetrack most other opposition measures. But the time when such tactics would succeed was rapidly passing and by late 1931 it was obvious to everyone but the President and his close followers that the "second program" could meet only a few of the problems confronting the nation. Nowhere was this realization more evident than among businessmen. His desertion by the progressive business leaders probably embittered Hoover more than any other single development, but it also marked a new stage in the campaign for unemployment prevention.

Business Takes the Offensive

THE EARLY Depression years projected American businessmen into new and challenging roles. Though some of them, notably the bankers and financiers, were discredited in the stock market crash and the ensuing financial crisis, many others found themselves with increased public responsibilities, particularly in the area of unemployment measures, which they had actively promoted and apparently shown unusual competence for in the 1920's. The Hoover Administration advanced, at least for a time, the idea that responsible businessmen were best qualified for this leadership, and many business leaders like Swope and Folsom took full advantage of their new opportunities. To a large degree these men were found among the membership of the United States Chamber of Commerce, which retained much of the Boston influence of its early years, influence that had involved it in many management reforms of the pre-Depression period. The influence of the progressives, moreover, increased after 1929. Under the aegis of the Hoover Administration the balance tipped in their favor; for several years the chamber's leaders, with nominal support from other businessmen's organizations, stood in the front ranks of those who demanded a positive unemployment policy, one that would prevent the recurrence of the problems they faced.

Before the Depression the Chamber of Commerce had endorsed the New Emphasis and frequently exhorted its members to stabilize their production and employment. In a statement entitled "Principles of Business Conduct" adopted in 1924, the chamber advocated "continuity of operation, bettering conditions of employment and increasing the efficiency and opportunities of individual employees."[36] More specifically it sponsored cost-accounting systems and personnel reforms for trade associations and company managers. Reflecting current interest in employment regularization, it publicized the experience of progressive employers and detailed the steps that all employers might take. Julius H. Barnes, who was the most influential leader of the chamber during this period, summarized the sentiment of many leaders of organized business when he wrote that "unemployment is a private charge on the responsibility of business leadership."[37]

Hoover's creation of the National Business Survey Conference, with Barnes at its head, presented the executives of the chamber with an unprecedented opportunity to implement these ideas on a nationwide scale. From the experiences of individual employers in rationalizing their operations, they envisioned an orderly economy, premised on the concepts of cooperation and stability. Such a goal understandably struck a responsive chord among hard-pressed executives faced with new uncertainties and competition after a decade's efforts to regulate production, prices, and markets. As Barnes emphasized, "business is learning that the measure of its own advancement is the common pace, that advantage is not to be weighed in terms of destroyed competitors, meager wages, and exploited consumers but in terms of efficiency, of economic achievement and that production, distribution and consumption go forward together or not at all."[38] The economic debacle threatened these goals as no other event of the century had done.

"Stabilization" in the terminology of 1930 meant the elimination of price and wage cutting, of unnecessary competition, and of the ill effects of these, unleashed by the Depression throughout the country. But, under the voluntary plan that Hoover endorsed, stability depended on the actions of the individual employer. It was therefore necessary to build from the ground up to convince the ordinary businessman that orderly progress was in his interest, while also imposing cooperation from the top down through trade associations or a national planning council. This dual requirement forced business leaders to consider the methods of progressive management while at the same time devising larger cooperative schemes. And a basic step in past efforts had been the prevention of unemployment, with or without the provision for a specific reserve fund. As Barnes explained on another occasion, "there is a realization that intelligent direction of industry must spread and stabilize employment against the crests and depressions of former years."[39]

At first the NBSC followed the President's example in emphasizing the remedial value of expanded construction, both public and private, during hard times. To achieve its goal of stabilizing production and employment, though "on a far larger scale than most of the previous movements," the Survey Conference emphasized the need for businessmen to undertake contemplated plant expansion and repairs, to maintain their regular orders, and to urge salesmen to "sell" the idea of continued prosperity.[40] This amalgam of construction and exhortation was not, however, merely an emergency move; it fit neatly into the overall pattern. Since production had outstripped consumption, the businessmen argued, the need to balance these forces was paramount. Stability could be obtained by channeling activity into construction rather than into industrial production. "The immediate problem," Barnes explained, was "to alter the course of industry without reducing its speed."[41]

By late 1930 many businessmen had begun to develop misgivings with the President's policy. Despite continuous assertions to the contrary from the White House and the Survey Conference, business had not improved. Conditions had worsened, joblessness had increased, and wages and prices had declined. As time passed it became more and more apparent that the public relations approach had failed. Only a perpetual optimist could contend that individual firms had stabilized their operations, much less tried, and the attempt to promote cooperation through trade associations had been even less successful. Many business leaders concluded that the antitrust laws were the major hindrance to industry-wide or interindustry cooperation. In any event, neither the President's policy nor the activities of the Survey Conference provided much solace to executives struggling with the disruptive force of the Depression.

The first overt signs of impatience with the Administration became evident in early 1931. Beginning in January the board of directors of the Chamber of Commerce formulated plans for independent studies of unemployment prevention measures. Barnes himself presented a resolution calling for the creation of a committee "to study all phases of employment stabilization, employment assurance, unemployment insurance and helpful contact between industries."[42] The chamber also approved an employment-office system that closely resembled the one provided for in Wagner's bill. As for the proposed stabilization committee, the executive board, meeting in March, suggested that it devote its energies to "finding practicable means by which industry can mitigate periodical recurrence of unemployment." Specifically, this meant devising ways of industrial planning to permit year-long work.[43]

The annual convention of the Chamber of Commerce, which met in April, marked a turning point in the relationship between organized business and the Hoover Administration. Recognizing the seriousness of the growing economic crisis, the delegates devoted their attention to the two-fold problem of stabilizing the individual firm and the economy. In a major address, which was "gone over carefully" by Hoover, Commerce Secretary Lamont urged the continuation of existing wage rates and the reduction of working hours. He was less specific, however, in endorsing industrial stabilization and only vaguely suggested the creation of unemployment reserves.[44] On the other hand Senator Couzens, a former chamber official, set the tone for the convention discussions with a scathing attack on business for failing to cope with unemployment. Couzens warned that if employers did not establish their own reserves systems, government would enact compulsory unemployment insurance.[45]

On both aspects of the stabilization question the businessmen went further than the Administration would have desired. To promote nationwide cooperation by other than rhetorical means, the delegates promised "the most vigorous offensive ever undertaken for revision of the Sherman antitrust laws." Together with representatives from the American Bar Association they condemned the "legal chains that prevent fair cooperation."[46] With these appeals against the ravages of unregulated competition, they sowed the most important seeds of dissension with the Administration. The delegates were less certain about their position on unemployment insurance and the role of the state or national government in it. Most of them condemned compulsory insurance as the "dole," but others, notably E. A. Filene, reminded the representatives that only the creation of company reserves could avert state action. A high point of the convention was a round-table discussion of employment stabilization featuring Folsom, Leeds, Filene, and Joseph H. Willits, a leading New Emphasis proponent from the Wharton school of business.[47] As a consequence of these discussions and the cry for antitrust revision, the delegates agreed to establish a special committee closely resembling the one which the executive board had proposed in March. This body, called the Committee on Continuity of Business and Employment, was assigned the task of studying both facets of the stabilization problem. To head it the officers chose Henry I. Harriman, former president of the Boston Chamber of Commerce, friend of the Massachusetts management reformers, and an advocate of the New Emphasis. To aid him they selected a large group of businessmen, including Dennison, Leeds, and James Gleason, an architect of the Rochester plan.[48]

While the chamber committee deliberated and worked out its report, sentiment within the business community for a comprehensive stabilization program spread rapidly. Talk of revising the antitrust laws, promoting large-scale cooperative activities, and providing job security for hard-pressed workers became commonplace. This approach appealed in particular to those employers who had undertaken similar programs on their own initiative. As a promoter of cooperation between the electrical manufacturers in the 1920's, the New Emphasis, and welfare capitalism, Gerard Swope was perhaps the best qualified of all employers to judge the merits and implications of regularized operations. Having completed his unemployment insurance plan, he began to turn his attention to bigger problems in late 1930. In October, for example, he urged the President to adopt a vigorous program of public works, relief, unemployment insurance, and old age pensions based on deficit spending.[49] But his major effort began in January 1931, when he worked out a comprehensive industrial stabilization program that had relatively little economic significance but an immense political impact. After showing his plan to Owen D. Young and Newton D. Baker, he proposed it in a speech to the National Electrical Manufacturers Association in September 1931.[50]

The Swope plan, as this document came to be called, was designed to satisfy the business demand for stabilization from above through the creation of powerful trade associations, while requiring individual firms to stabilize production and employment. Swope proposed anti-trust revisions and tax inducements to encourage employers to join the appropriate associations. His purpose was no secret: it was to place "the same social burden on companies competing in various parts of the United States." The trade association would coordinate production and consumption, providing a form of national regulation without increased taxation. Anticipating charges of attempting to curtail production, he pointed to the "great advantages of standardization and mass production" while contending that the prevention of "overproduction" was a legitimate goal.[51] As for the employees, Swope included provisions for employee life and disability insurances, pensions, liberal workmen's compensation benefits, and unemployment insurance financed by joint contributions. Of these features "the most important matter is stabilization of employment. . . . The result of taxing industry for a portion of the cost will be to put a premium on industry's finding ways of stabilizing employment. The collateral effects, therefore, of unemployment insurance will be much more important . . . than unemployment insurance itself."[52] Swope envisioned, moreover, a reciprocal effect between industrial cooperation and individual plant stabilization. The former would make possible steadier employment, while stable production and employment were essential preconditions for continued cooperation. These provisions brought immediate and generally favorable response from other business leaders. Silas Strawn, president of the Chamber of Commerce, remarked that the Swope plan "is entirely along the lines of one which the United States Chamber of Commerce has been working on."[53]

No sooner had Swope publicized his ideas than the Harriman committee, after months of deliberation, published its report. This document also reflected the influence of the progressive managers, but it differed in two important respects.[54] Rather than placing ultimate power in the hands of the trade associations, it called for the creation of a national economic council composed of representatives of various business interests and financed by private contributions. And because it sought to satisfy a large, heterogeneous constituency that wanted order but had no taste for compulsion, the Harriman committee suggested only voluntary compliance. In other ways the report differed little from the Swope plan. It suggested revision of the antitrust laws, official sanction of cooperative agreements, and permission to curtail production in natural resources. It also reported in detail on unemployment insurance and made several important observations. One subcommittee studied the British and German systems and decided, not unexpectedly, that the European plans were actuarially unsound.

But, unlike most business executives, the members of the subcommittee were surprisingly tolerant of government competition. They concluded that both the European approach and the poor relief and charity systems of the United States were inadequate, although they agreed that "at the moment we have no better substitute to suggest." Instead they enumerated the principles of a desirable unemployment insurance program: maximum coverage, limited liability, prevention incentives, and administration by the employers and employees.[55]

Another subcommittee—on unemployment reserves—took these recommendations seriously. Instead of a compulsory system it endorsed voluntary reserve funds modeled after the Rochester plan, as an integral part of an overall stabilization program. "Individual planning," the final committee report stated, "offers very definite promise to many branches of industry as a means of eliminating waste, curtailing excess production, anticipating seasonal fluctuations, and maintaining a scheduled rate of production throughout the year."[56] The subcommittee similarly justified unemployment reserves as a prevention measure. "The question of benefits," it stated, "is secondary. . . . such a plan . . . will give incentive to stabilize and thereby reduce unemployment. In many cases the benefits to the employer resulting from the greater stabilization will outweigh the cost of the benefit plans."[57] As this report indicated, unemployment prevention had taken on a larger meaning by 1931; it had been incorporated as part of a well-considered program of national planning and rationalized production.

Businessmen, however, were not alone in sensing the need for new direction and control over the economy. By 1931 national planning was a popular idea and the subject of a plethora of plans, some by crack-brained reformers, others by experts in their fields. But Hoover was deaf to all appeals. Rather, the Senate, at the initiative of Senator Robert M. La Follette, Jr., took up the question of national planning and the subsidiary issue of unemployment prevention. As the expert on unemployment and industrial stabilization among a group of dissident congressional progressives, La Follette planned his investigation with the aid of Sidney Hillman, George Soule, Harlow Person of the Taylor Society, and other academicians familiar with the problems of industrial reform.[58] The hearings on a national economic planning council which he conducted in October, November, and December, 1931, indicated widespread favorable support for this idea, especially from the business community. Of the employers who testified, nearly all had been associated with the New Emphasis campaigns of the 1920's.[59] Unlike the Wagner-Hebert hearings, which were conducted at the same time, those of the La Follette subcommitee proceeded without hindrance. The results nevertheless were the same. From business-men, labor leaders, and students of industrial relations the demand for reform, along lines that the management experts had pioneered in the 1920's, overwhelmed the Hoover Administration.

Meanwhile the Swope plan and Harriman committee report brought relations between the Administration and the progressive em-ployers to a crisis stage. In direct contradiction to the President's "sec-ond program," the business leaders demanded that the ideas implicit in the work of the Survey Conference of 1930 be respected and ex-tended. For his part Hoover reacted as he had to the advocates of un-employment insurance who had taken his rhetoric too seriously. He condemned the Swope plan, had his attorney general privately attest to its unconstitutionality, and relegated it to his lengthening list of "col-lectivist ideas gleaned from the Socialists, the Communists, and the Fascists."[60] To a cabinet officer he denounced "price fixing and control of distribution," the "organization of gigantic trusts," "complete mo-nopolies," and "decay of American industry" implicit in the Swope plan.[61] Together with the growing demands for federal relief, national planning, unemployment insurance, and various other costly—and com-pulsory—legislative proposals, the defection of the Chamber of Com-merce, which had been his handmaid of voluntary cooperation the pre-vious year, angered and embittered the President. Though he may have been correct in his accusations, he realized too late that he could not, with his modest program, direct the reform movements which he had helped initiate in 1929–30.

This split between progressive management and the White House widened appreciably during Hoover's last year in the Presidency. Rather than relenting, the heretical businessmen only intensified their activities, and other more conservative business leaders joined them. The NAM and the National Industrial Conference Board, in addition to advocating unemployment reserves as a stabilization device, gener-ally endorsed the planning proposals of Swope and the Harriman committee.[62] But the conflict between the Chamber of Commerce and the President overshadowed Hoover's relations with the rest of the business community. The election of Harriman to the chamber's presi-dency in 1932 did not help the situation; advocating a strong program of government action as well as the 1931 report on stabilization, Harri-man soon broke with the President. Hoover later recalled: "During the campaign of 1932, Henry I. Harriman . . . urged that I agree to sup-port these proposals [the Report on Continuity in Business and Employment] informing me that Mr. Roosevelt had agreed to do so. I tried to show him that this stuff was sheer fascism . . . and refused to agree to any of it. He informed me that in view of my attitude, the business world would support Roosevelt with money and influence."[63] Denied the opportunity to introduce their plans under a Republican Administration, many progressive businessmen worked for the election of a Democratic President. Their search ended with the National Industrial Recovery Act, participation in the planning councils of the National Recovery Administration and the Commerce Department, and, finally, a voice in the formulation of the unemployment insurance provisions of the Social Security Act.

New Opportunities for Reform

REFORMERS AND social workers felt the impact of the Depression in much the same way as politicians and business leaders. Increased unemployment forced new responsibilities upon them, but it also provided opportunities for constructive action. After a decade of relative obscurity, reformers found they had an audience, and social workers, clergymen, and other promoters of humanitarian causes gained new prestige in handling the massive relief efforts. Gradually these groups turned from the problems of the moment to more basic reforms, particularly reforms that would provide economic security for the workingman. After studying the tragedies of enforced idleness firsthand, they resolved to find a substitute for the makeshift, charity "doles" of the early Depression years. Almost without exception they turned to unemployment insurance as a permanent device for alleviating the hardship of the jobless. At first they accepted the New Emphasis, albeit without much enthusiasm. But as time passed unemployment prevention seemed increasingly inappropriate to the needs of the jobless. To the distress of Andrews and his business allies, the economic developments which made reform possible also created countervailing forces that threatened the work of a decade and a half.

Between 1928 and 1930 the proponents of unemployment insurance legislation displayed a rare willingness to cooperate in approaching their common goal. By virtue of his tireless efforts to promote labor legislation during the unfriendly 1920's, Andrews became the acknowledged spokesman of this rejuvenated movement. He brought to this role his long experience and a belief in the feasiblility of unemployment prevention that had been formed twenty years before and tested in the interim. Not that dissident voices were entirely absent from the uppermost ranks of reformers. Wolman, thought the author of the Amalgamated's plans, was skeptical of the Huber bill. It overemphasized prevention, he maintained, and a few other economists shared his doubts.[64] Leiserson, despite his Wisconsin training and his experience with the ACWA, expressed even stronger reservations about the New Emphasis. He bemoaned the fact that while employment stabilization produced higher, more stable incomes for skilled workers, it also reduced the opportunities for marginal employees. He expected increased relief demands from the "older, slower and less efficient workers.[65] And a young reformer, Abraham Epstein, who was schooled in the old age pension movement, criticized the "beclouded atmosphere" which resulted from Andrews' emphasis on prevention.[66] Yet in 1930–32 these objections were restrained and failed to disturb the activities of the Association for Labor Legislation.

Andrews took advantage of this unparalleled opportunity to formulate an unemployment insurance plan that would put his united backing to good use. While the association was publicizing the Wagner bills of 1930, he began to consider a bill that permitted the states considerable latitude in drafting specific legislation, and urged Couzens and Wagner to study such a scheme. The initial battle, Andrews well knew, would be waged in the state legislatures; hence the importance of a model bill that would command the support of reformers throughout the country and yet be acceptable to hesitant or conservative legislators. The exigencies of the political atmosphere of 1930 thus determined the nature of the "American plan" for unemployment insurance.

Under Andrews' guidance the AALL sponsored a series of conferences during 1930 to draw up a suitable state bill. Included in these discussions, which began in the spring and ran intermittently until late autumn, were most of the officers and advisors of the association. Primary responsibility for the actual drafting fell to Joseph Chamberlain of Columbia University, Bernard Shientag, former New York Commissioner of Labor, Bryce Stewart, Olga Halsey, and Wolman. But many others, including Paul Douglas, Hillman, Draper, Leeds, Dennison, Miss Perkins, and Commons, and even William Beveridge, took part in the discussions. Although the product of these deliberations was necessarily a compromise plan, Andrews exercised his influence and position to good advantage. He later recalled one occasion when they considered the basic provisions for a state bill: "At the opening of the conference . . . I made a statement . . . which . . . directed the discussion from the very beginning to the advantages of the Wisconsin [Huber] plan."[67] Because of Andrews' efforts and the commitment of many AALL members to the prevention theory, the bill that resulted closely resembled the Huber approach, despite the former's boast that "very great improvements" had been made. By late September the work was virtually completed, although the American plan was not officially released to the public until December. As Andrews maintained, this bill was based on the idea of "applying our practical American experience with accident compensation to the problem of unemployment."[68]

Yet the fact that the American plan was a "composite and represents the reasoned conclusions of the group" proved a weakness rather than a strength.[69] On two key issues, the type of state fund to be established and the question of contributions—who should make them and at what rate—the AALL found that it was impossible to reach a consensus among reformers. On the former the committee members decided that individual company reserves (i.e., the future Groves bill) should be opposed in favor of a single state-wide fund with refunds to employers who prevented unemployment, and exemptions for others who could meet the established rates. They reached this decision at the August meeting when Chamberlain, Shientag, William Mack, the former impartial chairman of the Cleveland clothing industry, and Douglas were present. None of these men were employers and Douglas in particular was rapidly becoming disillusioned with the New Emphasis. Andrews explained the reasoning behind their decision: "As for the financial stimulus to prevention, the Association is relying upon the refund to employers upon their individual experience. . . . I realize the premiums varying with the risk in the industry and in the individual plant would carry this incentive still further but it has been omitted because of the tactical advantage of assuring employers in advance of a definite and modest cost."[70] Employers closely associated with the AALL such as Draper, Lewisohn, and Leeds took a different view of the "tactical advantage" of such a scheme. Draper reflected their dissatisfaction with this provision when he complained that the American plan did not explicitly punish the wasteful employer, the primary purpose of all unemployment prevention plans.[71]

On the second proposition, "assuring employers," as Andrews explained it, "of a modest cost," the American plan also ran into trouble. The AALL experts agreed that the benefit payments should be based entirely on the contribution of employers; at the same time they set the employer's rate at a modest 1.5 percent of his payroll. While the fixed figure worried the management representatives, the low rate and meager benefit provisions (60 percent of wages not to exceed $10 weekly for a maximum of thirteen weeks a year) annoyed the social workers and economists who were more interested in adequate compensation than incentives for employers. In later years, when fierce battles raged between the reformers over these provisions, observers unfamiliar with the nature of the disputes wrongly credited them to the hair-splitting of "theorists" and impractical professors. While personal animosity inevitably became involved, more basic issues were at stake. Upon the outcome of these conflicts rested, in large degree, the long-cherished premises of management-oriented reform and unemployment prevention.

For the time being, however, Andrews won a respite from the impending conflict. The American plan, released to the press in December, received the paeans of reformers as an important step toward the establishment of compulsory unemployment insurance. The AALL convention, held in Cleveland in conjunction with the meetings of the American Association for the Advancement of Science, the American Association of Social Workers, and similar groups, marked the high point of Andrews' influence in the drive for unemployment reform legislation. He presided over informal gatherings of social insurance experts ranging from Leiserson and Douglas to Commons and Wolman, and personally arranged the impressive public sessions. His presence was felt not only in the AALL meetings but in those of the other social science groups. "Running through the three days," a local newspaper predicted, "there will be almost constant references to a bill . . . [to establish] unemployment reserve funds by the same procedure now used for workmen's compensation."[72] The climax of the convention was a banquet on the final evening and the discussion of "Immediate Problems in Unemployment Legislation." A number of prominent people attended and a host of labor-legislation experts spoke, but the position of honor was reserved for the reformers' congressional spokesman, Senator Wagner. Characteristically, he demanded greater "organization and control" to prevent unemployment while he bemoaned the degradation of the jobless worker, all to the immense satisfaction of his audience.[73]

Events soon showed that the spirit of goodwill and harmony, so evident at the Cleveland convention, could not hide the basic theoretical differences that split the reformers' ranks. An indication of the weakness of Andrews' consensus and the compromised position that the American plan had placed the association in was the reaction of the new generation of Wisconsin reformers. Much to Andrews' annoyance, Raushenbush attacked the American plan as a distortion of the prevention principle, which was at that time receiving a new and more drastic formulation in the Groves bill.[74] Andrews was shocked at the intransigent position of the Wisconsin group; after all, the AALL plan was little more than a modified Huber bill. This conflict, while short-lived, was nevertheless symbolic; as the economic situation worsened, reform sentiment polarized around extreme positions. Andrews found it more and more difficult to maintain his balance between the two sides, and suffered accordingly.

Indicative of the growing strength of the reformers who emphasized the wage-earner rather than the businessman in planning legislation was the outcome of a unique experiment at Swarthmore College. As early as 1925 Morris Cooke had, on the advice of Justice Brandeis, discussed the possibility of an unemployment research center with Frank Aydelotte, president of Swarthmore. But no substantive action was taken until 1929, when Swarthmore authorities obtained large contributions for the project from Samuel Fels, a businessman-philanthropist, and most likely from Leeds and other Philadelphia employers also.[75] In accordance with the business orientation of the project, Fels, Cooke, and Harlow Person were selected for the advisory committee.[76] During the spring of 1930 Aydelotte tried to get Leiserson to direct the study but turned to Douglas when he refused. The latter's work as head of the Swarthmore unemployment research center in 1930–31 established his reputation as an authority on unemployment insurance. He advised numerous state bodies on legislation and drew up several reports. But it also established him as an articulate supporter of insurance rather than reserves. As he reported in *The Problem of Unemployment*, unemployment insurance was no different from any other method of "providing financial protection against great risk through the accumulation of pooled reserves."[77] Thus the Swarthmore project, initiated by New Emphasis businessmen, ultimately provided additional backing for the promoters of a European-style system of social insurance.[78]

Yet the threat to the AALL and the New Emphasis reformers was less a result of desertions from their ranks than the awakening or growth of previously apolitical or politically insignificant groups. Social workers, women's clubs, and religious leaders had taken stands on social reform measures before the war, though seldom on unemployment insurance. During the 1920's they turned away from the arena of politics to continue their humanitarian work in other areas. But the Depression overwhelmed the private and municipal social welfare agencies and undermined much of their past progress. Finally, often reluctantly, many social workers and clergymen turned to the state and federal governments for relief and, in many instances, for reform. Besides their need for financial assistance, they often turned back to politics in order to vent their indignation at an economic system which permitted the Depression—a response characteristic of many clergymen. While only infrequently embracing political radicalism, they vigorously expressed their alienation from the business culture of the past decade. All of this spelled additional trouble for the American plan and unemployment prevention.

No group of American reformers felt the impact of the Depression more directly than the settlement workers. While most concerned with relief problems, they also discussed, studied, and eventually endorsed unemployment insurance legislation. This process began with a session on unemployment at the 1928 convention of the National Federation of Settlements where, after listening to Person and Isaac M. Rubinow, the delegates created a committee, headed by Helen Hall and Irene Hickok Nelson, to report on the problem of unemployment. The committee published reports in 1929 and 1930 that revealed the shocking degree of joblessness during the early Depression years. Yet the NFS study was short on specific solutions; it called for a federal employment office system, "employment stabilization," and "some form of insurance against . . . unemployment" without suggesting details.[79] Though the NFS did not officially endorse a federal social insurance program until 1933, many of its members were outspoken advocates of unemployment insurance legislation after 1930.[80]

The National Conference of Social Workers, a larger group than the settlement leaders, followed a similar course. The social workers first considered jobless benefits at their 1931 convention; Andrews was pleased that the American plan was the "one most generally supported."[81] A more objective observer probably would have concluded, however, that the social workers favored any system that promised results. As John A. Lapp, one of the delegates, maintained, unemployment was a "social disease" that could be combated through national planning, public works, and insurance to maintain purchasing power.[82] Two years later the National Conference endorsed national planning, unemployment insurance legislation, and other welfare reforms without taking a stand on a particular unemployment system.[83] By that time the nation's social workers were a united force for unemployment insurance, preferably a national plan that would provide maximum benefits to the jobless.

While the settlement leaders and social workers were determining their policies, other groups of a similar character also endorsed unemployment insurance. Florence Kelley of the National Consumers League had long been an advocate of jobless benefit payments and had publicly backed the Huber bill. She stated in 1930 that the league was "committed to the form of unemployment insurance advocated by Dr. Commons."[84] Members of the Consumers League aided the AALL's state campaigns in the early 1930's. Yet the most vigorous attack on the American plan and the prevention theory, the Ohio movement of

1930–36, was organized and directed under the auspices of the Consumers League of Ohio. The league's main concern like that of most women's groups was immediate aid to the jobless, rather than the promotion of internecine conflicts among the experts. In 1932–33 the League of Women Voters, the Young Women's Christian Association, and the National Federation of Business and Professional Women's Clubs endorsed unemployment insurance without advocating a specific plan.[85]

Among organizations which were associated with or sought the support of the labor movement there was often greater willingness to accept unemployment insurance than in the unions themselves. The Women's Trade Union League endorsed it in 1922 after a brief discussion of the merits of government versus industry-financed plans. Two years later the convention reaffirmed its support "in principle," but took no action until 1931–32.[86] At that time most of the members favored a prevention plan but, to avoid dissension, the executive board merely noted that the league had supported some form of benefits for a decade.[87] There was less equivocation on the part of the People's Lobby, a haphazard reform group founded in 1931 by John Dewey and Benjamin Marsh. The lobby had little patience with anything favored by businessmen; it demanded a national system of benefits that would alleviate the suffering of the poor and jobless.[88] Finally, the leaders of the Socialist Party, Norman Thomas and James Maurer (Maurer had endorsed Andrews' bills while president of the Pennsylvania State Federation of Labor), called for unemployment insurance in their 1928 and 1932 platforms.[89] Although this demand probably added few votes to their slim total, it indicated the growing radical tenor of the campaigns for jobless benefits.

Probably of even greater significance was the increased interest of the nation's religious leaders. The Federal Council of Churches and the Catholic Bishops had supported unemployment insurance as part of their postwar reconstruction programs, but in the 1920's even the liberal religious organizations had neglected social welfare legislation or had become involved in programs, such as prohibition, of dubious merit. The Depression, however, brought a remarkable resurgence of progressive and even radical sentiment. In late 1930 the National Catholic Welfare Conference issued a report calling for "unemployment insurance established by organized industries and failing that, state unemployment insurance."[90] The Federal Council followed this lead in 1931, when it rejected the employers' contentions that out-of-work benefits were too costly and demanded an insurance system.[91] The Central Conference of Jewish Rabbis also endorsed state-sponsored unemployment benefits.

Among the individual Protestant denominations there developed considerable enthusiasm for unemployment insurance between 1930 and 1932. As early as 1925 the Congregationalists had adopted an advanced program of social aims that advocated unemployment and other forms of social insurance, but most groups did not act until the Depression. The Methodist bishops took a strong pro-labor stand in 1930 and called for various forms of social insurance in their official statement of 1932. In 1931 the Northern Baptist Convention, Unitarian Churches, and Protestant Episcopal bishops concurred, and the Reformed and Presbyterian churches followed suit in 1932.[92] Commenting on the growing interest among religious leaders, the editors of the *Christian Century* noted the radically changed outlook of the denominations. "Two years go," they wrote, "such a system for guarding against the wastes of industry would have been greeted with derision."[93]

The awakening of social workers, professional reformers, and religious leaders to the plight of the unemployed and the necessity for social insurance, in the period between 1930 and 1932, was widespread but uncoordinated. Many voices demanded unemployment insurance; yet in the first years of the Depression there was no central organization to articulate these appeals except the AALL. Partly in response to this need, a number of liberal economists and labor-legislation experts took up the fight individually on behalf of the social workers and others who found the American Plan inadequate. In a few states such as Ohio these people formed a strong organization. In most areas, however, they spoke singly until 1933, when the American Association for Old Age Security, which Abraham Epstein had organized in 1926, changed its name to the American Association for Social Security and took up the fight for unemployment insurance. The groups that were dissatisfied with the low benefits and business approach of the AALL plan coalesced around Epstein and his organization. With the assistance of the labor movement, which had been going through a transformation more radical than that of the other groups, they formed a powerful alternative force to Andrews and the New Emphasis orientation of his work.

Organized Labor in Transition

WHILE THE Depression increased the numbers and prestige of the reformers, social workers, and clergymen, it had precisely the opposite effect on the American labor movement. Union membership, already decimated by the decline of coal, textiles, and other man-ufacturing industries, dropped even further after 1929. The threat of extermination was a factor in revising AFL policy toward government interference in employment conditions. But more significant than the absolute loss in numbers was the incidence of unemployment. Many craft workers who had enjoyed steady employment or had been subject to predictable layoffs now fought for their very jobs—and often lost. This process eventually undermined the federation's traditional policy and provided many recruits for the social workers' approach to unem-ployment insurance. Ironically, this development occurred after the old guard in the AFL had completed its identification with the New Emphasis.

The enthusiastic acceptance of the businessmen's approach by the AFL executive council between 1928 and 1930 bore many of the same characteristics as its earlier policy shifts. Rather than a carefully con-ceived move to reform employment conditions, it was clearly a reaction to mounting unemployment among trade union members. The execu-tive council admitted in 1928 that "reports of unemployment reached headquarters with insistence and frequency," and Green, noting the rise in technological displacements, concluded that "this is the kernel of the unemployment problem."[94] The executive council called for "an approach to the problem that promises more lasting results than all others—stabilization of industry. Responsibility for solving this prob-lem devolves primarily upon management. However . . . by coopera-tion with management in eliminating wastes and development of better technical procedure, the trade unions can help develop a stabiliza-tion of production that will bring regularity of work."[95] Green, more-over, now went a step further. In 1928 he argued not only that stabili-zation was the "final answer" but that "something must be done to protect those who suffer each year from loss of work." In 1929 he pro-posed out-of-work benefits and regularized work as the "two main ap-proaches" to alleviating unemployment.[96] Still, neither he nor the other federation officers systematically developed the idea that unem-ployment insurance could induce stabilization. At best they took a greater interest in the plans devised by individual unions, publishing descriptions of them in the *American Federationist* and suggesting that the constituent unions consider these methods.

Just as many of the management reformers opposed compulsory un-employment insurance before the Depression, so the AFL leaders con-tinued to adhere to voluntarism, despite their belated interest in union-financed plans. The question of jobless insurance did not arise in 1928–29, but the AFL leadership did consider old-age pension laws, and these discussions provide many clues to the federation's later stand on unemployment benefits. In 1929 the AFL convention's committee on resolutions, headed by Matthew Woll and Victor Olander, two old-guard leaders, recommended an agressive campaign for state pension legislation. To John Frey's objection that this would divert attention from organizing and fighting the yellow-dog contract, Woll asked: "Am I to understand . . . that we should not take any interest in that form of social legislation or any other? Surely they affect all life and the conditions of life of the wage earners." But Frey warned of the dangers of such an approach: "We might well keep in mind the fact that we have in our country many well-minded people who advocate a state sick insurance and who advocate unemployment insurance, and much of the argument which would support one of these forms of insurance would support the other."[97] The convention, however, endorsed the committee recommendation, proving once again that voluntarism meant what the officers decided it meant.

Green and the federation hierarchy gave their support to the New Emphasis just in time to back many of the business-oriented proposals of 1929–30. The unionists were pleased with the President's call for the maintenance of existing wage levels and Green thought that Hoover's inspirational meetings with businessmen had definitely improved the economic situation.[98] At the same time the union leaders backed Wagner's three unemployment bills, which included much of their program of 1928–29. Green even maintained that the federation was giving its "earnest attention" to the question of unemployment insurance. But the obstacles, he added, were formidable; a constitutional amendment would be necessary for federal legislation but, since workers moved from state to state and would lose their claims to benefits, federal legislation was necessary for uniformity.[99] In fact, the impediments to legislation were so great that he gave no hint that the federation's "earnest attention" would have any practical effect. The executive council, meeting in September 1930, agreed that "we cannot afford to commit the Federation to any definite conclusion until the subject is thoroughly studied."[100] This attitude, as well as the views of many AFL leaders, would have commanded a sympathetic hearing at many a Chamber of Commerce meeting.

The 1930 AFL convention revealed the wide disparity between the executive council's unemployment proposals and the actual endorsement of unemployment insurance legislation. "Labor's Unemployment Program," drawn up by the executive council, recited the ill effects of joblessness on the labor movement. It maintained that 21 percent of all union members were idle and in desperate need of relief. But, as

Green stated, the unionists must take a wider view of the problem. "Surely we can regularize the situation . . . so that men can be employed."[101] To achieve this end the executive council recommended reduced hours, more efficient management, public employment exchanges, better statistics, planned public works, vocational guidance and retraining, and a study of technological unemployment. Not a word on unemployment insurance appeared in "Labor's Program."

Several delegates, notably representatives of the Rhode Island State Federation of Labor, the International Wood Carvers' Union, the United Textile Workers, and the American Federation of Teachers, all of which had endorsed insurance legislation or were giving it serious consideration, noticed this discrepancy and called it to the delegates' attention. But their resolutions in favor of unemployment insurance legislation brought immediate objections from the officers. Olander attacked such schemes in the traditional terms; he predicted government control of the labor force, registration of the workers (he should have read Wagner's employment bureau bill more closely), and the loss of the worker's freedom.[102] Frey gave a more realistic explanation for the prejudice of the old guard. Recalling to a colleague the struggles of former years, he asserted "that my social and political, as well as my economic understanding, are practically the opposite of those held by socialists."[103]

The reasoning of the federation hierarchy, whether explicit or implicit, failed to satisfy many delegates. Henry Ohl expressed their impatience when he compared unemployment insurance legislation to accident compensation and denied it had any relation to the dole. But before the situation got out of hand Green intervened. He pointed out that the British system had failed and that American unionists, who were less powerful, would be unable to improve on the British record. He also explained the threat that union members would be forced to take jobs in nonunion industries. Finally he returned to the Gompers tradition: "The American workman, proud of his freedom and his liberty, is not yet willing to make himself a ward of the government."[104] The convention referred the disputed resolutions to the executive council for study, thus temporarily ending the incipient revolt. The consequences of this short confrontation were nevertheless far-reaching. Indeed, these few dissenters had begun the key debate over the most important issue affecting the labor movement since the 1890's—the future of voluntarism.

The most vocal challenge to the executive council's unemployment insurance policy in 1930–31 came from an admittedly radical group, the Conference for Progressive Labor Action. Largely composed of

unionists and intellectuals associated with the labor-education movement of the 1920's, persons like A. J. Muste and Israel Mufson, the
CPLA was formed in 1929 to "educate the workers to demand a complete program of social insurance."[105] By mid-1930 the radicals had
narrowed this objective to the immediate aim of winning unemployment insurance legislation. In June the CPLA launched a "national
campaign," complete with street-corner speeches, a model bill (which
was apparently a copy of the AALL bill for a federal-state system that
Wagner introduced in December), and a cross-country auto trip designed to publicize unemployment benefits and to undermine the executive council's position.[106] Due to the CPLA's meager financial resources this campaign quickly aborted and Muste, Mufson, and the
other radicals confined their efforts to the New York area. Henceforth
this noisy faction was more a nuisance than a threat to the AFL—stag-
ing meetings to discuss the weaknesses of the federation's program and
creating dissatisfaction among the more radical or desperate union
members.

Far more significant was the conversion of a large number of ortho-
dox union leaders to unemployment insurance legislation in 1930–31.
The International Association of Machinists, the first major conservative AFL union to take this step, had approved the Huber bill in 1927
and officially endorsed unemployment insurance a year later.[107] Arthur
Wharton, president of the Machinists, thereafter became a leading advocate of unemployment insurance legislation at executive council
meetings. The Teachers, Hosiery and Textile Workers, Lithographers,
Telegraphers, Pocket Book Makers, Railroad Clerks, and Wood Carvers joined the Machinists and Ladies' Garment, Fur, and Cap Workers
in backing compulsory unemployment insurance in 1930.[108] Many state
and city labor organizations were even more enthusiastic. City centrals
in Indianapolis, Flint, Elmira, Schenectady, Newport, and Providence;
the United Hebrew Trades of New York; and state federations in New
York, Pennsylvania, Minnesota, Montana, Rhode Island, Utah, and
California, in addition to Wisconsin, adopted resolutions favoring unemployment insurance legislation in 1930. The Massachusetts State
Federation of Labor and, significantly, the influential Teamsters and
Printing Pressmen joined this growing list the following year.[109] Even
the powerful Illinois State Federation of Labor, Olander's usually loyal
constituency, decided "not to entirely close the subject until after the
American Federation of Labor acts."[110] Clearly the AFL would have to
act or face further defections.

Green, an able politician if not a dynamic leader, adopted an ambiguous position with statements objecting to unemployment insurance

on practical rather than philosophical grounds. "As authorized by the Boston [1930] convention we are giving the matter careful thought and study. We do not want to jump at conclusions regarding legislation of this kind in advance of an analysis of different plans proposed. Many recommendations have been made by well-meaning people but which we consider impracticable. Labor . . . must not have forced upon it something which on the surface appears to be practical and workable but which would in operation rob it of economic freedom."[111] In reply to Andrews' persistent inquiries he explained that the AFL disliked the British scheme but had no alternative. "Until we have concluded our study," he explained, "we are not prepared to express approval of any plan."[112] In the meantime he led the executive council in considering various proposals, despite the skepticism of many members. Noting that many of labor's friends favored unemployment insurance legislation "because it seems to appeal to an ideal, perfect and workable," Green warned nevertheless that many unionists would support it at the 1931 convention unless the federation could convince employers to reduce the work week. He joined the other old-guard members in calling for an ultimatum to business: create jobs or be prepared for compulsory unemployment insurance.[113]

The officers' report to the 1931 convention reflected both their skepticism and their awareness of the growing pressure from the rank and file for some type of unemployment insurance. The council members contrasted unemployment prevention with "policies that crystallize unemployment and habits of accepting it as inevitable," meaning the British and German experiences which they judged to be "unsuited" to the United States. They asserted that management would be responsible if jobless insurance laws were passed, and concluded that the only alternative, and from their point of view the only satisfactory policy, was a shorter work week.[114]

But the delegates, at least a third of whom strongly favored unemployment insurance legislation, were in no mood for equivocation. Dissatisfied with the timidity of the federation, they were also encouraged by the action of the metal-trades department, which had virtually endorsed compulsory unemployment benefits at its preconvention meeting.[115] The dissidents were thus incensed when the resolutions committee, under Woll and Olander, not only agreed with the executive council but added a long antagonistic statement on the inviolability of the workers' freedom. In return for "a slice of bread—a mess of pottage," the report cried, the workers were "to yield up their birthright." James A. Duncan of the Seattle Central Labor Council dismissed the work of Woll and Olander as a "ghost story," since many

AFL bodies had already endorsed unemployment insurance legislation. This charge and Woll's reply, which was as melodramatic as the resolutions report, ignited one of the most explosive debates in AFL history. Charges and accusations were hurled by both sides. Andrew Furuseth, the ageless leader of the seamen, foresaw the "destruction of existing governments" if unemployment insurance was adopted. Yet he agreed that the resolutions committee "does not tell us how to get bread nor does the Executive Council." Representatives of the Teachers, Street Railway Workers, and Post Office Clerks led the opposition to the old guard. But Daniel Tobin of the Teamsters, ostensibly a supporter, provided little assistance in a vague and ambiguous speech.[116]

At the end of the debate Green cast his vote with the executive council and resolutions committee—at least temporarily. In an emotional speech he decried the evils of the public employment offices that would accompany unemployment insurance. State officials, he charged, would place unionists in nonunion shops. Yet he remained sufficiently ambiguous to straddle both positions. "Let us build our nation first," he proposed, "and then think about coming forward along more progressive social-justice lines."[117] Unlike other federation leaders, Green offered the delegates an immediate alternative to unemployment insurance. He promised to get "millions, billions if necessary" from Congress in relief appropriations. This speech settled the issue, at least for 1931, and the convention approved the resolutions committee's report.[118]

But the old guard had little reason to celebrate. The continuation of the Depression made all union members more conscious of the need for some measure of economic security. The powerful United Mine Workers, moreover, endorsed unemployment insurance in February 1932. Internal dissension, inability to control more than a fraction of the total number of mine workers, and the political conservatism of John L. Lewis, the Miners' president, had kept the UMW from considering it in the past. At their 1932 convention, however, the Miners called on their officers and the AFL for action. It was, as the chairman of the resolutions committee had predicted, "the most important question that will come before this convention." Thomas Kennedy, secretary of the UMW, indicated the significance of this move for the labor movement: "I speak for the International officers as a whole—we are going into the American Federation of Labor Convention for the purpose of putting this program over."[119] The desertion of the Miners from the voluntarists' camp, coupled with the continued decline of the economy, had a decisive impact on AFL policy.

When he learned of the Miners' decision, Green saw the handwriting on the wall. By April, in contrast to his past position, he considered unemployment insurance an immediate issue. "If we can formulate some constructive plan through the creation of reserves . . . without endangering the standing, efficiency and propriety of our labor movement," he wrote to Frank Duffy, a member of the executive council, "I am quite willing to subscribe to such a plan." He proposed to bring up the subject at the July executive council meeting "in a very clear and definite way."[120] It was Duffy, however, who first warned the council members that they had better act. Green also urged that they adopt a more positive policy "because of the growing demand to do something."[121] After Wharton suggested that the AFL favor federal rather than state legislation, the council assigned Green to prepare a bill for introduction in Congress which would protect the rights of unionists to refuse open-shop jobs and retain their benefit rights. Beyond this point the AFL leaders were undecided, and Green shared their indecision. "Whether I shall propose that the Federal Government contribute as well as employers and employees I cannot say at this time," he told reporters. "It may be that it will be sufficient for industry and the workers to make joint contributions."[122] Despite his previous enthusiasm for unemployment prevention, the federation's president had absorbed little of the businessmen's theory.

Once the executive council had acted, Green wasted no time in implementing their decision. With remarkable diligence for a long-time foe of unemployment insurance, he pursued his task, writing Duffy that "it is my intention to go into the subject of unemployment insurance in a very comprehensive and careful way."[123] By late September he had completed his study and, according to Andrews, had given up the idea of a national plan.[124] To help in the preparation of a specific bill Green invited a group of prominent economists and labor legislation experts, including Witte, Raushenbush, Leiserson, Chamberlain, Frankfurter, Donald Richberg, the labor lawyer, and Francis Sayre of Harvard University, to meet in Washington in mid-October. In a statement drafted by Sayre, this group endorsed state legislation with the "underlying object" of securing "compensation for those temporarily out of employment" until Witte and several others, unhappy at this peremptory rejection of the prevention approach, prevailed upon Green to delete this section.[125] The final AFL plan called for state legislation and employer contributions, but stated no preference between the reserves and pooled systems.

Although the supporters of unemployment insurance legislation now had the upper hand, the old guard waged a desperate rear-guard struggle to preserve the principle of voluntarism at the 1932 convention. Woll and Olander, who controlled the all-important resolutions committee, directed this effort. Obviously the old-guard leaders would have little chance to sway the delegates with appeals to principle in the face of increased rank-and-file pressure for government action. But their veto power over convention resolutions might enable them to emasculate the executive council's plan. When the prospect of Woll and his associates thwarting the delegates' will became known, the convention was thrown into turmoil. John L. Lewis, attacking the men whose views he had long shared, pledged to fight to the end for unemployment insurance. More diplomatic was Green, who urged the resolutions committee to adopt a conciliatory approach. The long-awaited document emphasized the need for "continuity of employment" together with safeguarding "the freedom and liberty" of the worker. This was a clue to the following section: "In recommending general approval of the foregoing proposals, we do so in the light of the previous declarations by conventions . . . and we recommend that where there is found to be conflict with previous declarations, that the Executive Council be authorized to alter such proposals in accordance with previous declarations."[126] On the convention floor Olander, Furuseth, and Charles Howard fought for this position. Frey then offered a crippling amendment providing that until the states actually enacted jobless benefit laws, the AFL would confine its activities to reducing the work day and raising wages. Kennedy, representing the insurgents, objected that Frey's proposal was out of order and Green, reconciled to the new policy, agreed with him.[127]

Green's action was indicative of the mood of the convention. Unlike 1930 or even 1931 the majority of delegates realized, perhaps reluctantly, that rank and file pressure, expressed through the actions of the individual unions and city and state organizations, could no longer be ignored. Robert Watt, president of the Massachusetts State Federation and a leader of the younger, more militant, unionists, summarized the exasperation of the local leaders. He objected not only to the intransigence of the old guard but to the irresolute policy of the executive council. "There are many, even of the union men . . . who will never see it brought about; that is, if we go about it at the same rate we have gone with other pieces of special legislation."[128] In contrast to Watt were the moderate UMW leaders whose belated affirmation of unemployment insurance symbolized the growing restlessness of the workers. Lewis, Kennedy, and Philip Murray, the Miners' vice-president, had earlier issued a statement asserting that insecure employment was the greatest impediment to their organizing efforts. Opposition to unemployment insurance was, in their words, a "foolish" policy; instead they chose the "sane, sensible step."[129] Green also reflected the moderate approach in his speeches. He mollified the old guard with reassurances that jobless insurance was the best way to protect organized labor and that labor would only support bills that protected union membership, placed the full financial burden on industry, and paid substantial benefits. After what must have seemed to many an interminable debate, Green put the question to a vote. The conclusion was foregone; he declared that the convention approved unemployment insurance legislation by an "overwhelming margin."[130]

With this decision the AFL ended a long history of opposition to social insurance legislation. It also began a new era in which its leaders often fought as hard for labor legislation as they had previously fought against it. But there was another, narrower but hardly less significant meaning of labor's new policy. Voluntarism, sometimes referred to as labor's version of laissez faire, paralleled labor's version of the New Emphasis. Just as the Depression forced reconsideration of the former, so it dictated a reevaluation of the latter. Increasingly after 1932 the state labor leaders abandoned the businessmen's approach to unemployment reform and allied themselves with liberal politicians, social workers, and other humanitarian groups. As pressure for legislative action mounted in the states, their demand was for benefits first, and prevention if and when it was feasible.

8 | LEGISLATION IN THE STATES

DESPITE THE impact of Senator Wagner's work in Congress, the awakening of politicians, reformers, businessmen, and union leaders to the importance of unemployment insurance was apparent first on the state level. While Congress debated the modest Wagner bills and their successors, the state capitals became the scenes of long and often bitter conflicts over the feasibility of unemployment insurance and, more significantly, over whether or not it should be designed to coerce the employer as well as compensate the worker. In Wisconsin, where reformers were able to achieve and maintain reasonable unity, the campaign quickly resolved into a contest between the state's organized employers and the Commons-Raushenbush-labor coalition. In other states the situation was more complex, as formidable divisions appeared in the ranks of both the reformers and their opponents. These divisions often involved local issues and personalities, but ultimately centered around the all-important question in the struggle for unemployment insurance legislation—the validity of the New Emphasis tradition of the 1920's. Several examples are particularly illustrative of these problems: reformers in Massachusetts and Ohio took extreme positions on the question of unemployment prevention while those of New York, the nation's foremost industrial state, were forced to wage a more complex campaign—one that indicated the wide range of difficulties that inhered in such an undertaking.

New Yorkers were not entirely unfamiliar with unemployment insurance on the eve of the Depression. Pre–World War I reformers had considered it on various occasions. The 1912 Progressive Party had endorsed unemployment insurance as part of an overall program of social insurance, and the Second New York City Mayor's Committee on Un-

162

employment of 1916–17 concluded in its January 1917 report that unemployment insurance was "inapplicable" in the United States until a better employment office system was developed. In a second report published in December the Mayor's Committee proposed that employers plan their operations to reduce employment fluctuations but concluded that unemployment insurance might still be required.[1] During the 1920's at least five bills were introduced in the New York legislature, none of which attracted appreciable support. Opposition from the labor movement, the absorption of progressives in less ambitious tasks, and public apathy doomed unemployment insurance legislation in New York, as they did elsewhere.

Overshadowing these activities after 1929 was the presence of Franklin D. Roosevelt, who as governor was responsible for promoting a host of new ideas for combating the Depression. Although a former progressive politician, Roosevelt's unemployment policies, insofar as they had an historical basis, were the product of his business experiences during the 1920's.[2] While he had, as head of the building industry's trade association, condemned irregular employment, his career as an insurance executive was also important in its effect on his thinking. He once wrote, somewhat facetiously, that "the little tin god I worship is called 'actuarial table,'" and described himself as a "hard boiled" insurance man.[3] For the most part, however, his business activities were ephemeral and his interest superficial. Several events of his pre-Depression gubernatorial career of 1929–30 probably did more to familiarize him with current thinking on industrial stabilization and social insurance. The ladies' garment industry dispute of 1929, which arose over the breakdown of contract negotiations, brought calls from the Governor for "stabilization" and more regular work. With the help of Herbert Lehman, his lieutenant governor, he appointed a new mediation group that eventually worked out an amicable settlement.[4] More important was Roosevelt's interest in a genuine old-age pension system, an interest that led him to appoint an advisory committee in 1929 and work for pension legislation in 1930. Abraham Epstein felt he had "assumed remarkable leadership" in this endeavor.[5] Particularly in view of Roosevelt's later insistence that pensions and unemployment insurance be combined in a single bill, his activities of 1929–30 were noteworthy, and revealed his eclecticism and humanitarian spirit.

The Governor's first response to the Depression again indicated his penchant for immediate action and his regard for the conservatism of the electorate. He suggested a number of relief measures of unprecedented scope, but for long-range solutions he turned to industry and the New Emphasis. He compared employment stabilization with the accident prevention campaign of an earlier period and defined his purpose as desiring "to assist employers of this state in gradual progress toward stabilization based on authentic American business experience."[6] To this end he appointed a Committee on Stabilization of Industry for the Prevention of Unemployment, consisting of several industrial leaders familiar with employment problems—Henry Bruere, Ernest Draper, and John Sullivan, president of the New York State Federation of Labor. When the Bruere Committee presented its preliminary report calling for adoption of the slogan, "steady work the year around" by employers, and recited the achievements of Procter, Hapgood, and other New Emphasis businessmen, he praised it as a "splendid" study and pledged his support for the work of the committee.[7]

Roosevelt continued his identification with the stabilization movement through 1930 by his association with the Bruere Committee, his official voice on unemployment prevention. Bruere and his colleagues publicized the efforts of imaginative employers and emphasized the industrial nature of joblessness. They called for voluntary activities reminiscent of the management-reform campaigns of the 1920's: the stimulation of off-season demand, continuous production based on planning and budgetary control, the development of "fill in" products, and a flexible work day in lieu of the layoff. They also reviewed company-financed unemployment insurance plans and warned that the state would act if industry hesitated.[8] Roosevelt encouraged this activity by stressing the necessity for "equilibrium of production and consumption," and added his voice to the increasingly common cry among employers for a planned economy.[9] His willingness to accept the rhetoric and endorse the program of the reformer-businessman accounted in large measure for sizable defections from Republican ranks in 1932 and afterward.

Without significantly expanding on these modest gestures Roosevelt used unemployment insurance—together with the host of other issues the Depression raised—to indicate his opposition to Hoover and to establish himself in the following months as a politician of national repute. His most daring move in this period came in a speech to the Governors' Conference in Salt Lake City during June, when he combined an attack on Republican extravagance with an appeal for old age pensions and unemployment insurance. Aligning himself with progressive businessmen, he rejected the "dole" and urged a self-supporting system based on employee and employer contributions. Although this speech provided valuable ammunition for reformers, it revealed neither a firm grasp of the issues involved nor a commitment to immediate action.[10] In August he made a similar plea to the New York

State Federation of Labor convention which was equally affirmative and equally noncommittal. He cited the European plans but once again rejected the "dole"; he called for tripartite contributions but compared unemployment benefits with workmen's compensation; and he demanded action along "business lines" but offered no specific suggestions. Finally he qualified his support by advocating an investigation rather than immediate legislation.[11] The convention endorsed "the sentiment expressed by the Governor" and the principle of compulsory jobless benefits.[12] In addition to having the desired political effect, this activity produced one concrete result, an Interstate Conference of Governors called to begin a "highly conservative study of the whole subject" of unemployment measures.[13] While the conference too had obvious political overtones, it promised to attack the problem of interstate competiton—the fear that new taxes on industry would only drive business to other states where production was less costly. A close observer, W. A. Warn, writing in the *New York Times,* reported that "some formula may be evolved at the Conference through which the leading industrial states in the East may take the lead for the inauguration of a nation wide system of unemployment insurance."[14]

The Interstate Conference of February 1931, the first regional attempt to deal with unemployment, made some progress toward fulfilling these expectations. The governors of Connecticut, Massachusetts, Rhode Island, and New Jersey attended in person, and Governors Gifford Pinchot of Pennsylvania and George White of Ohio sent representatives. Under Frances Perkins' direction Henry Bruere, Paul Douglas, and Paul Kellogg, editor of the *Survey,* drew up an agenda that covered every type of unemployment measure—public works, employment offices, relief, and unemployment insurance—but was weighted heavily toward the latter.[15] Bryce Stewart, Leo Wolman, William Leiserson, Joseph Chamberlain, Douglas, and other experts appeared to report on various aspects of unemployment insurance plans. But it is unlikely that their reports clarified Roosevelt's views—if indeed he wished to clarify his position. The conflict over unemployment prevention, which was emerging at that time, resulted in many differences of opinion among the experts. Leiserson, who spoke "with the greatest thoroughness and least shyness," rejected the idea of abolishing unemployment, although he did not dismiss the prevention theory: "we can diminish [unemployment] and we can mitigate the attendant suffering. Unemployment insurance is designed to do both." At the end of his statement Roosevelt asked how unemployment insurance related to old age pensions, and Leiserson, somewhat perplexed, replied that industry would contribute to both.[16] Wolman was less equivocal. He recited the

Amalgamated experience and stressed the virtues of the American plan, including the desirability of a reserves system over a pooled fund of unsegregated contributions. On the other hand Douglas represented the opposition to prevention. Skeptical of industry's ability to reduce unemployment, he emphasized the stabilizing effect of jobless benefits on purchasing power and minimized the value of the incentives provided by such a scheme.[17] The result was a firm affirmation of the need for unemployment insurance, but considerable dissension over the desirable features of a specific plan.

Though the Interstate Conference foreshadowed the serious differences that disrupted legislative campaigns in New York and elsewhere, it served Roosevelt's purposes remarkably well. As convener of the meeting he became known as an alert politician, sympathetic to the needs of the jobless, without alienating conservative Democrats. He also convinced his colleagues to appoint a committee, consisting of one representative from each state, to make the long-range study he had called for. He assured them that this group, which ultimately included Wolman, Leiserson, and A. Lincoln Filene, would contemplate no "dole" system of government subventions.[18] To his brother-in-law G. Hall Roosevelt he expressed his belief that unemployment insurance should be approached "from a business-like point of view."[19] In short he guided the conference toward his objectives without directly challenging the timidity—and prejudices—of the politicians involved.

While Roosevelt was getting political mileage from unemployment insurance, his activities helped stimulate interest in the New York legislature. The state's insurance companies sponsored legislation in 1931 to permit them to write protection against unemployment. The Dunmore bill, as their proposal was called, passed both houses in early April only to receive Roosevelt's veto on the grounds that it would preempt the Interstate Conference study.[20] At the same time Andrews was organizing a campaign for the American plan. To help in this effort he established the New York Conference for Unemployment Insurance Legislation, which for several years remained a major force in the state movement for unemployment insurance. Under the leadership of John Fitch, a writer and social worker, the conference opposed the efforts of the private insurance firms.[21] At the same time Andrews and his supporters persuaded State Senator Seabury C. Mastick and Assemblyman Irwin Steingut to introduce the American plan. At a hearing in late March an impressive group of reformers and a number of social workers favored the Mastick-Steingut bill. But the State Federation of Labor, under pressure from the AFL executive council, opposed it. Andrews bitterly complained that the "weak attitude" of the union leaders had doomed his bill.[22] As a consequence of the hearing the legislators scrapped the American plan and used Roosevelt's request for an investigation as a pretext to create a legislative committee headed by Assemblyman William L. Marcy to study unemployment insurance.[23]

By this act the lawmakers further confused an already complicated situation. In late May, shortly after the formation of the Marcy Committee, the interstate representatives held their first meeting to hear Miss Perkins call for the "retention of the best features" of the New Emphasis. Significantly, Leiserson was the only one of the experts who had reservations about unemployment prevention, and he was relegated to studying American plans and European experiences. Filene, on the other hand, headed the subcommittee on the "essential features of a sound insurance plan."[24] At the same time the Bruere Committee submitted its final report, which reviewed the efforts of various New York firms to stabilize employment, and the problems involved in the formulation of a system of unemployment insurance.[25]

As if these efforts were not sufficiently redundant, Roosevelt sent Labor Commissioner Perkins to Great Britain to study the "dole" in the summer of 1931. Mary W. Dewson, president of the New York Consumers League, contended that he took this step after she had appealed to Mrs. Roosevelt for action.[26] While private requests such as Miss Dewson's may have been a factor in the Governor's decision, it was characteristic of Roosevelt to create interest in a measure through simultaneous activity in many directions. In this case his action was particularly important, for Miss Perkins returned "fighting for unemployment insurance."[27] Rejecting the widespread belief that the British plan had corrupted the wage-earning class, she concluded that this system was "the basis of the tremendous improvement in the health, standard of living and morale of the English working people." Yet she admitted that the British had erred; poor relief was confused with insurance, actuarial principles had been disregarded, and politicians had expanded the coverage without regard for contributions. To remedy these evils she recommended concentration on cyclical rather than seasonal joblessness, limited payments, and the relation of benefits to reserves in accordance with insurance principles. But her most important conclusion, as far as future American efforts were concerned, was that "the technique of prevention of unemployment [is not] well enough understood at the present time, nor sufficiently encouraged by our economic system to make it wise or just to insist upon each industry bearing along the full cost of its unemployment. This is a social as well as an industrial problem, and the cost should be spread as widely as possible."[28]

Of greater immediate impact, however, were the efforts of the Interstate Conference Committee and the Marcy Committee. Whereas Miss Perkins, as head of a private investigation, concerned herself with social and economic considerations, these groups had, from their origin, realized the political implications of their studies. Wolman, as chairman of the Interstate Committee, was particularly sensitive to this fact. A favorable report, he explained, would "strengthen Roosevelt's hands considerably" in dealing with the legislature.[29] It might also have a positive effect on the Massachusetts stabilization committee, which favored unemployment prevention but sought added support. For this reason he was particularly disturbed when Leiserson refused to accede to Filene's recommendation of individual reserves. In the meantime most reformers suspected that political partisanship would make any positive recommendation by the Republican-dominated Marcy Committee unlikely. From the beginning Andrews had judged the legislative commission "heavily loaded against progress."[30] Yet the committee's hearings, which occupied most of November and December, had produced so many expressions of support for unemployment insurance that the nature of the lawmakers' report remained uncertain until early 1932.

The interstate representatives meanwhile submitted their recommendations on February 12, apparently before the Marcy Committee had completed its work. In what was undoubtedly the most important official endorsement of unemployment prevention, they gave their unequivocal support (except for Leiserson) to the New Emphasis approach. "A purpose of our proposal," the report read, "is to encourage the adoption of measures of prevention. The employers' financial liability under our plan should operate as a continuous incentive to prevent unemployment so far as practicable." In accord with this aim the report proposed an employer-financed individual reserve system similar to that provided in the Wisconsin law. It suggested the eventual possibility of industry-wide funds, but only after considerable experience with the reserves plan: "In so far then as unemployment is due to careless or indifferent management . . . the pooling of reserves may have the effect of perpetuating such uneconomic practice."[31] Roosevelt, in customary fashion, praised the report without committing himself to its provisions. He noted its "radical" departure from European schemes but denied that unemployment insurance could prevent recurrence of the Depression. "One definite thing it can do," he remarked, "is to alleviate . . . the extreme suffering which economic crises always occasion."[32] He did nevertheless urge the legislators on February 15 to take immediate action on the report and give the committee plan "a trial at the earliest possible moment."[33]

In a surprise move that negated much of the effect of Roosevelt's message, the Marcy Committee sent its report to the legislature on the same day. Unlike the Interstate Committee report, this document took an intermediate position: it rejected immediate enactment of a compulsory plan but did not rule out the eventual necessity for a reserves law. Instead, the Marcy study proposed a number of stopgap measures, including legislation to encourage voluntary employer-reserve systems and an appropriation to continue its investigation for another year.[34]

Andrews, who had worked with the minority Democrats on the Marcy Committee and realized the probable effect of its negative proposals on the Mastick-Steingut bill, decided that concessions were in order if unemployment insurance was to be salvaged in 1932. To take advantage of support for the Interstate Committee report, he redrafted the Mastick bill in late February to form a "merged bill including Mastick and Wisconsin features," but which made the all-important gesture to the Wisconsin reformers of including the individual reserves provision.[35] From this point unemployment prevention generally became synonymous with unemployment reserves and the differences between the advocates of prevention and the spokesmen for European-style unemployment insurance became more easily distinguishable. Roosevelt approved the new measure and Mastick and Steingut introduced it on February 2, only to find that the Republicans had united in favor of the Marcy report, with the hope of preventing the passage of any legislation.[36] When the Senate Finance and Labor Committees held hearings, Andrews led a large contingent of economists, social workers, and reformers in support of the bill, but their efforts proved futile; the legislature adjourned without acting, except to appropriate additional funds for the Marcy Committee.[37]

With the end of the legislative session Andrews immediately began to reorganize his battered coalition. Now committed to the compromise Mastick-Steingut bill, he attempted to align conservative support behind it. His first overtures were to Swope, whom he believed had sufficient influence over up-state lawmakers to determine the fate of any legislation. But the stubborn industrialist flatly refused to back any compulsory plan unless it included employee contributions. When Andrews protested that organized labor objected to contributions from the employees, Swope replied that he had talked to Matthew Woll and William Green and they had "nothing to present with reference to unemployment compensation," that "their opposition was largely based upon prejudice."[38] Andrews then conferred with Chamberlain, Paul Raushenbush, and leaders of the New York Conference on his next moves. They considered the possibility of obtaining the active support of the New York State Federation of Labor, but here too the prospects were bleak. J. M. O'Hanlon, secretary-treasurer of the state federation, consistently backed the AFL policy. At the 1931 hearings, for example, he had said that organized labor "is in the position of not supporting, but at the same time not opposing" the Mastick-Steingut bill.[39] There was strong sentiment for unemployment insurance legislation among the rank and file of the New York unions, which was reflected in demands for immediate action once the AFL had changed its policy, but it did Andrews little good in 1931. He was no more successful in forming a business-labor-reformer coalition in New York than he was on the national level.

If Swope was stubborn and the unionists ambiguous, at least the Marcy Committee offered a slight hope to the reformers. Assemblyman Marcy stated positively that his group would report for immediate passage of an unemployment insurance bill in 1933. The only question, he maintained, was whether to endorse a reserves plan or a genuine insurance system. In any event, Marcy predicted, the committee would present a "workable bill" to the legislature.[40] Raushenbush, who conferred with Marcy in late November, reported that the legislators would adopt the Wisconsin approach.[41] Thus the reformers' indignation was understandably great when they learned of the committee's "shocking somersault." The Marcy report, submitted in February 1933, rejected all proposals for unemployment insurance legislation on the grounds that such action would lead to the dismissal of thousands of part-time employees. Equally distressing was the fact that organized labor's representative on the committee agreed with the majority view. Wolman and Andrews charged duplicity. Howard Cullman, a New York businessman who had succeeded Fitch as head of the New York Conference, condemned the report as a "smoke screen for delay."[42]

Added to this blow was the performance of the new Democratic governor, Herbert Lehman, whose initial commitment to unemployment insurance was, at best, half-hearted. During his election campaign Lehman had, like the unionists, supported unemployment insurance in principle without specifying when a law should go into effect. Wolman had finally convinced him to pledge his support for immediate legislation to become effective when the state labor department declared that economic conditions had improved.[43] But Lehman's first annual message to the legislature called only for "a program looking toward a system of unemployment insurance." He told Mary Simkovitch, a prominent social worker, that he wanted a "broadly flexible formula with regard to the date and manner in which the law is to be administered, and particularly with reference to the date of the beginning of employers' contributions."[44] Andrews suspected that these qualifications might be merely excuses for continued inaction: ". . . we have become accustomed to liberal Governors and I fear we are in for some disappointment during this administration."[45]

In retrospect it seems likely that Andrews' worries were more a reflection of his personal disappointment than an objective assessment of the situation. Indeed, the *New York Times* reported that it was difficult to find anyone except the conservative manufacturers who overtly opposed unemployment insurance legislation.[46] The growing support for unemployment insurance legislation and the extent of Andrews' personal problem became apparent in early 1933 when new bills were introduced in the legislature. In addition to the Mastick bill, which Andrews again backed, State Senator William Byrne submitted a bill on behalf of the State Federation of Labor. The Byrne bill provided for individual reserve funds, liberal out-of-work benefits, and, in an unusual clause, unemployment payments to strikers. Andrews found the unionists "wholly evasive" on the strike benefit provision and suspected that it was part of an old-guard conspiracy to kill the measure. Woll, who was no less vehement in his opposition to unemployment insurance after the 1932 AFL convention than before, told him that O'Hanlon could justify this clause "before his own union" if not before a legislative committee. Raushenbush stated his suspicions more explicitly. Referring to the strike benefit provision, he asked, "Is this sabotage by Matthew Woll?"[47]

Potentially more dangerous, at least to the AALL, was a third bill introduced by State Senator Albert Wald for Epstein and his followers. Professor Herman Gray of New York University had drafted the Wald bill, which was based on the Ohio plan and the European experience. It called for the pooling of all contributions and for generous benefit payments. Leiserson complained that it too closely resembled a relief plan.[48] Although it received no consideration in 1933, the Wald bill represented a fundamental threat to Andrews' work; for, as Douglas argued, "our plan is so much more preferable that . . . it will win popular support and replace the others."[49] In the meantime the Democratic senate passed the Byrne bill—the only one the legislature considered in 1933—complete with the strike benefit clause.[50] When it reached the assembly, however, the Republican-dominated rules committee adamantly refused to report out any bill.[51]

But this setback in the assembly was much less important, in the long run, than the emergence of the antiprevention group. The significance of this development became apparent during the summer and autumn, as the unions and Epstein's Permanent Conference on Social Security gradually joined forces to fight for unemployment insurance and against unemployment reserves. The first step in the formation of this informal alliance was the decision by the convention of the State Federation of Labor in August to throw its "full support behind a drive for unemployment insurance."[52] Elmer Andrews, Lehman's Industrial Commissioner, then created a committee including representatives of Andrews' and Epstein's rival organizations, and Jeremiah Ryan and George Meany, vice-presidents of the state federation, to work out a new bill.[53] While the conflict between Andrews and Epstein prevented the committee from performing its stated functions, the experience deeply influenced Ryan and Meany. Epstein's arguments became more appealing as rank and file demands for benefits grew louder and louder and union members became concerned that plant reserves would tie the workers to their jobs and promote company unions. Ryan and Meany, reporting to the state federation convention in 1934, reflected these sentiments: "Your committee members studied this matter very carefully and decided as the result not only of their own deliberations but after consulting other officers of the Federation . . . [that] we would declare in favor of a hundred percent pooled fund."[54]

By December 1933 the die was cast. The state federation's executive council voted to sponsor a bill to pool all contributions, and Meany, charged with drafting the new measure, assured Epstein that he would adhere to his mandate.[55] In January Lehman promised the union leaders that he would sign any bill that reached his desk.[56] The Byrne-Condon bill, as the labor measure was called, apparently had the backing of the majority of the legislators. The public hearings also confirmed the growing popular support for unemployment insurance in general and the Byrne bill in particular. Epstein headed a large group of reformers who endorsed the pooled-fund plan. Andrews, on the other hand, could not prevent many of his followers from supporting the Byrne bill. The result was a great victory for unemployment insurance and, equally important, a major defeat for unemployment reserves. Epstein happily reported: "The advocates of the company reserves plan one after another capitulated and practically endorsed the Byrne-Condon Bill. . . . The leaders of the New York Conference . . . reported that they were completely split on the issue."[57] In April the senate passed the Byrne-Condon bill, but the assembly rules committee, still under Republican control, again refused to report any measure.[58] These obstructionist tactics, while in no way lessening the prospect of eventual passage, strengthened the labor-liberal coalition in 1934–35 just as they had helped to create and sustain it in 1932–33.

By late 1934 there was no doubt about the dominant influence among the reformers or what type of bill would eventually pass.

Meany, elected president of the state federation in 1934, maintained that the reserves plan "would seriously handicap trade unionism."[59] Cullman bowed to the inevitable and endorsed the pooled fund. Lehman, who favored the reserve plan but wanted unity above all, organized a special committee to work out an acceptable bill. Chamberlain and Gray represented the divergent schools of thought, but with Meany as its most prominent member, the outcome of the committee's work was never in doubt. The November elections, in which the voters elected a Democratic majority to the assembly, insured favorable consideration for Lehman's program; Senator Byrne predicted that "our unemployment insurance bill will be among the very first enacted into law."[60]

The Byrne-Killgrew bill, as the old Byrne bill was now called, had an impressive list of supporters when the legislature considered it in 1935. Even Andrews, perhaps tired of backing losing causes, spoke in behalf of the bill. Epstein was pleased at this turn of events, although he was also angry at the unionists for opposing employee contributions and at Lehman for agreeing to an amendment which permitted gradually increased employer contributions.[61] Much of the opposition came from employers like Folsom, who now doubtless wished they had been more flexible in 1931 or 1932. Andrews noted with irony that they had helped kill the 1933 bill "after it had passed the Senate with the very provision for which they are now contending."[62] The assembly, under Democratic leadership, passed the Byrne-Killgrew bill on March 20 by better than a two to one margin. The senate, chafing at pressure from Lehman, delayed action for two weeks but voted on April 7, 1935, to make New York the second state to enact unemployment insurance legislation.[63] During the three years since the passage of the Wisconsin act, however, much had changed. Unemployment prevention, the New Emphasis, and individual reserves had been forgotten. A revolution had occurred in the Empire State, and its impact—and that of similar transformations in other states—was very great indeed.

Continuity and Change in Massachusetts

MASSACHUSETTS WAS in many ways unlike New York. It had experienced the problems of industrialization at an earlier date and had been among the first states to pass progressive labor legislation. It had, however, entered a period of relative decline: many of the old textile firms and shoe companies had moved south or otherwise dispersed their operations. Nor had the social reform organizations which played an active role in New York politics a parallel in the Bay State. But in one respect Massachusetts had the edge in the 1920's: her manufacturers led the nation in developing new management techniques that introduced greater order and rationality into their operations. They played leading roles in evolving the New Emphasis and were among its chief propagandists. Their endorsement of the Huber bill was their first major excursion into unemployment politics, but it was not their last. As they had for the past decade and a half, Massachusetts employers advanced the New Emphasis as an antidote for the Depression in the early 1930's. In New York it was a tribute to Andrews' tenacity that unemployment prevention persisted as long as it did; in Massachusetts the surprising fact was that it did not last longer.

Beginning in 1916 the Massachusetts legislature appointed several groups to investigate unemployment prevention. The 1916 AALL bill and the widespread interest in social insurance legislation had, of course, resulted in the creation of a commission to consider various insurance measures.[64] But no further action was taken until 1922, when Andrews persuaded Henry Shattuck, an association member, to introduce a measure resembling the Huber bill. As part of the ensuing campaign Dennison and Commons recounted their experiences for the legislators at a public hearing in March 1922, but the consequence was the same as 1916—an investigation authorized by the legislature. Whether the 1922 commission was designed like its predecessor to explore the possibilities of unemployment insurance, or merely to sidetrack legislation, is impossible to judge, but it effectively performed the latter function. By autumn 1922, when the commission began to operate, public interest in unemployment had waned. The lawmakers nevertheless made a thorough study of the causes and results of joblessness, concluding that the "strongest emphasis possible" should be placed "on means for the prevention of unemployment."[65] To further this end they stressed the experiences of progressive businessmen, especially Dennison, whose activities they praised. They also commended Shattuck for submitting a bill that was "drawn with much care. . . . It indicates serious thought and study."[66] But they concluded that "compulsory indemnification during unemployment is not consistent with American principles." After a long tirade against "so-called" social insurance, the commission added that "the adoption of any form of state insurance against unemployment would neither be to the interest of Massachusetts industries nor to the permanent advantage of Massachusetts wage earners."[67] Its acceptance of the New Emphasis and rejection of legislation accurately summarized the viewpoint of most Americans in the 1920's.

An additional reason for the existence of this attitude in Massachusetts was the absence of any effective challenge, particularly from organized labor. Seasonal and technological unemployment were unusually high in the Bay State during the 1920's, but the Massachusetts State Federation of Labor offered few suggestions for remedial action. In 1928 the unionists called for labor-management cooperation and use of the "machinery of government" to solve the unemployment problem. "Some unions," the convention report added, "offer their members unemployment insurance and this plan has been helpful."[68] But the executive council had little to add in 1929 and in the following year, with joblessness rapidly increasing, called only for reform and relief without indicating the details of specific measures.[69] Like their brethren in other states, Massachusetts unionists reconciled the conflict between the wage earners' needs and voluntarism with platitudes.

With the legislature controlled by foes of state action and the labor movement reluctant to defy AFL policy, the initiative in advancing anti-Depression measures fell to the state's business leaders. At the time that the Hoover Administration adopted the New Emphasis for combatting unemployment, the Massachusetts Department of Labor and Industries appointed a large citizens' committee to study prevention measures. This group, which included many prominent management reformers—Richard Feiss, William T. Foster, Ben M. Selekman of the Russell Sage Foundation, Edwin S. Smith, and Raymond L. Tweedy, executive secretary of the Manufacturers Research Association—conducted a thorough study of unemployment. Unlike many such committees it made no attempt to gloss over the seriousness of the situation; yet its January 1931 report suggested few innovations. It called for creation of an information bureau to keep records of regularization efforts, revision of the insurance laws to permit commercial companies to write unemployment insurance, establishment of a special commission on stabilization, and improved public employment offices.[70]

After some hesitation the legislature created the Special Commission on the Stabilization of Unemployment called for. The new Democratic governor, Joseph Ely, appointed a number of prominent citizens, including Stanley King, who became chairman, Dennison, Henry Kendall, Edwin S. Smith, Karl T. Compton, president of the Massachusetts Institute of Technology, and two union officials, to fill the new posts. Not only did these selections fix public attention on the commission's work, but more importantly they placed supporters of unemployment prevention in command of the reform machinery, insuring continuity with the earlier efforts of Massachusetts employers.

The preliminary work of the commission, which occupied the rest of

1931 and early 1932, revealed its commitment to the doctrine of unemployment prevention. The members began the collection of information "concerning methods for permanently reducing unemployment," studies of public and private employment offices, an investigation of public works laws, and a study of company reserve funds "as an incentive to the regularization of employment."[71] Their basic approach was summarized in the statement that "stabilizing employment means stabilizing industry."[72] Kendall was even more explicit: "We are going to do what we can in an educational way to show industry its responsibility and get it to go as far as it can to put its own house in order. . . . Then I would not be at all surprised if we fathered some bill coming out of the suggestions in the very interesting Wisconsin bill."[73] Though this commitment precluded serious consideration of a European-style unemployment insurance system, the commission nonetheless made a detailed investigation of various approaches and consulted Raushenbush, Andrews, and other experts. In all, twenty-two meetings were held, including joint sessions with legislative commissions from Connecticut and New Hampshire.

The report of Roosevelt's Interstate Committee on unemployment insurance, published in early 1932, added a new dimension to the work of the Massachusetts committee. Dennison, Kendall, King, and probably Compton were already supporters of individual reserves; but the interstate report raised the prospect of eliminating interstate competition—a major barrier to favorable action by the Massachusetts legislature. King talked to reform leaders in New York, while Dennison and H. A. Wooster, an advisor, tried to persuade the Ohio Commission members to align their group behind the interstate plan. Wooster wrote that "it would be helpful to us here, and I think it might be to you in Ohio, if the two states were known to be working along similar lines."[74] The outright refusal of the Ohio reformers to consider individual reserves, the debacle in the New York legislature resulting from the *volte-face* of the Marcy Committee, and the conservatism of the New England commissions were serious setbacks to the Massachusetts commission. Because of these obstacles the opportunity for a concerted, interstate drive for unemployment prevention was lost, and Massachusetts politicians remained sufficiently wary to think long and hard before taking the first step alone.

In spite of the failure to create a common front with reformers from other industrial states, the Massachusetts commission report, published in December 1932, unequivocally endorsed unemployment prevention. It called for planned public works, unemployment office reform, vocational guidance and training, shorter working hours, and above all, compulsory company reserves along the lines of the Wisconsin act. Noting that voluntary action had had insignificant results, the members recommended a modest program to cover firms with ten or more workers, financed by a 2 percent payroll tax which would pay no more than $10 per week to the unemployed. All contributions were to be kept in separate accounts. The purpose of such a system, the commission explained, was to prevent joblessness. "We believe the effect of this bill when enacted into law will be a substantial decrease in the amount of unemployment. . . . There is need for a 'safety first' movement for labor turnover similar to that stimulated by workmen's compensation." On the other hand the commission explicitly opposed a pooled fund based on uniform contributions: "It is decidedly undesirable that the chosen system exert influence in a direction opposite to preventive measures."[75]

Although unemployment insurance bills had been introduced in the 1931 session of the legislature, the 1933 session was the first time since 1922 that a measure with substantial backing came before the Massachusetts lawmakers. The King bill, incorporating the commission's recommendations, was drafted by Raushenbush, Felix Frankfurter, and John Plaisted, Wooster's successor, and had the active backing of the committee members who volunteered to continue their work on an informal basis. Plaisted also recruited A. L. Filene and secured the endorsements of the Massachusetts Federation of Women's Clubs, the Massachusetts Civic League, and the Federation of Churches of Greater Boston.[76] However, his most important achievement was obtaining the nominal support of the Boston Chamber of Commerce. Even the leaders of the Associated Industries of Massachusetts, the employers' organization which led the opposition, admitted that the King bill had many good features; in fact they objected to the plan only on the general grounds of state interference in labor-management relations.[77] Governor Ely also endorsed the commission bill, although with the qualification that contributions be delayed until the economic situation had improved.[78]

Supported by the state's best known businessmen, the governor, and many civic leaders, the New Emphasis reformers reached the apex of their power in 1933. Hearings to consider the King bill as well as another measure sponsored by the socialists were held in February and March. Compton was the chief spokesman for the stabilization committee; he upheld the reserves plan but admitted, under pressure, that it might cost seasonal workers their jobs.[79] At the same time Plaisted lobbied for the bill, particularly with the members of the committee on labor. By early March he reported that the committee would favorably report the King bill, amended to delay the beginning of contributions in accordance with the Governor's request.[80] But the other lawmakers were less well-disposed toward the measure. After considerable debate they resolved the question by killing both bills and voting a new appropriation to continue the work of the stabilization commission until the next session.[81]

Throughout this period organized labor had refrained from any active role in promoting unemployment insurance legislation. But unionists in Massachusetts, like their counterparts in other states, became more vocal in their demands for reform as unemployment increased. The executive council of the state federation, finally bowing to rank and file pressure, rejected voluntarism in favor of a "new policy" in 1931. Despite the appearance of Green at the convention, the officers, led by Robert Watt, proposed that Massachusetts unionists back unemployment insurance and other social reform measures.[82] In their 1932 report the officers further clarified their position; they stressed that some form of insurance "must be evolved," since unemployment would continue to menace the workers for many years—perhaps permanently. The AFL endorsement of unemployment insurance, which Watt helped secure, removed the final barrier.[83] But the immediate effects of this shift were unclear, since labor generally, and the militant Watt in particular, were in no mood for the modest King bill.

The results of labor's new policy toward unemployment insurance were first apparent in 1934, when the legislature again considered the King bill. With Andrews' assistance the stabilization committee members widely publicized their approach. King and Compton appeared at the public hearings in favor of the reserves bill and with A. L. Filene conducted a vigorous propaganda campaign.[84] Yet the reluctance of the Associated Industries' officials to endorse the King bill until Congress passed uniform national legislation hurt the businessmen's efforts. On the other hand, the Socialist bill, which provided for higher benefits, received more attention than in past years. Watt and his followers supported it in principle.[85] After several months of deliberation the lawmakers again vacillated. In what proved to be a decisive defeat for the stabilization commission, they created another committee, consisting of four legislators and three public representatives, including Watt, to reexamine the conflicting proposals for unemployment insurance.

The legislative interim committee adopted an entirely different approach from its predecessor. Because of its composition it was more amenable to popular pressure than to carefully devised theories. This meant that the legislators would listen to the growing demands, directed in large part by Watt, for a measure providing higher benefit payments.[86] Consequently the committee concluded that "unemployment is due to political, social and economic causes beyond the control of an individual employer" and rejected the reserves plan in favor of a pooled fund which it regarded as "the soundest way of making the fund financially secure and of guaranteeing an adequate reservoir from which those unemployed through no fault of their own may draw benefits which will be *far more adequate* than would be possible under any individual reserve plan."[87] The legislators, however, recommended postponement of an actual law until the nature of the pending federal legislation became clear. Significantly, the employer representative who had supported the King bill refused to sign the report.[88]

Although Massachusetts' legislators hesitated while Congress deliberated, the debate over the provisions of the proposed law resumed in the spring as the prospect of federal legislation appeared more certain. The legislative commission had continued to meet informally during the winter of 1934–35 and drew up a new bill in May which provided for an insurance rather than a reserves system, and exemptions for existing company plans. An anomaly of the 1935 campaign was the opposition of employers like Kendall and A. L. Filene to a provision for employee contributions which Watt approved.[89] There was no contention, however, on the basic issue: labor flatly refused to support any bill which incorporated the reserves plan. One federal official reported that "Bob Watt has become very violent in his opposition to employer reserves. He thinks that they are part of some nefarious company union scheme."[90] Congressional action spurred the Massachusetts lawmakers; on August 12, before President Roosevelt signed the Social Security Act, Massachusetts became the fifth, and after New York the second most important, industrial state to enact unemployment insurance legislation. Despite their long experience with economic reform, the Bay State's progressive employers had been prevented by the impact of the Depression from completing their long campaign. The provisions of the August 1935 act marked a sharp deviation from the twenty-year struggle for "prevention" in Massachusetts.

New Perspectives: The Ohio Campaign

TO A greater degree than in either New York or Massachusetts, the line between support and opposition to unemployment insurance was clearly drawn in Ohio. This was partly because the state's employers had shown relatively little interest in the management reforms of the 1920's and identified, at least for political purposes, with the conservative farmers in opposing increased taxation. But it was also because there existed strong latent support for an advanced program of social welfare legislation in Ohio. Progressivism had been an urban phenomenon in Ohio; it had emphasized social justice legislation and "gas and water" socialism as much as economic efficiency and electoral reform. Ohio reformers had, consequently, enacted one of the nation's best accident compensation laws, and had created the most efficient employment office system in the country. Nor had their efforts slackened in the 1920's. In Cleveland, Toledo, Columbus, and Cincinnati social workers, clergymen, and university professors continued to agitate for better working conditions. And because it was this group, generally alien to the ideology of the New Emphasis, who backed unemployment insurance, rather than the businessmen, the Ohio campaign acquired distinctly different characteristics from similar movements in New York and Massachusetts.

Interest in unemployment insurance grew out of the activities of the Consumers League of Ohio, an organization of social workers and reformers that emphasized political lobbying and education.[91] In April 1928 Alice Gannett and Elizabeth S. Magee, respectively president and executive secretary of the Ohio League, arranged for a conference on unemployment to meet in Cleveland. As chief speaker they chose Rabbi A. H. Silver, a long-time supporter of labor legislation. This meeting and others that followed led to the formation of an unemployment committee under the auspices of the Consumers League.[92] The committee members worked hard to promote public interest in joblessness during 1929, but one incident illustrates the difficulties they faced in Ohio. After many months of recruiting, they persuaded several businessmen to join their unemployment committee. Then "the name of 'Consumers League' was inadvertently mentioned in one of the notifications of meetings [and] nearly all of the businessmen promptly resigned leaving us at the point at which we started!"[93]

Beginning in 1930 the focus of the committee's work shifted significantly. "We are turning to the group which has been . . . discussing unemployment," wrote Miss Magee in April 1930, "and asking them to take the responsibility for studying various kinds of unemployment insurance, looking toward working out a bill for Ohio."[94] The following summer the Consumers League committee became the Cleveland Committee for Unemployment Insurance, with Silver as its head. For the next six months the members discussed various legislative proposals, including the Huber bill. Leiserson, by that time an economics professor at Antioch College and a member of the board of directors of the Consumers League, suggested modeling a bill after the workmen's compensation act. But Douglas, then associated with the Swarthmore unemployment project, advised abandonment of the Wisconsin-type plans for a pooled fund with employee contributions.[95] The reformers' desire for higher benefits insured an enthusiastic reception for these ideas.

By late 1930 the Ohio reformers had decided to introduce a bill in 1931 "with the idea of getting the principle of unemployment insurance before the legislature and the people of the state."[96] To draft a specific measure they enlisted the aid of Marvin C. Harrison, a Cleveland attorney. Following Douglas' suggestions he produced a measure that provided for a single statewide fund and employee contributions, two distinctive provisions that suggested the different philosophy of the Ohio reformers. In late October the Consumers League announced that it would introduce a contributory unemployment insurance bill, and a surprising number of people responded favorably to the idea.[97] In December the Ohio reformers conferred with Andrews and Leo Wolman at the Cleveland AALL convention but never gave serious consideration to the American plan. The bill which Senator James Reynolds submitted to the Ohio legislature January 21, 1931, reflected as clearly as any act of the early Depression years the revival of interest in social insurance.

The Reynolds bill was in many ways an unqualified success. The only unexpected negative response was that from two of the state's progressive businessmen: S. P. Bush, a Columbus manufacturer who headed the governor's ineffectual stabilization committee, and William C. Procter. In other quarters the response was so encouraging that the Cleveland committee formed a state organization, the Ohio Committee for Unemployment Insurance. Among the members of the Ohio Committee were Leiserson, Rubinow, now living in Cincinnati as executive secretary of B'nai B'rith, Silver, Harrison, Professor H. Gordon Hayes of Ohio State University, Max S. Hayes, a Cleveland newspaperman, Gardner Latimer, a Columbus businessman, and Amy Maher, head of the Toledo Consumers League. Thomas J. Duffy, former chairman of the Ohio Industrial Commission and a Democratic politician, became its chairman. In hearings during February and March the Ohio Committee spokesmen maintained that unemployment insurance would end the existing haphazard methods of relief and that it would not lead to the "English dole." Organized labor, while uncommitted, at least did not oppose the bill. Thomas Donnelly, secretary of the Ohio Federation, recalled that "I remained neutral . . . explaining to those who interrogated me that I was not in a position to advocate or oppose the proposition."[98] The reformers also received a favorable response from the new Democratic governor George White. Miss Magee reported: "The Governor has told [Reynolds] . . . that when the matter is finally settled he will send a message to the legislature suggesting . . . the appointment of a commission to study unemployment insurance and report to the next legislature."[99] White kept his promise and though the legislature did not act on the bill itself, it did ultimately pass a resolution calling for a study of unemployment insurance.[100]

From this point the reformers pursued two parallel courses. They intensified their program of agitation and education, and through Reynolds and Duffy, friends of White, they pressured the Governor for a commission favorable to unemployment insurance. As part of this effort Reynolds submitted a list of "approved" names to the Governor for appointment to the commission. By September he was able to hint to Miss Magee that White would appoint a commission acceptable to the Ohio Committee. This prospect was, she wrote to Leiserson, "too good to be true!"[101] Yet when no announcement was made the reformers began to worry. To Duffy's inquiry in mid-October the Governor repeated his intention to appoint a liberal group.[102] Finally their work paid off: White selected Reynolds, Leiserson, H. Gordon Hayes, Rubinow, Miss Maher, and Rabbi Silver, all from the Ohio Committee; and Donnelly, Stephen Young, a Democratic politician, and Stanley Mathewson, secretary of the Springfield Chamber of Commerce, who were at least potential sympathizers. Only J. F. Lincoln, a manufacturer, and W. F. Kirk, Master of the State Grange, remained as possible opponents of unemployment insurance legislation.

Seldom in the annals of state political history has there operated a more enlightened group of experts—or for that matter one more unified on a highly controversial issue. Under the vigorous leadership of Leiserson, Rubinow, and Miss Magee (selected as executive secretary), the commission pursued its work with dedication and dispatch. During the period of the commission's deliberations, lasting from January to May 1932, only Lincoln seemed reluctant to follow their lead, and after finding himself outvoted on several early proposals, notably one to consider solutions other than unemployment insurance, he seldom attended.[103] Leiserson, who became chairman in the spring, adopted a moderate but firm approach, particularly on the question of a pooled fund. Miss Magee was also a valuable asset to the commission. She collected the numerous bills that had been introduced in state lesgislatures since 1916, organized the public hearings, and handled much of the administrative work. But Rubinow was in some respects the most important of the commission's members. Drawing on his experiences as an actuary, he computed the rates necessary to maintain the solvency of the fund and avoid a dole, thereby neutralizing the frequent attacks by employers' organizations on the financial soundness of unemployment insurance. After studying the existing statistics on joblessness in Ohio, he concluded that "there are no insurmountable obstacles from an actuarial point of view to the operation of an employment scheme."[104] His estimate was that a total 3 percent contribution, including 1 percent of the wage earner's pay, would permit the payment of sixteen weeks of benefits annually.

The opponents of unemployment insurance legislation made no attempt to influence the work of the commission, apparently on the premise that the outcome was inevitable. Lincoln tried to arrange a meeting between representatives of Ohio manufacturers and the commission, but the Manufacturers Association refused to cooperate because they "decided that nothing good would come of it."[105] Other employers' organizations also boycotted the hearings that the commission conducted throughout the state.[106]

As employer opposition to unemployment insurance in Ohio solidified, the labor movement took a different tack. Pressure among rank and file unionists for a long-range unemployment program was growing in Ohio as in other states. In April the Cleveland Federation of Labor endorsed unemployment insurance. To help obtain a similar statement from the state federation, Donnelly asked Miss Magee to prepare a series of articles for distribution among trade unionists. His invitation to Leiserson to address the federation's convention provided a clue to his strategy: "If you address the Convention on Tuesday morning or Tuesday afternoon, your address will no doubt be delivered before resolutions on the subject of Unemployment Insurance are considered by the committee . . . and will be helpful in giving the Committee and the delegates a larger understanding of the subject."[107] Leiserson's stirring appeal for unemployment insurance was effective, and the delegates voted their official support for the commission proposals.[108] With this endorsement the Ohio reformers added an important—perhaps indispensable—group to their list of backers.

From the beginning of the commission's deliberations there was no doubt that it would endorse unemployment insurance; the only question was what type of plan it would propose. The Reynolds bill of 1931 naturally served as a starting point in this process; yet it was not until the commission began to decide on the specific provisions of a desirable bill that the extraordinary influence of the Ohio Committee members became fully apparent. At an important meeting in late May the members voted to retain the principal features of the Reynolds bill, a single pooled fund and employee contributions. Leiserson was in full control. He argued that charity was necessary for unemployables but that industry must support able workers. And he added: "If industry can't support such people then those industries ought to be chucked into the Atlantic Ocean."[109] Particularly important was Donnelly's acceptance of employee contributions on the grounds that wage earners must retain their self-respect. Leiserson then incorporated these fundamentals in a draft bill which called for a total 3 percent contribution, an employee contribution of 1 percent, a statewide pooled fund, a maximum of sixteen weeks of benefits, and merit rating to take effect in 1937, three years after the start of contributions. The members voted on this draft at their October 26 meeting. "One might say," Rubinow suggested, "that the entire fate of our Bill is involved in that meeting."[110] The result was, however, never in doubt. With the exception of Lincoln and Kirk, who had already indicated their opposition to anything the commission might recommend, the members approved Leiserson's draft. Two days later representatives from the commission presented their recommendations to Governor White, who remarked that the report was timely, but prudently waited until after the November election to release it to the press.[111]

Published in mid-November, the Ohio Commission report marked a turning point in the conflict over unemployment prevention. Not only was it a dramatic counterattack against the conservative businessmen and politicians who offered nothing "except the present method of puting the unemployed on the dole," but it was also the best critique of the Wisconsin plan. "There is no pooling of risks," the report stated, referring to the Groves act. "The essential principle of insurance, that all who are subject to the risk shall pay premiums and those who actually suffer the risks shall receive the stipulated benefits is discarded." Instead the commission suggested a different type of stabilization: ". . . if a large insurance fund is accumulated during years of prosperity and paid out to supply purchasing power to the unemployed during periods of depression, far more order and stability will be maintained in the business world." Unemployment insurance would, therefore, permit society to "safely face" the economic problems of the future. In his dissenting statement Lincoln attacked the increased costs involved in such a program, and weakly proposed a back-to-the-farm movement. Kirk offered little more; he counseled greater thrift and a national system. Mathewson added a statement attacking the Ohio Chamber of Commerce for its "do nothing" policy. Harrison, now a member of the state senate, subsequently introduced the commission bill.[112]

The reception of the report among advocates of unemployment insurance was, to say the least, enthusiastic. Rubinow happily exclaimed that it "is making a sensation throughout the country." "The Wisconsin plan," he added, "is dead."[113] Even Andrews admitted that the "report is presented in fine style. It should be effective."[114] In Ohio the reaction was also generally favorable: Cleveland and Columbus newspapers gave it front page coverage, other papers commented sympathetically, and several business leaders, including officials of the Cleveland and Cincinnati Chambers of Commerce, expressed their approval. Mathewson's attack on the Ohio Chamber drew considerable attention. Harrison felt that Lincoln's "childish vituperation" would add "a good deal of additional force to the majority report."[115] White approved the principles of the report but said little else. Professor Hayes, his informal advisor, thought the Governor was a "little lukewarm" due to the "terrific pressure for economy and lowering of taxes."[116]

To counteract the commission's strong presentation, the opposition, particularly the Ohio Chamber of Commerce, Ohio State Grange, and the Ohio Farm Bureau, resorted to wildly exaggerated and often vicious attacks. George B. Chandler, secretary of the Ohio Chamber, led the opponents' campaign, charging that the insurance fund would quickly become insolvent, that the burden would then be shifted to property taxpayers, and that unemployment benefits "would ultimately destroy the fiber of the people."[117] More insidious were the chamber's attempts to smear members of the commission. Rubinow was the special object of this attack; he was publicized as an imposter because he was not a member of the life underwriters actuarial society—despite the fact that he had founded the association covering his main field of health and accident insurance. Another argument *ad hominem* was the accusation that the Russian parentage of Rubinow, Leiserson, and Silver indicated the presence of a subversive influence on the commission. Leiserson suspected a disguised appeal to anti-semitism: "Lazarus [a leading Columbus retail merchant and Jewish layman] and other men like him should be informed about this stuff."[118]

But the attacks of the conservative farm and business groups were the least of the reformers' immediate problems. To their consternation, White's message to the 1933 legislature endorsed their report in principle but recommended postponement of any legislation for the duration of the Depression. Claiming he had "no patience" with opponents who failed to offer suitable substitutes, the Governor proposed a joint legislative committee to make another study and report in 1935.[119] Professor Hayes and Mathewson knew that White was disturbed about beginning contributions in 1934, but they never imagined he would propose such drastic action. Rubinow was "stunned" that the Governor had "double-crossed" the commission, and the others were equally shocked.[120] Rather than publicly attacking the Governor, however, they attempted to resolve their differences and win him to their side. "It is necessary . . . to show the Governor where the real sentiment lies," Leiserson concluded. "We need to have as many prominent people as possible . . . urge immediate enactment of the bill."[121]

Once they decided that the timid White would only react to pressure, the reformers began a concerted campaign to change his mind. Harrison, Leiserson, Reynolds, Mathewson, and Donnelly, leading a delegation of unionists, called on him. They argued that unemployment would last for many years and that without unemployment insurance the state would have to raise its taxes to pay the increasing relief costs.[122] By February their efforts had had a modest effect. White stated specifically that contributions should begin in 1935. He explained that "I am definitely committed to unemployment insurance," a statement Miss Magee found "very encouraging."[123] Yet the Governor made no effort to push the commission bill, and his lack of initiative was reflected in the legislature. The House insurance committee did not report the bill until mid-March and the Democratic leaders showed no inclination to bring the measure to a vote. Harrison concluded that an appeal from Roosevelt or Labor Secretary Perkins "would be the only possible means of shaking him loose from his present attitude."[124]

In the meantime the reformers also attempted to mobilize public sentiment behind the commission bill. They pressured the legislators, testified at public hearings, and spoke to numerous civic groups. Leiserson conducted a series of public debates with Howard Odom, formerly an official of the National Metal Trades Association, whom the Ohio Chamber had employed to lead its fight against the commission bill. Unfortunately for the business leaders Odom adopted a more conciliatory approach than they had anticipated. He praised the commission report and repudiated the chamber's scurrilous attacks. To Leiserson's delight he merely argued that unemployment insurance was impractical and would not alleviate the immediate situation. Leiserson concluded that "the Chamber of Commerce is now quite on the defensive."[125]

But White's ambivalent position and the strength of the opposition still posed considerable obstacles to passage. The assembly passed the commission bill in June by a wide margin, but the senate conservatives were not so easily moved. As early as March Harrison reported that "the pressure that is being brought in opposition to the bill is tremendous, and I am quite skeptical as to the ability of the Committeemen to resist it."[126] In June, with the session coming to a close and the labor committee still reluctant to report the commission bill, the reformers played their last trick. Through Secretary Perkins they persuaded Roosevelt to make a personal appeal to White. On June 8 the President notified the Governor that unemployment insurance "is in accord with our platform."[127] White resented this interference, later claiming that he was not going to be made the "goat" by helping to enact unemployment insurance legislation.[128] He did, however, belatedly urge the senate to act, but to no avail. The commission bill died in committee. Harrison concluded—and most of the reformers would have agreed—that the bill "would have passed the Ohio Senate and would be the law in Ohio today . . . had it not been for the fact that George White . . . who was elected on a platform committing him to unemployment insurance . . . simply concluded that this was not the time to carry out that platform pledge and used all the vast influence of his office to defeat the bill."[129]

Between 1933 and December 1936, when the legislature finally approved unemployment insurance legislation, the Ohio campaign differed only in detail from similar efforts in other states. After the 1933 defeat the commission ceased to act as a unit: Leiserson moved to Washington to accept a federal post, and Rubinow died in 1936. The labor movement, with Donnelly as its chief spokesman, then took over the burden of lobbying for unemployment insurance. This remained a formidable job. The growing militancy of the labor movement in Ohio insured continual support for unemployment insurance legislation, but also created new problems. In 1935, for example, Donnelly backed the commission bill, but many left-wing union members supported another measure that was little more than an extended relief program. The commission bill failed in that session partly because a legislative committee appointed to study the bills favored the radicals' plan.[130] By September 1935 this pressure forced Donnelly to accept the deletion of employee contributions in the future. Not until Ohio employers were faced with compulsory contributions under the federal act was Donnelly able to work out the compromises that secured the final legislative victory.

If labor provided most of the backing for unemployment insurance after 1933, the businessmen continued to provide most of the opposition, as they did in virtually all the states. As the demands of organized labor became more extreme, employers generally came to see unemployment insurance in terms of dollars and cents rather than as part of a broad program of industrial reform. This transition was perhaps less evident in Ohio than in states where the New Emphasis tradition had been stronger, but it did, nevertheless, occur. While the Manufacturers Association and Chamber of Commerce, true to their tradition, opposed all legislation, the Retail Merchants Council, guided by its wily secretary George Sheridan, faced the inevitable and endorsed unemployment reserves. After speaking to a convention of department store executives in 1935, Rubinow observed that the merchants made "no pretense" about accepting the New Emphasis. "All this talk about the possible prevention and regularization effect is all no more than hooey," he reported. "If department stores can get their own fund for the entire industry, they, as department stores, are going to save a good deal of money."[131] In the special session of December 1935 the Retail Merchants Council made a concerted attempt to substitute the Wisconsin plan for the commission bill.[132] To strengthen their case Sheridan invited officials from the General Electric Company, the director of the Milwaukee office of the Wisconsin Industrial Commission, and H. W. Story of Allis Chalmers to testify for the reserves plan.[133] Only the conservative state senate, ill-disposed toward any legislation until it was absolutely necessary, discouraged a more formidable effort on behalf of unemployment reserves in 1936.

Ultimately, however, it was the obstructionist tactics of the legislators rather than the activities of either business or labor that prolonged the Ohio effort. Opposed in principle to unemployment insurance, the state senators employed one device after another to delay, frustrate, and defeat a series of bills. Their most successful excuse for inaction was, ironically, the prospect of federal legislation, and they used it both before the passage of the Social Security Act and after, when the possibility of an adverse court decision made further delay expedient.[134] But the lawmakers usually found it easier to create fact-finding committees and study groups than to register their outright opposition. This tactic was used with remarkable success in 1935 and 1936, when the impending federal payroll tax of 1937 reduced the issues to a matter of timing. There remains, however, some question whether the senate would have acted at all if the labor and business interests had not worked out a compromise plan in December 1936. Finally, when Donnelly acceded to the businessmen's demands for a more liberal merit-rating provision than the Ohio Commission bill provided, enough senators reversed themselves to pass a modified form of the 1932 measure.

The Ohio unemployment insurance act of 1936 consequently resembled many other state laws: it provided for a pooled fund, contributions only from employers, a maximum benefit of $15 a week for a total of sixteen weeks, and the adjustment of the employer's tax rate to his employment record. The governor signed the bill into law on December 12, ending the seven-year struggle for unemployment insurance in Ohio. If the results of this effort were little different in Ohio than in other states, the struggle itself had been important, for the Ohio campaign, the first concerted legislative challenge to prevention, had marked a decisive step in the shift away from the business-oriented schemes which the Wisconsin act had come to symbolize.

Other State Legislation

Two UNDERLYING themes, the importance of the labor movement and the ability of conservative legislators and employers to block legislation, were evident in the remaining state drives, much as they appeared in the four campaigns that have been reviewed. In no instance was a law passed that labor opposed. This fact explains in large measure the modest progress of unemployment insurance legislation before 1932 and the importance of the AFL decision to abandon voluntarism. The unionists, moreover, largely determined the major features of the laws that were enacted. They dictated, above all, the abandonment of the reserves approach in favor of more adequate benefit payments. But the relative weakness of the unions in the early Depression years also gave obstructionist legislators and businessmen the advantage they needed to delay if not destroy the programs of the reformers. The progressive employers, on the other hand, after brief prominence in many states, were literally forced out of the struggle and back to their factories, where they undoubtedly watched with mixed emotions as the legislatures debated and altered their proposals.

Yet the lines sharply drawn in New York and Massachusetts were less clear in other states. Only in Pennsylvania were the ingredients for a similar transformation, from an employer-oriented to a union-oriented movement, present. Following the pre-Depression work of the Philadelphia Chamber of Commerce, the state manufacturers association and the Pennsylvania Unemployment Commission publicized unemployment prevention in 1930–31. With the assistance of Leeds and Cooke these efforts generated considerable interest but resulted in little action.[135] In 1931 the State Federation of Labor again endorsed unemployment insurance legislation and in 1932, under the leadership of the United Mine Workers, began to work actively for a compulsory measure.[136] By 1933 they enjoyed the support of the Pennsylvania Security League, the Philadelphia Consumers League, and other social welfare groups. A reserves bill introduced in 1933 by antilabor legislators led to the creation of a committee on unemployment reserves; but the opposition of the employers' representatives on the commission to any type of unemployment insurance doomed the chances for a Wisconsin-type law.[137] Their tactics delayed passage of any legislation until December 1936, although the law that did result was, from the wage earners' point of view, one of the most favorable passed in any state.

In other industrial states the absence of progressive businessmen made passage of unemployment insurance legislation largely dependent on the support of union leaders. Spurred by the California State Federation of Labor, which endorsed insurance in 1931, the California legislature followed Massachusetts in enacting unemployment insurance legislation in 1935. On the other hand the Minnesota State Labor Federation, which had first backed a Huber-type bill in 1923, was unable to push a bill through the legislature until 1936, despite the assistance of the radical Governor Floyd Olson. Organized labor in New Jersey actively worked for legislation as early as 1933, but was unable to overcome the resistance of conservative employers until 1936. Michigan unionists were less interested; their lack of enthusiasm helped insure the postponement of legislative action for more than a year after the passage of the Social Security Act. In Illinois, despite the aid of a formidable group of social workers and reformers, Victor Olander gave only nominal attention to unemployment insurance until 1935. By then the stubborn employers, working through the Illinois Manufacturers Association, had determined to halt legislation at any cost. Only in 1937, after the federal government began collecting the payroll tax, did the Illinois legislature finally capitulate—the last in the nation to do so.

Although union enthusiasm varied from state to state and conservative legislators delayed action in every instance, virtually all the bills passed after the Groves act had one common characteristic: their principle aim was to sustain the unemployed worker rather than to force the employer to prevent unemployment. No state except rural Nebraska followed Wisconsin's example and created a system of individual reserves, although a few nonindustrial states permitted company reserves when a specified percentage of the employer's contribution was pooled. California and Massachusetts permitted employers to withdraw from the state pool under certain circumstances, but this small concession provided little satisfaction to progressive employers. Twenty-two states (but not New York, Pennsylvania, or Massachusetts) made a final, significant concession to unemployment prevention by including provisions for merit- or experience-rating in their original acts. One other vestige of employer influence—of the Swope rather than the Dennison variety—was the inclusion of employee contributions in several of the early acts. As the unionists became more assertive, however, these provisions were excluded or dropped from laws already passed.[138]

A profound change had thus occurred between 1931 and 1935. To some degree the abandonment of prevention reflected popular disillusionment with business leadership in general and the superficial, rhetorical acceptance of the New Emphasis. But it also indicated a different conception of the purpose of unemployment insurance. As defined by the management reformers of the 1920's, the primary objective had been the stabilization of production and employment. As defined by labor leaders and many of the reformers in the bleak and often desperate years of the early 1930's, it was the provision of benefits to unemployed workers. While the unemployment insurance plans of the 1930's were in no way designed to help wage earners already out of work, their creators looked forward with the conditions of the Depression, rather than the prosperous 1920's, foremost in their minds. Still, it should be added that the states could reject the businessman's approach only because it had been accepted to a degree on the national level. For a variety of reasons, among them the pressure of the supporters of unemployment prevention, the federal Social Security Act permitted considerable discretion on the part of the legislatures, including the right to enact or preserve both the old and the new forms of employer incentives—experience rating and individual reserves.

9 | THE NEW DEAL

WHILE THE battles over unemployment insurance legislation raged in the states, there was a parallel struggle in Washington over a federal program. Increased unemployment, the failure of voluntary relief and recovery efforts, and the rising radicalism of the early 1930's resulted in demands for long-term reform as well as short-term relief. The political alignments were much the same in this effort as they were in the states. Although the Democratic victory of 1932 (Roosevelt ran on a platform vaguely endorsing unemployment insurance legislation) eliminated many of the die-hard opponents of all legislation, many obstacles remained. Above all, it was necessary for reformers to reach some agreement on the role businessmen would play and on the related question of state or national control, a requirement that was made more difficult by the existence of three fairly well-defined factions that sought to influence congressional action between 1933 and 1935.

First, there were those who assigned a central role to the businessman, who believed in prevention as a legitimate goal but who also emphasized the employer's desire to be responsible only for his own workers. The most important spokesmen for this group of businessmen and intellectuals were Andrews and Raushenbush. The former, by virtue of his long experience and many contacts, was particularly effective in Washington; yet Andrews' leadership was impaired by his attempt to hold together his 1930 coalition. After the completion of Roosevelt's Interstate Committee report, he had thrown in his lot with the sponsors of individual reserves. But in 1933, in response to the Ohio Commission report and the growing strength of social insurance advocates, he once again shifted gears and announced two important clarifications in the American plan. He added provisions urging voluntary employee contributions and permitting industries to pool their funds if they desired. Likewise, the administrative authorities might demand pooling in any circumstance to insure the safety of the reserves. The revised plan, he argued, provided "a practical safeguard" against the dangers of the Wisconsin plan and, at the same time, "takes advantage of the greater preventive stimulus in establishment reserves."[1]

As a result of Andrews' compromises, it was Raushenbush who most clearly supplied the intellectual stimulus for prevention after 1932. Respected by Andrews as the "intellectual dynamo" behind the Wisconsin movement, Raushenbush operated from his strategic position as administrator of the Wisconsin act. Either in cooperation with the AALL or alone, he articulated the principles behind the Wisconsin experiment more forcefully than any other individual. Implicit in his statements was the thinking of Commons and Brandeis. Contrasting the NRA with the Wisconsin plan he explained: "It's [the NRA's] job is primarily the emergency job of getting people back to work. Unemployment reserve legislation designed to promote more regular employment is a long run job of steadying employment, with a view to preventing, at least in some measure, the occurrence of the type of catastrophe we have had during the last 3 or 4 years."[2] But he added, "The time must come when those business units which fail to meet the true social costs of their irregular operation will no longer be considered either socially or financially solvent." The trouble with pooled funds was that they "would thus tend to perpetuate and encourage the survival of the socially least fit."[3]

Though the intellectual backers of unemployment prevention were relatively few in number, the growing ranks of the businessmen who accepted their approach made up for this shortcoming. By 1932 nearly every national employers' organization had reported favorably on some type of prevention plan. The more cynical of these groups, such as the NAM and NICB, frankly favored such action to obviate the demand for legislation. "The most effective way to combat objectionable proposals of legislation," stated a Conference Board report on unemployment insurance, "is to offer sound alternative proposals of a constructive character that will command the support of legislatures and the public generally."[4] But more broad-minded businessmen, especially those with an interest in economic planning, also saw unemployment reserves as an integral part of their stabilization efforts. Ernest Draper went so far as to contend that "our only hope" lay in company reserve funds.[5]

This combination of altruism and expediency was evident in the policies of the Chamber of Commerce as well as in those of other businessmen's groups. After 1931, when the Committee on Continuity of Business and Employment report urged voluntary reserve plans, the chamber officially took no further action. The 1934 convention reaffirmed the delegates' belief in voluntary plans—that is, continued inaction.[6] Yet articles on company reserves and insurance legislation were often featured in the chamber's publications, and Harriman privately admitted that unemployment insurance was inevitable. He urged reserves legislation to insure that wage earners would not "be thrown on the none too tender mercies of charity" and that employers would receive the necessary incentive to stabilize employment. These sentiments were also shared by the members of the Business Advisory and Planning Council, formed by Commerce Secretary Daniel C. Roper in June 1933, which became the center of business support for unemployment insurance.[7] There remained, however, one basic difference between the businessmen and the intellectuals: Harriman and his colleagues, unlike Raushenbush, did not seek to purify competition but to control and regulate it. They were never able, moreover, to escape the obvious fact that individual reserves would likely cost less than a genuine insurance system, particularly since more and more employers joined Swope in recommending employee contributions. Even with these qualifications Harriman's followers were far more enlightened in their social outlook than their predecessors—or their successors.

The views of these men had important implications for the formulation of federal legislation. For whatever else they may have wanted they insisted upon an unemployment insurance system tailored to the needs of the individual employer. Harriman wrote: "Industries which can so regulate themselves that . . . employment is reasonably constant should not be burdened in order to pay for the cost of reserves for less well managed industries."[8] Specifically, this meant a low tax rate and the adjustment of the employer's tax to his employment record. Whether this should be accomplished through state-enforced reserves plans or some other arrangement was a subject of considerable disagreement. But it was clear that the flexibility the employers demanded virtually ruled out any type of national system with uniform standards. Their demands thus tended to reinforce the opposition of the Congress and the Supreme Court to a significant extension of federal power.

Opposed to the businessmen and their allies were the intellectuals, social workers, clergymen, and reformers, who urged a comprehensive national system of social insurance modeled after the European efforts as the only realistic answer for the problems of unemployment and insecurity. Though they hoped that unemployment insurance would help stabilize the economy, their basic argument was, in the words of Rubinow, that "no theoretical considerations should stand in the way of an effective system of guaranteed benefits." This simple, straightforward approach, reminiscent of the ideas of Churchill and Beveridge twenty years before, won many converts in the early Depression years. Epstein increased the membership of the American Association for Social Security substantially in 1934 and 1935 and, since the Groves bill and the original American plan adhered to the New Emphasis tradition, broke openly with Andrews, the AALL, and the Wisconsin reformers. "I am absolutely opposed to the Wisconsin plan," he wrote, "not only because it is not workable . . . but because it is essentially contrary to all social insurance ideas."[9] To draw analogies between unemployment insurance and workmen's compensation was, Epstein maintained, "to mock ordinary intelligence."[10] For the AALL he had nothing but scorn. "Of course, Dr. Andrews does not like us, but a little more hate cannot hurt."[11]

At first glance the Epstein faction seemed to have a significant advantage. While Andrews faced a constant struggle to reconcile and direct his followers and to exercise some influence over the business community, Epstein's task was somewhat easier. His supporters were alike in their alienation from the New Emphasis and their agreement that the solution to the unemployment problem, insofar as there was one, lay in a genuine insurance program. And though they praised the Ohio plan and were most successful on the state level, they knew that their success ultimately depended on the creation of a national system with uniform benefit standards. In the meantime they demanded the pooling of all contributions in accordance with the theory that the risks should be spread as broadly as possible. They also wanted employee contributions, not as Swope did, to give the worker a sense of responsibility, but to increase the amount of money available for benefit payments. Their views carried a sense of immediacy and the rejection of all-inclusive reform theories. They agreed with Rubinow that "the far reaching effects may work out, if at all, only in the long run . . . ."[12]

But there was one point on which they did disagree—the value of adhering to insurance principles, particularly the contributory method. Epstein in particular realized the immense psychological value of the Depression to his cause. He endorsed the British system and believed "the sooner we get away from our fine distinctions of insurance versus relief the better off we will be."[13] Among his important followers Douglas probably came the closest to agreeing with him. The Chicago reformer favored the British plan of state contributions; yet he maintained that until Congress enacted a progressive income tax, this provision would, through the property tax, shift the burden of unemployment compensation to the farmers and small property owners.[14] Leiserson and Rubinow, on the other hand, took a wholly different view. They realized that their support came from those who were basically interested in a more adequate system of relief; yet they insisted on the retention of insurance principles. Leiserson complained of the "fatal error" of varying benefits according to the size of the wage earner's family. "Such a provision completely changes the character of the law so that it becomes a relief measure," he wrote Epstein. "I will go along with you on any plan of Unemployment Insurance, but I do not want to mix relief measures with insurance legislation."[15] Rubinow was no less intransigent. Mixing relief and insurance was, in his opinion, the sure road to disaster: "Noncontributory unemployment insurance is bound to degenerate into some sort of dole."[16]

Between 1933 and 1935, however, far more serious practical problems overshadowed these theoretical differences. The strong suspicion of Americans toward any type of social insurance was a major obstacle. Passage of any social insurance program on the national level would be difficult; but the competition of the prevention approach in this case was likely to prove disastrous. Epstein and his backers could only succeed if they mobilized their potential supporters and demonstrated to Congress that the nation favored an unemployment insurance system that was modeled after the European rather than the "American" approach. But in this task they also faced a serious problem, for the leaders of organized labor, their major sources of political support in the states, were both independent and in some respects uncommitted. In particular the union leaders opposed employee contributions.[17] This left Epstein and his supporters in a precarious position. Yet they were prepared to fight a rearguard action and, if need be, to act as critics in the event an undesirable bill neared passage.

While this dichotomy oversimplifies the complex relationships that developed in 1933–35, it does illustrate the dilemma that faced the third group, the politicians and administrators who were responsible for devising an unemployment insurance program for the Roosevelt Administration. It seemed that if they submitted a bill that the businessmen would support, Epstein and his followers would surely protest and perhaps stop any action. But if they submitted a bill providing for a strong national system, they would just as surely lose the support of the businessmen and have to face even more determined opposition in Congress and possibly the judiciary. It was little wonder that their consciousness of the demands of the moment—the need for immediate action, the constitutional question, the limitations on what in fact Congress was willing to do, and the necessity for maintaining the support of as many of the erstwhile proponents of unemployment insurance as possible—overshadowed whatever personal interest in theoretical considerations or long-term goals they might have had.

Congressional Campaigns, 1933–1934

ROOSEVELT'S INAUGURATION in March 1933 heralded an assault on unemployment unlike anything the federal government had previously engaged in. The program of the Hundred Days aimed directly and indirectly at solving the problems of the unemployed. Yet the objective of this legislation was the re-employment of those who were out of work and the relief of the unfortunate, not specifically an attack on the long-range threat of joblessness. In this situation Congress gave relatively little consideration to the politically controversial question of unemployment insurance; indeed, probably no issue of such potential significance received less attention. With the exception of a few reformers who had taken a direct interest in unemployment reform during the Hoover years, most politicians and administrators showed by their lack of interest their feeling that such measures should be deferred for future consideration.

One of those few congressional leaders who maintained an active interest in unemployment insurance was Senator Robert F. Wagner. For him the Hundred Days marked no breathing spell, at least as far as his unemployment insurance program was concerned. Carefully maintaining his contacts with the reformers, he accepted the counsel of both groups and, in the months that followed, backed a succession of measures to encourage the states and private employers to establish unemployment insurance systems. While this approach had the advantage of permitting him to remain aloof from the struggle among his supporters, political expediency was not his only motive. "Unemployment insurance," he explained, "should depend on the particular industrial conditions in a state . . . It is a variable thing."[18]

In March 1933 Wagner introduced the two measures that he had proposed in his dissenting statement to the 1932 Hebert Committee report. His bills provided for a coordinated federal-state employment office system and tax incentives to employers who established private insurance funds. The latter measure, a highly conservative approach to unemployment insurance, was introduced, as Miss Perkins recalled, "for educational purposes."[19] Despite Roosevelt's endorsement and the aid of David J. Lewis, a Maryland congressman who introduced the same bill in the House, it was forgotten in the rush of the Hundred Days. But in June 1933 Congress did pass the Wagner-Peyser Act, which established the employment office system that the Senator had originally proposed in 1928. Although a revamped public employment office network was necessary to handle personnel for the Public Works Administration, it also marked an important step toward an unemployment insurance system. The Wagner-Peyser Act provided the administrative framework that was required for such a program—a fact that was hardly noticed in the summer of 1933. It was, moreover, another victory for Wagner's step-by-step approach to unemployment legislation, which he had begun in 1928 and would not complete for many years.

One additional measure in this progression drew even less attention than the tax-exemption bill. On June 19, a few days after Congress approved the Wagner-Peyser Act, Wagner introduced Andrews' revised American plan for the District of Columbia. Designed to promote the "middle way" between the Wisconsin and Ohio plans, this bill was the last in a series of federal measures drawn up by Andrews. It also indicated, perhaps better than the other Wagner bills, the reformers' wariness of the constitutional issue. Conservatives and progressives alike generally believed that labor legislation that was national in scope and provided for uniform enforcement would not survive a court test. The actions of the Supreme Court between 1933 and 1936 increased the likelihood of this outcome. But the federal government obviously controlled the District of Columbia and the 1933 Wagner bill was only the first of several measures that were designed in part to avoid an adverse court decision.

The next move in the congressional campaign for unemployment insurance reflected both this respect for the judiciary and the continued influence of the Wisconsin reformers. Since the passage of the Groves bill, the Raushenbushes had been seeking ways of encouraging reserves legislation in other states. They had been unsuccessful until 1933, when Senator Wagner's bill to promote voluntary reserves through business tax-incentives gave them a new idea. During the latter months of 1933 Raushenbush worked on a more ambitious version of the Wagner bill, under which Congress might "encourage or virtually compel the enactment of state laws." In October he wrote that another Wagner bill or "even more compelling tax devices may receive serious consideration in the 1934 Congress."[20] The "more compelling" device that he came up with was the "tax offset," which had first been used in the 1926 Federal Estate Tax law and which had been ruled constitutional by the Supreme Court. Under the tax-offset idea, Congress would adopt a payroll tax on employers, uniform for all the states, with the additional provision that employers in states enacting suitable legislation could credit their state-tax payments against their federal obligation. Such an act would have two important effects: it would limit interstate competition, since all employers would be subject to the federal tax, and it would base the unemployment insurance system on state rather than national legislation. By permitting a wide variety of state systems it would also protect the Wisconsin act from compulsory pooling.

Having decided that the tax offset was the best means of encouraging state legislation while preserving the Wisconsin act, Elizabeth Brandeis arranged, with the help of her father and A. L. Filene, a Washington meeting (Raushenbush remained in Wisconsin) to sell the idea of federal legislation to other businessmen and Administration leaders. Who participated in this meeting, held in early January, 1934, at the home of Filene's daughter, is the subject of controversy, but probably Frances Perkins, Wagner, Filene, and New Deal lawyers Thomas H. Eliot, Assistant Solicitor of the Labor Department, and Thomas G. Corcoran, were there.[21] Their enthusiastic response prompted Elizabeth Brandeis to ask Raushenbush to wire a draft bill and then, when long-range communication proved difficult, to arrange for him to discuss the tax-offset plan with Miss Perkins' staff.

With the aid of Charles Wyzanski, Jr., Raushenbush and Eliot drafted a bill in January 1934 which incorporated the tax-offset plan and a uniform 5 percent federal tax on employers' payrolls. It provided, however, that if the states should enact unemployment insurance laws with certain minimum benefit standards, the employers would receive full credit against their federal tax payments. Even if their contributions under the state laws amounted to less than the stipulated 5 percent because of merit or experience-rating clauses in the state laws, they would retain their full exemption from the federal tax. It was no wonder that this flexible approach received a sympathetic hearing from Administration officials, whose interest in unemployment insurance was tempered by their respect for the Court and their desire to avoid the controversy among the reformers. Senator Wagner and Representative Lewis introduced the bill on February 5, 1934.

While the Wagner-Lewis bill was intended to protect the Wisconsin experiment, it provided equal protection for plans such as the one contemplated in Ohio. The inherent impartiality of the measure held a strong appeal for Wagner and others who wanted to bridge the gap between the feuding reformers. As Edwin E. Witte argued, "this is one measure on which the supporters both of unemployment insurance and unemployment reserves can present a united front."[22] Andrews vigorously backed the Wagner-Lewis bill, throwing the full resources of the AALL behind the congressional campaign. Epstein was less enthusiastic; he finally backed the bill while continuing to work for a national system. Later he confessed: "There was no hearty support for the Wagner-Lewis bill except a political situation which caused most of us to feel, 'What are we going to do?' Here was an administration measure. It was very poor. We felt it was our job to line up with the administration and support the thing."[23]

That the conflict between the reform groups had passed the conciliatory stage was evident in the following weeks. In an attempt to win expert support for the Administration's program, Secretary Perkins scheduled, as part of a conference on labor legislation in mid-February, a session on unemployment insurance, to which she invited representatives from both sides, omitting only the more vocal and irreconcilable reformers such as Raushenbush, Miss Brandeis, Rubinow, and Epstein, in an attempt to avoid a new breach that might endanger the Wagner-Lewis bill. When Epstein learned of the conference, particularly the fact that Andrews had been invited, he was outraged. He concluded that the Association for Social Security had been deliberately left out: "My investigations . . . lead me to the firm conclusion that the exclusion order came directly from the Secretary of Labor."[24] Mobilizing his followers he protested so loudly over this apparent slight that Miss Perkins, fearful of alienating his supporters, quietly arranged a last-minute invitation. This unpleasant altercation, nevertheless, foreshadowed more serious problems that would arise in the future.

The conference of February 14–15 soon revealed the superficial nature of the new unanimity the reformers professed over the Wagner-Lewis bill. Miss Perkins opened the session on unemployment insurance with a highly conciliatory statement. Admitting that the Wagner-Lewis bill did not provide "the 100 percent perfect answer," she called for the support of all the factions. Douglas, who had never publicly shared Epstein's rancor, followed with a strong plea for harmony. The Wagner-Lewis bill, he maintained, was "federalism at its best," and expressed the hope that the individuals present would firmly resolve to work for its passage. He then summarized the arguments for the insurance approach, emphasizing the benefits of a pooled fund and employee contributions. John Fitch immediately called for the deletion of Douglas' personal views. Although Arthur J. Altmeyer suggested that Andrews explain the provisions of the Wisconsin act as a way of offsetting Douglas' statements, Andrews refused to defend the reserves approach. His obstinance and intimation that the social insurance reformers did not deserve an answer did nothing to preserve harmony among the reformers.[25] Douglas angrily noted that the AALL head "made an ass of himself by bitterly complaining about the slights which he had experienced."[26]

Epstein, as Miss Perkins had anticipated, did not share Andrews' reticence. While endorsing the Wagner-Lewis bill, he made a vigorous statement in favor of the "social insurance approach." He offered no compromise. His backers, he announced, pledged not "to give up our fight for an adequate plan of unemployment insurance in the different states." Attacking reserves plans as "little better than other company welfare schemes," he rejected any consideration of the Wisconsin plan. Instead he called for tripartite contributions and adequate benefits for the unemployed.[27] Though characteristic of Epstein's manner, this outburst only exacerbated the conflict that Douglas and Andrews had opened. The conference ended with the factions further apart than ever.

But it was the President rather than the reformers who provoked the greatest concern among backers of the Wagner-Lewis bill. Though he had shown little understanding of the economics of unemployment insurance and no inclination to choose between the various plans that were offered, he had fairly definite views on certain aspects of the subject. Frightened, perhaps, by denunciations of the British system, he insisted on strict adherence to insurance principles. This insistence meant not only a contributory plan divorced from government financial aid but employee contributions as well. He wrote in 1931 that he favored joint contributions despite the objections of his "social welfare friends," and stated this preference on several later occasions.[28] Only partially, however, was this view based on actuarial principles. Like Swope, Roosevelt thought that a small contribution would give the wage earner a sense of responsibility, a vested interest in unemployment insurance. But he also envisioned a broader program than most of the reformers. At least since his governorship, the President had been interested in a comprehensive social security plan. His ignorance of the technical problems of insuring against unemployment was matched by his indignation at the plight of the old, the poor, and the handicapped. He shocked Secretary Perkins on one occasion by proposing that "every child, from the day he is born," should be included in the system. "From the cradle to the grave they ought to be in a social insurance system."[29]

Roosevelt was consequently somewhat less than enthusiastic about the Wagner-Lewis bill. In late January he told Representative Lewis that he wanted a commission to study "the whole field of old age dependency and unemployment."[30] A month later he expanded on his position to Rexford Tugwell: "In regard to the Unemployment Insurance Bill, I have told Miss Perkins and Bob Wagner that I have no objection to its being reported by the committees, but I do not think the adjournment of the Session should be held up by it. As you say—it will require a good deal of overhauling and would necessarily cause much debate."[31] But he did agree, after considerable badgering from Miss Perkins and her aides, to endorse it publicly. In a letter written by Miss Perkins' staff and released on March 23 just after the House Ways and Means Committee began hearings on the measure, he expressed his dedication to unemployment insurance, called jobless benefits a "stabilizing device," and maintained that the Wagner-Lewis bill fulfilled the 1932 Democratic platform pledge.[32]

The hearings of March–April indicated that many people, including some high Administration officials, were more enthusiastic about the bill than the President. Miss Perkins and Harry Hopkins, the Federal Relief Administrator, presented the official point of view. They took no specific stand on the question of unemployment prevention but stressed the elimination of interstate competition. To their relief the reformers emphasized their support of the bill rather than describing their differences. The insurance advocates, including Epstein and several representatives of the Ohio Commission, clearly outnumbered Andrews and his followers. Although Epstein could not entirely suppress his displeasure with the reserves idea, his tone was moderate and conciliatory. An additional asset was the appearance of William Green, who endorsed unemployment insurance as a method for stabilizing purchasing power and helping the worker retain his self-respect.[33]

Thomas Eliot, Miss Perkins' associate, on the other hand encountered great difficulty in lining up employers to speak for the bill. Most of the businessmen who had experimented with voluntary plans agreed to testify, but the majority of them expressed reservations over the 5 percent payroll tax and considered any immediate action precipitate.[34] Swope and Folsom voiced the prevailing sentiment among executives when they urged delay and the scaling down of the employers' tax. Folsom spoke for many of his colleagues when he explained that most businessmen "have so many problems to consider in the present depression that they cannot be very interested in providing reserves for future depressions."[35]

These objections were indicative of the growing opposition among businessmen to unemployment insurance legislation. Detecting the first signs of an economic upturn in the spring of 1934, many executives became increasingly wary of new taxation. Others, confusing the Wagner-Lewis bill with the Wagner labor-disputes bill, equated unemployment insurance with a union resurgence. Under these circumstances the statements of Folsom and Swope advising delay were prophetic. In March the manufacturers committee of the Chamber of Commerce denounced the Wagner-Lewis bill, in a masterpiece of illogic, as an "unwarranted encroachment upon the privilege of each state to deal individually with the problems affecting the welfare of its citizens . . . ."[36] The chamber convention endorsed this position, although it reiterated its support for voluntary plans. Harriman attempted to assure Roosevelt that business appreciated his recovery program, but his statements had a hollow ring in the face of mounting opposition.[37] Various other employers' organizations, including the New York Merchants Association, the Automobile Chamber of Commerce, and a large group of Connecticut manufacturers, backed the chamber by registering their opposition to the Wagner-Lewis bill.[38]

No less important was the growing popular pressure on the New Deal being generated from both the political right and left. Senator Huey P. Long and Gerald L. K. Smith, through the Share Our Wealth Society, and Father Charles E. Coughlin of Detroit, through the National Union for Social Justice, exploited the popular unrest and dissatisfaction with the progress of the New Deal among the millions to whom their leadership appealed. The old-age pension movement of Dr. Francis E. Townsend had taken on the proportions of a crusade among the elderly hit by the Depression. Demands for increased government spending for the poor and aged could not be overlooked for long without provoking even angrier reactions. The Communists and their allies were pushing for the passage of the Lundeen bill, a radical relief measure offered to Congress, under the leadership of social worker Mary Van Kleek, as an alternative to the Administration bill; and though there was little sentiment in Congress for this measure, it further complicated an already difficult situation.

Pressured by jittery business executives on one hand and radicals on the other, Roosevelt also encountered divisions among his advisors. Tugwell urged postponement of the Wagner-Lewis bill until a thorough study could be made. Like many businessmen he warned of the dangers of rapidly liquidating the reserve funds accumulated under an unemployment insurance act during some future depression, a fear that was widespread in the spring of 1934 and undoubtedly worried the President.[39] At the same time Secretary Perkins intensified her efforts to gain Roosevelt's active support for the Wagner-Lewis bill. Her determination was evident in a message of April 17: "Don't forget this, will you? You wrote a letter which has gone all over the country and everyone has relied on that as an indication that it will go through. It

is probably our only chance in twenty-five years to get a bill like this.
. . . It is very important—do please telephone the Chief Performer on
the Hill at once that this must come out of Committee and be
passed."[40] This remonstrance was apparently successful—at least for the
time being. After conferring with the President, Wagner reported that
his bill would probably pass, although with a 2 rather than a 5 percent
tax.[41] On April 21 Roosevelt asked Lewis to assure the House members
of his support. And in early May he sent a message to Chairman Robert Doughton of the Ways and Means Committee asking for passage of
the Wagner-Lewis bill.[42] Despite this last minute flurry of activity, reports of the President's reservations persisted. Andrews was gravely disappointed at these rumors and the continued inaction of Doughton's
committee. Rubinow noted bitterly that "beyond writing his somewhat
innocuous letter a month or two ago, [Roosevelt] . . . has apparently
refused to make it part of his program."[43]

By late May it was apparent that Roosevelt had indeed decided to
drop the Wagner-Lewis bill. His stated reasons were twofold: he
doubted "the probability of its passage at this session," and argued
that "we can properly prepare for the next session an even more comprehensive plan for social insurance."[44] To eliminate these problems
he then proposed an interim study, much as he had done in New York.
The delay would permit time for congressional backing to develop,
and the study committee he hoped would piece together a "larger"
program, while reconciling the various groups with an interest in social insurance. On June 8 he announced to Congress that the "great
task of furthering the security of the citizen and his family through social insurance" would begin in 1935. To prepare the way he would establish a committee to draw up a long-term program to combat insecurity, based on a "maximum of cooperation between States and the
Federal government." Such a program would be financed, he emphasized, "by contribution rather than by increase in general taxation" and
would be "national in scope."[45] The Wagner-Lewis bill subsequently
died in Doughton's committee, and unemployment insurance was
turned over to the new Committee on Economic Security for inclusion
in a "more comprehensive plan for social insurance."

The Roosevelt Program Emerges

FOR SEVEN months, from June 1934 to January 1935,
Roosevelt's advisors labored diligently to devise a wide-ranging social
insurance program. Their job was complicated by the sheer scope of
their assignment. In addition to unemployment insurance or old age

pensions, both of which had created enough controversy to occupy the time of any committee for many months, they had to consider many other plans—assistance to the aged, handicapped, and needy, and health insurance. Their major problem would clearly be one of organizing these proposals into a single package that would be palatable to the President and the Congress. The obstacles to success were formidable; Roosevelt seemed to be indecisive, many congressmen were suspicious, the courts were hostile, and the reformers were impossibly divided. The answer—if indeed there was any satisfactory answer—was to move ahead with as little friction as possible, in short to present a program that would alienate the smallest number of people. It did not take Roosevelt's aides long to recognize this fact or to act accordingly.

When it became obvious that Roosevelt was determined to have an interim study of social insurance, Secretary Perkins adjusted her strategy to meet the new situation. To insure rapid progress in preparation for the new Congress, which would open in January, she suggested a committee of cabinet members assisted by experts and advisors representing various interest groups.[46] Once Roosevelt had agreed to this proposal, she and Altmeyer, the Assistant Secretary of Labor, immediately began the background work. During the next three weeks Altmeyer worked out the details of the organization. His completed plan called for a formal cabinet committee, consisting of the Secretaries of Labor, Commerce (changed by Roosevelt to the Secretary of Agriculture), the Treasury, the Attorney General, and the relief administrator; a Technical Board, composed of federal officials who were experts in labor legislation; an Advisory Council whose members would be prominent employers, reformers, and labor leaders; and an executive director and research staff. On June 29 the President approved this proposal in an executive order creating the Committee on Economic Security.[47]

While ultimate responsibility under this plan rested on the cabinet officers, the crucial position was that of the executive director. Charged with guiding the day-to-day work of the committee and its advisors, the executive director could determine the pace of the work and the necessary deadlines. Upon his shoulders would rest, moreover, the assignment of maintaining unity among the feuding reformers who were anxious to project their pet projects and ideas into the federal bill. After considering several people, Miss Perkins and Altmeyer chose Edwin E. Witte, who at that time was the acting director of the unemployment compensation division of the Wisconsin Industrial Commission. He was notified of his appointment on July 24 and began his duties two days later.[48]

Witte was well qualified for his new job. Though a student of Commons, a University of Wisconsin professor, and a close observer of the Wisconsin unemployment insurance movement, he had been prevented, because of his official position, from overtly backing Groves and the Raushenbushes. From Witte's point of view this was not an unwelcome immunity, for he had grave reservations about the prevention theory. As early as 1921 he had argued with his mentor that "prevention is not the only argument in favor of unemployment insurance. . . . [It] is a method for better distribution of losses. Fluctuations in employment due to business conditions, I feel, are largely beyond the control of the individual employer." He admitted only that the prevention of seasonal unemployment was possible.[49] As the years passed, his skepticism toward the rationale of the Huber and Groves bills was moderated only by his admiration for the individuals involved. In 1932, when he helped compose the AFL recommendations on unemployment insurance, he advised against a declaration for a pooled-fund system, although he agreed that such a plan was more practical than the reserves approach. He frankly admitted that he preferred "an unemployment insurance bill on the British model."[50]

Yet above all Witte was a political realist. He had kept his heretical views to himself during the Wisconsin campaign in the interest of ultimate victory. His long experience as an administrator had taught him that it would be easier to amend a federal unemployment insurance act than to pass one and that the administrators could do much to determine the nature of the federal system. Thus, instead of concerning himself with the conflict over prevention, he assumed that the Wagner-Lewis approach would meet the least resistance and worried about the prospects of state action after passage of the federal bill. Since most state legislatures had scheduled only brief meetings in 1935, delay in Congress might mean postponement of state action until 1937. "This situation," Witte noted shortly before his appointment, "affords a strong reason for urging everybody who will have anything to do with the new national bill that . . . [it] should be in shape so it can be put through Congress in a hurry."[51]

A final consideration that reinforced the position of pragmatists like Witte and Secretary Perkins—since there were no precedents from the state campaigns—was the constitutional issue. The apparent opposition of the Supreme Court to many of the New Deal programs was a specter that haunted the committee from its origin. In the end it was probably as significant as political acceptability in determining the program that was devised. Everyone assumed that the Court would cast a skeptical eye on any unemployment insurance law that centered great power in the federal government at the expense of the states. Miss Perkins, moreover, had heard from Justice Harlan Fiske Stone that use of the taxing power to establish a jobless insurance system would be a legitimate exercise of federal power.[52] With this in mind she and Witte effectively argued that the Wagner-Lewis tax-offset plan would be likely to receive a favorable opinion from the Court. And even if it were struck down the state laws would remain, insuring the continuation of the system whatever the verdict of the High Court.[53]

Witte's job, at least as far as unemployment insurance was concerned, was thus fairly obvious. Since little more than the Wagner-Lewis bill could be proposed without running the danger of securing no law at all, his assignment was to run interference for Miss Perkins while she extracted the necessary recommendations from the cabinet committee. But even this would demand considerable patience, stamina, and personal courage, since Epstein and his supporters were certain to insist on a plan that would be inacceptable to businessmen and reserves supporters. To insulate himself from their attacks Witte had relatively little intellectual armor, at least if the idea of the COES as a totally impartial, objective body was to be maintained. He attempted to use Roosevelt's speech—"I entered upon my work . . . in the fixed belief that these statements of the President constituted definite instructions"—without much success.[54] It was, however, his dedication to the pragmatic viewpoint of Miss Perkins rather than collusion with the Wisconsin reformers, as Epstein, Rubinow, and other advocates of a national insurance system later charged, that led to his continued insistence on a federal-state system similar to that proposed in the Wagner-Lewis bill.

The first of many challenges to this position—in the form of demands for a more ambitious program of unemployment insurance—came from the Technical Board and the COES staff headed by Bryce Stewart. Stewart prepared a preliminary report on unemployment insurance in which he outlined a national system based on tripartite contributions. At its September 26 meeting the Technical Board approved this statement and incorporated it in a report which the cabinet committee considered at its October 1 meeting. The cabinet officials, however, quashed this attempt to embark on a more wide-ranging program; they referred Stewart's plan back to the Technical Board with instructions for continued study.[55]

Deliberations between Witte and members of the staff and Technical Board on the principles of an unemployment insurance system occupied much of the following month and a half. Several staff members, including Stewart, looked askance at the tax-offset idea and the reserves approach and insisted on a national system. In the course of these consultations an intermediate federal-state plan won considerable favor. This was called the subsidy system, because the taxes collected by the federal government would be returned to the states or other jurisdictions that established unemployment insurance programs. Many proponents of a national plan backed this approach as the next best alternative, since it would allow the inclusion of national benefit standards. Leiserson, for example, was at first a strong advocate of the subsidy plan.[56] But Witte and others who were worried about the constitutional question had grave reservations, since the subsidy plan would make the entire system dependent on a favorable court judgment. Further discussions failed to break the impasse.

By mid-October Witte was very "concerned about the long delay which has developed upon the question of national or state administration." "I fear," he admitted, "that we have already delayed too long to have any hope of having the state legislatures act in their regular sessions next winter." If his fear was realized "our only chance . . . is to work out a nationally administered system which makes the constitutional question the all-important one. On this point, we get little or no encouragement from some people who have as good a line on the Supreme Court as any one."[57]

Finally the approaching deadlines forced the Technical Board to act —or rather to admit that it was unable to act. Since it had reached no decision, the board submitted a summary of the three plans to the COES on November 9 without a recommendation. After some discussion, Harry Hopkins moved that the COES adopt some type of federal-state system. The cabinet members not only accepted this proposal but unanimously endorsed the Wagner-Lewis over the subsidy method. Apparently their main concern was the possibility that Congress would not agree to a national program. Witte explained that they reached their decision "on political, not constitutional grounds."[58]

There were other signs that progress might henceforth be more rapid. The Business Advisory Council, while not a part of the COES organization, included several important members of the COES Advisory Council. In September it submitted a report drawn up by Swope, Leeds, Walter C. Teagle, and other business leaders, that advocated legislation to eliminate interstate competition. The council implied its opposition to a national plan by favoring limited contributions and opposing any type of pooled fund. It also called for a "substantial incentive [for the employer] to stabilize his forces by operating on a shorter week, spacing his production schedule over a longer season and adopting other means of leveling the curve of employment."[59] Witte thought it "probable that support for a satisfactory unemployment bill can be gotten from this group . . . ."[60] Then in November, at the National Conference on Economic Security, a meeting Miss Perkins and Witte organized to publicize the work of the COES, Roosevelt seemed to endorse the direction his advisors were taking. He assured his audience that "unemployment insurance will be in the program" and that "state laws will also be needed."[61]

But if Witte and Miss Perkins had expected their luck to continue they soon realized their error. The Advisory Council, which met periodically after the National Conference, raised the old problems all over again. The difficulties that they had with the Advisory Council grew out of the fact that most of its members were familiar with unemployment insurance plans and had strong interests in particular approaches. Of the five employer members—Swope, Leeds, Folsom, Sam A. Lewisohn, and Teagle—all but Teagle had had experience with company plans; of the five labor leaders, Green and Henry Ohl fit in this category; and of the eight (later thirteen) representatives of the public, nearly all possessed some degree of expertise in the field, although Paul Kellogg of the *Survey*, Edith Abbott, a settlement worker, Raymond Moley, and Frank P. Graham, a southern progressive who served as chairman, played the most prominent roles in the work of the council. While the more controversial reformers like Epstein, Douglas, and the Raushenbushes were excluded, the composition of the council practically insured the projection of the reformers' disputes into its deliberations. This became a certainty at the first meeting, when the council debated unemployment insurance and resolved to make a detailed study—a development which Perkins and Witte had not originally contemplated.

Retreading the ground the Technical Board had recently traversed, the council soon became involved in the question of a national versus a federal-state system. At the first meeting Witte and Eliot explained the committee's objections to a national system, after which the council reached a consensus that such an approach was inappropriate. But many of the members were impressed with the advantages of the subsidy idea. The employers, while supporters of prevention, were receptive to the suggestion that "it is probably easier to establish industrial funds operating on a nationwide basis which are exempted from state laws . . . ."[62] For more than a month the council reconsidered the subsidy plan, only to encounter the same problems that the Technical Board faced and ultimately report a deadlock. Miss Perkins and Witte in particular were angry that they had wasted their time waiting for the council to act after they had already determined on the Wagner-Lewis approach. Shortly afterward, however, the council convened and voted nine to seven, with all five employers in the affirmative, for the subsidy method. This vote was taken after the employer representatives had met privately with Stewart and decided to endorse the subsidy scheme, which further angered the cabinet members when they learned of the intrigue.[63] On the other hand the subsequent actions of the cabinet officers made many council members feel their advice had been deliberately disregarded.[64]

The embarrassing dispute over the subsidy plan was not, however, the last problem posed for Witte and Miss Perkins by the council. The businessmen wanted employee contributions so, as Swope contended, the worker would regard "the plan as partly his own and not as something given to him as a gratuity," a moderate tax, and explicit sanction for individual reserves plans.[65] At its December 6 meeting the council rejected suggestions for a 5 percent tax on payrolls and compulsory employee contributions and endorsed a 3 percent levy. Although it never got to the actual question of reserves or pooling, it was split by the decisions it did make; Kellogg, Graham, and Helen Hall, the settlement leader, together with Green and Ohl, drew up a statement objecting to the low contribution rate, while the employers and Moley complained that the council had given insufficient consideration to their demands. The businessmen praised the philosophy of the Wisconsin act and the idea of industry-wide plans so "the cost of the less regular industries will be borne by such industries."[66] On these notes of disagreement the council implicitly acknowledged that it had no more power than other groups to reconcile the debate over the objectives of unemployment insurance.

Except for the one unhappy meeting on December 7 the Advisory Council had relatively little contact with the COES, which in the meantime had resumed its deliberations independently of the council. Indeed, after the council's subcommittee on unemployment insurance submitted its inconclusive report, the cabinet members paid relatively little attention to the council. While this inattention was in part a result of the council's inaction, it was also a product of divisions among the COES members. After Roosevelt's November speech the COES had, as a result of public criticism, reconsidered the possibility of a national system. At one point the members had reversed their decision for a federal-state plan only to shift back after further study. But with the opening of Congress rapidly approaching, Miss Perkins finally forced a showdown: ". . . one day during Christmas week 1934 I issued an ultimatum that the Committee would meet at eight o'clock at my house, that all telephone service would be discontinued at my house for the evening and that we would sit all night, if necessary, until we had decided the thorny question once and for all. We sat until two in the morning, and at the end we agreed . . . that for the present the wisest thing was to recommend a federal-state system."[67]

In other respects the COES also followed the inclinations of its more pragmatic members. To avoid any potential trouble with the courts the members decided that the final bill should allow maximum freedom to the states. Consequently they included no national benefit standards—a major setback for reformers of the Epstein persuasion who would now have to depend on the states to provide adequate payments. They also opposed employee contributions without forbidding the states to require them, and they placed no restrictions on individual reserves plans except to require that one-third of the employer's 3 percent tax be paid into a state pooled fund, a provision originally suggested by Altmeyer which partially placated Epstein and his followers. Their deliberations concluded, Miss Perkins and Hopkins informally reported to Roosevelt on December 24. He agreed to include their recommendations in his 1935 legislative program.[68] Though many disputes among the cabinet members and their advisors remained for Witte to settle, the basic decisions had been made; federal unemployment insurance legislation—in the form of a weakened Wagner-Lewis bill—now rested in the hands of the nation's lawmakers.[69]

In retrospect the work of the COES is difficult to assess. Certainly the committee report met the tests of political and constitutional acceptability that the Administration officials had considered so important. Moreover, because its preparation involved so many people, it gave reformers of various persuasions—undoubtedly at the expense of Mr. Witte's peace of mind—a vested interest in the Administration's program. The committee work also stirred public interest in the economic security bill. Whether these achievements were more desirable than an all-out fight for the Wagner-Lewis bill in 1934, the reintroduction of the Wagner-Lewis bill in 1935, or the introduction of a stronger unemployment insurance bill in 1935 is at least arguable. The absence of benefit standards in particular was to be the subject of growing criticism in the succeeding years. But to judge the Administration leaders or the committee members by what was or was not to happen in the future would be unfair. The fact was that sufficient opposition appeared to remain in Congress to make their conservative approach the logical one in the spring of 1935.

The Congressional Campaign of 1935

THE PURPOSE of the unemployment insurance provisions of the COES report, Roosevelt declared to Congress on January 17, was "to afford a requirement of a reasonably uniform character for all States . . . and encourage the passage of unemployment compensation laws in the states." The goal of such a system was "to afford every practicable aid and incentive toward the larger purpose of employment stabilization." As far as the federal government was involved, it "should not foreclose the states from establishing means for inducing industries to afford an even greater stabilization of employment."[70] With this speech the congressional struggle for jobless insurance resumed. Part of the "second New Deal" legislative campaign of 1935, it marked the start of the last decisive stage of the campaign for unemployment insurance in the United States.

The Administration's economic security bill, which Roosevelt announced in his message, incorporated the decisions of the COES. As drafted by Eliot, the unemployment insurance section provided for a uniform tax, beginning in 1936, which would reach the maximum level of 3 percent in 1938. Employers in states that enacted unemployment insurance laws would receive credit for as much as 90 percent of the gross federal tax. The remainder would be used to pay administrative costs. The states were free to enact either the Wisconsin or Ohio plan, providing that 1 percent of the employers' payroll went into a state pool. No benefit standards were included. In fact, beyond the requirement that one-third of the tax be paid to the state pool, and safeguards for trade union members, the bill contained almost no standards for state compliance. Moreover, as an incentive to employers, it allowed "additional credit" so firms with good employment records could be permitted to pay less under state experience-rating provisions than the 2.7 percent (3 percent minus 10 percent) standard tax after five years. At his insistence Doughton as well as Lewis introduced the measure in the House, while Wagner was its Senate sponsor.

Initial opposition to the bill resulted from its cautious approach. Most moderate political and economic groups favored it, but as Witte reported, "Our program apparently is a 'middle of the road' proposal, which is drawing fire from reactionary business interests and extreme conservatives on one hand, and on the other the Townsendites and the advocates of the Lundeen bill."[71] In early February he complained that businessmen, Communists, New York "high brows," and Townsendites were trying to sabotage the Administration's program.[72] Yet as the exemplar of the middle-of-the-road approach, Witte was particularly sensitive to the possibility of increased opposition from other quarters. "There are a great number of cross currents and a vast undercover opposition," he warned in January. As a result "the legislation will not be through Congress much before the end of February."[73]

Though Witte correctly recognized the dark clouds on the horizon, he underestimated the strength of the bill's critics. This was a natural miscalculation, for the "vast undercover opposition" consisted of the friends rather than the enemies of unemployment insurance. The proceedings of the Advisory Council had foreshadowed this problem. And the council had represented the less vocal partisans of jobless insurance. When the COES bill reached Congress, the reports of divisions within the council exacerbated the existing split. In no case did this conflict involve the principle of unemployment insurance. Rather the industrialists on the one hand and the "perfectionists" (as Witte called them in derision) on the other welcomed the idea and condemned the details of the Administration program or, for that matter, any plan which differed from their own conceptions of a suitable approach. The inability of these groups to reach a satisfactory compromise was neither a new nor surprising development. Based on differing conceptions of the objective of unemployment insurance that made fundamental concessions impossible, the dispute between the employer- and the employee-oriented reformers grew more bitter as the stakes increased.

The paradox of the friends of unemployment insurance refusing to accede to a specific plan became painfully apparent to Administration backers during the hearings which the House Ways and Means and Senate Finance Committees conducted on the economic security bill during January and February. For the employers an impressive list of New Emphasis managers testified. The best informed of these was undoubtedly Folsom. He explained why the employer representatives of the Advisory Council favored the subsidy plan; nevertheless, he acknowledged that they accepted the Wagner-Lewis approach. Their remaining objections, he added, were not to the tax-offset provision but to the absence of incentives for stabilization and of employee contributions. Under the Administration bill, the 1 percent pooled fund and certain guarantees of adequate reserves would prolong the period before the time when the employer's contribution could be reduced. Folsom estimated that this would not occur before 1946. "My contention," he told the Senate committee, "is that no employer is going to do anything now to reduce his fluctuation of employment or to stabilize employment on the chance that in 1946 he might get a reduction in rate."[74]

Other employers reiterated these views. A. L. Filene, H. W. Story, and Samuel W. Reyburn, head of the National Retail Dry Goods Association, endorsed both unemployment insurance and Folsom's objections. But the most influential business spokesman to appear was Henry I. Harriman of the Chamber of Commerce. He had developed a close relationship with Witte during 1934 and had pledged to help win the support of businessmen for the Administration's program. Speak-

ing for the liberal faction among the chamber's members, he supported
the economic security bill, yet advised certain amendments to make the
bill more palatable to the business community. Like Folsom he suggested a small employee contribution, not to provide more substantial
benefits but "so that the employee will help to keep the fund solvent
by seeing that those who do not deserve the fund will not receive it."
He also asked that existing company plans with provisions at least as
liberal as those provided in the bill be permitted to continue.[75]

Harriman's testimony reflected the position, widely held among
members of the chamber, that "nothing—except how to make a profit
—is concerning American business just now as much as unemployment
insurance."[76] In March the chamber's committee on social reserves submitted a long-awaited report which amplified the businessmen's view
of unemployment insurance. This document generally endorsed the
Administration's program, although it favored the subsidy plan. More
important was its assertion that "no legislative measure should operate
to discourage experimentation by individual employers with methods
for regularizing employment."[77] This pronouncement marked a long
step forward since 1934, when the chamber convention refused to approve compulsory unemployment insurance. It was, however, one of
the last victories of progressive employers. The movement for congressional action on unemployment as well as other reform measures that
impelled businessmen to rethink their position produced a negative
reaction to all New Deal measures. The time when Harriman could
appear before a congressional committee to back a program such as the
economic security bill was rapidly running out.

But the businessmen's objections to the economic security bill, at
least when compared to those of many dedicated reformers, were relatively innocuous. For many social workers and labor legislation experts
who had devoted long years to the social insurance movement, Roosevelt's program was a major disappointment. On the verge of victories in
the state legislatures, they sensed betrayal at the highest level. Stewart
and Kellogg had expressed this sentiment during the preparation of
the bill. Kellogg then took his case directly to the President, arguing in
a series of letters for a national system and higher contributions. Roosevelt, perhaps annoyed at these complaints, explained the political lia-
bilities of his argument: "We would all like to see better standards but
it is a matter of finance and we cannot eat the whole cake at one
meal."[78] The reformers' displeasure increased when the economic security bill was submitted to Congress. Of the men who directed the attack on prevention in the state campaigns, Leiserson, who shared
Witte's pragmatism, and to a lesser extent Douglas, made their peace

with the Administration. But Rubinow and Epstein, neither of whom had been consulted at any stage in the preparation of the bill, remained implacable. Rubinow wrote that he "wouldn't shed one tear" if Congress struck out the unemployment insurance provisions of the economic security bill.[79]

Epstein, the most dogmatic of all the reformers, could not be similarly contained. First at the hearings and later as an informal advisor to the Senate Finance Committee, he systematically attempted to sabotage the economic security bill. As an advocate of a national plan based on the British system, he opposed the bill with the same intensity and uncompromising zeal with which he fought Andrews and the Wisconsin reformers. "We may as well speak frankly," he told the senators. "I do not want to see the country go off on a bad way and have another Congress repeal the whole thing because of rotten thinking." Referring to the unemployment insurance provisions he confessed that he desired their defeat. "And," he added, "we will fight and fight to repeal it for the next couple of years, because it will just put us off on a tangent that will get us nowhere and we will have to ask for its repeal."[80] Though relatively few of Epstein's supporters shared his bitterness, his tactics were a source of considerable satisfaction to the conservatives who hoped to block or emasculate the bill.

Less antagonistic but similarly estranged from the Administration was organized labor, which was at that time playing a vital role in the passage of state unemployment insurance legislation. While the AFL continued to support a federal social insurance program—Green had, in fact, aligned with the proponents of federal or subsidy plans while serving on the Advisory Council—it gave little assistance during the congressional struggle. This passive role was largely a result of Roosevelt's collective bargaining policy, especially his acquiescence in the growth of company unions. During the spring of 1935, at Wagner's initiative, Congress was moving toward the passage of pro-union legislation, but the union leaders' displeasure with the Administration temporarily deprived the economic security bill of their wholehearted backing. Green's testimony revealed little enthusiasm and his remarks were commonly interpreted as criticism. Since positive labor support was becoming an ever more important ingredient in the passage of reform legislation, its absence in this case was a serious blow to backers of the bill.

With their forces in disarray, Administration supporters had to face an additional obstacle, the irascibility of Chairman Doughton and the members of the House Ways and Means Committee. At the conclusion of the public hearings it appeared the committee might kill the entire bill. Witte feared impending disaster due to the "terrific snag" that the measure had encountered in the House committee.[81] In early March Epstein was informed by his Washington friends that the bill would not be reported, and Witte, as late as March 23, found the situation "not very favorable."[82] But the committee was less interested in killing the bill than in demonstrating its power. A series of important amendments were added in March and early April. Because of the states rights disposition of the Ways and Means Committee members, the controversy over the subsidy plan did not arise. The committee did, however, strike out the provision allowing an "additional credit"—one representative shrewdly asking Witte why, if the bill was to eliminate interstate competition, experience rating was permitted—the only incentive to unemployment prevention in the federal bill and therefore a politically necessary feature to insure employer support. Then the House draftsman, in rewriting the measure, prohibited individual reserve funds. Less serious but equally annoying were amendments that exempted more classes of workers; fixed the contributions at 1 percent in 1936 and 2 percent in 1937; permitted the states certain flexibility in using public employment offices to administer the act; and to the embarrassment of Miss Perkins took administration of the entire act away from the Labor Department and created an independent Social Security Board.[83]

To prevent complete emasculation of the bill, if not its actual defeat, the moderates concluded that Roosevelt's intervention was necessary. But this was precisely what he was determined to avoid. Sensitive to rising cries of Presidential dictation, he resisted the entreaties of the bill's backers through most of March, telling them "not to worry about the form in which the bill goes through the House, since the real important thing is to get it before the Senate Committee at the earliest date possible."[84] In the end, however, Doughton's loyalty to the Administration and a concerted publicity drive initiated by Miss Perkins and Andrews got the bill reported out of committee. Of the latter effort Witte later recalled that "this activity . . . came at the most critical time and marked a distinct turning point in the history of the measure."[85]

Once the bill was brought to the House floor Roosevelt was more forceful. In early April he placed it on the Administration's "must list" and warned the opposition, which consisted of reactionary Republicans and of Townsendites dissatisfied with the old age pension provisions, that he would fight for passage of the unemployment insurance and old age features of his bill.[86] By the time debate began on April 12, it was apparent that neither the Republicans nor the Townsendites could muster sufficient support to overrule the majority Democrats. The House speeches, despite more than the usual histrionics, had no direct effect on the outcome. On April 19 the House rejected amendments that would have substituted the radical Lundeen and Townsend plans, and proceeded to enact the Ways and Means Committee version of the social security bill (as the economic security bill was now called) by the overwhelming margin of 372 to 33.[87]

In the Senate, where the bill's supporters had anticipated considerable opposition from southern conservatives, there was relatively little interest in unemployment insurance. The danger to the bill came less from the senators' antagonism than from their leisurely approach. After the conclusion of hearings in February, the Finance Committee dropped the social insurance program until April and made no report until May 20. In the meantime the opposition of the erstwhile friends of unemployment insurance grew more vocal, if not more effective. Witte was most worried about Epstein, whom he contended had "the confidence of the Senate Committee more than anyone else."[88] Doubtless Epstein would have been flattered to hear Witte's remarks, for he too was having problems with the Finance Committee. The senators, it seemed, were not particularly interested in outside advice, whether it came from the friends or enemies of the bill.[89]

A far more real and serious threat was the defection of the business community. As economic conditions improved and support for compulsory collective bargaining and increased taxation grew, the nation's business leaders became increasingly disenchanted with the New Deal. The threats they foresaw were both economic and political: increased taxation would retard recovery, while bureaucrats and trade union officials would intervene in the management of their affairs. By the spring of 1935 these fears, which were not wholly without substance, caused near hysteria among business leaders. At its May 1935 convention the Chamber of Commerce repudiated Harriman, elected a staunch opponent of business-government cooperation to succeed him, and blasted the Administration's reform program, including unemployment insurance legislation. The Business Advisory and Planning Council, including many leading New Emphasis employers, called on Roosevelt to reject the stand of the chamber. But the pro-Administration employers were now definitely outnumbered, and the fate of the social security bill was further jeopardized.[90]

With the conservative forces apparently mobilizing to defeat or greatly weaken the bill, the moderates renewed their efforts to force the Finance Committee to act. Perkins and Witte brought together a small group of people, quietly obtained their financial support, and enlisted Andrews to conduct a propaganda campaign. The latter flooded his friends with appeals to write the Senate Committee urging passage of the bill with, incidentally, the provisions allowing individual reserves restored. As a result of this effort the senators received several hundred letters from labor legislation experts.[91] At the same time Miss Perkins pressured Roosevelt to intervene with the Finance Committee. He was again reluctant, especially since his wishes were well known, but he did include a section in his "fireside chat" of April 28 endorsing the unemployment and old age provisions. Significantly, he not only urged support for unemployment insurance but noted that such a plan should provide an incentive to employers to prevent unemployment.[92]

In the end, the Finance Committee and the Senate proved more cooperative than the reformers had expected. On May 17 the committee approved the bill with certain important changes, including an amendment proposed by Senator Robert M. La Follette, Jr., permitting individual reserves funds—a major victory for the Wisconsin plan. In addition, the senators dropped the compromise 1 percent pooled-fund feature, a deletion which remained in the final act, allowing the states considerably greater leeway in adjusting the tax rates of individual employers. The senators also restored the original provisions regarding the size of firms that would be required to participate, and returned the administration of the act to the Labor Department, although they retained the Social Security Board.[93] In this form the social security bill went to the Senate floor, where it met surprisingly meager opposition. On June 19 the Senate, by a seventy-six to six vote, approved the social security bill, insuring the start of a federal-state system of unemployment insurance in the United States.

For more than a month the House and Senate conferees squabbled over the differences between their respective measures. Their discussions centered on the old age insurance system but did, nevertheless, result in one important decision affecting the unemployment insurance program. The House members at first rejected the extended credit feature, but in return for the creation of an independent social security board they finally accepted the Senate interpretation of the individual reserves provision. They compromised on the other disputed provisions in their respective bills. The act, as it was sent to Roosevelt, allowed almost complete freedom to the states to settle the question of reserves versus pooled funds—which by that time had ceased to be an issue in most states—and permitted the states to enact merit or experience rating in either case. On August 14 the President affixed his signature to the Social Security Act, the most important program of its type in American history. It included provisions for a national old age pension plan, old age assistance, federal grants for dependent children, the handicapped, and disabled, and a federal-state unemployment insurance program.

These activities brought to an end the first phase of the development of unemployment insurance in the United States. Though more than a year passed before the states had complied with the provisions of the Social Security Act, there was no longer any question of choice in the matter. Soon administrators had replaced most of the men whose names appear prominently in this study as the key figures in the development of unemployment insurance. The work was far from over —as the performance of the new system in the depression year of 1938 indicated. But unemployment insurance legislation had become a reality in the United States. Finally, it seemed, the public had become convinced that compulsory measures were needed if either the workers or employers were to benefit from unemployment insurance.

Epilogue

IT IS difficult to summarize, much less generalize about, the development of unemployment insurance without merely repeating the story that has already been told. The impact of the British legislation, the failure of a parallel effort in this country, the numerous voluntary plans, and the prevention theory of the postwar decade, and finally the effects of the Depression and the political struggles of 1930–36—all these were important milestones in the creation of a nationwide system of unemployment insurance in the United States. But to detect a unifying theme, a simple formula, to explain what happened is more difficult. At first the paradoxes spring to mind: the wide acceptance of unemployment insurance in principle, the opposition of the labor movement, and the support of businessmen all contradict the popular notions of support and opposition for social welfare legislation. Yet these should probably be regarded as rather superficial manifestations of a more basic theme, the long-term effort by reformers to accommodate a European program to American conditions, to reach a middle ground between the need for something besides relief and the popular willingness to allow businessmen to cope with complex industrial problems. For only when this gap had been bridged was there strong support for an obligatory program.

The lack of enthusiasm for the European program was a forecast of the difficulties that any such social welfare legislation would face in the United States. The mere fact that most American reformers accepted without hesitation the idea that the British act would have to be modified to meet American conditions is perhaps the best evidence of this. Even in the period before World War I, when political progressivism was at its height, there was relatively little enthusiasm for social insurance or unemployment insurance legislation. In part, this apparent indifference to the unemployed was a product of ignorance, the sheer lack of information on the number of the jobless. But even when information was available it had little impact as opposed to the powerful "colonial or frontier philosophy" that the editor of the *Independent* had identified in 1908. While there was gradual progress in the general field of social insurance in the 1920's, only the devastating unemployment of the 1930's produced a feeling that the European approach to unemployment insurance should be reexamined. By then the prevention idea had become so entrenched that anything remotely resembling the original British or German acts was almost out of the question.

But to attribute to intangibles the failure of American legislators to consider, much less pass, unemployment insurance legislation designed principally to aid the jobless worker is hardly satisfying. It is, therefore, reassuring to be able to point to specific obstacles to such a program. Certainly the inarticulateness of the unemployed and the lack of interest shown by the labor movement were important factors in this situation. It is hard to see how strong unions, representing large numbers of workers who were subject to periodic unemployment, could have resisted the demand for concerted action as long as the AFL did. The case of the needle trades unions seems to bear out this point. Thus the basic impediment to legislation may have been the lack of contact between the unemployed and the unions. But there were still large numbers of AFL members who, though relatively well paid, did suffer from seasonal and technological unemployment. Their failure to articulate their grievances, at least before the 1930's, is apparently an indication of their belief either that government could do nothing or that nothing was preferable to what government could do. The difference between this view and the general American predisposition against unemployment insurance legislation was small indeed. Only the effects of five or six years of unprecedented unemployment insured the inclusion of anything resembling adequate worker-benefit provisions in the original state legislation.

The general unpopularity of the European approach stands in stark contrast, of course, to the acceptance given businessmen's ideas in the development of unemployment insurance. While the layoff of workmen was the immediate reason for considering unemployment insurance, it did not necessarily follow that the relief of these workmen was the only or even the most important goal that reformers had in mind. Many of them, as has been noted, viewed layoffs as a sign of economic disorganization as well as an indication of social distress. They stressed, more than many businessmen would have desired, the responsibility of business for unemployment and the ability of business to correct this defect in its organization. They were responsible for the long series of compromises—in Massachusetts in 1916, in Wisconsin in 1921 and 1931, in Congress in 1934–35—that helped transform the original British act into the American federal-state system. Although this interest in the potentialities of the employer was surely stronger among academic reformers than among businessmen themselves, the latter were agreeable to certain aspects of the prevention idea, notably those which might permit them to reduce their costs to an unemployment insurance fund. In fact, as actual prevention itself came to be recognized as something of a chimera, the accountability of the individual employer for his unemployment costs became an important argument for the retention of experience rating—an argument that apparently continues to have a strong appeal to the competitive instincts of the average employer.

The acceptance of certain aspects of the prevention idea today also suggests the responsive chord that it struck at a time when actual prevention seemed to many a panacea for the problem of economic disorganization. The idea that unemployment was a problem of industry so accurately coincided with the existing belief in the businessman's potentialities, that unemployment insurance seemed for a time the key to solving the problem. Although this view might have won considerable approval at any time, it was particularly successful in the 1920's. The effort by employers and their intellectual followers to attack the apparent inefficiencies of the factory system had been growing for many years. It reached a new high after the war when improved technology and new interest in management methods resulted in greatly increased productivity and dislocations in the work force. The prevalent "business philosophy" of the postwar era did, of course, nothing to retard this sentiment. There remained innumerable employers who disavowed an ability to control their destinies with anything like the precision that the reformers suggested, but they did not object too strenuously. Who would, after all, reject such a reputation for foresight and insight, particularly when it cost nothing?

The development of unemployment insurance before the institution of the federal-state system thus involved a combination of ideological commitments, political maneuvers, social myths, and that elusive substance, national character. It indicated why unemployment insurance was a complex issue then and, I suspect, partly why it is a complex issue today. It had a successful conclusion, if the passage of legislation in every state can be considered such, but it achieved that ending only when the proposed legislation was reconciled to the prevailing ideas of what unemployment insurance should do. In a democracy of diverse interests and reasonable freedom it would be unrealistic to expect that any other conclusion would have been reached when men began to study the unemployment problem and contemplate what should be done beyond providing mere relief.

Reference Matter

APPENDIX 1

Excerpts from the Wisconsin Unemployment Compensation Act of 1932

CHAPTER 108. UNEMPLOYMENT RESERVES AND COMPENSATION

108.01 PUBLIC POLICY DECLARATION. As a guide to the interpretation and application of this chapter the public policy of this state is declared as follows:

(1) Unemployment in Wisconsin has become an urgent public problem, gravely affecting the health, morals and welfare of the people of this state. The burden of irregular employment now falls directly and with crushing force on the unemployed worker and his family, and results also in an excessive drain on agencies for private charity and for public relief. The decreased and irregular purchasing power of wage earners in turn vitally affects the livelihood of farmers, merchants and manufacturers, results in a decreased demand for their products, and thus tends partially to paralyze the economic life of the entire state. In good times and in bad times unemployment is a heavy social cost, now paid mainly by wage earners. Industrial and business units in Wisconsin should pay at least a part of this social cost, caused by their own irregular operations. To assure somewhat steadier work and wages to its own employes, a company can reasonably be required to build up a limited reserve for unemployment, and out of this to pay unemployment benefits to its workers, based on their wages and lengths of service.

(2) The economic burdens resulting from unemployment should not only be shared more fairly, but should also be decreased and prevented as far as possible. A sound system of unemployment reserves, contributions and benefits should induce and reward steady operations by each employer, since he is in a better position than any other agency to share in and to reduce the social costs of his own irregular employment. Employers and employes throughout the state should cooperate, in advisory committees under government supervision, to promote and encourage the steadiest possible employment. A more adequate system of free public employment offices should be provided, at the expense of employers, to place workers more efficiently and to shorten the periods between jobs. Education and retraining of workers during their unem-

Wis. Laws Spec. Sess. 1931, ch. 20.

ployment should be encouraged. Governmental construction providing emergency relief through work and wages should be stimulated.

.   .   .   .   .

108.04 ELIGIBILITY FOR BENEFITS. (1) No employe shall be deemed eligible for benefits for partial or total unemployment unless he gives the notification of such unemployment required under subsection (1) of section 108.08, or unless such notification is waived by the commission in accordance with such section.

(2) No employe shall be deemed eligible for benefits on account of either partial or total unemployment during any calendar week unless such employe was physically able to work and available for work whenever with due notice called on by his employer to report for work. Nor shall any employe be deemed eligible for benefits for total unemployment for any calendar week in which he has suitable employment, as defined in subsection (6) of this section; provided, that nothing in this section shall render an employe ineligible for total unemployment benefits for any calendar week on the ground that such employe is employed on a governmental unemployment relief project under section 108.25.

(3) An employe shall be deemed partially unemployed in any calendar week, and shall at once be eligible for benefits for such partial unemployment, whenever his week's wages are less than the amount of weekly benefit to which he would be entitled under this chapter if totally unemployed.

(4) An employe shall be deemed totally unemployed in any calendar week when he performs no services whatsoever for his current employer during such week. An employe thus unemployed shall be eligible for benefits for total unemployment for each week of total unemployment occurring subsequent to a waiting period of two such weeks. No benefit shall be or become payable for this required waiting period, but not more than two such weeks of waiting period per employer shall be required of any employe in any twelve months in order to establish his eligibility for total unemployment benefits under this section. The commission may approve, in an approved voluntary unemployment benefit plan, such longer or shorter waiting period as will comply with the requirements of subsection (2) of section 108.15.

(5) An employe shall not be deemed eligible for any benefits for total unemployment based on his past weeks of employment, and no such benefits shall be payable to the employe, under any of the following conditions:

(a) If he has lost his employment through misconduct;

(b) If he has left his employment voluntarily without good cause attributable to the employer;

(c) During any period for which he has left and is out of employment because of a trade dispute still in active progress in the establishment in which he was employed;

(d) For any period during which he is out of employment because of an act of God affecting his place of employment;

(e) If he has received in wages fifteen hundred dollars or more during the twelve months preceding the date on which he became totally unemployed;

(f) If he is ordinarily self-employed, but has been temporarily (for not more than five months) employed in an employment subject to this chapter and can, at the termination of such temporary employment, reasonably return to his self-employment;

(g) If he attended a school, college or university in the last preceding school term, and has been employed by his employer only during the customary summer vacation of schools, colleges and universities.

(6) A claimant shall no longer be eligible for total unemployment benefits and the liability of his past employers to pay him such benefits based on his past employment shall cease for any period after he has without good cause refused to accept suitable employment when offered to him, or has failed to apply for suitable employment when notified by the district public employment office. Suitable employment shall mean either employment in his usual employment or other employment for which he is reasonably fitted, regardless of whether it is subject to this chapter; provided such employment is in the vicinity of his residence or last employment, and gives him wages at least equal to his weekly benefit for total unemployment or provides him work for at least half the number of hours normally worked as full time in such occupation or establishment; and provided, further, that whenever in any specific case the commission finds that it is impracticable to apply any of the foregoing standards, the commission may apply any standard reasonably calculated to determine what is suitable employment.

(7) Nothing in this section shall require an employe to accept employment; nor shall any employe forfeit his right to benefits by refusing to accept employment under either or both of the following conditions:

(a) In a situation vacant in consequence of a stoppage of work due to a trade dispute;

(b) If the wages, hours and conditions offered be not those prevailing for similar work in the locality or are such as tend to depress wages and working conditions.

(8) No employe shall be deemed eligible to receive benefits under this chapter on account of any period of partial or total unemployment unless such employe has been a resident of Wisconsin for the two years preceding the beginning of such period of unemployment or has been gainfully employed in the state for forty weeks within such two-year period; provided, that an employe's ineligibility under this subsection shall modify his employer's benefit liability only as specifically provided in subsection (5) of section 108.06.

108.05 AMOUNT OF BENEFITS. (1) Each eligible employe shall be paid benefits for total unemployment at a rate of ten dollars a week or fifty per cent of his average weekly wage, whichever is lower; except that when fifty per cent of such wage is less than five dollars a benefit of five dollars a week shall be paid.

(2) The benefit payable for partial unemployment in any week shall be the difference between the eligible employe's actual wages for the week and the weekly benefit to which he would be entitled if totally unemployed.

(3) Benefits shall be paid to each employe for the calendar weeks during which he is totally or partially unemployed and eligible for benefits; but no employe shall ever receive in any calendar year more than ten weeks of benefit for total unemployment, nor more than an equivalent total amount of benefits either for partial unemployment or for partial and total unemployment combined.

(4) The amount of benefits payable to any eligible employe shall be limited also by the benefit liability of his employer's account, as provided in sections 108.06 and 108.07.

108.06 BENEFIT LIABILITY OF EMPLOYER'S ACCOUNT. (1) An employer's account shall be liable to pay benefits to an employe in the ratio of one week of total unemployment benefit (or an equivalent of partial unemployment benefit) to each four weeks of employment of such employe by such employer within the fifty-two weeks preceding the date on which such employe last performed services for such employer. But no liability for the payment of benefits to an employe shall accrue unless the employe has been employed more than two weeks by the particular employer within such preceding year, or, in the case of an employe employed on a fixed monthly salary, unless the employe has been employed more than one month by the particular employer within such preceding year.

.   .   .   .   .

. . . In each calendar month an employer's account shall be liable to pay the benefits otherwise due his eligible employes for their weeks of unemployment occurring within such month only in accordance with the following schedule:

(a) When its reserve at the beginning of the month amounts to fifty dollars or more per employe, the account shall be liable for and shall pay in full all valid benefit claims for unemployment during the month;

(b) When such reserve amounts to over forty-five dollars but less than fifty dollars, all such valid benefit claims shall be paid, except that no eligible claimant shall receive for total unemployment a benefit of more than nine dollars per week;

(c) When such reserve amounts to over forty dollars but less than forty-five dollars, no claimant shall receive a benefit of more than eight dollars per week;

(d) For each further periodic drop of five dollars in the reserve per employe, there shall be a corresponding further drop of one dollar in the maximum benefit per week payable to any claimant for total unemployment.

(5) Any employe who has neither been a resident of Wisconsin for the past two years nor has been gainfully employed in the state for forty weeks within such two-year period, and who is, therefore, under subsection (8) of section 108.04 ineligible to receive benefits under this chapter, shall be known as "a nonqualified employe". Whenever such a nonqualified employe loses his employment, under conditions other than those enumerated in subsection (5) of section 108.04, his employer's account shall be at once liable to pay in lieu of benefits to such person a lump sum amount to the commission. This payment shall be made at the rate of five dollars for each four weeks of employment of such person by such employer during the period of employment just ended; but not more than five dollars shall be so payable for each five dollars reserve per employe in the employer's account at the beginning of the current calendar month. . . .

.   .   .   .   .

108.11 AGREEMENT TO CONTRIBUTE BY EMPLOYES VOID. (1) No agreement by an employe or by employes to pay any portion of the contributions required under this chapter from employers shall be valid. No employer shall make a deduction for such purpose from wages. An employe claiming a violation of this provision may, to recover wage deductions wrongfully made, have recourse to the method set up in section 108.10 for settling disputed claims.

(2) But nothing in this chapter shall affect the validity of voluntary arrangements whereby employes freely agree to make contributions to a fund for the purpose of securing unemployment compensation additional to the benefits provided in this chapter.

.   .   .   .   .

108.15 EXEMPTION. (1) The commission shall exempt, from the provisions of this chapter, except sections 108.12, 108.14, 108.15, 108.19, 108.21, 108.22 and 108.24, any employer who guarantees, under a plan approved by the commission, to all his eligible employes (and to each new eligible employe who is continued in employment after a probationary period of one month), in advance for a stated one-year period, at least forty-two weeks of work or wages, for at least thirty-six hours in each such week, if satisfied that the employer can and will make good such promise under all circumstances. . . .

(2) The commission shall exempt, from the provisions of this chapter, except sections 108.03, 108.04, 108.07, 108.101, 108.12, 108.13, 108.14, 108.15, 108.19, 108.21, 108.22, 108.23, 108.24, 108.25 and 108.26, any employer or group of employers submitting a plan for unemployment benefits which the commission finds: (a) makes eligible for benefits at least the employes who would be eligible for benefits under the compulsory features of this act; (b) provides that the proportion of the benefits to be financed by the employer or employers will on the whole be equal to or greater than the benefits which would be provided under the compulsory features of this act; and (c) is on the whole as beneficial in all other respects to such employes as the compulsory plan provided in this act. . . .

.   .   .   .   .

108.16 UNEMPLOYMENT RESERVE FUND. (1) For the purpose of carrying out the provisions of this chapter there is established a fund to be known as the "Unemployment Reserve Fund", to be administered by the state without liability on the part of the state beyond the amount of the fund. This fund shall consist of all contributions and moneys paid into and received by the fund pursuant to this chapter and of properties and securities acquired by and through the use of moneys belonging to the fund.

(2) A separate account shall be kept by the industrial commission with each employer contributing to said fund, and this separate employer's account shall never be merged with any other account except as provided in subsection (3) of this section.

(3) Whenever two or more employers in the same industry or locality desire to pool their several accounts with the fund, with a view to regularizing their employment by cooperative activity, they may file with the commission a written application to merge their several accounts in a new joint account with the fund. If in its judgment the plan has merit, the commission shall establish such a joint account, provided that the several employers each accept such suitable rules and regulations not inconsistent with the provisions of this

chapter as may be drawn up by the commission with reference to the conduct and dissolution of such joint accounts.

. . . . .

(5) The unemployment reserve fund shall be invested by the annuity and investment board in the readily marketable obligations of the United States of America, of any of its forty-eight state governments including this state, and of any city, county or other governmental subdivision of this state, all having a maturity of not over five years from the date of purchase. The investments of the fund shall be so made that all the assets of the fund shall always be readily convertible into cash when needed. When so directed by the industrial commission, the board shall dispose of securities belonging to the fund to secure cash needed for the repayment of benefits. All expenses of the annuity and investment board in the investment of the unemployment reserve fund shall be paid from the interest earnings of said fund, as provided in subsection (1) of section 20.725.

. . . . .

108.18 CONTRIBUTIONS TO THE UNEMPLOYMENT RESERVE FUND. The contribution regularly payable by each employer into his account with the fund shall be an amount equal to two per cent per annum of his payroll. (In order that reserves shall be built up for all employes potentially eligible to benefits, "payroll" shall include all wages, salaries and remuneration paid to employes subject to this chapter; except that it shall not include the amount paid to an employe or officer employed on a contractual basis for a fixed period at a fixed monthly salary, which will aggregate at least fifteen hundred dollars if said period is less than twelve months, or amount to at least fifteen hundred dollars per annum if such period is twelve months or more, provided such contract is duly reported to the commission by the employer; nor shall it include any salary or wage of three hundred dollars or more per month.) During an employer's first two years of contribution payments, and whenever thereafter his account amounts to less than fifty-five dollars reserve per employe, the employer shall make contributions to the fund at the rate of two per cent per annum on his payroll. If the employer has been continuously subject to this chapter during the two preceding years, the rate of contributions may be reduced or suspended under the following conditions:

(1) Whenever the employer's account amounts to fifty-five dollars but less than seventy-five dollars reserve per employe, such employer shall pay contributions to the fund at the rate of one per cent per annum on his payroll.

(2) Whenever and while the employer's account has a reserve per employe of seventy-five dollars or more, no contributions to the unemployment reserve fund shall be required of such employer.

108.19 CONTRIBUTIONS TO THE ADMINISTRATION FUND. Each employer subject to this chapter, including every employer exempted under section 108.15, shall regularly contribute to the unemployment administration fund created in section 108.20 at the rate of two-tenths of one per cent per annum on his payroll as defined in section 108.18. But the commission may prescribe at the close of any fiscal year such lower rates of contribution under this section, to apply to classes of employers throughout the ensuing fiscal year, as will in the commission's judgment adequately finance the administration of this chapter, and as will in the commission's judgment fairly represent the relative cost of the services rendered by the commission to each such class.

. . . . .

108.25 USE OF UNEMPLOYMENT RESERVE FOR PUBLIC WORKS. (1) If the state or any of its political subdivisions during a period of unemployment either directly or through a contractor provides work which in the opinion of the commission is an unemployment relief measure and which conforms to standards of wages and conditions prescribed by the commission, such work shall be deemed suitable employment within the meaning and subject to the limitations of subsection (6) of section 108.04; provided, that an employe who accepts such work for any calendar week in which he would otherwise be totally unemployed and eligible for benefits shall be entitled to receive such benefits in the form of wages paid him for such governmental work. To this end the state or subdivision giving such work and wages to such employe in any calendar week shall receive his benefits for such week, for the purpose of partially financing such employe's work and wages on such governmental unemployment relief project.

. . . . .

108.26 VOCATIONAL EDUCATION. When any employe is unemployed and eligible for benefits under this chapter, he may be recommended by the superintendent of the district employment office to attend vocational or other school during his unemployment. If he attends school under conditions approved by such superintendent and does satisfactory work in his classes he shall be eligible for an additional benefit of one dollar per week, to be paid from the administration fund. The education shall be furnished at public expense and any fee which may customarily be charged for attendance at such classes must be paid by the town, village or city in which such employe resides.

. . . . .

SECTION 3. VOLUNTARY SYSTEMS OF UNEMPLOYMENT COMPENSATION. (1) In accordance with the legislative intent expressed in section 1 the compulsory features of section 2 and section 5 of this act shall not take effect until July 1, 1933, nor shall they take effect on that date if the commission finds that on or before June 1, 1933, employers then employing in the aggregate at least one hundred seventy-five thousand employes as defined in section 108.02 shall have established plans previously approved by the commission as plans which would be entitled to exemption under section 108-15 of the compulsory act.

. . . . .

APPENDIX 2

Excerpts from the Report of the Ohio Commission, 1932

X. THE PROVISIONS OF THE PROPOSED BILL

. . . . .

2 Compulsory Insurance

. . . . .

. . . Compulsory insurance is the only organized means available by which it can be guaranteed that industry and its employees will have funds on hand to support the unemployed.

3 An Insurance Fund, Not Individual Reserves

The same considerations, in our judgment, condemn the proposal advocated in some states that there be substituted for the principle of insurance a system of compulsory reserves, to be kept separately by each employer or by the state in a fund with separate accounts for each employer. Under these plans the benefits drawn by employees who are without work are limited to the reserves set aside by their own employers. There is no pooling of risks, no purchasing of insurance. The essential principle of insurance, that all who are subject to the risk shall pay premiums and those who actually suffer the risks shall receive stipulated benefits is discarded. Therefore, the reserves of each employer would be locked up, so to speak, and the amount that each employer could afford to set aside in this way would be too small to provide anything like adequate benefits.

The maximum usually suggested is $10 a week for a total of 10 weeks. But even this meager benefit cannot be guaranteed. Growing industries using new inventions and having little unemployment could provide the $10 maximum. Other industries, suffering much unemployment because of the new inventions and having but meager reserves, could pay the unemployed less than $10 a week or nothing at all if their particular reserves were depleted or ex-

Ohio Commission on Unemployment Insurance, *Report* (Columbus, 1932).

hausted. Thus people with the same earning power working for different employers would have varying degrees of protection, and the protection to none would be adequate. Therefore, the burden of maintaining the able-bodied unemployed would still have to be borne by the public and the taxpayers, and the essential need presented by distress from unemployment would not be met.

4 *The Unemployment Insurance Fund*

These are some of the considerations which, in the judgment of the Commission, require that the state establish an unemployment insurance fund, similar to the workmen's compensation fund, in which substantially all industries and all employees regularly attached to those industries be required to insure their risks of unemployment.

An unemployment insurance fund in which substantially all employers and employees in the state must carry insurance is therefore provided in the bill that we recommend, and the Treasurer of the State of Ohio is made custodian of the fund.

The premiums paid into the fund and any earnings it may have are to be invested in bonds or other securities of the United States and of the State of Ohio, and in city, county, village and school district bonds within the State of Ohio. These investment provisions of the bill are modeled closely after the provisions of the Probate Code of the state.

5 *Employers' Premiums*

The bill proposes that payment of premiums into the fund shall begin on January 1, 1934, but that the law itself shall become effective immediately on its adoption. This would allow those charged with the administration of the law six or eight months in which to do the necessary preparatory work and to organize the system of insurance. It is the judgment of the Commission, however, that if business is not on the upgrade by January 1, 1934, and employment is not increasing, then the date when premium payments shall begin should be postponed until it is clear that the period of business recovery has begun.

Our recommendations are designed to prepare for future unemployment for the next depression, and cannot be helpful in dealing with the distress that now besets us because we did not prepare in the past. While employers and employees are still suffering from the industrial policies of the pre-depression era, they are not in a position to incur additional expenses for insurance. But as soon as the upward movement in employment and business is begun, as soon as industry begins to call back the employees whom the taxpayers have been supporting, then both employers and employees should be made to purchase insurance as a protection against the repetition of any such experience. With increased business, rising prices and increasing employment, the premiums required will be an excellent investment at small cost to purchase necessary protection and to make secure the human values invested in industry.

When the payment of premiums does begin, we recommend that employers be charged 2 per cent of the wages paid to their insured workers, for the protection afforded to industry and its employees. In addition, the eligible employees are to be charged 1 per cent of their weekly earnings. Our acturial calculations show that for the total of 3 per cent, a reasonable amount of protection can be purchased that will care for such unemployment as is caused by technological developments and the rise and fall of firms and industries, for the unemployment that comes during minor depressions every 3 or 4 years, and for that which comes with the severe depressions about every 10 years.

Two per cent from the employers cannot be considered burdensome. The Wisconsin law fixes the employers' contributions at 2 per cent with an additional 2/10 of 1 per cent for administrative expenses. Most of the bills introduced in the legislatures of the leading industrial states propose a premium rate of 2 per cent to be paid by employers, and the unanimous recommendation of the Interstate Unemployment Insurance Commission, appointed by the governors of the six leading industrial states of the Northeast, was also 2 per cent.

6 Merit Rating

We propose, however, that after January 1, 1937, when there will be enough experience and records to determine the variations in the unemployment risks of different industries and employments, the employers who provide more steady work may have their premium rates reduced as low as 1 per cent, while those who furnish the most unsteady work and cause the most unemployment may have their rates increased above 2 per cent according to the risk, but not in excess of $3\frac{1}{2}$ per cent. In other words, the insurance commission is authorized to classify industries and employments and to fix and publish rates on a merit rating system, after the manner of the workmen's compensation rates. As in industrial accident insurance, this will more justly distribute the cost of insurance and provide incentive for stabilizing work and preventing unemployment as far as possible.

Whether employers should be permitted to carry their own insurance is an open question. The Commission is of the opinion that satisfactory information about the effect on the state fund of permitting such self-insurance will be lacking until the records of 2 or 3 years of payments to the fund and expenditures from the fund in behalf of specific industries are available. . . .

7 Employees' Contributions

While theoretically the cost of insurance is properly a charge against the industries which use labor only intermittently and an essential part of the cost of production, like interest charges on idle plant and idle machinery, there are social and practical reasons for requiring employees to pay some part of the insurance premiums. The Commission therefore proposes that they contribute 1 per cent of their weekly earnings. This will make possible more adequate insurance payments to the unemployed than the employers' 2 per cent could purchase; and it will stimulate the feeling of self-support and self-respect that comes from providing for one's own protection. Moreover, it is desirable to give working people as well as employers an interest and a voice in conserving the insurance funds. Equally important is the need of a quick and simple method of distinguishing the unemployed who are eligible for insurance benefits from those who are not. If an unemployed workman has paid regularly into the fund, there can be no question about his title to benefits, if he is otherwise qualified.

8 No State Contributions

We have already indicated that the unemployment insurance fund is to be administered by the state as a trustee without liability beyond the amounts paid in by employers and employees and the moneys earned by the fund. While there is much to be said in favor of the state assuming certain administrative expenses of the unemployment insurance fund, as it does of workmen's compensation, we do not recommend this because we are strongly convinced that one of the most important functions of unemployment insurance is to relieve taxpayers of the burden of supporting able-bodied unemployed. Our bill provides that all expenses, including administration, shall be paid out of the insurance fund. It provides also that the State-City Free Employment Offices, which now cost the state and local governments something like $150,000 a year, be transferred to the unemployment insurance fund, and the tax burden be directly reduced by this amount.

9 Insurance Benefits

We provide in the bill that an insured employee when he is totally unemployed shall receive 50 per cent of his normal weekly wages, but not to exceed $15 per week, and that the maximum period for which benefits will be paid shall be 16 weeks in any one year. The $15 limitation is necessary to conserve funds so that an adequate reserve may be built up, and also to make possible the payment of the benefits to the unemployment for a longer period each year. If maximum benefits were not limited to $15 per week, the period during which the unemployed could receive benefits would have to be less than 16 weeks.

For those who are only partially unemployed, no benefits are to be paid unless there is a loss of more than 40 per cent of normal weekly wages. At first glance it seems unnecessary to provide benefits for those who have 3 days work each week, since such part-time work enables them to earn as much as the benefits that the totally unemployed receive. It is necessary, however, to stimulate unemployed workers to accept part-time work, and this can be done only by making the combined income from part-time earnings and partial benefits always greater than the benefits for total unemployment. A schedule is therefore included in the bill varying the amounts to be paid in benefits to those partially unemployed, so that they may always receive more than the wholly unemployed and thus be stimulated to accept part-time work whenever it is available.

10 Qualifications for Benefits

To assure efficient and practical administration of the unemployment insurance system, it is necessary that certain qualifications for benefits and disqualifications be stipulated in the law. Thus we provide that in order to qualify for benefits an insured employee must have been at work and paid premiums for at least 26 weeks during the 12 months preceding his application, or for a period of 40 weeks in the 2 preceding years. He must be capable of and available for employment, and unable to obtain work at his usual employment or at any other for which he is reasonably fitted. Also he must register at an employment office or other designated agency.

Disqualifications cover those unemployed because of strikes or lockouts, those failing to register or report at the designated employment offices, or those refusing to accept an offer of employment for which they are reasonably fitted. It is provided, however, that no one shall be disqualified because he refuses to take work where there is a strike or lockout, or where wages, hours and conditions of labor are substantially lower than those prevailing in the locality.

A waiting period of 3 weeks is provided during which no insurance benefits are to be paid. In this recommendation we differ from the proposals made in most of the insurance bills that we have examined. A 2 weeks waiting period is the most common provision. We recommend 3 weeks, however, because it is desirable to pay a minimum of benefits for seasonal unemployment and to conserve funds as much as possible for other forms of unemployment. Working people usually are able to make some provision themselves against regularly recurring seasons of idleness, and information collected by the Commission shows that most families applying for charitable relief do so usually after more than 3 weeks of self-support. In the interest of proper discipline and as a deterrent to thoughtless quitting of jobs, it is provided that the waiting period shall be 6 weeks for those who are discharged for just cause and for those who leave their employment without just cause.

· · · · ·

APPENDIX 3

Excerpts from the Federal Social Security Act of 1935

TITLE IX. TAX ON EMPLOYERS OF EIGHT OR MORE

Imposition of Tax

SECTION 901.   On and after January 1, 1936, every employer (as defined in section 907) shall pay for each calendar year an excise tax, with respect to having individuals in his employ, equal to the following percentages of the total wages (as defined in section 907) payable by him (regardless of the time of payment) with respect to employment (as defined in section 907) during such calendar year:

(1) With respect to employment during the calendar year 1936 the rate shall be 1 per centum;

(2) With respect to employment during the calendar year 1937 the rate shall be 2 per centum;

(3) With respect to employment after December 31, 1937, the rate shall be 3 per centum.

Credit Against Tax

SEC. 902.   The taxpayer may credit against the tax imposed by section 901 the amount of contributions, with respect to employment during the taxable year, paid by him (before the date of filing his return for the taxable year) into an unemployment fund under State law. The total credit allowed to a taxpayer under this section for all contributions paid into unemployment funds with respect to employment during such taxable year shall not exceed 90 per centum of the tax against which it is credited, and credit shall be allowed only for contributions made under the laws of States certified for the taxable year as provided in section 903.

49 Stat. 620 (1935).

237

Certification of State Laws

SEC. 903. (a) The Social Security Board shall approve any State law submitted to it, within thirty days of such submission, which it finds provides that—

(1) All compensation is to be paid through public employment offices in the State or such other agencies as the Board may approve;

(2) No compensation shall be payable with respect to any day of unemployment occurring within two years after the first day of the first period with respect to which contributions are required;

(3) All money received in the unemployment fund shall immediately upon such receipt be paid over to the Secretary of the Treasury to the credit of the Unemployment Trust Fund established by section 904;

(4) All money withdrawn from the Unemployment Trust Fund by the State agency shall be used solely in the payment of compensation, exclusive of expenses of administration;

(5) Compensation shall not be denied in such State to any otherwise eligible individual for refusing to accept new work under any of the following conditions: (A) If the position offered is vacant due directly to a strike, lockout, or other labor dispute; (B) if the wages, hours, or other conditions of the work offered are substantially less favorable to the individual than those prevailing for similar work in the locality; (C) if as a condition of being employed the individual would be required to join a company union or to resign from or refrain from joining any bona fide labor organization;

.   .   .   .   .

Unemployment Trust Fund

SEC. 904. (a) There is hereby established in the Treasury of the United States a trust fund to be known as the "Unemployment Trust Fund", hereinafter in this title called the "Fund." The Secretary of the Treasury is authorized and directed to receive and hold in the Fund all moneys deposited therein by a State agency from a State unemployment fund. Such deposit may be made directly with the Secretary of the Treasury or with any Federal reserve bank or member bank of the Federal Reserve System designated by him for such purpose.

.   .   .   .   .

(e) The Fund shall be invested as a single fund, but the Secretary of the Treasury shall maintain a separate book account for each State agency and shall credit quarterly on March 31, June 30, September 30, and December 31, of each year, to each account, on the basis of the average daily balance of such account, a proportionate part of the earnings of the Fund for the quarter ending on such date.

(f) The Secretary of the Treasury is authorized and directed to pay out of the Fund to any State agency such amount as it may duly requisition, not exceeding the amount standing to the account of such State agency at the time of such payment.

Allowance of Additional Credit

SEC. 909. (a) In addition to the credit allowed under section 902, a taxpayer may, subject to the conditions imposed by section 910, credit against the tax imposed by section 901 for any taxable year after the taxable year 1937, an amount, with respect to each State law, equal to the amount, if any, by which the contributions, with respect to employment in such taxable year, actually paid by the taxpayer under such law before the date of filing his return for such taxable year, is exceeded by whichever of the following is the lesser—

(1) The amount of contributions which he would have been required to pay under such law for such taxable year if he had been subject to the highest rate applicable from time to time throughout such year to any employer under such law; or

(2) Two and seven-tenths per centum of the wages payable by him with respect to employment with respect to which contributions for such year were required under such law.

(b) If the amount of the contributions actually so paid by the taxpayer is less than the amount which he should have paid under the State law, the additional credit under subsection (a) shall be reduced proportionately.

(c) The total credits allowed to a taxpayer under this title shall not exceed 90 per centum of the tax against which such credits are taken.

Conditions of Additional Credit Allowance

SEC. 910. (a) A taxpayer shall be allowed the additional credit under section 909, with respect to his contribution rate under a State law being lower, for any taxable year, than that of another employer subject to such law, only if the Board finds that under such law—

(1) Such lower rate, with respect to contributions to a pooled fund, is permitted on the basis of not less than three years of compensation experience;

(2) Such lower rate, with respect to contributions to a guaranteed employment account, is permitted only when his guaranty of employment was fulfilled in the preceding calendar year, and such guaranteed employment account amounts to not less than 7½ per centum of the total wages payable by him, in accordance with such guaranty, with respect to employment in such State in the preceding calendar year.

(3) Such lower rate, with respect to contributions to a separate reserve account, is permitted only when (A) compensation has been payable from such account throughout the preceding calendar year, and (B) such account amounts to not less than five times the largest amount of compensation paid from such account within any one of the three preceding calendar years, and (C) such account amounts to not less than 7½ per centum of the total wages payable by him (plus the total wages payable by any other employers who may be contributing to such account) with respect to employment in such State in the preceding calendar year.

(b) Such additional credit shall be reduced, if any contributions under such law are made by such taxpayer at a lower rate under conditions not fulfilling the requirements of subsection (a), by the amount bearing the same ratio to such additional credit as the amount of contributions made at such lower rate bears to the total of his contributions paid for such year under such law.

(c) As used in this section—

(1) The term "reserve account" means a separate account in an unemployment fund, with respect to an employer or group of employers, from which compensation is payable only with respect to the unemployment of individuals who were in the employ of such employer, or of one of the employers comprising the group.

(2) The term "pooled fund" means an unemployment fund or any part thereof in which all contributions are mingled and undivided, and from which compensation is payable to all eligible individuals, except that to individuals last employed by employers with respect to whom reserve accounts are maintained by the State agency, it is payable only when such accounts are exhausted.

(3) The term "guaranteed employment account" means a separate account, in an unemployment fund, of contributions paid by an employer (or group of employers) who

(A) guarantees in advance thirty hours of wages for each of forty calendar weeks (or more, with one weekly hour deducted for each added week guaranteed) in twelve months, to all the individuals in his employ in one or more distinct establishments, except that any such individual's guaranty may commence after a probationary period (included within twelve or less consecutive calendar weeks), and

(B) gives security or assurance, satisfactory to the State agency, for the fulfillment of such guaranties,

from which account compensation shall be payable with respect to the unemployment of any such individual whose guaranty is not fulfilled or renewed and who is otherwise eligible for compensation under the State law.

(4) The term "year of compensation experience", as applied to an employer, means any calendar year throughout which compensation was payable with respect to any individual in his employ who became unemployed and was eligible for compensation.

ACWA   Amalgamated Clothing Workers of America
AHR   *American Historical Review*
AJS   *American Journal of Sociology*
ALLR   *American Labor Legislation Review*
Annals   *The American Academy of Political and Social Science. Annals.*
BLS   Bureau of Labor Statistics
BTS   *Bulletin of the Taylor Society*
COES   Committee on Economic Security
Couzens Hearings
    U.S. Congress, Senate, *Hearings Before the Committee on Education and Labor*
CUNA   Credit Union National Association
HBR   *Harvard Business Review*
ILGWU   International Ladies' Garment Workers' Union
JASA   *Journal of the American Statistical Association*
JBEH   *Journal of Business and Economic History*
JBUC   *Journal of Business of the University of Chicago*
JPE   *Journal of Political Economy*
MFL   Massachusetts State Federation of Labor
MLR   *Monthly Labor Review*
NCCC   National Conference of Charities and Corrections
NCSW   National Conference of Social Work
NYFL   New York State Federation of Labor
PSQ   *Political Science Quarterly*
SHSW   State Historical Society of Wisconsin
USCC   United States Chamber of Commerce
Wagner-Hebert Hearings, 1931
    U.S. Congress, Senate, *Hearings Before a Select Committee on Unemployment Insurance*
WFL   Wisconsin State Federation of Labor

NOTES

CHAPTER 1

1 "Insurance Against Unemployment," *Independent*, 64 (Mar. 19, 1908), 647.
2 Leah Hannah Feder, *Unemployment Relief in Periods of Depression* (New York, 1936), esp. ch. 12.
3 Kansas Bureau of Labor and Industry, *11th Annual Report, 1895* (Topeka, 1896), p. 187.
4 Sidney Fine, *Laissez-Faire and the General Welfare State* (Ann Arbor, 1956), pp. 322–23.
5 *Ibid.*, p. 323; Joseph Dorfman, *The Economic Mind in American Civilization*, 5 vols. (New York, 1946–59), 3:76–77; Paul Monroe, "Insurance Against Non-Employment," *AJS*, 2 (May 1897), 772.
6 U.S. Congress, House, *Report of the Industrial Commission* (59 Cong., 1 Sess., House Doc. 183, Washington, 1901), 14:34 and xliv.
7 John R. Commons, "The Right to Work," *Arena*, 21 (Feb. 1899), 141.
8 *Report of the Massachusetts Board to Investigate the Subject of the Unemployed* (House Doc. 50, Boston, 1895), p. xxi.
9 Kansas Bureau of Labor and Industry, *11th Annual Report*, p. 198.
10 Dorfman, *Economic Mind*, 3:379.
11 Richard T. Ely, *Socialism and Social Reform* (Boston, 1894), pp. 331–32. See also Fine, *Laissez-Faire*, pp. 327, 329.
12 Charles A. Tuttle, "The Workman's Position in the Light of Economic Progress," *Publications of the American Economic Association*, 3rd series, 3 (Feb. 1902), 199–212. For the discussions see pp. 213–34, esp. pp. 217–19, 221, 232.
13 Abraham Epstein, *Insecurity, a Challenge to America* (New York, 1933), pp. 325–26. See also Constance A. Kichel, *Unemployment Insurance in Belgium* (New York, 1932) pp. 87–105, 289–90.
14 William H. Beveridge, *Unemployment, A Problem of Industry* (London, 1910), pp. 3, 193.
15 William H. Beveridge, *Power and Influence: An Autobiography* (London, 1953), p. 64.

243

16 Beveridge, *Unemployment,* pp. 219–20, 230.

17 Beatrice Webb, *Our Partnership* (London, 1948), p. 385.

18 Sidney Webb, *The Prevention of Destitution* (London, 1916), p. 139.

19 Sidney and Beatrice Webb, *English Poor Law Policy* (London, 1910), p. 300.

20 Webb, *Prevention,* pp. 114–41.

21 Bentley B. Gilbert, "Winston Churchill Versus the Webbs: The Origins of British Unemployment Insurance," *AHR,* 71 (Apr. 1966), 846–62; Bentley B. Gilbert, *The Evolution of National Insurance in Great Britain: The Origins of the Welfare State* (London, 1966), ch. 5.

22 Webb, *Our Partnership,* pp. 416–17 and 404.

23 Beveridge, *Power and Influence,* p. 86.

24 *Ibid.,* p. 83.

25 Cyril Jackson, *Unemployment and Trade Unions* (London, 1910), pp. 30–31.

26 Mary Gilson, *Unemployment Insurance in Great Britain* (New York, 1931), p. 42; Webb, *Our Partnership,* p. 468.

27 William M. Leiserson, "The Problem of Unemployment," *PSQ,* 31 (Mar. 1916), 1–2.

28 Henry R. Seager, *Social Insurance* (New York, 1910), pp. 92, 111–12.

29 Louis D. Brandeis, "Workman's Insurance—the Road to Social Efficiency," *Proceedings of the NCCC,* 38 (June 1911), 158, 161.

30 Elbert H. Gary, "Unemployment and Business," *Harper's Magazine,* 131 (June 1915), 71.

31 William M. Leiserson, "The Fight Against Unemployment in the United States," Conference Internationale du Chromage, Sept. 1910, William M. Leiserson Papers (State Historical Society of Wisconsin, Madison), Box 48. For an evaluation of Leiserson's career see J. Michael Eisner, *William Morris Leiserson: A Biography* (Madison, 1967).

32 "The International Conference on Unemployment, 1910," *Journal of the Royal Statistical Society,* 74 (Dec. 1910), pt. 1, pp. 67–70.

33 New York Commission on Employers' Liability, *3rd Report, 1911,* app. 1, Report of the Committee on Unemployment (Albany, 1911), p. 27, 66.

34 Isaac M. Rubinow, *Social Insurance* (New York, 1913), pp. 442, 455. Rubinow made the same point in several articles of the same period. See Isaac M. Rubinow, "Subsidized Unemployment Insurance," *JPE,* 21 (May 1913), 431, and "The Problem of Unemployment," *JPE,* 21 (Apr. 1913), 331.

35 For Common's role in the Wisconsin unemployment insurance campaign see Chapter 6.

36 Andrews to Olga Halsey, Jan. 27, 1915, John B. Andrews Papers (New York State Library of Industrial and Labor Relations, Ithaca), Box 12.

37 Charles R. Henderson, *Social Elements* (New York, 1898), pp. 152, 220.

38 Charles R. Henderson, "The Right of the Worker to Social Protection," *Proceedings of the NCCC,* 41 (May 1914), 359. See also Charles R. Henderson, *Citizens in Industry* (New York, 1915), p. 164.

39 Henderson to Andrews, December 26, 1914, Andrews Papers, Box 10; Charles R. Henderson, "The Right of the Worker to Social Protection," *Proceedings of the NCCC,* 41 (May 1914), 359.

40 William Hard, "Unemployment As a Coming Issue," *ALLR*, 2 (Feb. 1912), 93–100; Charles R. Henderson, "Recent Advances in the Struggle Against Unemployment," *ALLR*, 2 (Feb. 1912), 105–10; "Annual Business Meeting," *ALLR*, 2 (Feb. 1912), 155.

41 William Hard, "Report of the Committee on Unemployment," *ALLR*, 3 (Feb. 1913), 137.

42 Andrews to William Hard, Dec. 20, 1912, Andrews Papers, Box 6.

43 Andrews to Thomas Nixon Carver, Nov. 9, 1912, Andrews Papers, Box 6.

44 Andrews to Leiserson, May 1, 1913, Leiserson Papers, Box 1.

45 Isaac M. Rubinow, "First American Conference on Social Insurance," *Survey*, 30 (July 5, 1913), 479.

46 "American Section of the International Association on Unemployment," Outline of Work, 1914, Andrews Papers, Box 9; "Notes of Selig Perlman, Meeting of the Unemployment Conference Feb. 27, 1914," Unpublished Report, United States Industrial Relations Commission Papers (State Historical Society of Wisconsin, Madison), pp. 1–7.

47 *New York Times*, Mar. 1, 1914.

48 Andrews to Samuel McCune Lindsay, Mar. 16, 1914, Andrews Papers, Box 9.

49 "Memo on Unemployment," 1915, Edward A. Filene Papers (CUNA Archives, Madison), Unemployment Folder.

50 "Remedies for Unemployment," *Outlook*, 109 (Jan. 13, 1915), 54–55; Christina Merriman, "Unemployment and Compensation in a Pennsylvania Setting," *Survey*, 33 (Jan. 9, 1915), 402–3. *ALLR*, 5 (June 1915), contains the conference proceedings.

51 "A Practical Program for the Prevention of Unemployment in America," *ALLR*, 5 (June 1915), 189–91.

52 John B. Andrews, "Introductory Note," *ALLR*, 5 (June 1915), 169.

53 "Memo on Unemployment," 1915, Edward A. Filene Papers, Unemployment Folder.

54 Robert G. Valentine to Andrews, Feb. 1915, Andrews Papers, Box 46; Report of the Massachusetts Committee on Unemployment, Mar. 15, 1915, Andrews Papers, Box 12; Ordway Tead to Halsey, Jan. 15, 1916, Andrews Papers, Box 14; Feder, *Unemployment Relief*, pp. 231–32.

55 Hale to Andrews, Apr. 11, 1915, Andrews Papers, Box 12.

56 Andrews to Seager, Feb. 18, 1916, Andrews Papers, Box 14; Andrews to J. J. Handley, Sept. 24, 1920, Andrews Papers, Box 10; Hale to Andrews, Apr. 26, 1915, Andrews Papers, Box 12.

57 John B. Andrews, "Unemployment Insurance," *ALLR*, 5 (Nov. 1915), 591.

58 Tead to Halsey, Jan. 10, 15, 1916, Andrews Papers, Box 14.

59 Alfred E. Lunt to James A. McKibben, Mar. 14, 1916, including Lunt to Committee on Social Welfare, Mar. 9, 1916, Boston Chamber of Commerce Papers (Harvard Business School Archives, Cambridge), File 332-48-C; Massachusetts House of Representatives, *Journal of the House of Representatives*, 1916 (Boston, 1916), pp. 91, 1188. See also *Springfield* (Mass.) *Daily Republican*, May 27, 1916, June 1, 1916.

60 Massachusetts House of Representatives Special Commission on Social Insurance, *Report* (House Doc. 1850, Boston, 1917), p. 123.

61 Henderson to Andrews, Feb. 6, 1915, Andrews Papers, Box 12.
62 Charles R. Henderson, "Chicago," *AJS*, 21 (May 1915), 724–25.
63 Andrews to Henderson, Mar. 12, 1915, Andrews Papers, Box 12. See also Henderson, *Citizens in Industry*.
64 U.S. Commission on Industrial Relations, *Report and Testimony*, (Washington, 1916), 1: 345–47.
65 *Ibid.*, pp. 114–15.
66 *Ibid.*, p. 200.
67 U.S. Congress, House, Committee to Study Social Insurance and Unemployment, *Hearings Before the Committee on Labor* (64 Cong., 1 Sess., Washington, 1918), 11.
68 *Ibid.*, pp. 41, 44, 60, 73–74.
69 *Ibid.*, pp. 124–25.
70 John A. Ryan and Joseph Husslein, *The Church and Labor* (New York, 1920), pp. 222–23, 227–33.
71 State of New York, *Report of Governor Smith's Reconstruction Commission on a Permanent Unemployment Program* (Albany, 1919), p. 15.
72 John B. Andrews, "A National System of Labor Exchanges in Its Relation to Industrial Efficiency," *Annals*, 61 (Sept. 1915), p. 142; Don D. Lescohier, *The Labor Market* (New York, 1919), p. 166.
73 I. W. Litchfield, "United States Employment Service and Demobilization," *Annals*, 81 (Jan. 1919), 21.
74 Lescohier, *Labor Market*, p. 190; Don D. Lescohier and Elizabeth Brandeis, *A History of Labour in the United States* (New York, 1935), 3: 207.
75 Shelby M. Harrison *et al.*, *Public Employment Offices: Their Purpose, Structure, and Methods* (New York, 1924) pp. 132–33.
76 Otto T. Mallery, "National Policy—Public Works to Stabilize Employment," *Annals*, 81 (Jan. 1919), 56–60; Otto T. Mallery, "The Long Range Planning of Public Works," *Business Cycles and Unemployment* (New York, 1923), pp. 237–40.
77 See, for example, Sidney Webb, *When Peace Comes: The Way of Industrial Reconstruction*, Fabian Tract no. 181 (London, 1916).
78 Gilson, *Unemployment Insurance in Great Britain*, p. 3.
79 *Ibid.*, p. 63.
80 Quoted in Gilson, *Unemployment Insurance in Great Britain*, p. 61.
81 Harold J. Laski, "England Out of Work," *Survey*, 45 (Jan. 22, 1921), p. 594.
82 B. Seebohm Rowntree, "Unemployment and Its Alleviation," *Annals*, 100 (Mar. 1922), p. 99.
83 Molly Carroll, *Unemployment Insurance in Germany* (Washington, 1930), pp. 32–34.
84 *Ibid.*, pp. 48–49, 83.
85 Epstein, *Insecurity*, p 378.
86 Carroll, *Unemployment Insurance in Germany*, p. 112.
87 Ralph Hurlin and William A. Berridge, *Employment Statistics* (New York, 1926), p. 19. Also Irving Bernstein, *The Lean Years: A History of the American Worker, 1920–33* (Boston, 1960), ch. 2.
88 Hornell Hart, "Fluctuations in Unemployment in Cities of the United States, 1902 to 1917," *Studies from the Helen S. Trounstine Foundation*

(May 15, 1918), 1: 48. See William A. Berridge, "Cycles of Employment and Unemployment in the United States, 1914–21," *JASA*, 18 (Mar. 1922), 43; also the Sept. and Dec. issues.

89 Wesley C. Mitchell, "Review," *Recent Economic Changes* (New York, 1929), 2: 879.

90 Paul H. Douglas, *Real Wages in the United States, 1890–1926* (Boston, 1930), pp. 446–49, 459.

91 David Weintraub, "Unemployment and Productivity," *Technological Trends and National Policy* (Washington, 1937), p. 71.

92 Stanley Lebergott, *Manpower in Economic Growth* (New York, 1962), p. 186; "Annual Estimates of Unemployment in the United States, 1900–1954," *The Measurement and Behavior of Unemployment: A Conference of the Universities* (Princeton, 1957), p. 231.

93 Lebergott, *Manpower*, p. 185; also *Measurement and Behavior of Unemployment*, p. 229.

94 U.S. Congress, Senate, *Report on Conditions of Employment in the Iron and Steel Industry in the United States* (67 Cong., 1 Sess., Senate Doc. Vol. 20, Serial 6098, Washington, 1913), 3: 206. See also David Brody, *Steelworkers in America* (Cambridge, 1960).

95 Robert S. Lynd and Helen Lynd, *Middletown* (New York, 1929), p. 60.

96 David Weintraub, "The Displacement of Workers through Increases in Efficiency and their Absorption by Industry, 1920–31," *JASA*, 27 (Dec. 1932), 394, 399.

97 U.S. Bureau of the Census, *Historical Statistics of the United States, Colonial Times to 1957*, series P4 (Washington, 1960), p. 409.

98 Lebergott, *Manpower*, app. table A-5, p. 514.

99 See Solomon Fabricant, *Employment in Manufacturing, 1899–1939* (New York, 1942), p. 9.

100 Mills, *Economic Tendencies*, p. 230; also John W. Kendrick, *Productivity Trends in the United States* (Princeton, 1961), pp. 70–71.

101 Isaac M. Rubinow, "The Status of Social Insurance," *Survey*, 56 (May 15, 1926), 242–43. See also Roy Lubove's recently published book, *The Struggle for Social Security, 1900–1935* (Cambridge, 1968), which includes a chapter on unemployment and unemployment insurance and, I believe, tends to confirm the themes I have developed.

CHAPTER **2**

1 Henry S. Dennison, "Depression Insurance, A Suggestion to Corporations for Reducing Unemployment," *ALLR*, 12 (Mar. 1922), 32.

2 See Alfred Chandler, Jr., *Strategy and Structure* (Cambridge, 1962).

3 Howard Coonley, "Production Can Be Stabilized," *Nation's Business*, 18 (May 20, 1930), 44.

4 Herman Feldman, *The Regularization of Employment* (New York, 1925), p. 62; "New Emphasis" is taken from Feldman, *Regularization*, especially Chapter 2, "The New American Emphasis."

5 Alpheus T. Mason, *Brandeis—A Free Man's Life* (New York, 1946), pp. 143–44, 146; Louis D. Brandeis, *Business—A Profession* (Boston, 1912), pp. 5–9; Henry Greenleaf Pearson, *William Howe McElwain* (Boston, 1917), pp. 106–8.

6 Memorandum by Louis D. Brandeis on Irregular Employment, June 1911. In possession of Elizabeth Brandeis.

7 See A. Lincoln Filene, "Unemployment Reserves: The Underlying Theory," in the *New York Times,* May 20, 1934; Charles McCarthy to Emily Bodman, Mar. 12, 1912, Leiserson Papers, Box 42; Leiserson to Louis Brandeis, Nov. 12, 1914, Leiserson Papers, Box 4.

8 U.S. Commission on Industrial Relations, *Report and Testimony,* (Washington, 1916), 1: 995–96.

9 Feldman, *Regularization,* pp. xv, 366.

10 John R. Commons *et al., Can Business Prevent Unemployment?* (New York, 1925), pp. 2, 92, 157, 211.

11 Edwin S. Smith, *Reducing Seasonal Unemployment* (New York, 1931), pp. 6–7.

12 *Recent Economic Changes* (New York, 1929), 2: 862.

13 See John B. Andrews to John R. Commons, Nov. 14, 1921, Andrews Papers, Box 22; B. Seebohm Rowntree, *The Human Factor in Business* (London, 1921), pp. 33, 37; B. Seebohm Rowntree, *Industrial Unrest: A Way Out* (New York, 1927), pp. 17–20; B. Seebohm Rowntree, "Business Administration," *Atlantic Monthly,* 129 (Apr. 1922), 469–72. For examples of criticism, see Allen Bennet Forsberg, ed., *Selected Articles on Unemployment Insurance* (New York, 1926), pp. 253–390.

14 Feldman, *Regularization,* p. 49; Herman Feldman, "The New Emphasis in the Problem of Reducing Unemployment," *BTS,* 7 (Oct. 1922), 177–79; Herman Feldman, "Newer Methods in the Stabilization of Employment," *ALLR,* 16 (Mar. 1926), 55.

15 These are from Edward A. Filene, *The Way Out* (Garden City, 1924), pp. 11, 35–36; Feldman, *ALLR,* 16 (1926), 51.

16 Morrell Heald too readily accepts the type of Chamber of Commerce propaganda that most businessmen would have scoffed at. The employers' role in the unemployment insurance campaign is inexplicable if the "service motive" explanation is accepted. Morrell Heald, "Business Thought in the 1920's: Social Responsibility," *American Quarterly,* 13 (Summer 1961), 126–39; USCC, *Balancing Production and Employment Through Management Control* (Washington, 1930), p. 9.

17 A. Lincoln Filene, *Merchant's Horizon* (New York, 1924), p. 3.

18 Edward A. Filene to Royal Meeker, June 2, 1931. Edward A. Filene Papers, Unemployment Folder.

19 W. I. Clark to R. L. Tweedy, Feb. 25, 1924, Manufacturers' Research Association Papers (Baker Library, Harvard University, Cambridge), Case 2.

20 See ch. 6 for Commons' use of this idea in Wisconsin. Ch. 3 explores the practical application of unemployment prevention by employers.

21 National Industrial Conference Board, *Layoff and its Prevention* (New York, 1930), p. 75.

22 Joseph H. Barber, "Are Statistics Stabilizing Business?" *Management Review,* 15 (Aug. 1926), 232.

23 Henry S. Dennison, "Management," *Recent Economic Changes,* 2:524.

24 Henry J. Bruere and Grace Pugh, *Profitable Personnel Practice* (New York, 1929), p. 117).

25 Richard A. Feiss, "Personal Relationship as a Basis of Scientific Man-

agement," *Bulletin of the Society to Promote the Science of Management,* 1 (Nov. 1915), 12. See also "Scientific Management Applied to the Steadying of Employment and its Effect in Industrial Establishments," *Annals,* 61 (Sept. 1915), 103–11.

26   Morris L. Cooke, "Scientific Management as a Solution of the Unemployment Problem," *Annals,* 61 (Sept. 1915), 147; Morris L. Cooke, "Casual and Chronic Unemployment," *Survey,* 59 (May 1915), 199. See Harlow S. Person, "Scientific Management," *BTS,* 2 (Oct. 1916), 21; Harlow S. Person, "The Manager, the Workman, and the Social Scientist," *BTS,* 3 (Feb. 1917), 1.

27   Henry Eilbert, "The Development of Personnel Management in the United States," *Business History Review,* 33 (Autumn 1959), 348–49.

28   Robert N. Turner to Andrews, January 27, 1914, Andrews Papers, Box 9.

29   See, for example, Magnus Alexander, "Hiring and Firing: Its Economic Wastes and How to Avoid It," *Proceedings of the 20th Annual Convention, National Association of Manufacturers,* 1915, pp. 175–85; Paul H. Douglas, "Plant Administration of Labor," *JPE,* 27 (July 1919), 140.

30   Sumner Slichter, *The Turnover of Factory Labor* (New York, 1919), p. 140.

31   See, for example, George Gibb and Evelyn Knowlton, *The Resurgent Years* (New York, 1956), pp. 576–78.

32   Douglas, *JPE,* 27 (1919), 549–50.

33   Grosvenor S. Clarkson, *Industrial America in the World War* (New York, 1923), ch. 11; Feldman, *Regularization,* p. 157; A. W. Shaw, "Simplication: A Philosophy of Business Urgent," *HBR,* 1 (July 1923), 420–22.

34   J. Wainwright Evans, "Business Charts Its Course," *Nation's Business,* 5 (Oct. 1917), 11; Walter S. Gifford, "Business: Its New Job," *Nation's Business,* 5 (Oct. 1917), 33.

35   Harry A. Wheeler, "Industry's Congress for Reconstruction," *Nation's Business,* 6 (Dec. 1918), 10. See also Julius Barnes, "Government and Business," *HBR,* 10 (July 1932), 411–19.

36   Harlow S. Person, "The Opportunities and Obligations of the Taylor Society," *BTS,* 4 (Feb. 1919), 4.

37   Edward Eyre Hunt, ed., *Scientific Management Since Taylor* (New York, 1924), p. xii.

38   Morris L. Cooke, "Report of the Research Committee, Annual Business Meeting, December 5, 1919," *BTS,* 5 (Feb. 1920), 8; Morris L. Cooke, "Unemployment," *American Federationist,* 26 (Oct. 1919), 1034.

39   See Morris L. Cooke to Stanley King, Jan. 26, Feb. 4, 1921, Morris L. Cooke Papers (Franklin D. Roosevelt Library, Hyde Park), File 339; Henry S. Dennison, "A Dennisonian Proposition," *BTS,* 5 (Apr. 1920), 95–96.

40   Harlow S. Person, "Scientific Management and the Reduction of Unemployment," *BTS,* 6 (Feb. 1921), 51.

41   The AMA Board of Directors included Dennison, Lewisohn, Ernest G. Draper, and Marion B. Folsom at various times in the 1920's. See W. Wallace, "A Novel Unemployment Insurance Scheme," *American Man-*

agement Review—National Association of Corporation Training, 8 (Dec. 1921), 541–44; "Providing for a Plant's Unemployment," *ibid.*, 538–40; Bill Halley, "A Guarantee for Continued Employment," *American Management Review—Personnel Administration*, 11 (Feb. 1923), 7–12.

42 Willis Wissler to Leiserson, Mar. 10, 1926, Leiserson Papers, Box 45.

43 The overlap of Taylor Society and AMA functions resulted in conflict between the organizations in the late 1920's. See Cooke Papers, File 339, Dennison correspondence.

44 Edward Eyre Hunt, "1921 Forward," *Survey*, 62 (Apr. 1, 1929), 6.

45 Herbert Hoover to Warren G. Harding, Sept. 20, 1921, Warren G. Harding Papers (Ohio Historical Society, Columbus), Box 385.

46 *New York Times,* Aug. 29, 30, 1921.

47 "Advance Summary of the Report of the Economic Advisory Council," Sept. 22, 1926, Department of Commerce, Unemployment Conference, 1921, Herbert Hoover Papers (Herbert Hoover Library, West Branch, Iowa), 1-I/406.

48 Andrews to Edward E. Hunt, Sept. 2, 1921, Andrews Papers, Box 22.

49 Andrews to Hoover, Sept. 2, 1921, Dept. of Comm., Unemployment Conference, 1921, Hoover Papers, 1-I/406.

50 Andrews, "Unemployment Prevention Committee," Sept. 12, 1921, Andrews Papers, Box 22; Hunt to Hoover, September 8, 1921, Dept. of Comm., Unemployment Conference, 1921, Hoover Papers, 1-I/406.

51 "Advance Summary," Economic Advisory Council, Sept. 22, 1921, Dept. of Comm., Unemployment Conference, 1921, Hoover papers, 1-I/406.

52 President's Committee on Unemployment, *Report of the Unemployment Conference* (Washington, 1921), p. 167.

53 *New York Times*, Sept. 27, 1921.

54 *Report of the Unemployment Conference*, p. 27. See also Harding to Trigg, Sept. 22, 1921, Harding Papers, Box 285.

55 *Report of the Unemployment Conference*, pp. 19–21, 37–48; Hoover to Harding, Sept. 30, 1921, Harding Papers, Box 285; *New York Times*, Sept. 30, Oct. 1, 1921.

56 *Report of the Unemployment Conference*, pp. 23, 69–88, 89–110; *New York Times,* Oct. 5, 1921.

57 Andrews to Henry A. Harris, Oct. 14, 1921, Andrews Papers, Box 22.

58 William L. Chenery, "Mr. Hoover's Hand," *Survey*, 47 (Oct. 12, 1921), 255.

59 Andrews to Hoover, Oct. 24, 1921, Andrews Papers, Box 22.

60 Otto T. Mallery, "The Unemployment Conference," *Survey*, 47 (Nov. 12, 1921), 255.

61 Andrews to Commons, Nov. 5, 1921, Andrews Papers, Box 21. At the same time, Edward E. Hunt was trying to raise money for studies of company unemployment insurance plans. See Hunt to Leiserson, Nov. 25, 1921, Leiserson Papers, Box 17.

62 Hoover to Henry S. Prichett, Nov. 18, 1921, Dept. of Comm., Unemployment Conference, 1921, Hoover Papers, 1-I/407.

63 "Summary of Action Taken at the Meeting of the Business Cycle Committee at South Shore Country Club, October 2–3," Hoover Papers, Dept. of Comm., Unemployment Conference, 1921, 1-I/407.

64 "Meeting of Economists with Members of the Committee on Business Cycles, December 22, 1922," Hoover Papers, Report of the Committee on the Unemployment Conference, 1921, 1-I/407.

65 *Business Cycles and Unemployment*, p. xxxi.

66 Leo Wolman, "Unemployment Insurance," *Business Cycles and Unemployment*, p. 340.

67 Andrews to O. K. Cushing, Sept. 21, 1931, Andrews Papers, Box 46.

68 Henry S. Dennison, "The President's Conference, 1919," *BTS*, 5 (Apr. 1920), 81.

69 Henry S. Dennison, "What the Employment Department Should Be in Industry," BLS *Bulletin* 227 (Oct. 1917), 80.

70 Henry S. Dennison, "An Employer's View of Property," *Annals*, 103 (Sept. 1922), 58.

71 Dennison to Andrews, Mar. 2, 1915, Andrews Papers, Box 12.

72 Henry S. Dennison, "Regularization of Industry Against Unemployment," *Annals*, 100 (Mar. 1922), 104; See also Henry S. Dennison, "How I Use the Business Cycle," *Nation's Business*, 10 (Feb. 1922), 9–11.

73 Henry S. Dennison, "American Expansion and Industrial Stability," *Annals*, 109 (Sept. 1923), 289.

74 Henry S. Dennison, "The Applied Technique of Stabilization" in Lionel Edie, *Stabilization of Business* (New York, 1923), pp. 388–89.

75 See the Madison *Capital Times*, Feb. 21, 1923.

76 Henry S. Dennison, "Methods of Reducing the Labor Turnover," Proceedings of the Conference of Employment Managers Association of Boston, May 10, 1916, BLS *Bulletin*, 202 (Sept. 1916), 58.

77 Quoted in James T. Dennison, *Henry S. Dennison, New England Industrialist Who Served America* (Cambridge, 1955), p. 23.

78 This ran counter to the increasing conservatism of Massachusetts. See Richard Abrams, *Conservatism in a Progressive Era* (Cambridge, 1965).

79 Lawrence A. Jones, "Legislative Activities of the Greater Boston Chamber of Commerce," (Ph.D. diss., Harvard Graduate School of Business Administration, 1961), pp. 48–63. See also John W. Plaisted to Members, Industrial Relations Committee of the Boston CC, and the Boston *Journal* article, May 19, 1910, Edward A. Filene Papers, Workmen's Compensation Folder.

80 McKibben to E. A. Filene, January 3, 1913, Filene Papers, Boston CC Miscellaneous Folder; Robert Wiebe, *Businessmen and Reform* (Cambridge, 1962), pp. 35–36. James Prothro, *The Dollar Decade* (Baton Rouge, 1954), mistakenly equates the moderate U.S. Chamber of Commerce with the reactionary National Association of Manufacturers.

81 See Jane C. Williams, "The Reduction of Labor Turnover in the Plimpton Press," BLS *Bulletin*, 227 (Oct. 1917), 82–91; "Meeting of the Chief Executive's Committee," July 18, 1927, MRA Papers, Case 1; Henry P. Kendall, *The Kendall Company: 50 Years of Yankee Enterprise* (New York, 1953), pp. 8–10.

82 Henry P. Kendall, "Discussion of Address by Robert G. Valentine," *Bulletin of the Society to Promote the Science of Management*, 1 (Jan. 1915), 6.

83 See Filene, *The Way Out*, pp. 44–45.

84 E. A. Filene to Leiserson, Dec. 3, 1932, Leiserson Papers, Box 15. See also E. A. Filene to McMullin, May 20, 1931, Edward A. Filene Papers, Unemployment Folder; *New York Times,* Apr. 12, 1931, Jan. 1, 1933.

85 *New York Times,* May 20, 1934.

86 Howard Coonley, "The Control of an Industry in the Business Cycle," *HBR* 1 (July 1923) , 385-97; "A Manufacturer Averts Unemployment by Intelligent Planning," *ALLR,* 13 (Mar. 1923), 23.

87 Boston CC, *Current Affairs,* 8 (Aug. 20, 1917), 1; (Sept. 24, 1917), 1; (Oct. 29, 1917), 8.

88 *New York Times,* Sept. 11, 1921.

89 *Ibid.* See also Ernest G. Draper, "Can Unemployment Be Reduced?" *Outlook,* 132 (Sept. 6, 1922), 35-37.

90 See "Why Unemployment Insurance," Feb. 2, 1931, Ernest G. Draper Papers (Library of Congress, Washington) , Container 1.

91 Ernest G. Draper, "Prosperity and Unemployment," *Personnel,* 5 (May 1928), 196-97; "What Employers Are Doing to Combat Unemployment," [nd.], Draper Papers, Container 1; *Couzens Hearings* (70 Cong., 2 Sess., Washington, 1929), p. 30.

92 Ernest G. Draper, "Can Jobs Be Made More Steady?" Dec. 6, 1928, Draper Papers, Container 1.

93 See Ernest G. Draper, "Industry Needs Unemployment Reserves," *ALLR,* 22 (Mar. 1932), 29-32; Draper, "Design for Attack," Dec. 29, 1933, Draper Papers, Container 1.

94 William P. Vogel, *Precision, People, and Progress* (Philadelphia, 1949), pp. 26-35.

95 See Cooke to Robert W. Bruere, May 15, 1928, Cooke Papers; Bruere to Gifford Pinchot, Dec. 13, 1928, Cooke Papers, File 339.

96 *Couzens Hearings,* p. 210; Vogel, *Precision, People and Progress,* p. 48.

97 "National Conference on Unemployment," *American Industries,* 31 (Nov. 1930), 10.

98 For example, business was designed not for profit "but the well being of all." Sam A. Lewisohn, "The Living Wage and the National Income," *PSQ,* 38 (June 1923), 219.

99 Sam A. Lewisohn to Leiserson, Feb. 9, 1938, Leiserson Papers, Box 22.

100 Sam A. Lewisohn, *The New Leadership in Industry* (New York, 1926) , 75.

101 Sam A. Lewisohn, "Stabilizing Business Through Scientific Analysis," *Management Review,* 15 (Feb. 1926), 36.

102 *Couzens Hearings,* p. 25.

103 *New York Times,* Mar. 12, 1933; Sam A. Lewisohn, "New Aspects of Unemployment Insurance," *PSQ,* 50 (Mar. 1935), 3.

104 Owen D. Young, "Dedication Address," *HBR,* 5 (July 1927), 393.

105 Gerard Swope, "The Responsibilities of Modern Industry," *Industrial Management,* 72 (Dec. 1926), 336.

106 *1931 Wagner-Hebert Hearings* (72 Cong., 1 Sess., Washington, 1931), p. 117.

107 *Ibid.,* p. 116

108 Marion B. Folsom, "Future Protection of the Jobless," *Nation's Business,* 22 (Mar. 1934), 68.

CHAPTER 3

1 "Unemployment Benefit Plans in the United States and Unemployment Insurance in Foreign Countries," BLS *Bulletin,* 544 (July 1931), 5.
2 *Ibid.,* 6.
3 J. D. Brown, "Company Plans for Unemployment Compensation," *ALLR,* 23 (Dec. 1933), 176–77.
4 See, for example, Ellis Hawley, *The New Deal and the Problem of Monopoly* (Princeton, 1960) , chs. 1, 2. For the relation of this thought to unemployment insurance in the 1930's see ch. 8 of this book.
5 "Unemployment Benefit Plans," *MLR,* 35 (Dec. 1932), 1226.
6 Charlotte Heath, "History of the Dennison Manufacturing Company, II," *JBEH,* 1 (Aug. 1929), 164.
7 *Ibid.,* pp. 176–77.
8 John B. Andrews to Henry S. Dennison, Mar. 1, 1915, Dennison to Andrews, Mar. 2, 1915, Andrews Papers, Box 12.
9 Dennison admitted that "we have as yet no knowledge" of "just how this [find] can be used." Heath, *JBEH,* 1 (1929), 183.
10 Bryce M. Stewart, *Unemployment Benefits in the United States* (New York, 1930), pp. 464–65; *Couzens Hearings* (70 Cong., 2 Sess., Washington, 1929), pp. 12–13. One observer wrote regarding the six-month waiting period: ". . . the Dennison Company found, for example, that five months was the dividing point between the shifting and the steady classes." J. W. Helburn to R. L. Tweedy, Nov. 6, 1923, MRA Papers, Case 2.
11 Quoted in Stewart, *Unemployment Benefits,* p. 464.
12 Round Table on "Discussion of Shop Rules and Administrative Practices in Unemployment Insurance," John R. Commons Conducting, Dec. 29, 1923, John R. Commons Papers (SHSW, Madison), Box 5.
13 Heath, *JBEH,* 1 (1929), 174; Henry S. Dennison, "Regularization of Industry Against Unemployment," *Annals,* 100 (Mar. 1922), 104.
14 H. N. Dowse to Helburn, Aug. 22, 1923, MRA Papers, Case 2.
15 *Ibid.*
16 Stewart, *Unemployment Benefits,* pp. 476–77.
17 Dennison's views were shared by the experts. N. S. B. Gras wrote, after studying Dennison's activities: "There is now such a consciousness of policy, such an awareness of dangers, that the old-time swings are not likely to be repeated, at least in their extremes." N. S. B. Gras, *Industrial Evolution* (Cambridge, 1930), p. 169.
18 *MLR,* 35 (1932), 1227.
19 *Ibid.,* p. 1229; "United States Benefit Plans," BLS *Bulletin,* 544 (July 1931), 7.
20 William P. Vogel, Jr., *Precision, People, and Progress* (Philadelphia, 1949), pp. 27–35.
21 "Employer-Employee Plan," *Forbes* (Nov. 12, 1931), p. 12; Morris E. Leeds, "Democratic Organization in the Leeds and Northrup Company," *Annals,* 90 (July 1920), 13–14.
22 Robert Bruere, "Quaker Employer Builds a Company Union," *Survey,*

60 (Sept. 1, 1928), 546–47; Robert Bruere, "Quaker Employer on Democracy," *Survey*, 59 (Feb. 1, 1928), 569.

23 Vogel, *Precision*, pp. 42–43.

24 "Unemployment Insurance," *Nation's Business*, 10 (Sept. 1922), 50–52; Stewart, *Unemployment Benefits*, p. 528.

25 Charles S. Redding, "We Stick by Our Workers—And They Stick by Us," *Factory*, 38 (May 1927), 877.

26 *Ibid.*, p. 876; Stewart, *Unemployment Benefits*, p. 529.

27 *Forbes* (Nov. 12, 1931), pp. 13–14.

28 *Couzens Hearings*, p. 208.

29 *MLR*, 35 (1932), 1233.

30 *Ibid.*; also Vogel, *Precision*, p. 48.

31 Herbert F. Johnson, "Sales Doubled When We Made Our Product Easier to Use," *Sales Management*, 12 (Feb. 19, 1927), 307; Stewart, *Unemployment Benefits*, pp. 519–23.

32 *Couzens Hearings*, p. 134.

33 Stewart, *Unemployment Benefits*, p. 523; Anice Whitney, "Operation of Unemployment Benefit Plans in the United States up to 1934, Part I," *MLR*, 38 (June 1934), 1298.

34 Whitney, *MLR*, 38 (1934), 1297. See *Couzens Hearings*, p. 135.

35 Stewart, *Unemployment Benefits*, p. 512.

36 Ben M. Selekman, *Sharing Management with the Workers* (New York, 1924) contains details of the company's history.

37 *Ibid.*, pp. 13–16.

38 *Ibid.*, pp. 79–80.

39 Stewart, *Unemployment Benefits*, p. 439.

40 *Ibid.*, p. 495.

41 Selekman, *Sharing Management*, p. 129. Also compare p. 101 with Stewart, *Unemployment Benefits*, pp. 486–87 on the reduction of labor turnover.

42 "A Paper Company Plans Year-Round Employment," *Factory and Industrial Management*, 80 (Sept. 1930), 529.

43 *Ibid.*, p. 536; also Stewart, *Unemployment Benefits*, p. 519.

44 *MLR*, 35 (1932), 2342; Whitney, *MLR*, 38 (1934), 1296.

45 Stewart describes these plans in *Unemployment Benefits*, pp. 496–97, 554–61. See also W. W. Gates, "Personnel Activities of the Delaware and Hudson Railraod," *BTS*, 11 (Apr. 1926), 62–67; "Guarantee of Minimum Annual Income to Employees by Paper Company," *MLR*, 29 (Sept. 1929), 1235–36.

46 William C. Procter, "How We Divide With Our Men," *American Magazine*, 88 (Oct. 1919), 88. While he admitted the employees liked the profit-sharing system, Herbert Feis, after studying P & G labor relations, concluded "there has been produced no broadly diffused sense of ownership in the company. The employees continue to distinguish the real owners from themselves." Herbert Feis, "Workers as Capitalists," *Review of Reviews*, 77 (Apr. 1928), 404.

47 Most of this information comes from Alfred Lief, *"It Floats": The Story of Procter & Gamble* (New York, 1958), pp. 76–81, 123–33.

48 Quoted in Lief, *"It Floats,"* p. 86.

49 *Ibid.*, p. 135–39; Beulah Amidon, "Ivorydale—A Payroll that Floats," *Survey*, 64 (Apr. 1930), 19; W. C. Procter, "An Idea that Added Thou-

sands of Profits in 24 Months," *System*, 47 (May 1925), 597–98.

50 Herbert Feis, *Labor Relations: A Study Made in the Procter and Gamble Company* (New York, 1928), pp. 105–6.

51 *New York Times*, Aug. 5, 1923.

52 Feis, *Labor Relations*, pp. 97–98; Stewart, *Unemployment Benefits*, pp. 537–38.

53 William C. Procter, "An Experiment with Guaranteed Employment," *Review of Reviews*, 83 (Apr. 1931), 86; *Couzens Hearings*, p. 134.

54 Feis, *Labor Relations*, pp. 121–22.

55 Amidon, *Survey*, 64 (1930), 18; Harold B. Bergen, "Newer Methods of Employment Stabilization," *Personnel*, 8 (Nov. 1931), 59.

56 Paul H. Douglas, *The Columbia Conserve Company: A Unique Experiment in Industrial Democracy* (Chicago, 1926).

57 *Ibid.*, p. 1; *Couzens Hearings*, pp. 35–36.

58 Douglas, *Columbia Conserve*, p. 53.

59 *Couzens Hearings*, pp. 36, 44–45; William P. Hapgood, "The High Adventure of a Cannery," *Survey*, 47 (Sept. 1922), 657.

60 *Couzens Hearings*, p. 45.

61 Paul H. Douglas to Leiserson, Feb. 27, 1933; William R. Hapgood to Leiserson, Mar. 22, 1933; "Statement by the Committee of Four," June 24, 1933, Leiserson Papers, Box 8.

62 "Industrial democracy" lasted until 1942, when labor disputes forced a reversion to conventional managerial methods. See Russell E. Vance, Jr., "An Unsuccessful Experiment in Industrial Democracy: The Columbia Conserve Company" (Ph.D. diss., Indiana University, 1956).

63 "Unemployment Agreement Made with Workers," *Personnel*, 3 (Feb. 1921), 3; Stewart, *Unemployment Benefits*, pp. 499–502.

64 Stewart, *Unemployment Benefits*, p. 506; Whitney, *MLR*, 38 (1934), 1295–96.

65 *MLR*, 35 (1932), 1236–37.

66 Gerard Swope, "The Reminiscences of Gerard Swope," Oral History Research Collection (Columbia University, New York) p. 132. See also David Loth, *Swope of G. E.* (New York, 1958).

67 Swope, "Reminiscences," p. 66; Ida M. Tarbell, *Owen D. Young: A New Type of Industrial Leader* (New York, 1932), pp. 148–50.

68 *1931 Wagner-Hebert Hearings* (72 Cong., 1 Sess., Washington, 1931), p. 24.

69 U.S. Congress, House, *Hearings Before a Subcommittee of the Committee on Ways and Means* (73 Cong., 2 sess., Washington, 1934), pp. 122, 130; *MLR*, 35 (1932), 1238.

70 Whitney, *MLR*, 38 (1934), 1903.

71 Marion B. Folsom, "The Organization of a Statistical Department," *HBR*, 2 (Jan. 1924), 192–93.

72 Marion B. Folsom, "Program of Stabilized Production and Employment," *Annals*, 154 (Mar. 1931), 146.

73 Quoted in Governor's Commission on Unemployment Problems for the State of New York, *Report*, Part 2 (Albany, 1931), pp. 116–17. For the provisions see *New York Times*, Feb. 18, 1931.

74 Whitney, *MLR*, 38 (1934), 1306.

75 *Ibid.*, p. 1307.

76 *Ibid.*, p. 1304; *MLR*, 35 (1932), 1239–40.

77　The plan is described in "Unemployment Insurance and Savings Plan of
J. I. Case Company," *MLR*, 34 (Mar. 1932), 554–55; Whitney, *MLR*, 38
(1934), 1310. For the political implications of the plan see ch. 6.

CHAPTER 4

1　The independent Railroad Brotherhoods adopted various expedients to
assist unemployed members. The Locomotive Engineers established a
system of daily, and later monthly, pay guarantees in the 1880's and
1890's. They also paid extended strike benefits to unemployed engineers.
But apparently they did not consider a formal plan of unemployment
insurance until 1933. Reed C. Richardson, *The Locomotive Engineer,
1863–1963* (Ann Arbor, 1963), pp. 277, 334, 396. The United Mine
Workers, though a powerful AFL union in a "sick" industry, was preoccupied for many years with internal disputes.

2　Quoted in Gerald N. Grob, *Workers and Utopia* (Evanston, 1961), p.
144.

3　Louis S. Reed, *The Labor Philosophy of Samuel Gompers*, Columbia
University Studies in History no. 327 (New York, 1930), pp. 126–27.

4　Grob, *Workers and Utopia*, p. 142.

5　Quoted in Bernard Mandel, *Samuel Gompers* (Yellow Springs, 1963), p.
121.

6　Samuel Gompers, *Seventy Years of Life and Labor: An Autobiography*
(New York, 1925), 2: 5.

7　Mandel, *Gompers*, p. 490; also Samuel Gompers, "Voluntary Social Insurance vs. Compulsory," *American Federationist*, 23 (June 1916), 464.

8　This categorization, which perhaps oversimplifies the differences between policies, is, I believe, helpful in examining the issues involved in
the debate over unemployment insurance. Work sharing, for example,
which I have included in the second grouping, could be considered a
separate category.

9　See, for example, Norman J. Ware, *The Labor Movement in the United
States, 1860–90* (New York, 1929), pp. 299–319.

10　Jean T. McKelvey, *AFL Attitudes Toward Production, 1900–1932*, Cor-
nell Studies in Industrial and Labor Relations, 2 (Ithaca, 1952), ch. 1.

11　*Ibid.*, pp. 21–24; Milton Nadworny, *Scientific Management and the
Unions* (Cambridge, 1955), pp. 52, 88.

12　It was on this point that the socialist needle-trades unions deviated most
from AFL policy. See ch. 5.

13　Mandel, *Gompers*, pp. 122–23; also Samuel Gompers, "Labor History in
the Making—the 1915 A.F. of L. Convention," *American Federationist*,
23 (Jan. 1916), 31.

14　Bryce M. Stewart, *Unemployment Benefits in the United States* (New
York, 1930), pp. 242–53, 235–42, 227–28; Edward W. Bemis, "Benefit
Features of American Trade Unions," Department of Labor *Bulletin*, 22
(May 1899), 386–87; David P. Smelser, *Unemployment and American
Trade Unions* (Baltimore, 1919), p. 131.

15　Smelser, *Unemployment and American Trade Unions, pp.* 130, 139–44.

16　*Ibid.*, p. 146.

17　AFL, *Report of the Proceedings*, 44th Annual Convention, 1924, p. 5.

18 Reed, *Labor Philosophy*, p. 116.

19 *Ibid.*, p. 118; Fred Greenbaum, "The Social Ideas of Samuel Gompers," *Labor History*, 7 (Winter, 1966), 56.

20 The narrow distinctions inherent in these policies caused considerable difficulties for reformers. In commenting on a health insurance plan requiring no employee contributions, Andrews wrote: "It has required a great deal of educational work to get the trade unionists to realize the differences between workmen's compensation and health insurance in this respect, and I am wondering if you need to emphasize this point which is directly contrary to experience." Andrews to John R. Commons, Jan. 21, 1919, Andrews Papers, Box 19.

21 Mandel, *Gompers*, pp. 183–84.

22 AFL, *Proceedings*, 35th Conv., 1915, p. 144.

23 U.S. Congress, House, Committee to Study Social Insurance and Unemployment, *Hearings Before the Committee on Labor* (64 Cong., 1 Sess., Washington, 1918), pp. 175, 178.

24 See, for example, John S. Smith, "Organized Labor and Government in the Wilson Era; 1913–21: Some Conclusions," *Labor History*, 3 (Fall 1962), 267–70.

25 Gompers, *Seventy Years*, 2: 360, 362.

26 McKelvey, *AFL Attitudes*, pp. 37, 65–68. Cooke published an article in May citing the admission by AFL leaders that "in increased production lies one of the most hopeful routes to a higher social and economic status for those who work with their hands." Morris L. Cooke, "Who Is Boss in Your Shop?" *Annals*, 11 (May 1917), 172.

27 *Justice*, Aug. 9, 1919.

28 Samuel Gompers, "Labor Standards After the War," *Annals*, 81 (Jan. 1919), 183; AFL, *Proceedings*, 39th Conv., 1919, p. 72.

29 See Sidney Webb, "The Re-Organization of the British Labour Party," *New Republic*, 13 (Dec. 8, 1917), 149. The British platform was published as a special supplement to the *New Republic* entitled "Labor and the New Social Order." *New Republic*, 14 (Feb. 16, 1918), 1–12. For its influence on American unionists see Lewis L. Lorwin, *The American Federation of Labor* (Washington, 1933), p. 174; Paul U. Kellogg and Arthur Gleason, *British Labor and the War* (New York, 1919), pp. 125–26; and George Soule, *Prosperity Decade* (New York, 1947), pp. 188–89.

30 *New Republic*, 14 (1918), 5–7.

31 *New Majority*, Jan. 4, 1919. See also Illinois State Federation of Labor, *Proceedings*, 36th Conv., 1918, pp. 134, 262; IFL, *Weekly News Letter*, Mar. 23, 1918, Nov. 23, 1918; Eugene Staley, *A History of the Illinois State Federation of Labor* (Chicago, 1930), pp. 262–63.

32 *New Majority*, Apr. 19, 1919.

33 *New Majority*, Jan. 18, 1919; *Headgear Worker*, Jan.–Feb. 1919. J. M. Budish, an official of the Cap Makers' union, reported radical political affairs.

34 *American Labor Year Book*, 1919–20, p. 201.

35 *Headgear Worker*, Dec. 15, 1919, Jan. 2, 1920.

36 John P. Frey to Samuel Gompers, Sept. 8, 1919, John P. Frey Papers (Library of Congress, Washington), Box 10.

37 Gompers to Frey, Sept. 18, 1920, Frey Papers, Box 10.
38 See Staley, *History of the Illinois State Federation,* pp. 374–75. For the details of these developments see Robert S. Gabriner, "The Farmer-Labor Party, 1918–1924: A Study in the Dynamics of Independent Political Action" (M.A. thesis, University of Wisconsin, 1966).
39 The role of the unions in the postwar social insurance campaigns is covered in the following: John R. Commons and Arthur J. Altmeyer, "Health Insurance," app. 1, *Health, Health Insurance, Old Age* (1919), pp. 293, 301; *American Labor Year Book,* 1917–18, pp. 126–27; *American Labor Year Book,* 1918–19, pp. 236–40; Clark A. Chambers, *Seedtime of Reform* (Minneapolis, 1963), pp. 156–57; and the Andrews Papers, Box 16.
40 AFL, *Proceedings,* 41st Conv., 1921, p. 332; William Green to Andrews, Sept. 9, 1921, Andrews Papers, Box 22.
41 See ch. 6.
42 Frieda S. Miller to Andrews, Mar. 9, 1921, Andrews Papers, Box 9.
43 See Joseph P. Chamberlain to Andrews, Mar. 17, 1921; Andrews to Otto T. Mallery, Apr. 1, 1921; Morris E. Leeds to Andrews, Apr. 20, 1921; Andrews to Leeds, Apr. 22, 29, 1921, Andrews Papers, Boxes 22, 23.
44 See Reed, *Labor Philosophy,* p. 116; Address of Samuel Gompers, Sept. 6, 1921, AFL-Gompers Papers (SHSW, Madison), Series 11, File A, Box 48.
45 Gompers to Allen B. Forsberg, Nov. 10, 1921, Andrews Papers, Box 22.
46 AFL, *Proceedings,* 41st Conv., 1921, p. 376.
47 *Ibid.,* p. 377.
48 Gompers to Theodus W. Sims, Feb. 20, 1922, AFL-Gompers Papers, Series 11, File A, Box 43; also Samuel Gompers, "Unemployment, An Illusive and a Real Way Out," *American Federationist,* 22 (Apr. 1921), 311.
49 Samuel Gompers, "Statement for Newspaper Enterprise Association," Sept. 9, 1921, AFL-Gompers Papers, Series 11, File A, Box 48.
50 Samuel Gompers, "The Unemployment Conference—A Picture," *American Federationist,* 28 (Nov. 1921), 960.
51 Gompers, *Seventy Years,* 2: 17.
52 McKelvey, *AFL Attitudes,* pp. 72–78.
53 AFL, *Proceedings,* 42nd Conv., 1922, p. 76.
54 *Ibid.*
55 Matthew Woll, "Report on Business Cycles and Unemployment," *American Federationist,* 30 (May 1923), 386.
56 See Nadworny, *Scientific Management,* p. 130.
57 See the *American Federationist,* 34 (June 1928). Green's call for cooperation in solving the unemployment problem is reprinted in *BTS,* 12 (June 1927), 407–10.
58 "Labor's Unemployment Conference," *MLR,* 25 (Nov. 1927), 1073–75; BLS *Bulletin,* 365 (Sept. 1928), 53; AFL, *Proceedings,* 47th Conv., 1927, p. 38.
59 See Andrews to H. R. Rutherford, Feb. 6, 1925, Andrews Papers, Box 25; Staley, *Illinois State Federation,* pp. 491–92.
60 The unions did, nevertheless, undertake such interunion activities as life insurance programs.
61 See Anice Whitney, "Operation of Unemployment Benefit Plans in the

United States up to 1934, Part I," *MLR*, 38 (June 1934), 1288.
62 Stewart, *Unemployment Benefits,* pp. 295–96.
63 Whitney, *MLR*, 38 (1934), 1288.
64 *Ibid.*

CHAPTER 5

1 Elias Tcherikower, ed., *The Early Jewish Labor Movement in the United States* (New York, 1961), pp. 167–68, contains a systematic account of business organization in the needle trades. Also Leo Wolman, "Garment Industries," *Encyclopedia of the Social Sciences* (New York, 1931), 574–76, and Louis Levine, *The Women's Garment Workers* (New York, 1924), ch. 32. The problems of the women's garment industry in the 1920's are discussed in Governor's Advisory Commission, Cloak, Suit, and Skirt Industry, New York City, *Report* (Albany, 1925), and Governor's Advisory Commission, *Final Recommendations* (Albany, 1926).
2 The best account of Hillman's career is his "official" biography: Matthew Josephson, *Sidney Hillman* (Garden City, 1952).
3 Joseph Gollomb, "Sidney Hillman," *Atlantic Monthly*, 162 (July 1938), 48.
4 *Advance,* Mar. 25, 1921.
5 Leo Wolman *et al., The Clothing Workers of Chicago* (Chicago, 1923), p. 2.
6 Joseph Schlossberg to Louis Weiss, Oct. 18, 1919, ACWA Papers (ACWA Headquarters, New York).
7 *Advance,* Oct. 8, 1920.
8 Gollomb, *Atlantic Monthly,* 162 (1938), 49.
9 Jacob Potofsky to G. D. H. Cole, Dec. 15, 1919, ACWA Papers; also *Advance,* Dec. 20, 1919.
10 *Advance,* Jan. 23, 1919.
11 *Advance,* Aug. 8, July 25, 1919; *New York World,* July 27, 1919.
12 ACWA, *Documentary History of the ACWA: Proceedings,* 4th Biennial Convention, May 1920, p. 237.
13 Legal Statement by Leo Wolman, [n.d.], ACWA Papers; Josephson, *Hillman,* p. 197.
14 *Advance,* Sept. 12, 1919; "Arbitration Leads to Redistribution and Reduction of Burden of Unemployment," Sept. 17, 1919, ACWA Papers.
15 *Advance,* June 18, 1920.
16 Wolman, *Clothing Workers,* p. 159.
17 *Advance,* Sept. 3, 1920; also ACWA, *Documentary History: Proceedings,* 5th Conv., May 1922, General Executive Board Report, p. 130.
18 Sidney Hillman, "Views of an American Workman on Unemployment," *ALLR,* 11 (Mar. 1921), 28. In a letter to Hillman, Morris L. Cooke ably summarized the case for unemployment prevention. Cooke to Hillman, Dec. 29, 1919, Cooke Papers, Box 9.
19. Leo Wolman, "A Proposal for an Unemployment Fund in the Men's Clothing Industry," *Amalgamated Education Pamphlets,* 5 (New York, 1922), 12.
20 *Ibid.,* p. 21.
21 *Advance,* Aug. 26, 1927.

22 ACWA, *Documentary History: Proceedings,* 5th Conv., GEB Rept., p. 135.

23 "Memorandum of a Tentative Agreement Concerning Employment Fund between Messrs. Hillman, Wolman and Howard," Jan. 13, 1923, ACWA Papers.

24 *Advance,* Apr. 27, 1923.

25 *Advance,* May 4, 18, 1923; H. A. Millis, "Unemployment Insurance in the Men's Clothing Industry of Chicago." *University Journal of Business,* 2 (Mar. 1924), 163.

26 "Editorials," *Survey,* 51 (Nov. 1, 1923), 164.

27 ACWA, *Documentary History: Proceedings,* 6th Conv., app., pp. i–xi; *Advance,* Aug. 10, Sept. 28, Oct. 12, 1923.

28 See Bryce M. Stewart, "An American Experiment in Unemployment Insurance in Industry," *International Labor Review,* 11 (Mar. 1925), 319–23.

29 Bryce Stewart to Leo Wolman, Aug. 7, 1923, ACWA Papers; John R. Commons to William M. Leiserson, Aug. 25, Sept. 20, 1923, Leiserson Papers, Box 9; John R. Commons, *Myself* (Madison, 1964), pp. 198, 200.

30 *Couzens Hearings,* (70 Cong., 2 Sess., Washington, 1929), p. 224.

31 *Advance,* Sept. 4, 1925; ACWA, *Documentary History: Proceedings,* 8th Conv., 1928, pp. 198–99.

32 W. E. Hotchkiss to Commons, Apr. 30, 1925, Commons Papers, Box 3; *Advance,* Mar. 27, May 8, 1927; Josephson, *Hillman,* p. 283; Joel Seidman, *The Needle Trades* (New York, 1942), p. 266.

33 ACWA, *Documentary History: Proceedings,* 7th Conv., 1926, p. 30.

34 Charles E. Zaretz, *The Amalgamated Clothing Workers of America* (New York, 1934), p. 267.

35 *Couzens Hearings,* p. 223.

36 *Advance,* Jan. 4, Feb. 1, 1924; ACWA, *Documentary History: Proceedings,* 6th Conv., 1924, pp. 246, 277–78.

37 *Advance,* June 27, 1924.

38 *Advance,* July 4, 1924.

39 Theodore Draper, *American Communism and Soviet Russia* (New York, 1960), pp. 215–23; also Melech Epstein, *Profiles of Eleven* (Detroit, 1965), p. 291.

40 Earl R. Browder, "Amalgamated Clothing Workers Resist Reaction," *Labor Herald,* 3 (June 1924), 107.

41 A. Simon, "Ferment in the Needle Trades," *Labor Herald,* 3 (Aug. 1924), 175.

42 William Z. Foster, "The Left Wing in the Needle Trades Elections," *Workers Monthly,* 4 (Feb. 1925), 150. The struggle between the Foster and Ruthenberg wings of the Party was also an important factor in encouraging a "tough" line toward the socialist unions. See Draper, *American Communism,* pp. 75, 218–19, 222–23; Josephson, *Hillman,* pp. 274–75; David M. Schneider, *The Workers (Communist) Party and American Trade Unions,* Johns Hopkins University Studies in Historical and Political Science, series 46, no. 2 (Baltimore, 1928), p. 62.

43 *Advance,* Dec. 5, 1924.

44 *Ibid.*

45 These events may be followed in the *Advance,* especially Dec. 19, 1924, Feb. 20, 1925; Schneider, *Workers Party,* pp. 64–70; Josephson, *Hillman,* pp. 277–79; Joel Seidman, *The Needle Trades* (New York, 1944), pp. 176–78. For a typical statement of the "left" demands see *Daily Worker,* Dec. 16, 1924.

46 *Advance,* Dec. 5, 1924. See Jacob Potofsky to S. Kucharska, Jan. 23, 1925, ACWA Papers.

47 *Advance,* June 26, 1925. Josephson states that the 1926 contract provided for the establishment of unemployment insurance in 1928. Josephson, *Hillman,* p. 300.

48 *Advance,* June 29, 1928.

49 *Ibid.*

50 *New York Times,* July 1, 1928.

51 *Advance,* June 15, 1928.

52 *Advance,* June 29, July 27, Aug. 10, 1928, Feb. 1, Apr. 19, Nov. 15, 1929; *New York Times,* Nov. 29, 1929; ACWA, *Documentary History: Proceedings,* 9th Conv., 1930, GEB Rept., p. 66, 11th Conv., 1936, GEB Rept., p. 125.

53 *Rochester* (New York) *Times Union,* June 13, 1923.

54 Report, Apr. 12, 1928; Local 202 Meeting Report, Apr. 26, 1928, Rochester Joint Board Papers (New York State Library of Industrial and Labor Relations, Ithaca), Reel 2.

55 The influence of the national officers is suggested in the reports of Abraham Chatham, the Joint Board Manager. In late 1927 he stated that unemployment was a serious problem but that he had not decided what to do. Manager's Report, Dec. 1, 1927; also Manager's Report, Feb. 9, 1928, Rochester Joint Board Papers, Reel 2.

56 Anice Whitney, "Operation of Unemployment Benefit Plans in the United States up to 1934, Part I," *MLR,* 38 (June 1934), 1316; ACWA, *Documentary History: Proceedings,* 11th Conv., 1936, GEB Rept., p. 125.

57 ACWA, *Documentary History: Proceedings,* 9th Conv., 1930, p. 113.

58 Levine, *Garment Workers,* pp. 280–82, 285–86.

59 *Ibid.,* pp. 280–82.

60 *Ibid.,* pp. 285–86.

61 *Ibid.,* pp. 322, 325; *Justice,* July 23, 1920.

62 Levine, *Garment Workers,* p. 367.

63 *Ibid.,* pp. 375–77.

64 Morris L. Cooke to Henry S. Dennison, Mar. 25, 1925, Cooke Papers, File 339.

65 *Justice,* Feb. 4 ,1921.

66 *Justice,* July 2, 1920; see Bryce M. Stewart, *Unemployment Benefits in the United States* (New York, 1930), p. 375; Herman Feldman, *The Regularization of Employment* (New York, 1925), pp. 142, 368. Levine cites the Dec. 1920 Board of Referees meeting, rather than the July conference, as the origin of the unemployment insurance plan. Levine, *Garment Workers,* p. 271.

67 *Justice,* Apr. 29, 1921; Olga Halsey, "Employment Guaranteed," *Survey,* 47 (Jan. 14, 1922), 594. Levine sets the original fund at forty-one weeks. Levine, *Garment Workers,* p. 372.

68 Levine, *Garment Workers*, p. 378. For the statistics of the Cleveland plan see Stewart, *Unemployment Benefits*, p. 383; ILGWU, *Report of Proceedings*, 19th Convention, 1926; Meyer Perlstein, "Killing Two Birds (in Cleveland)," *Labor Age*, 12 (Dec. 1923), 5–6.

69 *Justice*, Jan. 13, May 19, 1922.

70 ILGWU, *Report of the GEB*, 19th Conv., 1928, pp. 217–18; "Unemployment Benefit Plans," *MLR*, 35 (Dec. 1932), 1245.

71 Feldman, *Regularization*, pp. 388–89. See also John R. Commons *et al.*, *Can Business Prevent Unemployment?* (New York, 1925), p. 201.

72 Fred C. Butler, "Guaranteed Employment in the Cleveland Garment Industry," *ALLR*, 14 (June 1924), 137; also William J. Mack, "Safeguarding Employment: The 'Cleveland Plan' of Unemployment Compensation," *ALLR*, 12 (Mar. 1922), 25–30.

73 *New York Times*, Sept. 10, 1922.

74 *Justice*, Oct. 15, 1920.

75 Benjamin Stolberg, *Tailor's Progress* (Garden City, 1944), p. 99.

76 *Justice*, Oct. 20, 1922.

77 ILGWU, *Report of Proceedings*, 16th Conv., 1922, pp. 97, 184.

78 The best account of the growth of factionalism is Levine's *Garment Workers*, pp. 352–57; also Schneider, *Workers Party*, pp. 88–89, and Stolberg, *Tailor's Progress*, pp. 109–23.

79 See, for example, Stolberg, *Tailor's Progress*, pp. 118–24; Levine, *Garment Workers*, pp. 257–58.

80 ILGWU, *Report of the GEB*, 17th Conv., 1924, p. 9. See also *Justice*, Nov. 2, 1923.

81 Levine, *Garment Workers*, p. 418.

82 *Justice*, July 6, 1923.

83 *Ibid.*, Apr. 20, 1923.

84 *Ibid.*, Mar. 14, 1924.

85 *Fur Worker*, Feb. 1923.

86 *Ibid.*, May 1923.

87 *Ibid.*, Nov. 1923.

88 *Ibid.*, Feb., May 1924.

89 *Ibid.*, Jan., May 1924.

90 *Ibid.*, Aug. 1924.

91 United Cloth Hat and Cap Makers, *Report of the Proceedings*, 12th Biennial Convention, 1919, p. 46.

92 *Headgear Worker*, Sept. 9, 1921, May 13, 1923; UCHCM, *Proceedings*, 14th Conv., 1923, pp. 59, 105.

93 ILGWU, *Report of Proceedings*, 17th Conv., 1924, p. 176.

94 Schneider, *Workers Party*, pp. 91–92; Stolberg, *Tailor's Progress*, pp. 125–26.

95 *New York Times*, June 19, July 2, 8, 14, Aug. 6, 1924; ILGWU, *Report of the GEB*, 18th Conv., 1925, pp. 9–24; *Justice*, June 20, 23, July 4, 1924. Approximately 27,000 dressmakers were covered under the agreement in 1925.

96 Governor's Advisory Commission, *Report*, p. 85; James A. Corcoran, "Unemployment Insurance in the Cloack, Suit and Skirt Industry of New York City, *MLR*, 22 (Apr. 1926), 889.

97 See *New York Times*, Feb. 5, 1925.

98 *Justice,* Oct. 3, 1924.
99 Stewart, *Unemployment Benefits,* p. 394; ILGWU, *Report of the GEB,* 18th Conv., 1925, pp. 139–40.
100 ILGWU, *Report of Proceedings,* 18th Conv., 1925, p. 177.
101 Governor's Advisory Commission, *Recommendations,* p. 8; see Stolberg, *Tailor's Progress,* p. 136; Benjamin Stolberg, "Collapse of the Needle Trades," *Nation,* 124 (May 4, 1927), 99.
102 *New York Times,* Sept. 5, 1926.
103 *Justice,* Feb. 11, 18, Mar. 25, Apr. 1, 1927. The dressmakers' unemployment insurance fund, which was provided in an April 1925 agreement but which remained relatively unimportant, was suspended in April 1926, when the "lefts" allowed it to lapse. *Justice,* Apr. 3, 1925, Apr. 16, 1926; ILGWU, *Report of the GEB,* 19th Conv., 1926, p. 275.
104 *Fur Worker,* Jan. 1925.
105 *Ibid.,* Mar. 1925.
106 *Ibid.,* May, June 1925; Schneider, *Workers Party,* p. 76; Philip S. Foner, *The Fur and Leather Workers Union* (Newark, 1950), pp. 147–53.
107 *Fur Worker,* July 1925.
108 Schneider, *Workers Party,* pp. 79–80; *Fur Worker,* Nov., Dec. 1925, Jan. 1926.
109 Benjamin Gitlow, *I Confess: The Truth About American Communism* (New York, 1939), pp. 337–46; Draper, *American Communism,* pp. 218–19, 222–23.
110 Schneider, *Workers Party,* pp. 81–85; "Beneficial Activities of American Trade Unions," BLS *Bulletin,* 1565 (Sept. 1928), 151; *Fur Worker,* June 1926.
111 *Justice,* Dec. 14, 1928, July 19, 1929, Feb. 14, 1930, May 21, 1931.
112 See Wilfred Carsel, *A History of the Chicago Ladies' Garment Workers' Union* (Chicago, 1940), pp. 180–81, 186, 196; ILGWU, *Report of the GEB,* 19th Conv., 1926, p. 184; *Justice,* Mar. 14, 1930.
113 *New York Times,* May 26, 1933; Foner, *Fur Workers,* p. 382.
114 *Headgear Worker,* Sept. 28, Oct. 26, Nov. 23, 1923; Cloth Hat, Cap and Millinery Workers, *Report of the Proceedings,* 15th Biennial Convention, 1925, p. 30.
115 CHCMW, *Proceedings,* 15th Conv., 1925, p. 30.
116 *Headgear Worker,* Nov. 23, Dec. 28, 1923.
117 See *Headgear Worker,* May 16, Aug. 8, 1924, Feb. 6, 1925; CHCMW, *Proceedings,* 15th Conv., 1925, p. 35.
118 *Headgear Worker,* May 24, 1924.
119 *Ibid.,* Mar. 21, 1924.
120 UCHCM, *Proceedings,* 16th Conv., 1927, p. 219; also *Headgear Worker,* Oct. 29, 1926.
121 *MLR,* 25 (1932), 1245–46.

CHAPTER **6**

1 John B. Andrews, "The Prevention of Unemployment," *Proceedings of the NCCC,* 1915, p. 552.
2 Joseph Dorfman, *The Economic Mind in American Civilization,* 5 vols. (New York, 1946–59), 4: 377.

3 John R. Commons, *The Distribution of Wealth* (New York, 1893), p. 81.

4 John R. Commons, "The Right to Work," *Arena,* 21 (Feb. 1899), 140–41.

5 Wisconsin Industrial Commission, *Report* (1901), 14: 34.

6 *Ibid.,* pp. xliv–xlv, 35–37.

7 William M. Leiserson, "How to Provide Against Unemployment?" Address to the State Conference of Charities and Corrections, Nov. 6, 1913, Leiserson Papers, Box 48.

8 John R. Commons to Emily Bodman, Mar. 4, 1912, Commons Papers, Box 2. See Commons to William M. Leiserson, Mar. 20, 1912, Leiserson Papers, Box 9; Leiserson to John A. Fitch, Nov. 1912, Leiserson Papers, Box 15.

9 Wisconsin Industrial Commission, *Bulletin,* 2 (Feb. 20, 1913), 69–70.

10 John R. Commons, *Myself* (Madison, 1964), p. 142.

11 John R. Commons, "Social Insurance and the Medical Profession," Address before the State Medical Society, Oct. 7, 1914, Unpublished Report of the U.S. Industrial Relations Commission (SHSW, Madison), p. 7.

12 John R. Commons, "Address Delivered at the Fifteenth Annual Meeting, National Tuberculosis Association, June, 1919," in *Trade Unionism and Labor Problems* (New York, 1921), p. 82.

13 See John R. Commons, "The True Scope of Unemployment Insurance," *ALLR,* 15 (Mar. 1925), 43.

14 John R. Commons, "Unemployment and Its Relation to Business Men's Organizations," U. of Wis. *Bulletin* no. 800, General Series 597 (July 1916), pp. 87–88.

15 John B. Andrews to Commons, May 13, 1915, July 15, 1915; David J. Saposs to Andrews, July 12, 1915; Andrews to Olga Halsey, Jan. 27, 1915, Andrews Papers, Box 12.

16 "Notes of the Conference Between Professor Commons and Mr. Andrews, Oct. 16, 1914, Andrews Papers, Box 9.

17 John R. Commons and John B. Andrews, *Principles of Labor Legislation* (New York, 1916), pp. 412–13.

18 For Wisconsin employment during this period see Citizens Committee on Unemployment and Public Employment Bureau of Milwaukee, *6th Report,* 1919, p. 5.

19 See John R. Commons, *Industrial Goodwill* (New York, 1919), pp. 58–59, 65; John R. Commons, "Bringing About Industrial Peace," Address to the Conference of the National Association of Employment Managers, Dec. 3, 1919, in *Trade Unionism and Labor Problems,* pp. 9–10.

20 Special Committee on Social Insurance, *Report* (Madison, 1919), p. 14.

21 Thomas W. Gavett, *The Development of the Labor Movement in Milwaukee* (Madison, 1965), pp. 96–97; also Edwin E. Witte, "Labor in Wisconsin History," *Wisconsin Magazine of History,* 35 (Winter 1951), pp. 139–140.

22 Wisconsin State Federation of Labor, *Proceedings,* 22nd Annual Convention, 1914, pp. 26–27; also WFL, *Proceedings,* 17th Conv., 1909, pp. 30–31; WFL, *Wisconsin Labor* (1924); "History of the Wisconsin State

Federation of Labor," [n.d.] Wisconsin State Federation of Labor Papers (SHSW, Madison), Box 10.

23 WFL, *Proceedings*, 26th Conv., 1918, pp. 36, 46, 68, 77–84.

24 WFL, *The Next Steps for Wisconsin* (1919), pp. 7–8. This concern was reflected in an earlier debate. See Minutes of the Executive Board Meeting, Jan. 17, 1919, WFL Papers.

25 *La Crosse Tribune*, July 27, 1920; WFL, *Proceedings*, 28th Conv., 1920, pp. 71–72, 88–89.

26 *La Crosse Tribune*, July 22, 1920.

27 Wisconsin Industrial Commission, *The Wisconsin Labor Market* [n.d], 2: 1.

28 *Ibid.*, (Aug. 1920), 1: 3.

29 *Ibid.*, (July 1921), 11: 2.

30 Interview with Jacob F. Friedrich, Aug. 24, 1966.

31 See Charles A. Myers, "Employment Stabilization and the Wisconsin Act" (Ph.D. diss., University of Chicago, 1939), fn. 20; "History of the Wisconsin State Federation of Labor," WFL Papers, Box 10.

32 J. J. Handley to Andrews, Sept. 20, 1920, Andrews Papers, Box 20.

33 J. J. Handley, "Unemployment Insurance," *Proceedings*, Wisconsin State Conference of Social Work, Oct. 13–15, 1920, pp. 150–51.

34 Gertrude Schmidt, "History of Labor Legislation in Wisconsin" (Ph.D. diss., University of Wisconsin, 1933), p. 336.

35 Record of the Proceedings, Federated Trades Council, Dec. 1, 1920, Federated Trades Council Papers (SHSW, Madison); Madison *Capital Times*, Dec. 9, 1921.

36 Allen B. Forsberg to Andrews, Feb. 1, 1921, Andrews Papers, Box. 21.

37 *Capital Times*, Feb. 1, 1921.

38 *Ibid.*, Feb. 15, 16, 1921; *Wisconsin State Journal*, Feb. 15, 1921.

39 John R. Commons, "Putting an End to Unemployment," *La Follette's Magazine*, 13 (Mar. 1921), 39; *Capital Times*, Feb. 16, 1921.

40 See, for example, *Milwaukee Sentinel*, Feb. 16, 1921.

41 Commons to Alvin H. Hansen, Mar. 22, 1932, Commons Papers, Box 4.

42 See *Equity News*, Apr. 1, 1921; *Capital Times*, Mar. 1, 1921.

43 Commons to Andrews, Mar. 16, 1921, Andrews Papers, Box 20.

44 *Capital Times*, May 3, 1921; Schmidt, "History of Labor Legislation," pp. 37–38.

45 *Capital Times*, May 26, 1921; *Wisconsin State Journal*, May 26, 1921.

46 Commons to Andrews, May 28, 1921, Andrews Papers, Box 22; *Wisconsin State Journal*, June 1, 1921.

47 *Capital Times*, June 2, 1921.

48 Edwin E. Witte to Andrews, Apr. 24, 1922, Andrews Papers, Box 25.

49 "President Philip A. Koehring Presents Annual Message to Association of Commerce Members," *Milwaukee*, 4 (Feb. 10, 1927), 2, 5; "Just a Few Legislative High Spots," *Milwaukee*, 4 (Mar. 10, 1927), 2.

50 See Gavett, *Labor Movement in Milwaukee*, p. 140.

51 Frederick H. Clausen, "The Obligations of Our Industry," Speech Before the Convention of the Farm Equipment Industry, Oct. 1921, Frederick H. Clausen Papers, (SHSW, Madison), Box 1.

52 John R. Commons, "Unemployment Compensation and Prevention," *Survey*, 47 (Oct. 1, 1921), esp. 8–9; John R. Commons, "Unemploy-

ment Prevention," *ALLR,* 12 (Mar. 1922), esp. 19–21. The latter was his speech to the AALL convention in December 1921.

53 Forsberg to Andrews, Feb. 20, Mar. 28, 1922, Andrews Papers, Box 25.

54 Commons to Andrews, Sept. 20, 1922, Andrews Papers, Box 25. See also Henry A. Huber to Halsey, Dec. 16, 1922, Henry A. Huber Papers (SHSW, Madison), Letter Book 1920–26.

55 Andrews to Royal Meeker, Feb. 16, 1922, Andrews Papers, Box. 25.

56 WFL, *Proceedings,* 30th Conv., 1922, pp. 30–31, 64, 92.

57 *Milwaukee Sentinel,* Jan. 13, 1923.

58 See Schmidt, "History of Labor Legislation," p. 339; Commons to W. A. Titus, Dec. 18, 1922, Commons Papers, Box 3.

59 *Capital Times,* Feb. 21, 1923.

60 *Wisconsin State Journal,* Feb. 21, 1923; *Milwaukee Journal,* Feb. 21, 1963.

61 *Wisconsin State Journal,* May 17, 1923. Essentially the same article appeared in the Dec. 1923 issue of the *ALLR.*

62 See, for example, *Equity News,* Apr. 15, 1923; *Wisconsin State Journal,* Apr. 5, 1923; *Wisconsin Farmer,* May 3, 1923. Commons often argued that most hoboes were farm boys who had been lured to the city.

63 Witte to Andrews, July 19, 1923, Andrews Papers, Box 18; also *Milwaukee Leader,* June 7, 1923; *Milwaukee Sentinel,* June 7, 1923. The "deal" was reported in the *Wisconsin State Journal,* June 5, 1923.

64 *Wisconsin State Journal,* June 6, 1923. For Blaine's alleged support see *Milwaukee Sentinel,* Feb. 24, 1923.

65 Witte to Andrews, July 14, 1923, Andrews Papers, Box 28; *Milwaukee Leader,* June 28, 1923. See also Thomas M. Duncan and Herman O. Kent, "The Progressives at Home," *Labor Age,* 12 (Oct. 1923), 4–6.

66 See Don D. Lescohier and Florence Peterson, *The Alleviation of Unemployment in Wisconsin* (Madison, 1930), pp. 9–17.

67 "The Farmer," *Milwaukee,* 1 (July 5, 1923), 2.

68 See, for example, Wisconsin Manufacturers Association, *Farm and Factory Facts,* Feb. 8, 1928; "Presents Interesting Talk on Taxation," *Milwaukee,* 1 (Feb. 21, 1924), 4.

69 WMA, *Farm and Factory Facts,* July 25, Oct. 10, 1928.

70 Frederick H. Clausen, "The Spirit of Deare," Moline Address, Mar. 31, 1927, Clausen Papers, Box 1.

71 WMA, *Farm and Factory Facts,* June 26, Sept. 18, 1929.

72 *Couzens Hearings* (70 Cong., 2 Sess., Washington, 1929), p. 212.

73 Commons, *ALLR,* 15 (1925), 42–43. He called his work in Chicago "about the most interesting enterprise I have ever engaged in." Commons to Willard E. Hotchkiss, May 11, 1925, Commons Papers, Box 3. But his emphasis on individual reserves confused some observers. See John R. Commons, "The Limits of Unemployment Insurance," July 25, 1924, Commons Papers, Box 3; *Wisconsin State Journal,* Aug. 31, 1924.

74 "Talks Made at the Unemployment Insurance Hearing," Mar. 12, 1925, 1–4; E. G. Draper, "Speech on Unemployment Insurance Before the Wisconsin Legislature," Mar. 12, 1925, Commons Papers, Box 6.

75 See Press Releases from the Unemployment Insurance Association, Legislative Reference Library (State Capitol, Madison); *Capital Times,* Mar. 11, 1925.

76 WFL, *Proceedings*, 33rd Conv., 1925, p. 97; "Interesting Legislative Gossip," *Milwaukee*, 2 (Mar. 5, 1925), 4.
77 Andrews to Isaac M. Rubinow, June 4, 1928, Andrews Papers, Box 39.
78 *Capital Times*, Mar. 21, June 6, 1929; WFL, *Proceedings*, 36th Conv., 1928, p. 85.
79 Commons to Mamie Barrett, Sept. 30, 1929, Commons Papers, Box 4.
80 Lescohier and Peterson, *Alleviation of Unemployment*, pp. 26, 101.
81 See "Unemployment Expert," *Milwaukee Commerce*, 9 (Sept. 12, 1930), 3.
82 W. F. Ashe to D. C. Everest, Sept. 18, 1930, D. C. Everest Papers (SHSW, Madison).
83 *Wisconsin State Journal*, Sept. 11, 1930.
84 Elizabeth Brandeis to Andrews, June 5, 1930, Andrews Papers, Box 31.
85 Commons to Andrews, July 7, 1930, Andrews Papers, Box 42.
86 Andrews to Commons, Jan. 5, 1931, Andrews Papers, Box 45.
87 Paul A. Raushenbush to Mrs. E. G. Evans, Jan. 1, 1931, Andrews Papers, Box 45. This critical document, like others, was read by Andrews.
88 *Capital Times*, Jan 21, 1931; Minutes of the Executive Board Meeting of the Wisconsin State Federation of Labor, Jan. 3, 1931, WFL Papers, Box 3.
89 Witte to Andrews, Dec. 19, 1930, Andrews Papers, Box 45.
90 Commons to Andrews, Jan. 15, 1931, Andrews Papers, Box 45.
91 *Milwaukee Leader*, Mar. 24, 1931; Official Bulletin of the Milwaukee Association of Commerce, Mar. 26, 1931, Legislative Reference Library.
92 See *Milwaukee Journal*, Mar. 5, 1931; *Milwaukee Leader*, Mar. 14, 1931; Radio speech by George F. Kull, Apr. 5, 1931, Legislative Reference Library.
93 Witte to Andrews, Feb. 28, 1931, Andrews Papers, Box 45.
94 See Witte to Andrews, Apr. 16, May 6, 1931, Andrews Papers, Box 45; W. Ellison Chalmers to Handley, May 2, 1931, Commons Papers, Box 10; Schmidt, "History of Labor Legislation," p. 353.
95 Andrews to Anna Bogue, June 25, 1931, Andrews Papers, Box 44.
96 Commons to Andrews, July 20, 1931, Commons Papers, Box 4.
97 Andrews to Morris E. Leeds, July 28, 1931; Leeds to Andrews, Aug. 5, 1931, Andrews Papers, Box 45.
98 Raushenbush to Andrews, Aug. 17, 1931, Andrews Papers, Box 45.
99 See Handley to Chalmers, June 29, 1931, Commons Papers, Box 4; WFL, *Proceedings*, 39th Conv., 1931, p. 66; Handley to Andrews, Aug. 22, 1931, Andrews Papers, Box 45.
100 See Ann Neal, "Person Appearing For and Against Unemployment Insurance at the Hearings Conducted by the Interim Committee on Unemployment, Nov. 1931," Legislative Reference Library, p. 1.
101 Andrews to Dr. Louis Bloch, Sept. 22, 1931, Andrews Papers, Box 46; Minutes of the Wisconsin Legislative Interim Committee on Unemployment, 1: Sept. 15, 1921, pp. 61–88, Sept. 16, 1931, pp. 2–56, WFL Papers, Box 16.
102 Minutes of the Wisconsin Legislative Interim Committee on Unemployment, 2: Sept. 29, 1931, WFL Papers, Box 16.
103 Andrews to Felix Frankfurter, Sept. 24, 1931; also Raushenbush to Andrews, Sept. 19, 1931, Andrews Papers, Box 45.

104 Elizabeth Brandeis to Andrews, Oct. 3, 1931, Andrews Papers, Box 45.
105 Merrill G. Murray to Andrews, Oct. 7, 1931, Andrews Papers, Box 46.
106 See, for example, *Equity News*, Nov. 15, Dec. 1, 1931.
107 *Capital Times*, Oct. 23, 1931; Murray to Andrews, Oct. 23, 1931, Andrews Papers, Box 46.
108 Elizabeth Brandeis, *History of Labour in the United States* (New York, 1935), 3: 618–19; also *Capital Times*, Oct. 28, 1931; *Milwaukee Leader*, Nov. 4, 1931. The Equity resolution explicitly protested the farmers' tax burden to support the unemployed and the need to raise urban purchasing power.
109 Wisconsin Legislative Interim Committee on Unemployment, *Report* (Madison, 1931), pp. 35, 38–40, 44, 69.
110 *Milwaukee Journal*, Nov. 18, 1931; also see "Manufacturers to Meet," *Milwaukee Commerce*, 10 (Nov. 13, 1931), 3.
111 *Milwaukee Journal*, Nov. 18, 1931; *Wisconsin State Journal*, Nov. 17, 1931.
112 Witte to Andrews, Dec. 24, 1931; Andrews Papers, Box 45; *Capital Times*, Dec. 21, 1931.
113 Witte to Andrews, Dec. 24, 1931, Andrews Papers, Box 45.
114 Witte to Commons, Mar. 9, 1934, Edwin E. Witte Papers (SHSW, Madison), Box 1; Interview with Harold Groves, Apr. 29, 1966. Gettleman later stated he had promised the League of Progressive Women to vote for the bill. *Capital Times*, Jan. 8, 1932.
115 Murray to Andrews, Jan. 8, 1932, Andrews Papers, Box 45; *Capital Times*, Jan. 8, 1932.

CHAPTER 7

1 William T. Foster to John Frey, Aug. 23, 1928, John P. Frey Papers (Library of Congress, Washington), Box 8; *New York Times*, Nov. 22, 1928.
2 See *Milwaukee Journal*, Feb. 19, 1923.
3 See Herbert Hoover to Samuel Gompers, Feb. 19, 1923, Hoover Papers, Secretary of Commerce, Herbert Hoover Personal File, Gompers File, 1-I/515.
4 Harry Bernard, *Independent Man: The Life of Senator James Couzens* (New York, 1958), p. 194; James Couzens to John Carson, Aug. 8, 1928; Couzens to C. O. Hardy, Sept., 1928; Carson to Couzens, Oct. 17, 1928, James Couzens Papers (Library of Congress, Washington), Box 58.
5 See, for example, Isador Lubin, "Let Out," *Survey*, 62 (Apr. 1929), 11–13.
6 *Couzens Hearings* (70 Cong., 2 Sess., Washington, 1929), pp. xi–xiii.
7 Couzens to William M. Leiserson, June 27, 1929, Leiserson Papers, Box 10.
8 Robert P. Lamont to Ernest G. Draper, July 9, 1929, Draper Papers, Box 1.
9 William Starr Myers, ed., *The State Papers and Other Public Writings of Herbert Hoover*, 2 vols. (Garden City, 1934), 1:183. See also Albert U. Romasco, *The Poverty of Abundance* (New York, 1965), pp. 44–49.

10 Myers, *State Papers,* 1: 391.
11 *Ibid.,* p. 394.
12 See *New York Times,* Feb. 16, Mar. 27, 28, Apr. 21, 1928.
13 Robert F. Wagner to Harold G. Moulton, Mar. 13, 1930, Robert F. Wagner Papers (Georgetown University, Washington).
14 Andrews to Wagner, Apr. 12, 1930, Wagner Papers.
15 See Irving Bernstein, *The Lean Years* (Boston, 1960), ch. 6.
16 Herbert Hoover, *The Memoirs of Herbert Hoover* (New York, 1951), 3: 47; Bernstein, *Lean Years,* 283–84.
17 Andrews to Couzens, Mar. 28, 1930; also Andrews to John R. Commons, Apr. 5, 1930; Andrews to Joseph P. Chamberlain, July 2, 1930; Andrews to Commons, July 2, 1930, Andrews Papers, Box 42. For Couzens' viewpoint see "Couzens Proposes Annual Salaries for Workman," *Business Week* (Apr. 9, 1931), 37–38.
18 Wagner to Andrews, May 28, 1930, Wagner Papers.
19 Wagner to Gerard Swope, July 27, 1930; Swope to Wagner, Dec. 12, 1930, Wagner Papers.
20 Press Release, Dec. 15, 1930, Wagner Papers. Wagner received favorable comments from many business leaders on his tax exemption plan. He was "surprised" at this response. Wagner to Meyer Jacobstein, Jan. 6, 1931, Wagner Papers.
21 *New York Times,* Nov. 12, Dec. 22, 1930.
22 See Wagner to Felix Hebert, Mar. 12, 1931; Hebert to Wagner, Mar. 18, 1931; Otis Glenn to Wagner, Mar. 16, 1931, Wagner Papers; *New York Times,* Mar. 21, 1931.
23 Romasco, *Poverty,* p. 186.
24 Myers, *State Papers,* 1: 579.
25 *New York Times,* Aug. 9, 1931.
26 *New York Times,* Aug. 11, 1931. Since most unemployment insurance proposals of the early 1930's merely enabled the states or individual employers to establish their own funds, Hoover's equation of them with the European "doles" is all the more incredible.
27 Swope to Hoover, Sept. 11, 1931, Hoover Papers, Presidential, Box 754; W. N. Doak to Hoover, Aug. 14, 1931, Hoover Papers, Unemployment, Box 273.
28 Hoover to Hebert, Sept. 11, 1931, Hoover Papers, Unemployment, Box 273. This exchange is recorded only in cross-reference notation. It is partially confirmed, however, in Lawrence Ritchey to Hebert, Sept. 15, 1931, Hoover Papers, Presidential, Box 754.
29 William Mitchell to Hoover, Nov. 21, 1931, Hoover Papers, Presidential, Box 892.
30 Hebert to Wagner, Oct. 3, 1931, Wagner Papers.
31 U.S. Congress, Senate, *Report of the Select Committee to Investigate Unemployment Insurance* (72 Cong., 1 Sess., Rept. 964, Washington, 1932), pp. 50–52.
32 *Ibid.,* p. 53. See also Isador Lubin to Simon H. Rifkind [n.d]; Wagner to Paul H. Douglas, Jan. 11, 1932, Wagner Papers.
33 *New York Times,* Dec. 28, 1930.
34 Wagner to A. J. Barbor, Feb. 10, 1931, Wagner Papers.
35 Wagner to Homer G. Shockley, Apr. 21, 1931, Wagner Papers.

36 Reprinted in USCC, "Balancing Production and Employment" (1930), p. 9.
37 *Ibid.*
38 Julius H. Barnes, "Facing the Larger Problems of Business Management," *JBUC*, 3 (July 1930), 277.
39 Julius H. Barnes, "The New Philosophy of Stabilization," *Nation's Business*, 18 (May 20, 1930), 19–20.
40 USCC, "Balancing Production and Employment," p. 55. Hoover stressed these activities in public and private messages. See Hoover to Julius H. Barnes, Dec. 7, 1929, Hoover Papers, Presidential, Box 273.
41 Barnes, *JBUC*, 3 (1930), 276.
42 USCC, Minutes of the 117th Meeting, Board of Directors, Jan. 23, 1931, Chamber of Commerce Archives.
43 USCC, Minutes of the 40th Meeting, Executive Committee, Mar. 21, 1931, Chamber of Commerce Archives.
44 *Wall Street Journal*, Apr. 30, 1931; *New York Times*, Apr. 30, 1931.
45 *New York Times*, Apr. 15, 1931. Couzens wrote to E. A. Filene, who as one of its founders wielded great influence within the Chamber of Commerce: "I have rather been relying . . . on private initiative solving this problem . . . but I have reached the point where I am discouraged about relying on industry." Couzens to E. A. Filene, Apr. 23, 1931, Filene Papers.
46 *New York Times*, Apr. 29, 1931.
47 *New York Times*, Apr. 30, 1931; Robert Smith, "How Business Builds its Platform," *Nation's Business*, 19 (Apr. 1931), 28.
48 See USCC, *Men Who Serve You*, 1931–32.
49 See Gerard Swope, "The Reminiscences of Gerard Swope," Oral History Research Collection (Columbia University), p. 101.
50 Swope, "Reminiscences," p. 123.
51 Gerard Swope, "Stabilization of Industry," reprinted in Charles A. Beard, ed., *America Faces the Future* (Boston, 1932), pp. 161, 162, 178–79, 181–84.
52 *Ibid.*, p. 184.
53 Quoted in *Ibid.*, p. 191.
54 Harriman presented his proposals to the board of directors on Oct. 3. The report was released to the public on Dec. 18. See USCC, Minutes of the 121st Meeting, Board of Directors, Oct. 23, 1931, Chamber of Commerce Archives.
55 Beard, *America Faces the Future*, p. 259; also *1913 Wagner-Hebert Hearings* (72 Cong., 1 Sess., Washington, 1931), pp. 304–5.
56 Beard, *America Faces the Future*, p. 207.
57 *Ibid.*, p. 225.
58 See Romasco, *Poverty of Abundance*, p. 218; George Soule, *Hillman* (New York, 1939), p. 158; ACWA, *Documentary History of the ACWA: Proceedings*, 10th Biennial Convention, 1934, pp. 16–17.
59 U.S. Congress, Senate, *Hearings Before a Subcommittee of the Committee on Manufacturers* (72 Cong., 1 Sess., Washington, 1932).
60 Hoover, *Memoirs*, 3: 36; Hoover to Solicitor General, Sept. 14, 1931; "Memo on the Swope Plan," Hoover Papers, Presidential, Box 892.
61 Hoover, *Memoirs*, 3: 334.

62 See *American Industries,* 31 (Oct. 1930), 39; *New York Times,* Apr. 12, Aug. 16, 1931; NICB, *Essentials of a Program of Unemployment Reserves* (New York, 1933).

63 Hoover, *Memoirs,* 3: 420.

64 See, for example, Leo Wolman, "The Future of Unemployment Insurance," *ALLR,* 13 (Mar. 1923), 41–42; E. M. Burns, "The Economics of Unemployment Relief," *American Economic Review,* 33 supp. (Mar. 1923), 32.

65 Leiserson to Beulah Amidon, Feb. 15, 1928, Leiserson Papers, Box 39.

66 Abraham Epstein to Jacob Billikopf, Nov. 30, 1928, Abraham Epstein Papers (Columbia University, New York), Box 8.

67 Andrews to Commons, Aug. 21, 1930, Andrews Papers, Box 42.

68 John B. Andrews, "Extracts from a Paper Before the American Academy of Political and Social Science, Dec. 5, 1930," Wagner Papers. This meeting of unemployment experts, ironically, indicated the wide differences in their views. See John B. Andrews, "Unemployment Reserve Funds. An American Plan to Stabilize Jobs and Purchasing Power," *Annals,* 154 (Mar. 1931), 117–23.

69 Andrews to Paul A. Raushenbush, Jan. 7, 1931, Andrews Papers, Box 45.

70 Andrews to Raushenbush, Jan. 15, 1931, Andrews Papers, Box 45; also Andrews to Commons, Aug. 21, 1930, Andrews Papers, Box 42. The text of the American plan appeared in the *ALLR,* 20 (Dec. 1930), 251–56.

71 Sam A. Lewisohn to Andrews, Oct. 20, 1930; Draper to Andrews, Oct. 23, 1930; Morris E. Leeds to Andrews, Dec. 26, 1930, Andrews Papers, Box 42.

72 Cleveland *Plain Dealer,* Dec. 29, 1930; Andrews to Leiserson, Dec. 8, 1930, Leiserson Papers, Box 1; Andrews to Chamberlain, Dec. 8, 1930, Andrews Papers, Box 43.

73 Andrews to Wagner, Aug. 7, 1930, Wagner Papers; Cleveland *Plain Dealer,* Dec. 29, 1930. Wagner's address is reprinted in *ALLR,* 21 (Mar. 1931), 11–17.

74 He aptly summarized the position of the Wisconsin reformers on Jan. 8: "As your bill now stands, I should 'applaud the effort, and vote against the measure.'" Raushenbush to Andrews, Jan. 8, 1931, Andrews Papers, Box 45.

75 See Morris Cooke to Elizabeth Brandeis, Apr. 5, 1927, Jan. 4, Mar. 14, 1929; Cooke to Robert Bruere, Mar. 14, 1929, Cooke Papers, Box 4.

76 See Leiserson to Billikopf, Apr. 12, 1930; Billikopf to Leiserson, Apr. 21, 1930, Leiserson Papers, Box 5; Cooke to Elizabeth Brandeis, Jan. 2, 1930, Cooke Papers, Box 4.

77 Paul H. Douglas and Aaron Director, *The Problem of Unemployment* (New York, 1931), p. 487.

78 This distinction with regard to the Swarthmore project can easily be exaggerated. Douglas dealt sympathetically with the businessmen's efforts (see, for example, *The Problem of Unemployment,* pp. 110–13), but was a firm supporter of true social insurance.

79 Clinch Calkins, *Some Folks Won't Work* (New York, 1930), pp. 159–63; also Clark A. Chambers, *Seedtime of Reform* (Minneapolis, 1965), pp. 144–45; Paul U. Kellogg, "The Unsettling Settlements," *Survey,* 60 (May 15, 1928), 217, 250; Helen Hall and Irene Hickok Nelson,

"How Unemployment Strikes Home," *Survey*, 60 (Apr. 1, 1929), 51.

80 See Chambers, *Seedtime of Reform*, p. 215; Gertrude Springer, "Partners in a New Social Order," *Survey*, 69 (July 1933), 249.

81 Andrews to Anna Bogue, June 25, 1931, Andrews Papers, Box 44.

82 John A. Lapp, "Is Unemployment Permanent?" *Proceedings*, National Conference of Social Work, 58th Annual Session, 1931, pp. 233–38; Gertrude Springer, "The Challenge of Hard Times," *Survey*, 66 (July 15, 1931), 318–82.

83 Gertrude Springer, *Survey*, 69 (1933), p. 246; Chambers, *Seedtime of Reform*, p. 243; "National Objectives for Social Work," *Proceedings*, NCSW, 60 (June 1933), 646–47.

84 Chambers, *Seedtime of Reform*, p. 173; Florence Kelley to Andrews, Oct. 2, 1930, Andrews Papers, Box 31.

85 Chambers, *Seedtime of Reform*, p. 220.

86 National Women's Trade Union League of America, *Proceedings*, 8th Biennial Convention, 1922, pp. 18–99, *Proceedings*, 9th Biennial Convention, 1924, p. 122.

87 Chambers, *Seedtime of Reform*, pp. 220–21.

88 *Ibid.*, p. 233.

89 See David A. Shannon, *The Socialist Party of America* (New York, 1955), pp. 194–95, 219.

90 Quoted in R. A. McGowan, "Catholic Work in the United States for Social Justice," *Catholic Action*, 17 (May 1936), 8; also Aaron I. Abell, *American Catholicism and Social Action: A Search for Social Justice 1865–1950* (New York, 1960), p. 236.

91 *New York Times*, June 20, 1931.

92 Robert M. Miller, *American Protestantism and Social Issues, 1919–39* (Chapel Hill, 1958), pp. 224–26, 230–44.

93 "Unemployment Insurance," *Christian Century*, 47 (Dec. 17, 1930), 1553.

94 AFL, *Report of the Proceedings*, 48th Annual Convention, 1928, p. 45; William Green, "Two Kinds of Unemployment," *American Federationist*, 35 (Apr. 1928), 403.

95 AFL, *Proceedings*, 48th Conv., 1928, pp. 48–49.

96 William Green, "Unemployment Insurance," *American Federationist*, 35 (Apr. 1928), 403–5; William Green, "Study of Unemployment," *American Federationist*, 36 (May 1929), 535.

97 AFL, *Proceedings*, 49th Conv., 1929, pp. 258, 260.

98 See William Green to John H. Walker, Jan. 3, 1930, AFL–William Green Papers (SHSW, Madison), Series 11, File B, Box 7.

99 Green to Helen A. Russell, Jan. 30, 1930, AFL-Green Papers, Series 11, File B, Box 7.

100 AFL, Executive Council Minutes, Sept. 12, 1930, quoted in Milton Lewis Farber, "Changing Attitudes of the American Federation of Labor Toward Business and Government, 1929–33" (Ph.D. diss., Ohio State University, 1959), p. 204.

101 AFL, *Proceedings*, 50th Conv., 1930, pp. 51, 305–8.

102 *Ibid.*, p. 311.

103 Frey to Sumner H. Slichter, May 24, 1930, Frey Papers, Box 15.

104 AFL, *Proceedings,* 50th Conv., 1930, pp. 312, 315.

105 "A Statement of Policy of the CPLA," *Labor Age,* 18 (June 1929), 6–7; also "A Challenge to Progressives," *Labor Age,* 18 (Feb. 1929), 6.

106 See "Unemployment Insurance—The Next Step," *Labor Age,* 19 (June 1930), 21; "Our Unemployment Insurance Bills," *Labor Age,* 19 (Oct. 1930), 22–23. The campaign is aptly summarized in James O. Morris, *Conflict Within the AFL* (Ithaca, 1958), pp. 133–34.

107 *Machinists' Monthly Journal,* 39 (Apr. 1927), 223–25; International Association of Machinists, *Proceedings,* 18th Conv., 1928, p. 50.

108 See American Federation of Teachers, *Report of the Proceedings,* 14th Annual Convention, 1930, p. 119; Emil Rieve, "Hosiery Workers' Union Favors Unemployment Reserve Funds," *ALLR,* 21 (Mar. 1931), 61; Mabel Walker, "Third Unemployment Survey," *ALLR,* 20 (Dec. 1930), 405; Phil E. Ziegler to Andrews, Oct. 16, 1930, Andrews Papers, Box 43.

109 See Walker, *ALLR,* 20 (1930), 405; New York State Federation of Labor, *Official Proceedings,* 67th Annual Convention, 1930, p. 146; Louis Francis Budenz, "Toward Unemployment Insurance," *Labor Age,* 19 (July 1930), 18; California State Federation of Labor, *Proceedings,* 31st Convention, 1930, pp. 14, 72.

110 Illinois State Federation of Labor, *Proceedings,* 49th Annual Convention, 1931, pp. 153–54; Massachusetts State Federation of Labor, *Proceedings,* 46th Annual Convention, 1931, p. 13; Bernstein, *Lean Years,* p. 349.

111 Green to Wagner, Jan. 19, 1931, Wagner Papers.

112 Green to Andrews, Jan. 9, 1931; also Green to Andrews, Mar. 15, 1931, Andrews Papers, Box 46.

113 AFL, Executive Council Minutes, Aug. 19, 1931, quoted in Farber, "Changing Attitudes of the AFL," p. 218.

114 AFL, *Proceedings,* 51st Conv., 1931, pp. 149–62.

115 AFL, *Proceedings,* 23rd Convention of the Metal Trades Department, 1931, p. 63.

116 *Ibid.,* pp. 368–71, 372, 378–79, 381, 382–85.

117 *Ibid.,* pp. 397–98.

118 *New York Times,* Oct. 15, 1931.

119 United Mine Workers of America, *Proceedings,* 32nd Convention, 1932, pp. 393, 402.

120 Green to Frank Duffy, Apr. 11, 1932, William Green Papers (New York State Library of Industrial and Labor Relations, Ithaca).

121 AFL, Executive Council Minutes, July 22, 1932, quoted in Farber, "Changing Attitudes of the AFL," p. 240.

122 *New York Times,* July 23, 1932.

123 Green to Duffy, Aug. 5, 1932, Green Letters.

124 Andrews to Dorothy W. Douglas, Sept. 21, 1932, Andrews Papers, Box 47; *New York Times,* Sept. 30, 1932.

125 "Draft Prepared by Professor Sayre," in Green to Edwin E. Witte, Oct. 17, 1932; Witte to Green, Oct. 19, 1932; Chamberlain to Witte, Oct. 21, 1932, Witte Papers, Box 1.

126 AFL, *Proceedings,* 52nd Conv., 1932, pp. 313, 319–20.

127 *Ibid.,* pp. 352–55.

128 *Ibid.,* p. 345.
129 *Ibid.,* pp. 135, 337.
130 *Ibid.,* pp. 346, 360, 442.

CHAPTER **8**

1 These relatively obscure events can be followed in William English Walling, *Progressivism—and After* (New York, 1914), p. 75; *New York Times,* Apr. 7, 1915, Mar. 19, 1916; Bruno Lasker, "How to Meet Hard Times," *Survey,* 45 (Feb. 5, 1921), v, x.
2 Frank Freidel, *Franklin D. Roosevelt* (Boston, 1954), 2: 153–54.
3 Franklin D. Roosevelt to S. N. Eben, Nov. 15, 1930, Franklin D. Roosevelt Papers (Roosevelt Library, Hyde Park), Governor, RG 12.
4 Press Release, July 2, 1929; Robert V. Ingersoll to Roosevelt, Aug. 1, 1929; Benjamin Schlesinger to Roosevelt, Feb. 6, 1930; Press Release, Feb. 4, 1930, Roosevelt Papers, Governor, RG 18.
5 Abraham Epstein to William M. Leiserson, Mar. 2, 1929, Epstein Papers, Box 28.
6 *Public Papers of Franklin D. Roosevelt,* 1930 (Albany, 1931), pp. 507–8. This statement was probably drafted by Frances Perkins. See Frances Perkins to G. T. Cross, Mar. 27, 1930, Roosevelt Papers, Governor, RG 18.
7 New York Committee on the Stabilization of Industry for the Prevention of Unemployment, "Preventing Unemployment," *Preliminary Report,* Apr. 21, 1930, p. 15; Roosevelt to Perkins, Apr. 23, 1930, Roosevelt Papers, Governor, RG 18. See also Bernard Bellush, *Franklin D. Roosevelt as Governor of New York* (New York, 1955), pp. 128–29.
8 Governor's Commission on Unemployment, New York, "Less Unemployment Through Stabilization of Operations," *Report* (Nov. 13, 1930), 1: 7–20.
9 Roosevelt to Henry Bruere, Oct. 8, 1930, Roosevelt Papers, Governor, RG 18.
10 *New York Times,* July 1, 1930; Freidel, *Roosevelt,* 3: 138–40. Cary A. Hardee, secretary of the conference, added "unemployment" to his original topic, "old age pensions." Cary A. Hardee to Roosevelt, June 18, 1930. Miss Perkins suggested the businessmen's experience. Perkins to Roosevelt, June 24, 1930, Roosevelt Papers, Governor, RG 18.
11 These statements appear in *Public Papers,* 1930, p. 752; New York State Federation of Labor, *Official Proceedings,* 67th Annual Convention, 1930, pp. 127–28.
12 NYFL, *Proceedings,* 67th Conv., p. 146.
13 Roosevelt to John B. Andrews, Sept. 13, 1930, Roosevelt Papers, Personal, RG 12; Roosevelt to Andrews, Dec. 29, 1930; Roosevelt to Jackson P. Olcott, Oct. 1, 1930; Roosevelt to Eben, Nov. 15, 1930, Roosevelt Papers, Governor, RG 18.
14 *New York Times,* Jan. 23, 1931.
15 Perkins to Roosevelt, Dec. 13, 1930, Roosevelt Papers, Governor, RG 18.
16 *Public Papers,* 1931, pp. 564, 567.
17 *Ibid.,* pp. 547–49.

18 *New York Times,* Jan. 26, Feb. 2, 1931.
19 Roosevelt to G. Hall Roosevelt, Feb. 24, 1931, Roosevelt Papers, Governor, RG 18.
20 Roosevelt had never before clearly stated his opposition to private insurance plans, in fact he occasionally seemed to encourage them by stressing insurance principles. See *New York Times,* Mar. 7, 1931; Roosevelt to G. Hall Roosevelt, Feb. 24, 1931, Roosevelt Papers, Governor, RG 18; *Public Papers,* 1931, p. 238.
21 Minutes of the Conference for Unemployment Insurance Legislation in New York State, Feb. 17, 1931, Andrews Papers, Box 47.
22 New York Times, Mar. 3, 19, 1931; Andrews to Gardner Latimer, Mar. 30, 1931, Andrews Papers, Box 46.
23 *Public Papers,* 1931, pp. 129–30.
24 *New York Times,* May 29, 1931; Leiserson to Governor George White, June 4, 1931, Leiserson Papers, Box 44.
25 Governor's Commission on Unemployment, "Less Unemployment Through Stabilization of Operations," *Report,* 2 (June, 1931).
26 Mary W. Dewson, "An Aid to an End," 1: 13, Mary Dewson Papers (Roosevelt Library, Hyde Park).
27 Andrews to Joseph P. Chamberlain, Nov. 20, 1931, Andrews Papers, Box 46.
28 Perkins to Roosevelt, Oct. 23, 1931, Roosevelt Papers, Governor, RG 18.
29 Leo Wolman to Leiserson, Feb. 4, 1932, Leiserson Papers, Box 16.
30 Andrews to Louis Block, Sept. 22, 1931; John A. Fitch to Andrews, Jan. 29, 1932, Andrews Papers, Box 46.
31 *Public Papers,* 1932, pp. 70–71.
32 *Ibid.,* p. 69; Press Release, Feb. 15, 1932, Roosevelt Papers, Governor, RG 18.
33 *Public Papers,* 1932, p. 69.
34 *New York Times,* Feb. 16, 1932.
35 Andrews to Paul A. Raushenbush, Feb. 11, 1932; Andrews to Perkins, Feb. 22, 1932, Andrews Papers, Box 47.
36 Andrews to Raushenbush, Mar. 1, 1932; Andrews to Perkins, Feb. 24, 1932, Andrews Papers, Box 47.
37 NYFL, *Proceedings,* 69th Conv., 1932, p. 81; *New York Times,* Feb. 27, 29, Mar. 2, 1932.
38 "Memorandum on Conference with Gerard Swope," June 14, 1932, Andrews Papers, Box 47.
39 NYFL, *Proceedings,* 68th Conv., 1931, p. 140; Andrews to Chamberlain, Nov. 20, 1931, Andrews Papers, Box 46.
40 Andrews to Raushenbush, Oct. 21, 1932, Andrews Papers, Box 47; *New York Times,* Oct. 19, 22, 1932.
41 Raushenbush to Andrews, Nov. 25, 1932, Andrews Papers, Box 47.
42 *New York Times,* Feb. 21, 1933.
43 Andrews to Wolman, Oct. 28, 1932; Andrews to Josephine Goldmark, Nov. 2, 1932, Andrews Papers, Box 47.
44 Herbert H. Lehman to Mrs. V. G. Simkovitch, Feb. 16, 1933, Andrews Papers, Box 47.
45 Andrews to Simkovitch, Feb. 21, 1933, Andrews Papers, Box 50.

46 See *New York Times,* Dec. 3, 1932, Jan. 8, 1933.
47 Andrews to Dorothy Douglas, Feb. 25, 1933; Raushenbush to Andrews, Feb. 23, 1933, Andrews Papers, Box 50.
48 Herman A. Gray to Leiserson, Mar. 13, 1933; Leiserson to Gray, Mar. 17, 1933, Leiserson Papers, Box 16.
49 Paul H. Douglas to Epstein, July 6, 1933, Leiserson Papers, Box 2.
50 *New York Times,* Mar. 3, Apr. 3, 1933; *Public Papers of Herbert H. Lehman* (Albany, 1933), p. 116.
51 A. L. Moffat to Andrews, Apr. 25, 1933, Andrews Papers, Box 50; *New York Times,* Apr. 9, 11, 1933. See also "Killing the Job Insurance Bills," *New Republic,* 74 (May 3, 1933), 339.
52 *New York Times,* Aug. 24, 1933.
53 NYFL, *Proceedings,* 70th Conv., 1933, p. 13.
54 NYFL, *Proceedings,* 71st Conv., 1934, p. 115.
55 George Meany to Epstein, Jan. 8, 1934, American Association for Social Security Papers (New York State Library of Industrial and Labor Relations, Ithaca), Box 28.
56 *New York Times,* Jan. 23, 1934.
57 Epstein to "Friend," Apr. 5, 1934, Leiserson Papers, Box 2. The report of the *New York Times,* Apr. 5, 1934, suggests that Epstein exaggerated his victory, although it confirmed that the Byrne bill was favored.
58 *New York Times,* Apr. 22, 24, 1934; NYFL, *Proceedings,* 71st Conv., 1934, p. 70.
59 *New York Times,* Oct. 28, 1934.
60 William T. Byrne to Epstein, Dec. 19, 1934, Epstein Papers, Box 42.
61 Epstein to Joseph Schlossberg, Mar. 1, 1932, American Association for Social Security Papers, Box 28.
62 Andrews to Lehman, Mar. 7, 1935, Andrews Papers, Box 55; also *New York Times,* Mar. 2, 1935.
63 *New York Times,* Mar. 29, Apr. 19, 1935.
64 Special Commission on Social Insurance, Mass., *Report,* Feb. 1917, House No. 1850 (Boston, 1917), pp. 121, 123.
65 Special Commission on Unemployment, Unemployment Compensation and the Minimum Wage, Mass., *Report,* Feb. 9, 1923, House No. 1325 (Boston, 1923), p. 26.
66 *Ibid.,* pp. 27, 28, 31, 38.
67 *Ibid.,* pp. 43–46.
68 Massachusetts State Federation of Labor, *Proceedings,* 43rd Annual Convention, 1928, p. 14. The Massachusetts Federation opposed the Shattuck bill. See Joseph Huthmacher, *Massachusetts People and Politics, 1919–33* (Cambridge, 1959), p. 60.
69 MFL, *Proceedings,* 45th Conv., 1930, p. 12.
70 Massachusetts Department of Labor and Industries, "Report of an Investigation as to the Causes of Existing Unemployment," *Special Report,* Jan. 1931, House No. 1298 (Boston, 1931), pp. 8, 14, 56–58.
71 Special Commission on the Stabilization of Employment, Mass., *Preliminary Report,* Dec. 1931, House No. 1100 (Boston, 1931), pp. 13–14.
72 *Ibid.,* p. 9. See *Boston Evening Transcript,* Dec. 5, 1931.
73 U.S. Congress, Senate, *Hearings Before a Subcommittee of the Committee on Manufacturers* (72 Cong., 1 Sess., Wash., 1932), 410.

74 H. A. Wooster to Elizabeth S. Magee, Apr. 21, 1932, Leiserson Papers, Box 25.
75 Special Commission on Stabilization of Employment, Mass., *Final Report* (Boston, 1933), pp. 23–27; *Springfield* (Mass.) *Republican,* Dec. 13, 1932.
76 John Plaisted to Andrews, Feb. 18, 1933, Andrews Papers, Box 50.
77 "Report of the Advisory Committee on Unemployment Reserves of the Associated Industries of Massachusetts," [Feb. 10, 1933], Andrews Papers, Box 50.
78 *Boston Evening Transcript,* Jan. 5, 1933.
79 See *Springfield Republican,* Feb. 24, 1933; *Boston Evening Transcript,* Feb. 23, Mar. 23, 1933.
80 Plaisted to Andrews, Mar. 6, 1933, Andrews Papers, Box 50.
81 See MFL, *Proceedings,* 48th Conv., 1933, pp. 14, 27–28, 31.
82 MFL, *Proceedings,* 46th Conv., 1931, pp. 13–14, 34.
83 MFL, *Proceedings,* 47th Conv., 1932, p. 21.
84 See W. L. Stoddard to Andrews, May 24, 1934, Andrews Papers, Box 54; Stanley King, "Unemployment Reserves and Insurance," *ALLR,* 23 (Dec. 1933), 171; Karl T. Compton, "Massachusetts Plan for Unemployment Reserves," *ALLR,* 23 (June 1933), 97.
85 J. S. Stone to Andrews, Apr. 6, 1934, Andrews Papers, Box 54.
86 MFL, *Proceedings,* 49th Conv., 1934, p. 58.
87 Special Commission Appointed to Make an Investigation of Unemployment Insurance, Reserves and Benefits, Mass., *Report,* House No. 386 (Boston, 1934), pp. 5, 11.
88 *Ibid.,* pp. 12, 38.
89 Special Commission Appointed to Make an Investigation of Unemployment Insurance, Reserves and Benefits, Mass., *Second and Final Report,* House No. 2225 (Boston, 1935), p. 4.
90 Thomas Eliot to A. Frank Reel, Apr. 26, 1935, E. A. Filene Papers.
91 For the background and activities of the league regarding unemployment see "Facts About Retail Stores," Consumers League of Cincinnati *Bulletin,* 3 (June 1916), pp. 3–4; Frances R. Whitney, *Employment Agencies in Cincinnati* (Cincinnati, 1928). For political progressivism in Ohio see Hoyt Landon Warner, *Progressivism in Ohio 1897–1917* (Columbus, 1964).
92 Minutes of the Meeting of the Consumers League (of Ohio) Board, Apr. 17, 1929, Oct. 9, 1928, Leiserson Papers, Box 9; Elizabeth S. Magee, "Ohio Takes Stock," *Proceedings,* National Conference of Social Work, 1932, p. 285.
93 Alice P. Gannett to Leiserson, Mar. 19, 1929, Leiserson Papers, Box 9.
94 Magee to Leiserson, Apr. 2, 1930, Leiserson Papers, Box 25.
95 Minutes of the Consumers League (of Ohio) Board Meeting, May 6, Oct. 7, 1930, Leiserson Papers, Box 9; Leiserson to Magee, Apr. 7, 1930, Leiserson Papers, Box 25.
96 Leiserson to Magee, Oct. 24, 1930, Leiserson Papers, Box 9.
97 Magee to Leiserson, Oct. 20, 1930; Minutes of the Consumers League (of Ohio) Board Meeting, Nov. 4, 1930, Leiserson Papers, Box 9.
98 Thomas J. Donnelly to John P. Frey, Aug. 12, 1931, Frey Papers, Box 8.
99 Magee to Leiserson, Mar. 13, 1931, Leiserson Papers, Box 25.

100 *Ohio State Journal,* Apr. 7, 1931; Cleveland *Plain Dealer,* Apr. 7, 1931.

101 Magee to Leiserson, Sept. 24, 1931, Leiserson Papers, Box 9.

102 Thomas J. Duffy to Leiserson, Oct. 19, 1931, Leiserson Papers, Box 10.

103 See Minutes of the Ohio Commission on Unemployment Insurance, Jan. 21, 1932, Leiserson Papers, Box 31.

104 Rubinow to Magee, June 24, 1932, Isaac M. Rubinow Papers (New York State Library of Industrial and Labor Relations, Ithaca), Box 9.

105 Leiserson to Magee, Mar. 31, 1932, Leiserson Papers, Box 25; Minutes of the Meeting of the Ohio Commission on Unemployment Insurance, May 24, 1932, Rubinow Papers, Box 9.

106 Elizabeth Magee, *Proceedings,* NCSW (1932), p. 389.

107 Donnelly to Leiserson, Sept. 20, 1932, Leiserson Papers, Box 25; Magee to Leiserson, Apr. 9, 1932, June 15, 1932, Leiserson Papers, Box 32.

108 Ohio State Federation of Labor, *Proceedings,* 49th Annual Convention, 1932, pp. 78–86; Leiserson to Paul U. Kellogg, Nov. 12, 1932, Leiserson Papers, Box 39.

109 Summary of Discussion at Commission Meeting, Ohio Commission on Unemployment Insurance, May 24, 1932, Leiserson Papers, Box 31.

110 Rubinow to Magee, Oct. 17, 1932, Rubinow Papers, Box 9.

111 See Magee to Leiserson, Oct. 28, 29, 1932, Leiserson Papers, Box 25.

112 Ohio Commission on Unemployment Insurance, *Report* (Columbus, 1932), 1: 11, 14, 19, 58–59, 60, 81, 89–97.

113 Rubinow to Magee, Dec. 28, 1932, Rubinow Papers, Box 9; Rubinow to Leiserson, Dec. 2, 1932, Leiserson Papers, Box 35.

114 Andrews to Leiserson, Nov. 25, 1932, Leiserson Papers, Box 1.

115 See Magee to Leiserson, Nov. 16, 19, Dec. 29, 1932, Leiserson Papers, Box 25; Marvin C. Harrison to Leiserson, Nov. 28, 1932, Leiserson Papers, Box 17; *Ohio State Journal,* Nov. 14, 1932.

116 Magee to Leiserson, Dec. 27, 1932, Leiserson Papers, Box 25; *Ohio State Journal,* Nov. 16, 1932.

117 *Ohio State Journal,* Nov. 15, 1932.

118 Leiserson to Charles J. Bauer, Dec. 19, 1932, Leiserson Papers, Box 10; Leiserson to Rubinow, Dec. 1, 1932, Rubinow Papers, Box 9; also *New York Times,* Dec. 4, 1932.

119 *Ohio State Journal,* Jan. 10, 1933.

120 Magee to Rubinow, Jan. 7, 1933; Rubinow to Douglas, Jan. 13, 1933; Rubinow to Magee, Jan. 10, 1933, Rubinow Papers, Box 9.

121 Leiserson to Frances Whitney, Jan. 28, 1933, Leiserson Papers, Box 9.

122 See Leiserson to Stanley Mathewson, Jan. 29, 1933, Leiserson Papers, Box 26.

123 White to Charles E. Chittenden, Feb. 10, 1933, Leiserson Papers, Box 15; Magee to Leiserson, Feb. 1, 1933, Leiserson Papers, Box 25.

124 Harrison to Leiserson, Aug. 16, 1933, Leiserson Papers, Box 17; also *Ohio State Journal,* Mar. 13, 1933.

125 Leiserson to John R. Commons, Mar. 21, 1933, Leiserson Papers, Box 9.

126 Harrison to Rubinow, Mar. 4, 1933, Rubinow Papers, Box 9.

127 *Ohio State Journal,* June 6, 7, 10, 1933; Perkins to Roosevelt, June 3, 1933; Roosevelt to White, June 8, 1933, Roosevelt Papers, Office Files, 121-A.

128 Magee to Leiserson, Aug. 29, 1933, Leiserson Papers, Box 25.

129   U.S. Congress, House, *Hearings Before the House Ways and Means Committee* (73 Cong., 2 Sess., Washington, 1934), pp. 2–516; also *Ohio State Journal,* June 8, 21, 1933; Roosevelt to White, June 15, 1933, Roosevelt Papers, Office Files, 121-A.
130   Magee to Leiserson, Apr. 1, 1935, Leiserson Papers, Box 9.
131   Rubinow to Magee, Apr. 14, 1936, Rubinow Papers, Box 9.
132   Magee to Leiserson, Jan. 20, 1936, Leiserson Papers, Box 9.
133   *Ohio State Journal,* Apr. 9, 16, 1936.
134   Magee to Leiserson, May 28, July 8, 1936, Leiserson Papers, Box 9; *Ohio State Journal,* July 8, 1936.
135   See, for example, M. L. Cooke to W. C. Byers, Dec. 11, 1930; J. W. Rawle to Cooke, Jan. 3, 1931, Cooke Papers, Box 20.
136   Pennsylvania State Federation of Labor, *Proceedings,* 31st Annual Convention, 1932, pp. 32, 51.
137   See *New York Times,* Apr. 2, 1933; "Report of the Committee on Unemployment Reserves, Pennsylvania," *MLR,* 37 (Aug. 1933), 277.
138   See George H. Trafton, "State Unemployment Compensation Laws," *ALLR,* 27 (Mar. 1937), 53–57.

CHAPTER **9**

1   "An American Plan for Unemployment Reserve Funds," *ALLR,* 23 (June 1933), 81.
2   "Discussions," BLS *Bulletin,* 609 (Nov. 1933), 115.
3   Paul A. Raushenbush, "The Wisconsin Idea: Unemployment Reserves," *Annals,* 170 (Nov. 1933), 72–73.
4   NICB, *Essentials of a Program of Unemployment Reserves* (New York, 1932), p. 40.
5   Ernest G. Draper to John H. Finley, July 30, 1931, Draper Papers, Box 1.
6   *New York Times,* May 5, 1934.
7   U.S. Department of Commerce, *Business Advisory Council for the Department of Commerce,* 1944, 1958, especially p. 8 (1944 edition), pp. 5–9 (1958 edition); "Opening Statement at the Meeting of the Business Advisory and Planning Council," by Gerard Swope, Nov. 1, 1933, Library, U.S. Department of Commerce (Washington).
8   Henry I. Harriman, "The Stabilization of Business and Employment," *American Economic Review,* 23 (Mar. 1932), 74; Henry I. Harriman, "Current National Problems," address, Sept. 21, 1934, Chamber of Commerce Archives. The effort within the chamber to reach an acceptable yet positive position can be followed in Minutes of the 130th (Jan. 13, 1933), 139th (May 2–3, 1934), and 145th (Mar. 1, 1935) Meetings, Board of Directors, CC Archives.
9   Abraham Epstein to Jacob Billikopf, Sept. 30, 1932, Epstein Papers, Box 8.
10   Abraham Epstein, *Insecurity, a Challenge to America* (New York, 1933), p. 248.
11   Epstein to William Haber, June 9, 1933, Epstein Papers, Box 4.
12   Isaac M. Rubinow, "The Movement Toward Unemployment Insurance in Ohio," *Social Service Review,* 7 (June 1933), 206.

13 Epstein to William M. Leiserson, Sept. 6, 1933, Leiserson Papers, Box 2.

14 Paul H. Douglas, *Standards of Unemployment Insurance* (Chicago, 1932), pp. 149–51; also Paul H. Douglas to Epstein, June 9, 1932, Leiserson Papers, Box 2.

15 Leiserson to Epstein, Sept. 4, 1933, Leiserson Papers, Box 2.

16 Isaac M. Rubinow to Elizabeth S. Magee, Sept. 7, 1934, Rubinow Papers, Box 9.

17 See, for example, William Green, "Unemployment Insurance," *American Federationist,* 40 (Mar. 1934), 247–48.

18 Robert Wagner to C. K. Chilberg, Nov. 20, 1933, Wagner Papers.

19 Frances Perkins, *The Roosevelt I Knew* (New York, 1946), p. 278.

20 Raushenbush, *Annals,* 170 (1933), 75; interview with Paul A. Raushenbush, May 9, 1967.

21 Paul A. Raushenbush, "Starting Unemployment Compensation in Wisconsin," *Unemployment Insurance Review,* 4 (April–May, 1967), 22; interview with Raushenbush, May 9, 1967. See also Arthur M. Schlesinger, Jr., *The Coming of the New Deal* (Boston, 1958), p. 302; Charles E. Wyzanski, Jr., "Brandeis," *The Atlantic,* 198 (Nov. 1956), 69; William Haber and Merrill Murray, *Unemployment Insurance in the American Economy* (Homewood, 1966), p. 72.

22 Edwin E. Witte to Epstein, Feb. 9, 1934, Witte Papers, Box 1.

23 U.S. Congress, House, *Hearings Before the House Ways and Means Committee on the Economic Security Act* (74 Cong., 1 Sess., Washington, 1935), pp. 666–67.

24 Epstein to Francis McConnell, Feb. 17, 1934, Leiserson Papers, Box 2.

25 National Conference for Labor Legislation, *Proceedings,* Feb. 14–15, 1934, in BLS *Bulletin,* 583 (Apr. 1934), 35–49, especially pp. 35, 43–45, 49.

26 Douglas to Rubinow, Feb. 22, 1934, Rubinow Papers, Box 2.

27 NCLL, *Proceedings,* in BLS *Bulletin,* 183 (1934), 52–53.

28 Roosevelt to G. Hall Roosevelt, Feb. 24, 1931, Roosevelt Papers, Governor, RG 18; also Schlesinger, *Coming of the New Deal,* pp. 308–9.

29 Quoted in Perkins, *Roosevelt I Knew,* p. 283.

30 David J. Lewis to Roosevelt, Jan. 20, 1934, Roosevelt Papers, OF 727.

31 "Memorandum from the President to the Assistant Secretary of Agriculture," Feb. 28, 1934, Roosevelt Papers, PSF Agriculture Department, Tugwell File.

32 Frances Perkins to Roosevelt, Mar. 21, 1934: Henry Morgenthau to Roosevelt, Mar. 21, 1934; Roosevelt to Robert Doughton, Mar. 23, 1934, Roosevelt Papers, OF 121-A; *New York Times,* Mar. 24, 1934.

33 *Hearings Before the House Ways and Means Committee,* 1934, pp. 45, 255.

34 See Thomas H. Eliot to Leon H. Keyserling, Mar. 9, 1934, Wagner Papers; Perkins to Draper, Mar. 24, 1934, Draper Papers, Box 1.

35 *Hearings Before the House Ways and Means Committee,* 1934, p. 70.

36 USCC Minutes of the 138th Meeting, Board of Directors, March 2–3, 1934, Chamber of Commerce Archives.

37 See Harriman to Roosevelt, May 10, 1934, Roosevelt Papers, OF 105.

38 See *New York Times,* Apr. 2, 7, 1934.

39 See Edwin E. Witte, *The Development of the Social Security Act* (Madi-

son, 1962), p. 4; Raymond Gram Swing, "Social Security in a Hurry," *Nation*, 139 (Sept. 19, 1934), 319.

40 Perkins to Roosevelt, Apr. 17, 1934, Roosevelt Papers, OF 121-A.

41 *New York Times*, Apr. 18, 1934.

42 M. H. McIntyre to Lewis, Apr. 21, 1934; McIntyre to Doughton, May 9, 1934, Roosevelt Papers, OF 121-A.

43 See John B. Andrews to Wagner, May 16, 1934; Epstein to Wagner, May 18, 1934, Wagner Papers; Rubinow to Royal Meeker, May 18, 1934, Rubinow Papers, Box 9.

44 Roosevelt to Meeker, May 24, 1934, Roosevelt Papers, OF 121-A.

45 Samuel Rosenman, ed., *The Public Papers and Addresses of Franklin D. Roosevelt*, 13 vols. (New York, 1938-50), 3: 291.

46 Perkins, *Roosevelt I Knew*, p. 279; Witte, *Development of the Social Security Act*, p. 5.

47 Perkins to Roosevelt, "Plan for Study of the Economic Security," June 29, 1934, Roosevelt Papers, OF 1086. See also *New York Times*, June 28, 1934.

48 Witte, *Development of the Social Security Act*, pp. 12–13; Arthur J. Altmeyer, *The Formative Years of Social Security* (Madison, 1966), p. 7.

49 Witte to John R. Commons, July 2, 1921, Witte Papers, Box 1.

50 Witte to William Green, Oct. 19, 1932; Witte to Mollie R. Carrol, Oct. 27, 1932, Witte Papers, Box 1.

51 Witte to Andrews, June 19, 1934, Witte Papers, Box 2.

52 Perkins, *Roosevelt I Knew*, pp. 286–87.

53 The state legislators also realized this. In nearly every case state legislation was won at the price of tying it to the constitutionality of the Social Security Act.

54 Witte, *Development of the Social Security Act*, p. 111.

55 Minutes of the Meeting of the Technical Board, Sept. 26, 1934; Minutes of the Meetings of the Committee on Economic Security, Oct. 1, 1934, Witte Papers, Box 65; also Witte, *Development of the Social Security Act*, pp. 112–14.

56 See, for example, Leiserson to Witte, Oct. 9, 1934, Leiserson Papers, Box 8. The strengths and weaknesses of the various approaches are described in Paul H. Douglas, *Social Security in the United States* (New York, 1936), ch. 2.

57 Witte to Leiserson, Oct. 17, 1934, Leiserson Papers, Box 8.

58 Witte to Charles E. Wyzanski, Jr., Nov. 10, 1934, Committee on Economic Security Papers (National Archives, Washington), Box 60; Minutes of the Meetings of the Committee on Economic Security, Nov. 9, 1934, Witte Papers, Box 65; Witte, *Development of the Social Security Act*, p. 118; Altmeyer, *Formative Years*, p. 231.

59 Business Advisory and Planning Council, Report of the Industrial Relations Committee, "Industry's Responsibility to Its Unemployed," Sept. 19, 1934, COES Papers, Box 1.

60 Witte, "Memorandum," Views of Messrs. Flanders, Leeds, and Julian, [n.d.], COES Papers, Box 17; Witte, "Report on Progress of Work During October," COES Papers, Box 1.

61 Rosenman, *Public Papers of Roosevelt*, 3: 452-53.

62 Advisory Council on Economic Security, Minutes of Meetings on Nov. 15, 1934, COES Papers, Box 48.

63 Advisory Council on Economic Security, Minutes of the Dec. 7 Meeting, COES Papers, Box 48; Witte, *Development of the Social Security Act,* p. 60.

64 See, for example, Raymond Moley, *After Seven Years* (New York, 1939), p. 303.

65 Gerard Swope to Witte, Dec. 10, 1934, COES Papers, Box 16.

66 Marion B. Folsom, Morris E. Leeds, Sam A. Lewisohn, Raymond Moley, Swope, and Walter Teagle to Perkins, Dec. 15, 1934, COES Papers, Box 60; also Paul U. Kellogg to Witte, Dec. 27, 1934, COES Papers, Box 15.

67 Perkins, *Roosevelt I Knew,* pp. 271, 292.

68 Witte, *Development of the Social Security Act,* pp. 125–27.

69 It is interesting that Epstein saw in the subsidy versus tax-offset plans a continuation of the debate over unemployment prevention. "The Wisconsin crowd," he wrote in December after talking to Stewart, "insists on putting over their little scheme. There is tremendous pressure on them [Advisory Council] to bring out a unanimous report which will of course be the type that Mr. Swope and the Wisconsin boys want." Epstein to Douglas, Dec. 6, 1934, Epstein Papers, Box 11.

70 Rosenman, *Public Papers of Roosevelt,* 4: 45.

71 Witte to Frank P. Graham, Feb. 1, 1935, COES Papers, Box 16.

72 Witte to Irma Hochstein, Jan. 28, 1935, COES Papers, Box 15; Witte to M. C. Otto, Feb. 7, 1935, COES Papers, Box 58.

73 Witte to Harry Jerome, Jan. 12, 1935, Witte Papers, Box 2.

74 U.S. Congress, Senate, *Hearings Before the Committee on Finance* (74 Cong., 1 Sess., Washington, 1935), pp. 555–59. He gave the same testimony to the House committee. See especially U.S. Congress, House, *Hearings Before the House Ways and Means Committee* (74 Cong., 1 Sess., Washington, 1935), pp. 991–92.

75 *Hearings Before the Committee on Finance,* 1935, pp. 913–15.

76 "What You Need to Know About Unemployment Reserves," *Nation's Business,* 23 (Jan. 1935), 41.

77 USCC Committee on Social Reserves, "Social Legislation," Mar. 1935, pp. 8–9, Chamber of Commerce Archives.

78 Louis Howe to Kellogg, Feb. 7, 1935, Roosevelt Papers, OF 1086.

79 Rubinow to Epstein, Feb. 20, Mar. 11, 1935, Epstein Papers, Box 51. At one point he suggested that Mickey Mouse be adopted as the symbol of the Administration's social insurance program.

80 *Hearings Before the Committee on Finance,* 1935, pp. 466–68, 470.

81 Witte to Grace Abbott, Feb. 21, 1935, COES Papers, Box 16.

82 Epstein to Rubinow, Mar. 8, 1935, Epstein Papers, Box 51; Witte to Graham, Mar. 23, 1935, COES Papers, Box 16.

83 See Witte, *Development of the Social Security Act,* pp. 130–40. As early as February Miss Perkins had registered her indignation, especially over the creation of the Social Security Board. She wrote: "I think you will have to speak on [the] telephone to Doughton about this." Perkins to Roosevelt, Feb. 23, 1935, Mar. 15, 1935, Roosevelt Papers, OF 121-A.

84 Quoted in Witte to Andrews, Mar. 29, 1935, COES Papers, Box 54.

85 Witte, *Development of the Social Security Act,* pp. 93, 96–97.

86 See *New York Times,* Apr. 11, 1935.

87 *New York Times,* Apr. 16, 19, 20, 1935; *Congressional Record* (74

Cong., 1 Sess., Washington, 1935), pp. 5709, 5779–82; Joseph P. Harris to Witte, Apr. 2, 1935, COES Papers, Box 16.

88 Witte to Harris, Apr. 19, 1935, COES Papers, Box 13; Witte to Roger Sherman Hoar, Apr. 23, 1935, COES Papers, Box 57; Witte to Andrews, Apr. 25, 1935, COES Papers, Box 54.

89 See, for example, Epstein to Billikopf, Apr. 18, 1935, Epstein Papers, Box 8.

90 Witte to O. V. Fragstein, May 7, 1935, Witte Papers, Box 2; *New York Times*, Apr. 29, May 3, 1935. Shortly before the repudiation by the chamber, the National Association of Manufacturers' convention had reiterated its opposition to the New Deal. For the split among chamber leaders see *Wall Street Journal*, Aug. 1, 3, 1935.

91 Witte to Andrews, Apr. 25, 1935, COES Papers, Box 54; Witte to John G. Winant, Oct. 7, 1935, Witte Papers, Box 2.

92 See Rosenman, *Public Papers of Roosevelt*, 4: 135.

93 See Witte, *Development of the Social Security Act*, pp. 140–42.

BIBLIOGRAPHICAL NOTE

THE SOURCES used in the preparation of this study are both varied and voluminous. Books, newspapers, scholarly and popular journals, publications of private and government organizations, and unpublished correspondence all provided a wealth of material, as the footnotes indicate. The manuscript collections are singled out for special attention in the following paragraphs because, unlike the other sources, their use involves considerable travel and expense.

No group in recent American history has left richer or more complete collections of correspondence than the economists and professional reformers who were responsible for much of the state and national labor legislation of the 1930's. The John B. Andrews Papers are an outstanding example of this fact and were indispensible for this study. Second only to the Andrews Papers in importance are the William M. Leiserson Papers, which provide almost day-to-day documentation of the Ohio campaign for unemployment insurance legislation, as well as extensive material on other aspects of Leiserson's career. The Isaac M. Rubinow Papers are much less extensive but also very helpful. They contain important information on the reform movements of the 1930's, particularly the Ohio campaign. The Abraham Epstein Papers reveal a great deal about Epstein but relatively little about his day-to-day activities, and were useful only for the period 1933–35. For this study the American Association for Social Security Papers and Mary Dewson Papers were of secondary value. The John R. Commons Papers, which probably contain more correspondence on this subject than any other, are nevertheless fragmentary and disappointing. The Edwin E. Witte Papers include many records and letters pertaining to the work of the Committee on Economic Security, though much of this material also appears in the Committee on Economic Security Papers. The typescript reports of the United States Commission on Industrial Relations, 1914–16, contain occasional references to unemployment.

Much less revealing but often as extensive are the papers of the politicians who were involved in the campaign for unemployment insurance. Of the three Presidential collections that were used, only the Franklin D. Roosevelt

285

Papers were of major importance. Yet most of the Roosevelt letters pertaining to unemployment insurance are readily available as quotations in the various biographical studies of Roosevelt. Of less importance were the Herbert Hoover Papers, which provide extensive documentation for Hoover's activities as Secretary of Commerce but almost nothing on his Presidency. The Warren G. Harding Papers show only that as President, Harding was not the master of his own destiny. Unfortunately the Robert F. Wagner Papers, a voluminous collection, contain relatively little about the Senator's role in the formulation of unemployment insurance legislation. The James Couzens Papers contain some informative material and the Committee on Economic Security Papers thoroughly document the efforts of Roosevelt's advisors to work out a congressional program on unemployment insurance. Two collections of Wisconsin politicians, the Henry A. Huber and John J. Blaine Papers, contain little that pertains to this subject.

Businessmen seldom leave extensive records of their activities, but there are several collections that are useful for the study of unemployment insurance. Ernest Draper was the only major "New Emphasis" employer whose papers are available, and they consist primarily of speeches and printed matter. But the Taylorites can be followed through the Morris L. Cooke Papers, and to a lesser degree through the Manufacturers' Research Association Papers. The A. Lincoln Filene Papers and the Edward A. Filene Papers are small, rather disappointing collections, although with the Boston Chamber of Commerce Papers they help document the early activities of the Massachusetts employers. The Gerard Swope Oral History Memoirs and the United States Chamber of Commerce Archives provide some insight into the planners' activities. The Frederick H. Clausen Papers contain a few letters and speeches pertaining to unemployment insurance legislation.

The labor collections used in this study varied in usefulness but generally added little that was not available through other sources. The American Federation of Labor Papers are fragmentary; they contain relatively little on the subject of unemployment insurance. The Minutes of the AFL Executive Council, which are quoted extensively in Milton Lewis Farber's dissertation, "Changing Attitudes of the American Federation of Labor Toward Business and Government, 1929–33" (Ohio State University, 1959), suggest that the AFL leaders made little effort to understand the issues of unemployment insurance. The William Green Papers (on microfilm at the New York State Library) are voluminous. Unfortunately the deterioration of the film has made them almost impossible to read. The John P. Frey Papers are enlightening, since Frey was among the most articulate and intelligent of the old guard leaders. But the Amalgamated Clothing Workers of America Papers are, like the AFL Papers, fragmentary; they contain almost nothing that casts light on Hillman's career. The Wisconsin State Federation of Labor Papers are valuable for Wisconsin labor's role in planning the Wisconsin campaign.

MANUSCRIPT COLLECTIONS

Amalgamated Clothing Workers of America Papers. ACWA Headquarters, New York.

American Association for Social Security Papers. New York State Library of Industrial and Labor Relations, Ithaca.

American Federation of Labor Papers. State Historical Society of Wisconsin, Madison.

Andrews Papers, John B. New York State Library of Industrial and Labor Relations, Ithaca.

Blaine Papers, John J. State Historical Society of Wisconsin, Madison.

Boston Chamber of Commerce Papers. Harvard Business School, Cambridge.

Clausen Papers, Frederick H. State Historical Society of Wisconsin, Madison.

Committee on Economic Security Papers. National Archives, Washington.

Commons Papers, John R. State Historical Society of Wisconsin, Madison.

Cooke Papers, Morris L. Franklin D. Roosevelt Library, Hyde Park.

Couzens Papers, James. Library of Congress, Washington.

Dewson Papers, Mary. Franklin D. Roosevelt Library, Hyde Park.

Draper Papers, Ernest G. Library of Congress, Washington.

Epstein Papers, Abraham. Columbia University, New York.

Everest Papers, D. C. State Historical Society of Wisconsin, Madison.

Federated Trades Council [Milwaukee] Papers. Microfilm. State Historical Society of Wisconsin, Madison.

Filene Papers, A. Lincoln. Harvard Business School, Cambridge.

Filene Papers, Edward A. CUNA Archives, Madison.

Frey Papers, John P. Library of Congress, Washington.

Green Papers, William. Microfilm. New York State Library of Industrial and Labor Relations, Ithaca.

Harding Papers, Warren G. Ohio Historical Society, Columbus.

Hoover Papers, Herbert. Herbert Hoover Library, West Branch, Iowa.

Huber Papers, Henry A. State Historical Society of Wisconsin, Madison.

Leiserson Papers, William M. State Historical Society of Wisconsin, Madison.

Manufacturers' Research Association Papers. Harvard Business School, Cambridge.

Rochester Joint Board [ACWA] Papers. Microfilm. New York State Library of Industrial and Labor Relations, Ithaca.

Roosevelt Papers, Franklin D. Franklin D. Roosevelt Library, Hyde Park.

Rubinow Papers, Isaac M. New York State Library of Industrial and Labor Relations, Ithaca.

Swope Papers, Gerard. Oral History Memoirs. Columbia University, New York.

United States Chamber of Commerce Papers. Chamber of Commerce Archives, Washington.

United States Industrial Relations Commission Papers. State Historical Society of Wisconsin, Madison.

United States Department of Commerce Papers. Department of Commerce Archives, Washington.

Wagner Papers, Robert F. Georgetown University, Washington.

Wisconsin State Federation of Labor Papers. State Historical Society of Wisconsin, Madison.

Witte Papers, Edwin E. State Historical Society of Wisconsin, Madison.

INDEX

Abbott, Edith, 209
Advance, 82, 84, 88, 89
Advisory Commission of the Council of National Defense, 68
Advisory Council COES: origin, 205; discusses issues, 209–10; mentioned, 213
Alexander, Magnus, 33
Altmeyer, Arthur J.: calls for compromise, 200; organizes COES, 205; proposes state pooled fund, 211; mentioned, 119
Amalgamated Clothing Workers of America: unemployment insurance plans, 81–92 *passim;* mentioned, 79, 93, 97, 99, 103, 114, 126, 166. *See also* Hillman, Sidney
American Association for Labor Legislation: origins, 13; Social Insurance Committee, 1913, 15; aids Massachusetts effort, 1916, 17; members favor London bill, 20; Dennison supports, 1915–16, 41; Draper member of, 43; postwar work with unions, 71; Cleveland convention, 1930, 148, 181; works with Consumers League, 150; faces competition in New York, 171; mentioned, 26, 42, 44, 72, 106, 108, 109, 113, 114, 123, 134, 137, 146, 147, 148, 152, 193, 195, 200. *See also* Andrews, John B.
American Association for Social Security, 152, 195, 200
American Association for the Advancement of Science, 319
American Association of Social Workers, 319
American Bar Association, 140

American Cast Iron Pipe Company, 56
American Catholic Bishops, 20
American Economic Association, 5
American Federationist, 153
American Federation of Labor: unemployment policies, 64–78; *passim;* Hoover addresses convention, 1930, 132; convention, 1930, accepts unemployment insurance legislation, 152–61, *passim;* accepts New Emphasis, 153; criticism of Roosevelt Administration, 215; mentioned, 206, 220
—Executive Council: unemployment policies, 153; hesitates on unemployment insurance, 154; challenged by Conference for Progressive Labor Action, 155; recommends unemployment measures, 1930, 155; Green discusses unemployment insurance, 157; endorses unemployment insurance legislation, 159
American Federation of Teachers, 155, 156
American Labor Legislation Review, 113
American Management Association: interest in unemployment insurance, 35; Lewisohn president of, 45; conflict with Taylor Society, 250n43; mentioned, 131, 132
American plan: prepared 1930–31, 146–48; reformers find inadequate, 152; Ohio reformers study, 181; Wagner introduces, 198; mentioned, 193, 195. *See also* Andrews, John B.
American Society of Equity: supported unemployment insurance, 125, 268n108; mentioned, 124
Amidon, Beulah, 58